1995

Israel Gershoni and James Jankowski examine the development of nationalism among the Egyptian middle class during the 1930s and 1940s, and its
growing awareness of an Arab and Muslim identity. Before the 1940s,
Egypt did not define itself in these terms, but adopted a territorial and
isolationist outlook. It is the revolutionary transformation in Egyptian
self-understanding which took place during this period that provides the
focus of this study. The authors demonstrate how the growth of an urban
middle class of traditionalist background, combined with Egypt's economic and political failures in the 1930s, eroded the foundations of the
earlier order. Alongside domestic events, the momentum of Arabism
abroad and the impact of regional events, such as the crisis in neighboring
Palestine, necessitated Egyptian involvement. Egypt's present position as
a major player in Arab, Muslim, and Third World affairs has its roots in
the fundamental transition of Egyptian national identity at this time.

Cambridge Middle East Studies

Redefining the Egyptian nation, 1930–1945

Cambridge Middle East Studies 2

Editorial board

Charles Tripp (general editor)
Shaul Bakhash, Michael C. Hudson, Deniz Kandiyoti, Rashid Khalidi,
Noah Lucas, Basim Musallam, Roger Owen, Shimon Shamir,
Malcolm Yapp

Cambridge Middle East Studies has been established to publish books
on the nineteenth- and twentieth-century Middle East and North Africa.
The aim of the series is to provide new and original interpretations of
aspects of Middle Eastern societies and their histories. To achieve disci-
plinary diversity, books will be solicited from authors writing in a wide
range of fields including history, sociology, anthropology, political science
and political economy. The emphasis will be on producing books offering
an original approach along theoretical and empirical lines. The series is
intended for students and academics, but the more accessible and wide-
ranging studies will also appeal to the interested general reader.

Redefining the Egyptian nation, 1930–1945

Israel Gershoni
University of Tel Aviv

and

James P. Jankowski
University of Colorado

CAMBRIDGE
UNIVERSITY PRESS

Published by the Press Syndicate of the University of Cambridge
The Pitt Building, Trumpington Street, Cambridge CB2 1RP
40 West 20th Street, New York, NY 10011–4211, USA
10 Stamford Road, Oakleigh, Melbourne 3166, Australia

First published 1995

Printed in Great Britain at the University Press, Cambridge

A catalogue record for this book is available from the British Library

Library of Congress cataloguing in publication data

Gershoni, I.
Redefining the Egyptian nation, 1930–1945 / Israel Gershoni and
James P. Jankowski.
   p.   cm. – (Cambridge Middle East studies; 2)
Includes bibliographical references.
ISBN 0 521 47535 X (alk. paper)
1. Nationalism – Egypt – History – 20th century.
2. Egypt – Politics and government – 1919–1952.
I. Jankowski, James P., 1937– . II. Title. III. Series.
DT107.82.G43 1995
320.5′4′0962 – dc20   94–31795   CIP

ISBN 0 521 47535 X hardback

CE

For
John and Ann
Michal and Nimrod

Contents

Illustrations

Preface

Studies of nationalism in modern Egypt have usually focused on the political struggle against Great Britain and the British Occupation of Egypt. The topics which bulk largest in such works are the changing relationship between occupier and occupied, the history of the various political movements striving for Egyptian independence, and the successive phases of the struggle for national liberation.

This work considers Egyptian nationalism from a somewhat different perspective. Although taking account of the external political conflict with imperialism, it emphasizes the social, the intellectual, and the internal political dimensions of nationalism. Its central concern is the creation and dissemination of new Egyptian national images and frameworks of identity. In part the history of Egyptian nationalism involves the contest for political authority and the competition among rival political forces; but it also involves the larger historical process of Egyptian collective self-definition.

In what follows, we address the evolution of Egyptian national identity on both the conceptual/intellectual and the operative/political levels. In terms of the former, we attempt to isolate and reconstruct the answers Egyptians gave to such fundamental questions concerning their national identity as "Who are we?" "What do we want?" "What are we to become?" In terms of the latter, we endeavor to determine the practical answers given by Egyptians to more concrete questions like "Where does Egypt fit in the world?" "Which policies best serve the interests of the Egyptian nation?" The complex and sometimes conflicting responses given to these questions by different Egyptians at different times, and the tactics by which different groups and forces attempted to impose their answers at the expense of others, are our subject-matter. In short, our work is an attempt to trace the evolving nationalist discourse of Egyptians in the period from 1930 to 1945. It is an essay in Egyptian self-understanding.

Basic to our task is delineating the various systems of Egyptian nationalist thought and action that were first articulated in this period. Each of the major new nationalist approaches of the era receives separate and extended attention. However, we also identify an overarching trend subsuming these individual nationalist variants. All the new forms of nationalist imagining and policy developed between 1930 and 1945 shared the common feature of being *supra-Egyptian* in character. In contrast to the territorially defined and exclusivist form of nationalism prevailing in Egypt in the 1920s, all shared an aspiration to connect Egyptian national identity or Egyptian-ness to peoples and regions beyond the Nile Valley. As an umbrella concept, supra-Egyptianism comprehends the several new definitions of Egyptian national identity which became prominent after 1930 – "Easternism," Islamicism, Arabism, and integral Egyptian nationalism. The first three linked Egyptian national identity to the external referents of the Islamic community, the Arab nation, and the "East"; the last expressed the conviction that Egypt had a role of leadership extending to the same peoples and regions. Both "supra" and "Egyptianism" are important; "supra-Egyptianism" denotes both the outward thrust of these approaches and their belief in a perduring Egyptian reality within the external arenas with which they saw Egypt as being affiliated.

Methodologically we have been guided particularly by Quentin Skinner's dictum that "a knowledge of the writer's intention in writing ... is not merely relevant to, but is actually *equivalent* [Skinner's emphasis] to, a knowledge of the meaning of what he writes."[1] Recovering authorial intent demands a two-pronged, "internal" as well as "external," strategy. An internal inquiry traces the evolution of a text within the conceptual field defined by prevailing symbolic conventions, linguistic usages, and ideological assumptions. An author intends that his text be recognizable and legitimate within the canonical parameters of communication about a given topic.[2] An external inquiry, on the other hand, examines the social setting of both author and text. An author is laden with the baggage of his or her environment; texts are conditioned by contexts.[3] There is, of course, space between these two variables for an author to exercise his or her discretion and originality. The parallel dynamics shaped by internal textual field and external social environment, along with the author's ability to maneuver within these frameworks, comprise the complex set of variables determining authorial intent.

But authors do not act in isolation in the generation of ideas. Authors or "producers" of ideas write (or at least publish) for audiences or "consumers" of ideas. Consumers do not always consume everything presented to them; some ideas are rejected. Nor is the consumption of texts by consumers a passive exercise. In the course of appropriating ideas, consumers engage in a conscious act of interpretation and sometimes even reproduction. The publics receiving ideas reconstruct meanings in terms that suit their norms and values and that complement their modes of feeling and expression. Such reconstruction can also reverberate back on the producers of texts. The manner in which ideas are received and reconstructed by audiences can in time create a feedback loop in which authors adapt their production to meet the demands of their consumers.[4]

Our study places special emphasis on the mechanism of the feedback loop between authors and audience, producers and consumers of ideas, in the generation of supra-Egyptian nationalism. In our view, the consumers of ideas played a crucial role in shaping the content of Egyptian nationalist thought and policy in the period under discussion. To a considerable degree the new supra-Egyptian nationalism of the era was sculpted from below, as both intellectual and political elites adapted themselves to the values and desires of a new Egyptian public emerging over the interwar period.

This feedback model which takes consumer influence into account in large part explains the eventual ascendancy of supra-Egyptian nationalist imaginings over the earlier territorial and Western-influenced nationalism embedded in Egypt's Pharaonic heritage which had been dominant in Egypt before 1930.[5] Egyptian territorial nationalism developed before the revolution in Egyptian literacy which brought larger and previously marginal social strata into active involvement in Egyptian public life. These strata were more deeply rooted in Arab-Islamic modes of expression than the smaller and more Westernized elite of the previous generation. As they entered nationalist dialogue, they naturally propounded a nationalist outlook in line with their values and background. They also influenced established opinion-makers. Upon their arrival in the public arena as a new audience with whom Egyptian intellectuals and politicians had to deal, the elite producers of nationalist concepts and policies found the inclinations of their audience reflected back upon them. In an ongoing negotiation, Egyptian nationalist ideologues and politicians alike adjusted their message to match the propensities of a changing audience.

Thus a major object of our inquiry is a consideration of precisely who these new consumers of Egyptian nationalism were, what criteria they used in selecting among the cultural and political options available to them, and what effect their outlook had on both the producers of Egyptian nationalist concepts and the formulators of Egyptian national policy. We also examine the crucial mediational role played by Egypt's secondary intellectuals – teachers, journalists, editorialists, organizational spokesmen – who, while not the most prominent articulators of new nationalist ideas or the primary shapers of new national policies, nonetheless were pivotal in transmitting concepts from the top down as well as relaying consumer reaction from the bottom up. Many of these secondary intellectuals themselves derived from newly participatory strata, and thus tended to imbue nationalist discourse with a more Arab-Islamic hue.

The emergence of a new audience of Egyptian nationalist consumers along with the feedback effects of their selective consumption of nationalist ideas and policies together played a central role in the gradual ascent of a more supra-Egyptian nationalist outlook. The capacity of newly literate and newly politicized Egyptians of a more Arab and Islamic background to assimilate nationalist concepts as their own depended on the redirection of those concepts into more Arab-Islamic channels. The entry of these middle strata into the negotiation over national identity was the decisive event shaping the evolution of Egyptian nationalism; it in large part accounts for its relentless Islamicization, Arabization, and "Easternization" on the one hand, its de-Westernization and "de-Pharaonicization" on the other.

Acknowledgments

We have incurred debts to many institutions and individuals in the process of working on this study. Financial and logistical assistance was provided at various points of time by the Fund for Basic Research of Tel Aviv University; by the Department of History and the Council on Research and Creative Work of the University of Colorado; and by the American Philosophical Society.

We wish to thank the staff of the Egyptian National Library (Cairo) and the Public Record Office (London) for their assistance on several research trips to those institutions. Much of the writing of the work was completed at the Middle East Centre of St. Antony's College, Oxford. We are indebted to the Warden and Fellows of the College, to the Director of the Centre Dr. Derek Hopwood and its Fellows Drs. Roger Owen, M. M. Badawi, and Celia Kerslake, and its staff members Elizabeth Anderson, Diane Ring, and Angela Mills, for making our stay in Oxford a pleasant as well as a productive one.

Many colleagues and friends provided advice and stimulation. The late Professor Albert Hourani was a source of wisdom and insight about the modern Middle East. The works and views on nationalism of the late Professor Elie Kedourie repeatedly stimulated our own thinking about the subject. Professor Emmanuel Sivan demonstrated concern and offered important counsel, Professor Itamar Even-Zohar was the source of invaluable theoretical insights, and Professor Avi Shlaim offered indispensable assistance in the process of publication. We also wish to thank Sa'id al-'Ashmawi, Haggai Erlich, the late Husayn Fawzi, Boyd Hill, Robert Hohlfelder, Robert Jancu, Philip Kennedy, Hafiz Mahmud, Ralph Mandel, Charles Middleton, Gabi Piterberg, Robert Schulzinger, Yaacov Shavit, Kenneth Stein, Ehud Toledano, and Ursula Wokoeck, all of whom provided information, advice, and/or support as our work progressed. The views and judgments found in the study are of course our responsibility, not theirs.

We are enormously grateful to the readers and staff of Cambridge University Press for their assistance in the process of evaluation, revision, and publication. The anonymous readers of the manuscript provided numerous valuable suggestions for refining the contents of the study. Marigold Acland has been a gracious and most helpful editor; her guidance has improved the work immensely. Margaret Deith did a meticulous job of copy-editing.

Our greatest debt is to our families, who put up with innumerable alterations and disruptions of their own lives and plans in order to facilitate our collaboration. Our work could never have been completed without the patience, encouragement, and support provided by Shoshi and Mary Ann. The demands imposed by the research and writing of this study have also shaped the lives of Michal and Nimrod, John and Ann (we hope for the better). Thank you all.

Abbreviations of Arabic periodicals

AA	al-'Alam al-'Arabi	MJ	al-Majalla al-Jadida
AD	al-Adib	MK	al-Makshuf
AH	al-Ahram	MQ	al-Muqtataf
AN	al-Ansar	MR	al-Manar
AR	al-'Arab (Jerusalem)	MS	Mir'at al-Sharq
ARB	al-'Arab (Cairo)	MSR	al-Musawwar
BL	al-Balagh	MSU	Mulhaq al-Siyasa
BU	al-Balagh al-Usbu'i	MT	Majallati
DS	al-Dustur	MU	al-Muqattam
FH	al-Fath	ND	al-Nadhir
FI	Filastin	NF	al-Nahda al-Fikriyya
HD	al-Hidaya al-Islamiyya	NI	Nur al-Islam
HI	al-Hilal	RA	al-Rabita al-'Arabiyya
HT	al-Hadith	RI	al-Risala
IM	al-Ikhwan al-Muslimun	RS	al-Rabita al-Sharqiyya
JA	al-Jami'a al-'Arabiyya	RY	Ruz al-Yusuf
JH	al-Jihad	SA	al-Sarkha
JI	al-Jami'a al-Islamiyya	SB	al-Shabab
JJ	al-Jil al-Jadid	SH	al-Sha'b
KI	al-Kitab	SI	al-Siyasa
KL	al-Khulud	SJ	al-Sharq al-Jadid
KM	al-Katib al-Misri	SM	al-Shubban al-Muslimun
KS	Kawkab al-Sharq	SQ	al-Sirat al-Mustaqim
KW	al-Kutla al-Wafdiyya	SU	al-Siyasa al-Usbu'iyya
LI	Liwa' al-Islam	TH	al-Thughr
MA	al-Ma'rifa	TQ	al-Thaqafa
MF	Misr al-Fatah	WM	al-Wafd al-Misri
MGQ	Majallat Ghurfat al-Qahira	WN	Wadi al-Nil
MI	al-Misri	ZA	al-Zahra'

1   The roots of supra-Egyptian nationalism in modern Egypt

The 1930s were a crucial decade in the evolution of modern Egypt. Many things changed in Egypt between the onset of the world depression in late 1929 and the outbreak of World War II ten years later. Not the least of these changes was a major shift in the character of Egyptian nationalism. In place of the exclusivist territorial nationalism which had marked the 1920s, the period after 1930 witnessed the development of new supra-Egyptian concepts of national identity.

Three processes laid the basis for the emergence of supra-Egyptian nationalism. One was the manifest economic and political difficulties of Egypt in the 1930s, difficulties which produced a widespread mood of disillusionment with the existing Egyptian order and which led many Egyptians to question the territorial nationalist premises upon which that order was based. A second development was the changing social composition of the articulate Egyptian public after 1930 – the physical growth and growing political importance of a larger urban and literate population which was less thoroughly Westernized than the smaller Egyptian elite of the previous generation, and correspondingly whose nationalist inclinations were toward greater identification with Egypt's Arab and Muslim neighbors. The third was the gradual growth of a variety of new institutional as well as personal contacts between Egyptians and other Arabs, contacts which over time reinforced an Egyptian identification with Arab nationalism in particular. It was the conjunction of the disillusionment and alienation of the 1930s, the emergence of a new generation different in both social composition and intellectual perspective from its predecessor, and the increasing integration of Egypt with the surrounding Arab world which together laid the foundations for supra-Egyptian nationalism

Egypt in the 1930s

After a decade of relative prosperity in the 1920s, the 1930s were a period of severe economic contraction in Egypt. The Great Depression had an almost-immediate impact upon Egypt. The world price of cotton, Egypt's main export, dropped from $26.00/*qantar* in 1928 to $10.00 in 1931.[1] Between 1928 and 1933, the relative value of all Egyptian exports is estimated to have declined by one-third.[2] With declining trade came a significant deterioration in Egyptian living conditions. According to Bent Hansen's calculations, the rise in real per capita income and disposable income which had characterized Egypt in the 1920s was reversed in the 1930s, with both declining by about 10 percent between 1929 and 1937 and with per capita income reverting to its immediate pre-World War I level by the late 1930s.[3] The average daily wage of an Egyptian laborer could buy 8 kilograms of maize in 1929, but only 3.5 in 1933; as a result, per capita consumption of both maize and beans, two Egyptian staples, declined by over 20 percent between 1929 and 1933.[4]

The Egyptian political system also experienced major difficulties in the 1930s. Something close to a Palace-oriented dictatorship emerged in 1930, when Isma'il Sidqi was appointed prime minister and dismissed the Wafdist-controlled parliament, abrogated the Constitution of 1923, introduced a more autocratic replacement in its stead, and rigged the elections of early 1931 to obtain a pliant parliamentary majority. The years of Sidqi's premiership from 1930 through 1933 were ones of political polarization, repression, and violence.[5] A major shift in Egyptian politics occurred late in 1935, when massive student demonstrations and the formation of a united front by Egypt's political parties forced the restoration of the Constitution of 1923; in the following year, free elections returned the Wafd to office. Although the party remained in power for a longer period than at any time in the past (May 1936 to December 1937), by late 1937 internal schism, opposition from its parliamentary rivals, violence between its supporters and its opponents, and the erosion of its position due to repeated conflicts with the young and popular King Faruq all combined to weaken the Wafdist ministry to the point where the king could dismiss it from office. From the beginning of 1938 until the eve of World War II, Egypt was ruled by unstable coalition ministries headed by the Liberal leader Muhammad Mahmud. Decisive power in Egyptian political life in 1938–9 did not reside in the ministry, however; it rested in the Egyptian Palace and the coterie of conservative and/or opportunist advisors around King Faruq, men whose political ideas revolved around the use of religious and traditionalist themes to institutionalize royal autocracy in Egypt.[6]

Both the economic difficulties produced by the depression and the factionalized, repressive, and often violent course of Egyptian public life through the 1930s had enormous repercussions for the mental outlook of Egyptians. In place of the optimism which had prevailed in the 1920s after the attainment of independence as a result of the Revolution of 1919,[7] a widespread mood of disillusionment set in in Egypt in the 1930s. The operational impotence of the Wafd *vis-à-vis* the Palace and the British; the inability of the electoral system to reflect popular wishes; the elite-dominated and self-serving nature of parliament; the factionalism and corruption of the country's political parties; the manifest inequalities of the socio-economic order – all these indicated the failure of the new Egyptian state to achieve its proclaimed goals of independence, modernity, and progress. The utopian expectations that the Revolution of 1919 had heralded the inauguration of a new era of freedom, prosperity, and national revival came crashing down under the dual impact of depression and repression.

Many of the specific discontents of Egyptians with the shape of their country in the 1930s were raised in a letter written by the young Jamal 'Abd al-Nasir in 1935.[8] As the future president of Egypt viewed the condition of his country in the mid-1930s, "the situation today is critical; Egypt is in a precarious state." The parliamentary regime was permeated by "corruption and bribery"; the constitution had been abrogated; "patriotism" and "dignity" were dead; another British protectorate threatened the country. "A life of despair and despair with life" now characterized the attitude of patriotic Egyptians. Most telling was Nasir's lament for the lost spirit of commitment and sacrifice which had inspired Egyptians during the Revolution of 1919: "Where is the patriotism which in 1919 ignited a fire in breasts? Where are those who by their words and the thoughts of their hearts defended the ramparts of this blessed, sacred nation, sacrificing their lives for the sake of independence?"[9]

In Egyptian critiques of the political order in the 1930s, two specific institutions came under greatest attack. The first was parliament, which increasingly came to be viewed as a corrupt, unrepresentative, and self-serving body concerned only with promoting the interests of its members and the class which they represented. Tawfiq al-Hakim is perhaps the outstanding example of a former enthusiast of the post-1919 Egyptian national order who by the 1930s was pointing out fundamental flaws in the parliamentary system. Hakim presented the Egyptian parliament as an instrument of one social formation – the large landowners of Egypt. Representatives of the class of large landowners had taken control of parliament, deprived it of any real democratic quality, and through the use of populist rhetoric had mobilized the country's resources for their own benefit.[10] The process through which the landed elite established its control of parliament was the electoral system. For Hakim, Egyptian elections were only "election shows" in which the established elite perpetuated its position through the use of a combination of money, power, and fraud.[11] His description of the electoral procedure followed by a rural official captures Hakim's contempt for the Egyptian electoral process: "This is what I always have done in elections. Total freedom. I let people vote for whomever they prefer until the voting is over. Afterwards I simply take the ballot box and throw it into the canal. In its place I put our box which we rig at our leisure."[12]

Other Egyptian intellectuals and publicists also denounced the corruption of the parliamentary system. For Muhammad 'Awad Muhammad, Egypt had a system of "parliamentary rule without real democracy"; the laws passed by parliament served to "guard the material interests of the upper classes only."[13] In the view of Ramsis Shahata, the promises so freely made in parliament were never kept; they were just "empty pretense whose only purpose was to blind the masses and to exploit them most shamefully and vilely."[14] After the rigged parliamentary elections of March 1938, Young Egypt's leader Ahmad Husayn was asserting that the electoral process as practiced in Egypt was driven solely by "lust for office" and "desire for personal gain"; as such, electoral results "cannot be considered as an expression of the will of the people."[15] Husayn's colleague Fathi Radwan was even more strident: "We despise the parliamentary system which prevents and hinders work, which turns the country into a stage for oratory and theatrics. The people are starving, yet the deputies wax eloquent; the country is threatened with danger from within and without, yet the minutes of the sessions contain only idle debates which delay more than they expedite affairs."[16]

Equally vehement criticism was directed at the organizations which had turned parliament into such a travesty of what it should have been, namely the established political parties of Egypt. The term which came to encapsulate the various accusations levelled at Egypt's political parties from the 1930s onwards was *hizbiyya* – "partyism" or "factionalism." *Hizbiyya* embodied the transformation of Egyptian politics into an arena for personal and factional power struggles devoid of any higher purpose. It came to be viewed as an incurable sickness in the body politic, "the sickness of factionalism [*marad al-hizbiyya*]" spreading through the body of the nation.[17] *Hizbiyya* had been rarely used in the 1920s; by the 1930s it was becoming a widely accepted term in the Egyptian political lexicon, a symbol of the bankruptcy of Egyptian public life.[18]

In the view of Tawfiq al-Hakim, Egypt's political parties had no economic, social, or even political program.[19] Their social concepts were limited to the idea of charity and the traditional *noblesse oblige* often manifested by elites; paternalism had taken the place of systematic economic and social policy.[20] Indeed, Egyptian parties were not really "parties" in the generally accepted sense of the term:

In Egypt there is no party [*hizb*] in the true sense of the word, a party as the word is understood and used in genuine democratic regimes. Rather, in Egypt there are separatist factions [firaq] called parties. None of these factions has a goal other than dividing up the seats in parliament, obtaining government office, and managing election campaigns through passing out ballots. But as for any program, none of them even thinks about it![21]

Hakim was not alone in his characterization of Egyptian politics as personalized, programless factionalism. A similar critique of the Egyptian political process as being nothing more than "a series of factional struggles which are won by individuals, not by principles, outlooks, or systems, as if politics were a boxing or soccer match," was expressed by Ibrahim al-Misri.[22] Spokesmen for the new anti-parliamentary movements of the 1930s were utterly convinced of the shortcomings of Egypt's political parties. Ahmad Husayn of Young Egypt assailed the Wafd as "not having any clearly defined program" other than that of attaining independence for Egypt.[23] The same was true of the parties which had split off from the Wafd and now competed with it. These parties "have no program and no defined aim except fighting with the Wafd and collaborating with the British as a means of gaining power; they have no interest, internally or externally, save awarding posts in office."[24]

The negative effects of hizbiyya reached beyond politics per se. In the view of 'Abd al-'Aziz al-Bishri, incessant partisan struggle and the rapid alternation of ministries which resulted from it had done enormous harm to the Egyptian administrative system. In effect, Egyptian bureaucrats had to respond to two masters; the incumbent minister as well as the minister whom they expected to replace him tomorrow. Bureaucratic success was dependent on duplicity; in this fashion, throughout the entire governmental system "morals are completely undermined and the character of men is utterly destroyed."[25] Both Salama Musa and Tawfiq al-Hakim saw repression as the natural result of partisanship. For the former, the bitter party struggles which characterized Egyptian politics meant that all respect for one's opposition was lost. With respect went restraint. Egyptian politicians had lost any sense of the rights of the opposition. Political hizbiyya in turn spawned cultural and moral hizbiyya; the stifling of freedom of expression of political opponents also resulted in the stifling of cultural expression and creativity.[26] Like Musa, Hakim saw factionalism and the quest for power as aggravating party rivalries and personal animosities to the point where the political opposition became delegitimized. The logical consequences were repression, the denial of freedom of expression to the opposition, and "waging war with every available weapon" by one faction against another.[27] "Our country is drowning in the blood of factionalist war [al-harb al-hizbiyya]," he lamented at one point.[28]

For Hakim, the evil effects of hizbiyya extended from politics to all areas of Egyptian life. From parliament and the parties, the twin vices of "opportunism [*wusuliyya*]" and "materialism [*maddiyya*]" had spread to the bulk of Egyptians, corrupting the entire social fabric.[29] Physicians do not treat the sick except for exorbitant fees; in their verdicts judges show partiality and pervert justice; teachers do not devote themselves to educating their students; materialism has infected religious functionaries.[30] Even the family had not escaped the taint of *hizbiyya*. As Egyptians "learned from the politicians" to concern themselves only with their own interests, "the family bond has dissolved and chaos has set in. Fathers have lost control over sons; youth have come to lead adults at home and in politics!"[31]

The failure of the Egyptian parliamentary system to function as a genuine democracy, the crassness of the Egyptian political establishment, and the sterile and destructive factionalism of the parties produced a contempt for politics among many Egyptians by the 1930s. Rather than being the forum for constructive national action, as had been the case in the 1920s, "politics [*al-siyasa*]" acquired a negative image as nothing more than an arena of personalized power struggles. Egyptian politics came to be viewed as lacking any meaningful content; they were a "politics of words" devoid of any real substance for Hakim as well as for Ahmad Hasan al-Zayyat, a politics of "silly talk" for Ramsis Shahata.[32] Politics became a term of abuse for disillusioned Egyptians by the 1930s. A similar discrediting of representative government occurred in Europe as well in the 1930s, where it also had the effect of spawning anti-parliamentary attitudes and movements. But in Egypt, this revulsion with "politics" had the additional effect of reverberating negatively upon the Western-inspired form of territorial nationalism which had taken hold in Egypt in conjunction with the parliamentary order.

The mood of discontent and frustration extended beyond politics. The terms often used by intellectuals to characterize Egypt in the 1930s were those denoting a country in "crisis [*azma*]," an Egypt experiencing social "confusion [*idtirab*]," intellectual "perplexity [*haira*]," emotional "anxiety [*qalaq*]," and moral "chaos [*fawda*]." A frequently expressed theme was that of the fragmentation of Egyptian worldviews and values into contradictory schools of thought. For Ahmad Hasan al-Zayyat, this cultural confusion manifested itself particularly among the younger generation of Egyptians who were torn between their native Egyptian traditions and the alien values of the West. The new Egyptian intelligentsia found itself living in "an oscillating culture [*thaqafa mudhabdhaba*]," an artificial and unsuccessful patchwork of European cultural values imposed upon an Eastern social structure.[33] Similarly Sayyid Qutb saw contemporary Egyptian culture as being in a state of "confusion [*idtirab*]" in which the values of the "materialist European civilization" spreading in Egypt did not fit with the country's beliefs and customs; the result was bound to be a prolonged period of "perplexity [*haira*]" and "anxiety [*qalaq*]."[34] As Amin al-Khuli put it, the differing outlooks coexisting but clashing in contemporary Egypt had produced a general condition of "intellectual confusion [*idtirab fikri*]."[35] For Fikri Abaza, the war between "tradition [*taqalid*]" and "imitation [*taqlid*]" presently being fought in Egypt was bringing "a social revolution that begins with chaos [*fawda*] and ends in dissolution [*inhilal*]."[36]

A central theme of these pessimistic representations was the perception that Egypt was losing its internal harmony and solidarity. Cultural division inevitably led to social schism. Thus the "intellectual confusion" which Amin al-Khuli perceived as prevalent in Egypt was also leading to "the severing of the bonds of conviviality and spiritual union, a severing that prevents the social cooperation that the homeland urgently demands of this generation."[37] 'Abd al-'Aziz al-Bishri found social disharmony in the wildly differing dress styles of Egypt; the diverse styles of dress found in contemporary Egypt reflected "life in a tower of Babel."[38] Muhammad 'Abd al-Wahid Khalaf saw the differences and conflicts between the old and new generations as an additional expression of the loss of Egyptian social harmony. The differences between these two generations – in life style, mentality, thought and behavior patterns, political philosophy, cultural and aesthetic taste – were so substantial as to divide Egypt into "two camps struggling with each other."[39] For Zaki Mubarak, Egypt was "suffering from a crisis the likes of which she has never known."[40] At the heart of the crisis were the social divisions which now prevailed in Egypt, the existence of "several publics" who viewed each other with mutual "anxiety and resentment."[41] A passage from Najib Mahfuz's later novel *Mirrors* sums up the sense of despair which had come to prevail among many Egyptians by the 1930s: "There was a crisis [*azma*] in which values sunk to the depths. The self-respect of many people was demolished . . . [It was] an age of earthquakes and erupting volcanos, an age of frustrated dreams and the rise of the two devils of opportunism and crime, an age of martyrs from all classes."[42]

The "new effendiyya" of the 1930s and 1940s

The archetypal Egyptian of the parliamentary era was Misri Effendi. As caricatured in the popular press, Misri Effendi was a short, stout, bespectacled, somewhat disheveled figure. With Western trousers and jacket, half-Western fez, and Eastern prayer beads, Misri Effendi contrasted visually with the even more portly, more elegantly Western-dressed pashas of the upper class as well as with the peasantry in their traditional galabiyyas. His function in the political journalism of the period was that of observer and/or interlocutor; a wry commentator on the follies of rich and poor alike.

العلم نور

(وزير المعارف) : مبسوط مني دلوقت ؟ ... زى ما انت شايف كل يوم بازور مدرسة أو دار للتعليم ...

(المصري افندى) : طيب اياك على الله تتعلم لك حاجة ...

'Knowledge is light' (*Ruz al-Yusuf*, 27 November 1933)

MINISTER OF EDUCATION: Are you satisfied with me now? As you see, every
    day I visit a school or teachers' college . . .

MISRI EFFENDI: Well, I hope you will learn something . . .

معلوم !

(المصرى أفندى) : ايه الحكايه ! . . . . كل ما واحد نائب يقدم سؤال نجروا وراه لغاية مايسحبه تانى ؟
(الوزراء) : معلوم ! ... لاننا أعلى وأسمى وأجعص وأكبر من أن ترفق الينا الشبهات !

'Of course!' (*Ruz al-Yusuf*, 7 March 1932)

MISRI EFFENDI: What's the story?! Every time an MP presents a question
to you, you run after him until he finally retracts it?

THE MINISTERS: Of course! We are too high and exalted, vain and high-
ranking for suspicions to be levelled at us.

'Best way to ease the pressure!' (*Ruz al-Yusuf*, 16 October 1933)
(The government declared it has designated a sum of E£1,000,000 to ease
the pressure off the fellahs and will look for the best means to this
purpose.)
MISRI EFFENDI: The fellah appointed me to tell you not to bother looking.
If you really want to ease the pressure on him, get off his back and let
him rest, and keep the million pounds!

Behind the caricature lay a complex social reality. "Effendi" (lit. *afandi*) was the term used in Egypt in the early twentieth century to refer to the urban, educated middle class of native Egyptians. In the Egyptian hierarchy of wealth and status the effendi on the one hand stood below both the indigenous political elite (many of Ottoman background, and for whom the Ottoman term *basha/bashawiyya* was employed) and the often European *haute bourgeoisie* who dominated much of the Egyptian economy; on the other side, the effendis of Egypt definitely stood above the country's urban working classes (the *'ummal*) and the masses of its rural peasantry (the *fallahin*).

In positive terms, to be an effendi meant several things. The visual hallmark of the effendi was European-style clothing; trousers, jacket, and fez (Eg. *tarbush*) were the customary uniform of an effendi. Central to the status of effendi was formal education. Egyptians educated in the newly developed, Westernized educational system were the quintessential effendis of early twentieth-century Egypt. Occupationally the term "effendi" spanned many groups: students in the Western-style secondary schools, higher institutes and the Egyptian University who were in the process of becoming effendis; perhaps most typically, civil servants in the bureaucracy and teachers in the modern educational system; clerks in the expanding commercial economy; depending on their dress and education, some of the merchants and employees in the more traditional sectors of the economy; and even a segment of the industrial workforce such as technical school graduates who perceived their education as distinguishing them from other workers.[43] Precise lines are impossible to draw with a term as broad and multifaceted as "effendi"; but its range covered "the bulk of the urban middle class and the petty bourgeoisie."[44] The effendi cohort was the embodiment of modern Egypt; those social formations thrown up by the massive changes of the recent past, and correspondingly most representative of what the nation was in the process of becoming.

What is the relevance of the effendi for Egyptian nationalism? In brief, our argument is that the processes of urbanization, educational expansion, and the formation of new occupational groups which occurred in Egypt under the parliamentary monarchy eventually resulted in the creation of a significantly different effendi population from that found in the early decades of the century. Larger in size as well as more traditional in outlook than the smaller, more Westernized educated upper and middle class of the previous generation who had been the authors and audience of the Egypt-ianist approach dominant in Egypt prior to 1930, this "new effendiyya" population was the most important social group responsible for the move-ment of Egyptian nationalist thought and action away from its earlier territorial nationalist perspective and toward the supra-Egyptianist outlook which emerged in the post-1930 period.

Of all the processes increasing the numbers of politically aware Egyptians under the parliamentary monarchy, urbanization and educational expansion were the most important. Cairo's estimated population of 790,939 in 1917 had increased to 1,312,096 by 1937; comparable figures for Alexandria in 1917 and 1937 are 444,617 and 675,736.[45] Over the same two decades, Egypt's twenty largest towns together increased their population by 54 percent.[46] By 1947, Cairo had a population of over 2 million (2,090,654), while Alexandria was approaching a million (919,024).[47]

The cumulative effects of urbanization had major consequences for Egyptian nationalism. As an (urban) observer noted in 1938, Egypt's rural majority did "not really participate in the national life of the country"; the rural masses were "dead as regards healthy nationalistic life."[48] As more and more Egyptians came to live in an urban setting where they were now exposed to educational opportunities, social pressures, and political stimuli which were absent or attenuated in the village setting, urbanization was an indispensable prerequisite for the enlargement of the nationally involved population of Egypt.

Education is central to the definition of the effendiyya category. The growth of the number of students enrolled in the state educational system from the 1920s to the 1940s was impressive:[49]

Year	Primary	Secondary	Higher
1925/6	210,123	16,979	3,368
1935/6	706,228	45,203	7,515
1945/6	1,039,177	75,096	13,927

Due to educational expansion, the percentage of literate Egyptians reported in the censuses taken in the period of the parliamentary monarchy increased from 13.8 percent in 1927 through 18.6 percent in 1937 to 22.8 percent in 1947.[50]

Increased urbanization and expanded education produced a new human geography in Egypt. One of the most important groups in Egyptian political life in the post-1930 era was the country's growing student population. Whereas in 1925–6 only 15 of every 1,000 Egyptians were enrolled in school, by 1940/1 the ratio had increased to 69/1,000.[51] Of greatest relevance for politics was the rapid increase in the secondary school and university population. Between 1925–6 and 1935–6, enrollment in state secondary schools nearly tripled and enrollment at the Egyptian University more than doubled; by 1945–6, there were more than four times the number of secondary and university students as there had been twenty years earlier. If secondary school and university students increasingly played a larger role in the public life of their country, one basic reason is that there were more of them to do so.

By the interwar period, the state educational system had eclipsed the parallel religious educational system centered on al-Azhar in both social and political importance. Al-Azhar experienced only minimal growth under the parliamentary monarchy (from 15,826 students in 1918–19 to 18,582 in 1948–9).[52] Smaller in numbers and concerned primarily with occupational issues, the students and graduates of al-Azhar were a declining force in Egyptian public life in the period under discussion, both in the political parties of the older generation and in the movements of the new effendiyya.[53]

The rapid expansion of secondary and higher education under the parliamentary monarchy eventually generated an appreciable Egyptian professional class. The number of doctors and engineers in Egypt each more than doubled from 1927 to 1947, while the number of lawyers nearly doubled.[54] Posts in the government bureaucracy grew by 61 percent over the period from 1940–1 to 1953–4, and grew particularly in the number of educated employees required (from 47,000 to 170,000).[55] Overall, in the decade from 1937 to 1947 the size of occupational groups of a primarily effendi character (government clerks; teachers; medical and legal specialists; engineers; "writers and journalists") is estimated to have increased by almost 40 percent (from 155,500 to 216,500).[56]

The metaphor of the marketplace is heuristically useful for understanding what these processes meant for Egyptian nationalism. Urbanization, educational growth, and occupational shifts combined to generate an ever-increasing number of "consumers" of modern, literate culture. In turn, the growth of the number of consumers of literate culture had major effects on the character of Egyptian cultural production. Quantitatively, the growth of a new and different body of consumers generated a growing volume of cultural production. If any statistic symbolizes the change in the size of Egypt's cultural arena by the 1940s, it is the massive growth reported in the number of "writers and journalists" from 1937 to 1947 (1,200 to 8,200).[57]

This new and larger body of consumers also influenced the content of Egyptian cultural production in the 1930s and 1940s. At the same time as the consumers of ideas are in part shaped through what is available for consumption, they also influence the market through the choices they make in the appropriation of some products and the rejection of others. On the one hand, this growing body of consumers soon generated its own producers of ideas, representatives of the new social groups in the process of formation who expressed ideas congruent with the outlook of the social strata from whence they had come. On the other hand, the growth of this population had a feedback effect, influencing spokesmen of the older generation to refine their product in order to reach an audience significantly different in social composition and intellectual inclination from that they had appealed to in the past.

The territorial nationalist orientation which prevailed in Egyptian public life in the early decades of the century had been the product of the country's small and intensively Westernized elite. It was this minority of the population of Egypt which provided both the producers and the consumers of the Western-derived and Egypt-centered nationalism of the period. Over time, however, the massive entry of new social groups into national life significantly altered the marketplace of ideas. The masses who abandoned the rural communities of Egypt and crowded into its cities found little of appeal in the Egyptianist outlook with its alien Western and archaic Pharaonic trappings which had little resonance in the Arab-Muslim culture in which they were still embedded. For the educated new effendiyya, the territorial nationalist outlook was found lacking for several reasons. On one level, its basis in Western models of community was problematic for a generation imbued with anti-imperialist sentiment. In addition, that territorial nationalism had taken an explicitly anti-Arab and anti-Muslim tone in the 1920s; for a population not as thoroughly Westernized and more attuned to Egypt's Arab-Muslim heritage, the anti-traditionalism of territorial nationalism was offsetting. Only a national culture based on Egypt's indigenous Arab-Islamic heritage was capable of serving as the foundation for a widely shared system of national values and priorities. Finally, the territorialist approach was increasingly perceived to have failed to achieve Egyptian independence and progress. In view of the Western-associated, anti-Arab and anti-Muslim, and ineffective nationalism represented by Egyptianism, a more authentic alternative was required.

Both Egyptian territorial nationalism and the new supra-Egyptian imaginings of Egypt were of course "invented traditions,"[58] in the sense that all were subjective mental constructs created at a specific point in time through a selective reading of the multi-layered Egyptian heritage. What made the former a flawed reading of that heritage in the eyes of the new effendiyya and the latter a correct or "authentic" one was a combination of the greater salience of Arab-Islamic symbols and referents for this particular cohort in contrast to the remoteness of the Pharaonic imagery upon which territorialism drew, and the clearly Western/imperialist influences found in Egyptian territorial nationalism. The supra-Egyptian imaginings of Egypt which appealed to the new effendiyya were by no means non-Egyptian; all accepted the reality of Egyptian identity. What they did, however, was to link that identity not to the distant Pharaonic past or to the imperialist West, but to the more meaningful and indigenous Arab, Islamic, and Eastern dimensions of Egyptian life. Even if supra-Egyptian nationalism was an invented tradition, at least it was a home-made invention.

What were the social characteristics and intellectual predilections of the "new effendiyya" which influenced their nationalist attitudes? The social background of the new effendiyya is an elusive issue. As the educated population of Egypt expanded, of necessity it drew its membership from broader and therefore less affluent strata of the population of the country. Several observers have concluded that Egypt's student population, the leading edge of the new effendiyya cohort, over time came more and more from middle-class and to some degree even lower-class segments of both urban and rural society.[59]

Some indication of how social background correlates with nationalist orientation can be obtained from a consideration of the social composition of the main organizations which championed a supra-Egyptianist outlook in the post-1930 period. The data available on the leadership and membership of the Young Egypt Society and the Muslim Brotherhood indicate a generally middle-class, usually urban, and primarily Western-educated activist core for both movements. 'Ali Shalabi's examination of the family backgrounds of the members of Young Egypt's several leadership bodies of the 1930s indicates that the movement had a heterogeneous social base; other than being predominantly composed of educated youth, its cadre ranged from a few individuals descended from large landed families through a plurality of members drawn from the middle peasantry and the urban bourgeoisie to a few representatives of urban lower-class background.[60] The data provided for the ten members of the party's Administrative Council in 1937 show a primarily Western-educated background for the movement's leadership; while at least three were lawyers, two graduates of other faculties of the Egyptian University, and two others had received their higher education in England, only one had been educated at al-Azhar.[61]

Estimates concerning the membership of Young Egypt in the 1930s indicate a primarily urban base for the movement. In mid-1937, Young Egypt itself claimed 1,536 *mujahid*s (wearers of its distinctive green shirt) in Cairo and another 384 in Alexandria; the report did not provide numbers for membership elsewhere, implying less of a following outside the two metropoles.[62] Nor was Young Egypt *'ulama'*-based; whereas in late 1937 its nominees received 124 votes in elections for the Student Union of the Egyptian University, in late 1938 it enumerated only fifteen members enrolled in the Faculty of Sacred Law at al-Azhar.[63] "Middle-class" social background, residence in the major cities of Egypt, and Western education – Young Egypt was solidly based upon the new effendiyya population emerging in the interwar period.

Much the same seems to have been the case with the Muslim Brotherhood. Despite its religious ethos, the Brotherhood was not an 'ulama'-led organization. Its founder and charismatic figure Hasan al-Banna was not an Azharite by training; rather, he received his higher education at the partially Westernized teachers' college Dar al-'Ulum.[64] Nor was the leadership of the Society dominated by 'ulama'. Of 112 delegates to the Brotherhood's annual conference in 1935, only 25 were shaykhs presumably educated at al-Azhar; nearly twenty years later, the 150 delegates to the Brotherhood's Consultative Assembly of 1953 included but 12 'ulama'.[65] The Brotherhood appears to have been primarily an effendi movement. Its spokesmen distinguished between what they viewed as more obscurantist forms of Islam and the modernist "message of the Muslim Brothers" which was explicitly defined as "the message of the effendi."[66] Ellis Goldberg's research on Brotherhood unionizing efforts indicates that the organization focused its appeal to labor, with considerable success, upon the upper strata of labor, the skilled workforce whose education in technical schools made them part of the new effendiyya.[67] Uri Kupferschmidt has suggested that even outside Egypt's largest cities the Brotherhood's main following was located in provincial towns rather than in villages proper, and has emphasized that the movement's scripturalist/normative approach to Islam had little resonance in the traditional village setting where the folk rituals of popular Islam prevailed.[68] Richard Mitchell's evaluation of the pattern of attendance at Brotherhood meetings after World War II found the "overwhelming majority" of its supporters to be from effendiyya elements such as "the student, the civil servant, the teacher, the clerk and office worker, and the professional in their Western suits."[69]

The environment and acculturation of the new effendiyya cohort produced conflicting stimuli in relation to concepts of national identity. On the one hand, much in their origins and education led them towards a system of values similar to that of the generation before them. On the other hand, variants in their social background and new circumstances in their surroundings were such as to lead them to reject some of the ideas of their predecessors. In terms of nationalism, the results were ambivalent; whereas some aspects of their upbringing led towards an acceptance of the new Egyptian nation-state, other elements in their socialization led them to question the premises upon which that state was based.

The atmosphere of urban Egypt in the interwar period was a heavily Westernized and in some respects an un-Arab, non-Muslim one. This was certainly the case with the state-controlled school system in which the bulk of educated younger Egyptians were being socialized. The emphasis of the curriculum of the state schools was on non-traditional, Western-derived, "modern" subject-matter. In the curriculum in effect through the mid-1930s for the first three years of secondary school, for example, only 20 of a total of 105 class hours were devoted to the study of religion and the Arabic language; the other 85 hours were allotted for the study of foreign languages, the natural and social sciences, and physical education.[70]

The same Western emphasis in education was even more pronounced at the Egyptian University. With its French academic structure, largely European teaching staff, and Western subject-matter usually presented in European languages, the "Egyptian" University in its early years was only nominally an Egyptian institution.[71] The natural result of both the structure and the content of Egyptian state education under the parliamentary monarchy was to produce a generation of Egyptians who, in the words of one of their teachers, were "Muslims only geographically ... Islam does not interest them much or little ... they simply imitate the Europeans in their living and behavior."[72]

At the same time as the state-controlled educational system worked to separate them from their Arab-Muslim heritage, the new effendiyya were being provided with an alternative, Egypt-centered referent for national identity. Courses in civics education were thoroughly Egyptianist in tenor; as a civics syllabus drafted in 1930 put it, the purpose of civics education was to "promote a sense of nationalism through the understanding that in spite of the successive invasions and foreign domination which plagued Egypt throughout its history, Egypt remained an independent and distinctive entity."[73]

Particularly important in molding Egyptian youth in an Egyptianist mold was the myth of the Revolution of 1919, with its aura of unified national struggle and its emphasis on the "complete independence" of Egypt from all external connections. The Revolution of 1919 appears to have been a central event in the lives of politicized younger Egyptians who lived through it. Thus Ahmad Husayn (b. 1911) of Young Egypt in his memoirs emphasized his participation – at age eight – in demonstrations in Cairo in 1919;[74] his colleague Nur al-Din Tarraf (b. 1910) recalls his having to be sent out of Cairo to prevent him from joining his older brothers in anti-British and potentially dangerous activity;[75] and the Wafdist youth leader Mahmud Yunis (b. 1912) remembers being so imbued with nationalist fervor during the Revolution as to have acquired a pistol for use against the British.[76] Ahmad Husayn's later oratory about the psychic effects of having been a youth during the nationalist turmoil of the post-World War I era may reflect a wider attitude among his demi-generation of Egyptians:

I joined in the ranks of the demonstrations, and my voice gave forth with the resounding cries "Egypt and the Sudan belong to us" – "Egypt for the Egyptians" – "complete independence or instant death." Yes, Gentlemen, I remember those images which instilled my spirit with strength and which taught me how to love our eternal mother Egypt and how one should consider life expendable for the sake of Egypt.[77]

Yet, for all their European-oriented education and the primarily Egypt-ianist environment in which they were being acculturated, in comparison to educated Egyptians of the previous generation the Westernization of the new effendiyya of the post-1930 period was on the whole more superficial. Other elements in their circumstances and surroundings oriented this cohort of educated Egyptians toward the indigenous Arab and Muslim traditions of Egypt.

One specific issue which increasingly concerned the educated middle classes of Egypt was that of inadequate occupational opportunity. By the early 1930s, warnings about "the crisis of the educated in Egypt," referring specifically to the lack of employment opportunities for the increasing numbers of educated younger Egyptians, were appearing in the press.[78] An estimate of 1937 placed the number of unemployed graduates of the higher educational system at 11,000.[79] The situation appears to have become worse over time: by the early 1950s, an official source estimated that the state bureaucracy could absorb only 13 percent of the college graduates produced from 1948 to 1952.[80] The result of this constriction of opportunity was student resentment and discontent. In 1936, the issue of employment generated public protests by students themselves.[81] Part of their frustration over uncertain occupational prospects was directed against the Egyptian government, which had traditionally hired many graduates of the state school system but which increasingly found itself unable to continue to do so.[82] Because a significant number of the better jobs in the private sector had long been controlled by Egypt's European minorities, frustration over dreary job prospects was contributing to the anti-European tone which often characterized the supra-Egyptian nationalist outlook.[83]

A significant phenomenon of Egypt in the early 1930s was the emergence of youth-based campaigns whose common purpose was the promotion of Egyptian economic autarky and/or industrialization. In 1931–2, the newly formed network of Young Wafdist Committees mounted an organized campaign for the boycott of foreign, particularly British, imports and the promotion of the sale of local products.[84] A parallel but non-Wafdist campaign was the Piastre Plan inaugurated by university students late in 1931 as a national fundraising drive to collect donations for the creation of new Egyptian industries.[85] The Piastre Plan was the direct forerunner of the Young Egypt Society, itself an organization with a heavy emphasis on economic independence. One of the Ten Principles drafted for the guidance of Young Egypt's followers in 1933 called on them "to buy only from Egyptians, to wear only what is made in Egypt, and to eat only Egyptian foods"; another instructed them "to scorn anything which is foreign, each one of you, and to cling steadfastly to your nationality, making it an obsession."[86]

Along with this economic nationalism went an intense nativism, a self-righteous moralism, and an insistence on Egyptian authenticity. These qualities were perhaps the central feature of the ethos of the new, explicitly Muslim politico-religious societies such as the Young Men's Muslim Association, the Muslim Brotherhood, and numerous others which emerged in Egypt from the late 1920s onwards. The programs and activities of these groups centered on the related issues of the reinvigoration of traditional Muslim mores within Egypt and the defense of the status and prerogatives of Muslims throughout the world. Thus the oath adopted by the Young Men's Muslim Association in 1930 committed its members "to revive the guidance of Islam," "to be active as a warrior fighting for the revival of the glory of Islam," and "to strengthen the ties of brotherhood among all Muslims."[87] Similar themes resonate through the list of goals adopted by the Society of Islamic Jihad in 1934: to promote solidarity among Muslims; to strengthen Islamic ethical values and moral behavior; to oppose irreligious doctrines and heresies; "to resist shameful actions in every possible way ..."[88] Despite its formally secular character, Young Egypt in many ways demonstrated the same spirit. The movement's original program of 1933 stated among its aims the intent to "elevate morals" and to "struggle against immorality, effeminacy, and drunkenness"; its coda of Ten Principles promulgated in the same year enjoined its members to "be pure" and to "abstain from liquor, prohibited entertainments, and foreign films."[89]

Equally important in the ethos of these new organizations was their fierce sense of activism, of the necessity for Muslims to take the initiative in reversing the unIslamic course of recent history. At the founding of the Muslim Brotherhood in 1928, Hasan al-Banna recalls having responded to the appeal of his friends for the formation of a new religious organization by summoning them to be "soldiers" for Islam and by reminding them of the necessity of struggle or *jihad* for its sake.[90] The necessity of commitment, of active striving for the good, of "maximal effort in word and deed," were central themes in the literature of both the Muslim Brotherhood and Young Egypt.[91]

The logical corollary of this dynamism and activism was an intensely political orientation on the part of the new effendiyya. Both the emphases of their formal education and the circumstances of their environment led younger Egyptians coming to maturity under the parliamentary monarchy to regard political involvement as a personal imperative. In its content, Egyptian civics education has been analyzed as being highly idealistic in nature, with the net result of its emphasis on both the rights and the duties of citizens of the new Egyptian state being to incline students toward a sense of political awareness and involvement.[90] Outside the classroom, the socio-psychological milieu of interwar Egypt reinforced a political orientation for the new effendiyya. Their select status as an educated minority in what was still a primarily illiterate country by default placed the psychological burden of responsibility for shaping the future of the country on educated youth. The broader culture's incessant emphasis on the clash between "ancient" and "modern," with its corollary that youth represented the latter, also drove the new groups being socialized in the interwar period toward involvement in Egyptian public life.[91] Perhaps most important in propelling these groups toward political activism was the vibrant political culture of Egypt under the parliamentary monarchy – competing political parties, raucous press, and incessant appeals by politicians addressed to the younger generation that the future of the nation was in their hands.

What may be termed a myth of youth developed in interwar Egypt, a rhetoric stressing the national role as well as the redeeming power of the "new generation." Egypt's premier cultural periodical *al-Hilal* devoted an entire issue to "The Youth [*al-Shabab*]" in 1936, justifying its publication of the same on the grounds that "at the present time youth have an influence in both the political and the social spheres; on their shoulders now rests [the responsibility for] new revivals in the East and the West."[92] An emphasis on youth received an enormous boost later in the same year when King Fu'ad was succeeded by his sixteen-year-old son Faruq, who in the later 1930s possessed an image of sincerity, piety, and promise unfulfilled by his subsequent performance as king.[93] The tendency to reify youth was most pronounced in the Young Egypt movement. On one side, its publicists repeatedly denounced the shortcomings and failures of "the old generation [which] has exhausted the last of its stock of vigor, of its ability to work and to rule and to produce."[94] On the other, as unsullied representatives of a generation politicized since their youth by absorption in the national struggle, they proclaimed their own greater competence: "we are the sons of the Revolution, believers in the glory of our country; therefore we can do what the older generation is incapable of."[95]

There were also more organizational outlets for political activity on the part of the new effendiyya as time progressed. With the rapid expansion of the school system in the interwar period, individual schools began to generate their own student associations. According to the memoirs of figures prominent in youth politics after 1930, such school clubs had been the forum where they first found an opportunity for political as well as cultural self-expression.[98] Egypt's main political parties – the Wafd, the Nationalists, and the Liberals – established organized youth affiliates in the 1920s.[99] A new trend of the early 1930s was the formation of new, student-based organizations which were largely independent of the established political parties. The Piastre Plan was one such group; although possessing an advisory committee of older notables, both its leadership and its membership were drawn from students of the Egyptian University and the secondary schools.[100] A similar youth-directed activity of the same period was the Eastern Students Conference, an abortive project spawned among the faculty and students of the Egyptian University for an international assembly of students from various "Eastern" countries to convene annually to discuss common problems.[101] The culmination of the trend toward independent organization and activism by educated Egyptian youth came in 1933, with the creation of an explicitly youth-oriented patriotic association, the Young Egypt Society.[102]

The most visible form of political activism by the new effendiyya in the 1930s was found in the paramilitary organizations which briefly obtruded into Egyptian public life in the mid-1930s. An essential feature of Young Egypt from its inception was its Green Shirt formations with their military organization, paramilitary drill, and vitalist ethos.[103] The Wafd established its parallel paramilitary Blue Shirt organization in the wake of the massive student demonstrations of late 1935–early 1936.[104] Together, the Green Shirts of Young Egypt and the Blue Shirts of the Wafd, with their mutual antipathy and periodic street clashes, were a major factor in the destabilization of Egyptian public life in the later 1930s, until a decree of March 1938 dissolved all paramilitary organizations.

The emergence of these political organizations for youth was paralleled by the establishment and growth of new religious societies which also played a larger and larger political role over time. The most prominent of these were the Young Men's Muslim Association and the Muslim Brotherhood.[105] The YMMA grew rapidly after its formation in Cairo in 1927, soon opening branches in Alexandria and several provincial cities; it had a reported 15,000 members before the end of the decade.[106] The 1930s were a period of rapid growth for the Muslim Brotherhood, whose local branches are estimated to have increased from perhaps four in 1929 to some 500 in 1939.[107] By the late 1940s, James Heyworth-Dunne reported some 135 separate societies of an Islamic character existing in Egypt.[108]

Despite their religious orientation and their general rejection of the premises of Egyptian territorial nationalism, this network of new Islamic movements should be regarded as part and parcel of the development of a modern national culture in Egypt. Largely urban, with a focus on youth and the educated middle class, and possessing a socially activist emphasis on promoting practical activities ranging from athletics to cooperative economic ventures, these societies represented a conscious attempt to adjust Egyptian life to the sweeping changes of the twentieth century by developing an outlook and lifestyle which would be both Muslim and modern. With their intellectual outlook which regarded all spheres of life as subordinate to religion, from their inception they became deeply involved in the main issues agitating Egyptian public life. When they did so, they did so on a Muslim-Arab basis.

Egyptian ties with the Arab world

The final major process which helped to promote supra-Egyptianist perspectives in Egypt after 1930 was a changing relationship between Egypt and its Arab neighbors. An extensive network of contacts between Egypt and the surrounding Arab world developed over the interwar period. In the Arab East in particular a unified cultural community, what Albert Hourani has termed "a shared world of taste and ideas" linked physically by better communication and mentally by increased intellectual interaction, took shape in the 1920s and 1930s.[109] The effect of these new ties between Egypt and its Arab neighbors was to erode the previous Egyptian sense of separation from the Arab world, replacing it with a heightened awareness of both the shared heritage and the common interests linking all Arabs.

The immediate arena of greater contact between Egyptians and other Arabs was within Egypt itself. A sizable Arab immigration to Egypt, particularly from Syria and Palestine, occurred in the late nineteenth and early twentieth centuries. The census of 1927 reported 72,934 foreign-born residents of Egypt from other Arab countries.[110] The Arab émigré community living in Egypt in the interwar period was an affluent and articulate one. Most relevant for the subject of nationalism is the prominent place in journalism and publishing held by Arabs of Fertile Crescent origin. Many of the leading publications of Egypt were operated by families of Syro-Lebanese extraction; numerous other Arabs of Fertile Crescent origin worked as journalists in Egypt.[111]

The political and cultural views expounded by these "Syrian" journalists active in Egypt during the interwar years ran the gamut from the secular modernism of journals like *al-Hilal* and *al-Muqtataf* to the religious conservatism found in *al-Manar* and *al-Fath*. On the whole, however, the perspective found in these Syrian-run publications converged in their emphasis on Egypt's integral linkage with the surrounding Arab and Muslim worlds. The reasons offered as the basis for such an affiliation often differed (Arab cultural bonds in *al-Hilal*; the economic and political benefits to be gained from Arab cooperation in *al-Muqattam*; the communal unity of all Muslims in *al-Fath*). But the overall effect was the same – making Egyptians aware of their connections with neighboring regions and peoples.

In the interwar period, Egypt served as a refuge and a base for many Arab nationalist activists who had been forced into exile from their own homelands by their opposition to imperialism. Prominent Arab spokesmen such as Shaykh 'Abd al-'Aziz al-Tha'alibi of Tunisia, Dr. 'Abd al-Rahman al-Shahbandar of Syria, or Muhammad 'Ali al-Tahir of Palestine spent years of residence in Egypt, where they were in frequent demand as commentators on Arab and Muslim affairs. Sometimes their efforts to encourage greater Egyptian attention to the conditions in the Arab world were met with Egyptian indifference. But in other instances they were able to influence the Egyptians with whom they came in contact to adopt a more positive attitude toward the Arabs. Shaykh Tha'alibi has been credited with helping to move the opinions of several leading Egyptians, including Ahmad Shafiq and Muhammad Lutfi Jum'a, toward a greater sympathy with Arab nationalism;[112] Hafiz Mahmud recalls having the seeds of his own concern for Arab questions planted in him through hearing a lecture by Dr. Shahbandar at the YMMA;[113] and Ahmad Husayn similarly remembers a speech by the Palestinian leader Is'af al-Nashashibi as one of the crucial events swinging him away from an exclusively Egyptianist orientation.[114]

Over time, Arab nationalists came to give greater attention to the relationship between Arab nationalism and Egypt. In contrast to the Arab nationalist indifference toward Egypt before and during World War I, the elimination of the Ottoman Empire in the aftermath of the war led other Arabs to look toward Egypt for regional leadership. As a manifesto by one of the short-lived Arab societies founded in Egypt in the early 1930s noted, whereas before the Great War the East had centered its attention on "the Ottoman state because it was the state of the Caliphate," after the war the whole East and the Arab East in particular began to see that "its intellectual leadership has [now] been entrusted to Egypt."[115] This was particularly the case with the younger generation of Arab nationalists. According to As'ad Daghir, a leading Arab publicist resident in Egypt for much of the interwar period, the Arab nationalists with whom he was associated believed that Egypt's isolation from Arab affairs harmed Arab nationalism, that "there is no Arabism without Egypt," and thus that "it is necessary for every Arab, Egyptian or non-Egyptian, to devote his strength to propagating and implanting the Arab idea in the minds of Egyptians."[116]

By the 1930s, Arab nationalists were actively promoting Egyptian involvement in Arab affairs. Arab émigrés and students living in Egypt took the lead in the formation of the first Arab-oriented societies established in Egypt in the early 1930s: an Arab Progress Society created by Palestinian students at al-Azhar in 1930, one of the aims of which was the promotion of "Arab unity";[117] the Society for Arab Unity (Jam'iyyat al-Wahda al-'Arabiyya) established at the Egyptian University in 1931, the central purpose of which was "strengthening the social bonds and the cultural connections between the Arab regions";[118] the Committee for the Spread of Arab Culture (al-Lajna li-Nashr al-Thaqafa al-'Arabiyya) set up by 'Abd al-Rahman Shahbandar and Ahmad Zaki in the same year.[119] Similar organizations were created, often with non-Egyptian Arabs playing a leading role, in the later 1930s: a revived Society of Arab Unity (Jam'iyyat al-Wahda al-'Arabiyya) formed by Arab and Egyptian students at the Egyptian University in 1936 on the premise that "there is no Arabism without Egypt, and no unity or independence save after her involvement with them [the Arabs]";[120] an Association of Arab Unity (Jama'at al-Wahda al-'Arabiyya) established by students at the Egyptian University in the autumn of 1938;[121] the Bond of Arabism (Rabitat al-'Uruba) created by Arab and Egyptian students at the same institution's Faculty of Law early in 1939.[122]

The most durable and important of these Arabist organizations of the 1930s was the Arab Bond Society (Jam'iyyat al-Rabita al-'Arabiyya). The goals of this officially non-political organization upon its creation in 1936 were "working for the spreading of Arabic culture by every possible and legal means" as well as the "strengthening of the scientific, social, and economic bonds and relations between Egypt, the remaining Arab regions, and the speakers of Arabic in various lands."[123] The new organization drew significant support from the Syrian community resident in Egypt, and students of the Egyptian University played an active part in its activities. Numerous Egyptian politicians and intellectuals sympathetic to Arab issues contributed to the association's journal *Majallat al-Rabita al-'Arabiyya* or participated in its meetings. Its cadre thus combined Arab émigrés sympathetic to Arab nationalism, Egyptian politicians and intellectuals moving in the direction of a more Arabist orientation, and representatives of the new effendiyya population. The society's main form of activity through the later 1930s was in the salon/*hafla* tradition of Egyptian cultural interaction; the hosting of receptions for Arab notables living in or visiting Egypt, events which were the occasion for speeches declaiming on the numerous bonds which linked the Arab peoples, the benefits of Arab interaction, and the need for Egyptian leadership of the movement toward Arab unity.[124]

The interwar period witnessed an appreciable increase in physical contact and intellectual interaction between Egyptian and other Arab students and professionals – the new effendiyya of the Arab world. Student groups from neighboring Arab countries began making organized visits to Egypt from 1926.[125] The frequency of these increased by the early 1930s, when school and scouting groups from Fertile Crescent areas visited Egypt annually during the summer months. Such tours were the occasion for receptions and meetings with Egyptian youth groups.[126] Arab youth visiting Egypt were not loath to remind Egyptians of the Arabness of Egypt: in 1932, upon touring the new factory being built by funds collected in the Piastre Plan and reading its motto of "Egypt Over All," the members of an Iraqi student delegation are reported to have responded with the cry "Arabism Over All!"[127]

Egyptian travel to Arab countries also increased over the interwar period. From the early 1920s and the stabilization of political conditions in the Middle East, growing numbers of Egyptians traveled in Arab Asia. The principal occasion for Egyptian travel to Arab Asia was the Muslim Pilgrimage. British estimates of the number of pilgrims traveling to the Hijaz from Egypt in the 1920s and 1930s range from a low of 2,500 in 1920 to a high of 16,000 in 1926, before the depression reduced the number to between 5,000 and 10,000 annually through the 1930s.[128]

What was novel was the range and frequency of visits by Egyptians to Arab areas for reasons other than the Pilgrimage. Some went for scholarly purposes, to search for manuscripts (Ahmad Zaki).[129] Others went as journalists, to sample and to write about the still somewhat quaint conditions in neighboring Arab regions (Mahmud 'Azmi, Ibrahim 'Abd al-Qadir al-Mazini),[130] or as proselytizers for Egyptian religious organizations (the Muslim Brotherhood leaders 'Abd al-Rahman al-Sa'ati and Muhammad As'ad al-Hakim).[131] Some went for political reasons, as did Ahmad Zaki and Muhammad 'Ali 'Alluba when they testified before the Wailing Wall Commission of the League of Nations in 1930.[132] Still others had business interests they wished to promote, Tal'at Harb of Bank Misr visiting the Fertile Crescent three times in the 1920s in order to establish foreign branches of the bank or Ahmad Shafiq going to the Hijaz on pilgrimage but taking the opportunity to attempt to obtain banking and mineral concessions from King ibn Sa'ud.[133] As a result of such Egyptian travel in the Arab world, in time a mini-genre of travel literature concerning Arab countries sprouted in Egypt.[134] Its emergence testifies both to the personal impact such travel was having on the Egyptians who undertook it as well as to the emergence of an Egyptian market for literature about the neighboring Arab countries.

Egyptian group travel to other Arab regions increased as well. The first organized educational tours by Egyptian students to the Arab lands date from 1929, when a group of Egyptian University students spent the summer in Syria and Lebanon.[135] Trips by Egyptian youth to Arab Asia became a regular occurrence in the 1930s, when Egyptian University student tours proceeded to all the countries of the Fertile Crescent as well as to the Hijaz and when Egyptian Boy Scout trips added to the flow in the summer months.[136]

The new sense of Egyptian affiliation with the Arab world developed particularly in university circles in the 1930s. For al-Azhar this was only to be expected; at this explicitly Islamic institution, a sizable proportion of the student body of which was drawn from other Arab and Muslim countries, a concern with Arab-Muslim issues was built into its curriculum as well as its constituency. But the secular Egyptian University, the students of which were the epitome of the new effendiyya population emerging in interwar Egypt, was also an important center for the development of a more supra-Egyptian nationalist outlook. Egyptian University students played an active part in the formation of many of the Arab unity societies which were created in Egypt in the 1930s, and were in the forefront of political agitation relating to Arab-Muslim issues such as Palestine in the later 1930s.[137] An Arabist journal was not far from the mark in 1937 when it stated that "the [Egyptian] University is now considered the leader of the Arabist movement in Egypt."[138]

In view of the prominent place of students and academicians in this network of expanding Egyptian–Arab contacts, it is not surprising that the main spheres of increased Arab interaction were those of cultural exchange and educational cooperation. By the 1930s, numerous organizations and projects for fostering Arab cultural and educational collaboration had been initiated in Egypt. Several organizations oriented toward the promotion of Arab greater cultural interaction were established in Egypt in the early 1930s: the Apollo Society (Jam'iyyat Apulu) of 1932–4 which, while primarily created to foster modernist literary activity, also had the strengthening of cultural cooperation among the Arab regions as an explicit part of its program;[139] the Arab Literary Union (Ittihad al-Adab al-'Arabi) headed by Dr. Muhammad Sharaf of 1933;[140] the Arab General Union (al-Ittihad al-'Arabi al-'Amm) founded by 'Ali al-'Inani in the same year, the purposes of which included strengthening the Arabic language and Arab culture.[141]

This current accelerated in the later 1930s. In 1936, a group of Egyptian intellectuals invited representatives from other Arab lands to come to Cairo to discuss inter-Arab cultural cooperation.[142] Subsequent meetings resulted in the formation of the Association for the Unification of Arab Culture (Jam'iyyat Tawhid al-Thaqafa al-'Arabiyya). Its activities were intended to encompass the entire Arab world from the Arab Peninsula through North Africa; its specific aims included "the strengthening and consolidation of the Arab cultural revival," the coordination of educational programs among the different Arab countries, the publication of a new Arab cultural journal, and the convening of Arab cultural conferences.[143] These contacts of 1936–7 came to fruition in 1938–9, with the establishment of a successor

committee of Arab intellectuals, the Society of Arabic Studies for the
Unification of Arab Culture (Jam'iyyat al-Dirasat al-'Arabiyya lil-Tawhid
al-Thaqafa al-'Arabiyya) headed by the Egyptian academician Ahmad Amin
and dedicated to "the consolidation of links between specialists from different Arabic disciplines of learning."[144]

Growing Arab cooperation was particularly visible in the realm of education. Increasing numbers of Egyptian academicians traveled to Arab
countries to teach and to advise on educational matters from the late 1930s
onwards; by 1945, some 360 Egyptians were reported to be teaching in
neighboring Arab lands.[145] Educational missions sent to Iraq appear to
have been of particular importance in fostering a more Arab-inclined attitude in Egypt. From the mid-1930s, when the Iraqi government requested
the dispatch of Egyptian University faculty to assist in improving Iraqi
higher education, numerous Egyptian academicians (among others, Ahmad
Hasan al-Zayyat, Zaki Mubarak, 'Abd al-Razzaq al-Sanhuri, and 'Abd al-
Wahhab 'Azzam) went to Iraq on temporary assignment.[146] Coming into
close contact with Iraqi colleagues such as Sati' al-Husri, Sami Shawqat,
and Fadil al-Jamali, the writings and public statements of Egyptians
serving in Iraq indicate a significant impact on their own nationalist
thought by the pan-Arabist ideology then in the process of formulation in
Iraq.[147]

Travel to or work in the Arab world was an important influence in
producing a new openness to ideas of Arab solidarity and cooperation on the
part of individuals who previously had been solely Egyptianist in outlook.
Mahmud 'Azmi was one such; as he put it in 1929, "I was personally
liberated from the bondage of 'Egyptianist Pharaonic' theory after I travel-
led to Palestine, Lebanon, and Syria, and discovered the reality of the
feelings of the people there towards Egypt and the extent of the relationship
of all the regions which speak the Arabic language and are linked by Arab
history."[148] Similarly Ahmad Husayn, a fervent Pharaonicist in his youth,
credits a trip to the Fertile Crescent as one of the major influences which
turned him from Pharaonicism toward Arabism; it "implanted in my soul
the love of Arabism and [the belief] that the future of Egypt was dependent
on its links to the Arab lands."[149] Ahmad Hasan al-Zayyat captured the
eye-opening effect of travel in the Arab world for Egyptians:

he [the Egyptian traveler] observes their hearts beating with the same feelings he
feels, their breasts heaving with his hopes, their tongues talking about his news, their
revival seeking guidance from his revival, their path pointing in the same direction as
his. For his journals are read, his books studied, his policies imitated, his leadership
followed. Moreover, his quarrel is their quarrel, his government is their government, his people the same people as their people, his country the *qibla* of their
country.[150]

It is no coincidence that several of the more vehement statements in support of Egypt's Arabness and the necessity for closer Egyptian interaction with other Arabs were made by Egyptians either while traveling in other Arab countries or immediately upon their return from such travel. Such was the case with Muhammad 'Ali 'Alluba's declaration that "the Arab countries are one nation bound by the same bond," uttered while in Damascus in 1930;[151] with Ibrahim 'Abd al-Qadir al-Mazini's articles advocating an Arab policy for Egypt, written after a trip to Syria and Iraq in 1934;[152] with Muhammad Tal'at Harb's statement that "Egypt and Iraq are one country," made at a reception in Iraq in 1936;[153] and with Zaki Mubarak's ringing affirmation that "Egypt is Arab in everything" in a speech in Baghdad in 1938.[154]

Conclusion

The cumulative force of these trends moving Egyptians away from an exclusivist Egyptian territorial nationalism and toward a more inclusive supra-Egyptian conceptualization of national identity appeared in the periodic controversies over the essential nature of Egypt which became a feature of Egyptian public life in the early 1930s. A well-attended debate over the issue of whether Egypt's culture was "Pharaonic" or "Arab" was held at the Egyptian University in December 1930. After a lengthy exchange in which Muhammad Lutfi Jum'a defended the essential uniqueness of Egyptian culture while Muhammad Rashid Rida – seconded by an emotional address by the young Ahmad Husayn – asserted its massive and determining Arab and Islamic character, the audience was polled; by a sizable majority (187 to 103), the Arabist position prevailed.[155] In 1931, the journal al-Hilal polled several Egyptian notables over the issue of whether Egypt's cultural heritage was primarily "Pharaonic or Arabic or Western." The dominant theme of the responses was to emphasize the Arab and Muslim dimensions of Egyptian life.[156]

The most extensive of these public disputations over the national character of Egypt took place in late 1933. In an article of 28 August, Taha Husayn made a passing reference to the "injustice" and "aggression" suffered by the people of Egypt at the hands of various invading groups, "the Arabs" included.[157] Husayn's remark set off a furious debate in the Egyptian press over the next several weeks.[158]

As might be expected, Husayn's equation of the Arabs with other "invaders" of Egypt came under fierce criticism from non-Egyptian Arabs.[159] Most Egyptian commentary was also critical of his position. At the least, the historical accuracy of his sweeping assertion about Arab oppression in Egypt was disputed. 'Abd al-Qadir al-Mazini maintained that all prolonged periods of rule by one group were bound to be a blend of positive and negative features.[160] To Hasan al-Banna of the Muslim Brotherhood, Arab rule in Egypt had been "a spiritual, enlightening, cultural imperialism."[161] The general consensus of most of those joining in the debate was stated by al-Balagh's editor 'Abd al-Qadir Hamza: "Dr. Taha Husayn is mistaken in what he has written concerning the Arabs."[162]

The controversy became the occasion for indictments of the entire Pharaonic orientation which had developed in Egypt in recent years, and with which Taha Husayn was (not totally fairly) identified by his critics. 'Abd al-Rahman 'Azzam simply denied that "the Egyptian nation" was the "continuation" of Pharaonic Egypt; in his view, modern Egypt had been shaped primarily by "Arab religion, customs, language, and culture."[163] Muhammad Amin Hassuna sarcastically compared Egyptians advocating Pharaonicism with Spaniards seeking to revive Arab culture in contemporary Spain; both approaches were equally anachronistic.[164] Ahmad Hasan al-Zayyat, after belittling Pharaonicism by maintaining that only "two or three" Egyptian authors promoted it, argued for the contingent nature of nationalism. One became part of a people when imprinted with their social and cultural characteristics. On this basis, over thirteen centuries of being Arab in religion, language, and culture had "eliminated the Pharaonic influence" for Egyptians; "as for the culture of the papyrus, it has no connection with Arab Egypt, neither with the Muslims nor with the Copts."[165]

Rather than viewing the Arabs as alien to Egypt, Husayn's critics maintained the undeniably Arab character of Egypt. For Hasan al-Banna, all Arab peoples shared the same blood, language, religion, customs, and culture; in his view any Arab, "whether one's land is Egypt or Iraq or Syria, must also consider himself a member of the body of a great nation unified by language, religion, sentiment, and goal. That is the Arab nation."[166] 'Ali al-'Inani held that Egyptians were members of a larger "Semitic Arab race," an immemorial historical entity including all speakers of Arabic from the Persian Gulf to the Atlantic Ocean. In his view "Egypt was never anything but Arab in flesh and blood."[167] The strongest assertion of Egypt's Arabness propounded in the debate of 1933 came from the figure who was already emerging as the leading exponent of Egypt's indissoluble connection with the Arab world, 'Abd al-Rahman 'Azzam. To 'Azzam, Egyptians had not only "accepted the religion, customs, language, and culture of the Arabs"; in addition, "most of the blood of its [Egypt's] people is traceable to Arab veins."[168] 'Azzam went on to assert a racial basis for Egyptian identification with the Arabs, arguing that Egypt had "become Arab" over a period of millennia and that the Arab conquest of Egypt in the seventh century itself had been facilitated by this "racial link" between Arabs and Egyptians.[169] 'Azzam therefore called on his fellow Egyptian Arabs to join the other Arabs in working for "the glorification of the race" to which they all belonged.[170]

Taha Husayn was not without his defenders in the debate. Husayn himself replied to his critics first by maintaining that he opposed neither the Arab revival nor Arab unity, then by qualifying his original remark with the gloss that Arab rule over Egypt had originally been beneficial but that it later deteriorated into "a mixture of good and bad, justice and injustice."[171] Hasan Subhi and Muhammad Zaki Ibrahim indirectly supported Husayn's position by presenting inclusive views of Egyptian national identity which saw the Arabs as only one of the many groups of outsiders who had entered Egypt and influenced its national personality.[172] Muhammad Kamil Husayn and Hasan 'Arif went even further than Husayn in distinguishing between Egyptians and Arabs, the former maintaining that "Egyptian life differs from the life of the Arabs" and that "Egyptians have their own mentality which differs from the mentality of the Arabs," the latter asserting that Egypt was "not Arab" and that it "differs from the Arabs in everything."[173]

Perhaps the most illuminating viewpoints expressed in the debate of late 1933 were those which attempted a reconciliation between Husayn's presumed Egyptianism and the Arabism of his critics. Muhammad Husayn Haykal presented an eclectic vision of Egypt and its long history, one which asserted the continuity and complementarity of all eras of Egyptian history.[174] For Haykal, there was no inherent contradiction between attention to Egypt's ancient Pharaonic heritage and the assertion of its present primarily Arab and Islamic character. Pharaonic strands and Arabo-Islamic elements were both part of the complex and multilayered Egyptian historical legacy; both deserved sympathetic study by contemporary Egyptians who wished to revive their nation in the present and future. Haykal's counsel to his readers was that "a present which has no past has no future"; the recognition and appreciation of the multiple historical legacies of Egypt as well as the other Arab countries was an indispensable part of the ongoing revival of these nations.

'Abd al-Qadir Hamza's presentation of Egyptian history developed the theme that the Egyptian national character combined two main strands: from Egypt itself came racial, local, and long-term historical influences; from the Arabs came language, religion, and culture. "Thus Egyptians are Egyptian in their homeland, their race, and their history, and at the same time they are Arabs in their religion, their language, and the genuine affection which they carry for their Arab brothers east and west." From this theoretical position Hamza called both on his fellow Egyptians to acknowledge the Arab community as their "second *watan*," but also on other Arabs to accept that the "first *watan*" of Egyptians was Egypt.[175]

One of the last major contributions to the debate was an essay by Mahmud 'Azmi evaluating the potential meaningfulness for Egypt of the alternative concepts of an Eastern, an Islamic, or an Arab orientation. The "Eastern bond" in 'Azmi's view was an arbitrary and artificial one which reflected neither meaningful distinctions between "East" and "West" nor any organic unity among the various regions comprising the "East"; as such, it was a "fantasy" which provided no genuine basis for solidarity or common action. The "Islamic bond," on the other hand, was a meaningful one; indeed, in the past it had been the strongest bond for Egyptians as well as others. But for 'Azmi it carried the drawback of potentially dividing the nation between religious groups and thus weakening national unity. Given these problems of either an Eastern or an Islamic affiliation for Egyptians, 'Azmi found the "Arab bond" the only one capable of providing a sound basis for future Egyptian action. Rooted firmly in a common language, culture, and shared "aspirations for independence and liberation," an Arab alliance was the most beneficial regional policy for contemporary Egypt.[176]

Several important points about the state of Egyptian opinion on the question of national identity emerge from this debate of 1933. The very fact that it took place is itself important; such discussions of the Egyptian-Pharaonic versus the Islamic-Arab character of Egypt had no precedents in the 1920s, when Egyptian territorial nationalism was preeminent within Egypt. By 1933, in contrast, the dominant nationalist paradigm of the 1920s was becoming problematic. The significance of the debate was captured in a private letter written by one of its main participants, 'Abd al-Rahman 'Azzam, to a British official in October 1933.[177] After reviewing how "the strength of the local patriotism" prevailing in Egypt in the 1920s had succeeded in "isolating Egypt from its co-religionists and brothers beyond its frontiers," 'Azzam's judgment was that this exclusivist Egyptian nationalism was now fading. In the past few years, he asserted, Egyptian public opinion had begun to move in the direction of the acceptance of Egyptian collaboration with the neighboring Arabs. The recent controversy over Egypt and the Arabs only confirmed this movement of public opinion toward a greater acceptance of Egypt's Arabness: in 'Azzam's view, "The debate was ended by an enormous vote in favour of Egypt [as] an Arab country. Dr. Taha felt defeated and closed the discussion but the topic is still in the Press and it is quite clear that [opinion in] Egypt on this subject is something very different from what it was ten years ago." The character and content of that very different view of Egyptian national identity is the subject of the following analysis.

Part I

The intellectual formulation and social
dissemination of new supra-Egyptian
orientations and ideologies

2 "Now is the turn of the East":[1] Egyptian Easternism in the 1930s

Orientations, ideologies, intellectuals

The following discussion of supra-Egyptian nationalism treats the phenomenon on two levels. The first is an analysis of the underlying nationalist orientations reinterpreting Egypt's place in the world which developed after 1930. The second is an analysis of the specific ideologies which built on those new orientations, instructing Egyptians as to how to behave in their reinterpreted environment.[2]

By "orientation" we mean the overall accounting people make of the place of themselves and their society in the wider world. Orientations are the global outlooks found in a society. On the one hand, they involve drawing lines: between us and them, self and other. On the other, they attempt to identify, in very broad terms, the network of symbols and values appropriate as the basis of the collective existence of a society. In content, orientations consist of a large body of overlapping, interrelated, and not necessarily totally consistent moods, attitudes, beliefs, and interpretations of reality. Generalized and diffuse in nature, they provide the basic assumptions and presuppositions about a society's relationship to its environment which are implicit in the specific arguments, theories, and debates occurring in intellectual and political circles.

While orientations are clearly a response to the temporal situation of a society, in and of themselves they do not offer a program for altering that situation. Orientations lack an operative, programmatic dimension. Both logically and historically, they precede attempts to define blueprints for current and future change. An orientation provides the bundle of fears and apprehensions, hopes and aspirations, which programmatic endeavors are directed to obviating or achieving.

As large and diffuse intellectual structures, orientations extend through much of the articulate population of a society. In the case of Egypt in the 1930s and 1940s, two new orientations set the terms of the nationalist discourse of the period. One was an identification with the peoples and cultures of the "East" rather than with those of the "West." The other was a renewed emphasis on the Islamic character and culture of Egypt. These interrelated Eastern and Islamic orientations were articulated by numerous Egyptians representing different generations, social strata, and educational and occupational backgrounds. They found expression in numerous sources – the daily press, journals of opinion from those representative of the Egyptian establishment to the more populist publications of the organizations of the new effendiyya, political propaganda, and creative literature.

By "ideology" we mean systematic bodies of thought formulated into a coherent intellectual structure and oriented toward action in the world. They are programmatic systems of symbolic meaning. Ideologies modify the inchoate perceptions expressed in orientations, incorporating them in a more analytical structure and giving them a critical character which attempts to explain social reality. An ideology is an attempt to find meaningful order in the multiplicity of reality, an effort to explain the logic behind experience. From the variety of life, an ideology selects specific events and moments to which it accords significance. Ideology seeks to fill the gaps between past and present, individual and group, thought and action, thereby providing a coherent framework through which people can relate to one another as well as to the world.

Central to our concept of ideology is its operative dimension. An ideology is simultaneously a response to strain and an attempt to overcome strain. Beyond understanding reality, it aims at altering it. First and foremost, an ideology is "a cluster of symbols and representations which facilitate the meaningful constitution and social integration of action."[3] Ideologies are praxis-oriented. They are intended as maps through the labyrinth of experience.

Ideologies are more discrete intellectual phenomena than the more generalized orientations which they reflect. This was the case in Egypt in the 1930s and 1940s. The Eastern and Islamic orientations which developed after 1930 in turn gave birth to three new supra-Egyptian nationalist ideologies – those of Egyptian Islamic nationalism, integralist Egyptian nationalism, and Egyptian Arab nationalism. Although not their exclusive creators, specific intellectuals and/or organizations of the period played the leading role in the formulation and dissemination of each of these new supra-Egyptian ideologies.

The distinction between orientations and ideologies is not always clear-cut. In content, these analytical categories overlapped in their historical evolution as well as in their symbols and substance. All were based on the same "external" environment; all drew from the same cultural reservoir in their reinterpretations of reality. In terms of their producers, Eastern, Islamic, and Arab attitudes were often expressed by the same authors in the same texts. Nonetheless, despite the overlap and mutual links between these bodies of thought, we believe that an analysis structured in terms first of the new overall orientations of the era, then of the specific ideologies to which these orientations gave rise, is a heuristically useful one for understanding the complex nationalist intellectual development of Egypt after 1930.

As might be expected with a complex and multifaceted phenomenon, numerous Egyptian intellectuals and publicists participated in the formulation and dissemination of the supra-Egyptianist orientations and ideologies of the post-1930 period. Older intellectual luminaries such as Ahmad Amin (b. 1886), 'Abbas Mahmud al-'Aqqad (b. 1889), Taha Husayn (b. 1889), and Muhammad Husayn Haykal (b. 1888), all of whom in the 1920s had been advocates of territorial nationalism, now redefined their nationalist thought to take account of changing conditions and a changing audience. Several other intellectuals of the same generation – Mansur Fahmi (b. 1886), Muhammad Lutfi Jum'a (b. 1886), 'Abd al-Wahhab 'Azzam (b. 1894), Ahmad Hasan al-Zayyat (b. 1885), Zaki Mubarak (b. 1891), 'Abd al-Rahman 'Azzam (b. 1891) – who had been less important in the territorialist milieu of the 1920s achieved the height of their prominence as spokesmen of the supra-Egyptianist outlook in the 1930s.

But it was particularly younger intellectuals and publicists drawn from the emerging new effendiyya population of Egypt who were central to the development of supra-Egyptian imaginings of Egypt. With their own avenues of dissemination of ideas relatively independent of established channels (their own societies and network of journals), individuals such as Hasan al-Banna (b. 1906), Salih Mustafa 'Ashmawi (b. 1905?), Ahmad Husayn (b. 1911), Fathi Radwan (b. 1911), Hafiz Mahmud (b. 1910), Sayyid Qutb (b. 1906), Ahmad Khaqi (b. 1908), Ahmad Sabri (b. 1910), Muhammad Sa'id al-'Aryan (b. 1905), and Sulayman Huzayyin (b. 1909), played the key role in both the articulation of supra-Egyptianist concepts and the diffusion of the new nationalist perspective through broader sectors of society.

Egyptian Easternism

The division of the world into two broad civilizational entities – the "West" equated with Europe and its colonial outliers, and an "East" composed of the traditions of Asia and Africa – had been a distinction accepted by various Egyptian thinkers since the late nineteenth century. In the 1930s, Egyptian speculation about the East–West dichotomy took on a new quality. On the one hand, there was a heightened insistence on the substantive differences separating East and West; on the other, a belief in the existence of a perennial and ineradicable conflict between the two civilizations became the norm.

The development of this new Easternist orientation of the 1930s can best be explained within the context of the general evolution of Egyptian national life. At the same time that the economic and political traumas experienced by Egypt after 1930 demonstrated the contradictions between Egyptian territorial nationalist theory and Egyptian reality, they also fueled a search for alternative interpretations of the causes of Egypt's internal and external difficulties. The Easternist speculation of the 1930s provided one such explanation. In emphasizing Egypt's "Eastern" character, it afforded both a convincing analysis of what was wrong with contemporary Egypt (its abandonment of its true essence in favor of an alien and inferior Western-ism) and an appealing prescription as to how to rectify the situation (through a return to authentic Egyptian = Eastern values).

The Easternist speculation of the 1930s also had a social basis. Its development was part of a process of adjustment on the part of the country's intellectual elite to the rapidly changing social structure of Egypt, specific-ally to the emergence of the larger literate new effendiyya population. Both the symbols and the substance of the more anti-Western, Eastern-oriented thought of the 1930s show its formulators to be responding to the intel-lectual and emotional demands of the new "consumer" groups from the urban middle class which were becoming the principal audience for cultural production. Thus the emergence of the Easternist speculation of the 1930s should also be understood in terms of the mutual feedback between the intelligentsia of Egypt and the evolving popular expectations to which intellectuals were becoming more sensitive and more receptive.

East is East and West is West

In the 1920s the need for Egypt to emulate the West in all facets of life in order to become a modern society had been widely accepted by the country's political and intellectual leadership. Modernization meant "Westernization [taghrib or istighrab]," and was construed as involving not only the adoption of Europe's material culture – its technology, economic institutions, and political structures – but also the absorption of the spiritual aspects of Western civilization – the customs, values, and mentality of the West.[4]

In the 1930s Egyptian intellectuals reconsidered these Westernizing assumptions. They now rejected the identification of modernization with Westernization and the conclusion that modernization necessarily must result in Egypt becoming similar to Europe. The desire for thoroughgoing Westernization was seen as being both a simplistic, uncritical approach to the issue of modernization, and in conflict with the basic Egyptian need to restore Egypt's authentic collective personality. Achieving the latter involved cultivating a national identity and culture rooted in indigenous traditions. Remaining authentically Egyptian was just as important as becoming modern.

These intellectuals went on to assert that there was a viable alternative to the course of wholesale Westernization which had been so popular in the 1920s. Greater selectivity in cultural borrowing than had been exercised in the recent past were incumbent on an East which wished to maintain its individuality and independence. Thus a great deal of Easternist commentary in the 1930s involved a critique of the uncritical efforts at Westernization of the past and an attempt to define an alternative, more discriminate course of modernization for Egypt in particular and the East as whole.

Spokesmen of an Islamic inclination were consistent critics of the idea of wholesale Westernization. For Yahya Ahmad al-Dardiri, Westernization was a destructive exercise which, by ignoring the fact that "the Western social order contains many elements that are incompatible with the Eastern Islamic spirit," was producing "moral chaos."[5] Hasan al-Banna maintained that Westernization was an "illusory reform [islah wahmi]" which "touched the outer shell but did not pierce to the heart" of European civilization.[6] Socially, it had generated a serious cultural schism between elite and mass in Egypt, thereby leading to a condition of "anarchy and disarray" in Egyptian society.[7]

More illustrative of new mood of the 1930s are the views of previously Westernizing Egyptian intellectuals. Ibrahim 'Abd al-Qadir al-Mazini addressed the issue of Westernization on practical grounds, challenging the feasibility of the assumption that Egyptians could become Westernized. To think that they could do so was both false and dangerous: false because Westernization could not extend beyond superficial and external aspects of life due to the inability of non-Westerners to internalize Europe's spiritual essence; dangerous because, in their infatuation with the West, Egyptians were losing their own cultural values.[8] For Ahmad Amin, the idea of wholesale Westernization was a superficial and simplistic approach to the current cultural encounter between East and West. In particular, Amin attacked the attitude of extreme Westernizers who praised everything Western while belittling all that was Eastern as a message of cultural despair bordering on self-hatred.[9] Asserting that "the Easterner has his own character and the Westerner his own character," Mansur Fahmi argued that "those urging Easterners to adopt the civilization of the Westerners are clearly in error."[10] In adopting the cult of Europe and becoming infatuated with every passing fashion of thought spawned in Europe, Egypt was suspended between two worlds, belonging to neither: "We lost ourselves in the face of her [Europe] ... We came to resemble the crow who wanted to imitate the peacock's strut but failed, and eventually forgot his own original way of walking. Thus he became the object of derision of both crows and peacocks."[11]

The threat to cultural authenticity inherent in unrestrained Westernization and the self-abasement implicit in the adoption of an alien culture received emphasis in the writings of Ahmad Hasan al-Zayyat and 'Abd al-Wahhab 'Azzam. In Zayyat's view, Westernization was a trap; in addition to entailing physical domination by the West, it also meant spiritual bondage and the obliteration of the East's own personality in self-effacing fusion with the West: "surely mental slavery is far more dangerous and injurious than bodily slavery."[12] 'Azzam similarly emphasized the destructive aspects of Westernization. In their zeal for things Western, the peoples of the East had lost their self-respect and developed "the character of slaves."[13] "They believe everything of theirs is false and everything European is the truth"; in so doing, "they were led to discard their own morals, religion, and culture."[14]

Assailing indiscriminate Westernization was merely the prologue to coping with the problem of tradition and change. Beyond demonstrating the flaws of wholesale Westernization, Eastern-oriented writers had the larger task of defining an alternative "Eastern" way to modernize Egypt in particular and Eastern countries in general. Most were not totally opposed to external stimuli and innovation. What was necessary was selective imitation congruent with the values and spirit of the East. The crucial task was to distinguish between permissible and impermissible borrowing from the West.

In their critiques of Westernization, Dardiri and Banna stated the basic premises of the selective approach to emulation of the West. Dardiri was a believer in the need for change, the necessity of "casting off stagnation and backwardness," and did not deny the benefits Western civilization offered in the areas of "scientific and industrial progress"; indeed, in these areas it was essential for the East to borrow "whatever it finds useful."[15] At the same time, he warned, "we must never forget that this [Western] civilization contains many social evils in the face of which we must exercise supreme vigilance."[16] Banna asserted that "in the entire Islamic East there is no one who opposes reform and espouses backwardness and stagnation."[17] Asserting that it was imperative to "distinguish between what merits borrowing and what it is essential to reject," Banna called for what he termed "genuine reform [islah haqiqi]" or "Eastern reform [islah sharqi]."[18] The prerequisite for such genuine and Eastern modernization was that whatever was adopted "not conflict with the Eastern spirit and not eliminate the civilization of the East and its glory."[19]

This distinction between the acceptable emulation of the material features of Western civilization and the unacceptable imitation of its spiritual elements was echoed by numerous Eastern-oriented writers. Mansur Fahmi was convinced that "the one [Western] thing which is undoubtedly of benefit to the East is industrial civilization."[20] But, while he approved of the imitation of the West's technological achievements, he also insisted on rejecting the spiritual dimensions of the West. Thus Fahmi called for the creation of "a pure Eastern culture [thaqafa sharqiyya khalisa]" which would be capable of borrowing from Western technology but would be based on the indigenous heritage of the East.[21] 'Abd al-Wahhab 'Azzam similarly demanded distinguishing between the West's "material culture," which the East could and should emulate, and its "spiritual culture" which had to be rejected.[22] "No difference whatsoever exists between East and West where mathematics, engineering, and chemistry are concerned," he elaborated; in contrast, "what a difference there is in creeds, temperament, social practices, and so forth."[23] For Ahmad Hasan al-Zayyat, "science has no homeland" and thus could be borrowed; culture and social practices, on the other hand, were both unique and vital to nations, and "by relinquishing them a nation gives up its self-identity."[24] Ibrahim 'Abd al-Qadir al-Mazini also approved of borrowing in the area of the sciences and material techniques, but rejected it with regard to the spiritual dimensions of life, cultural creativity, or the ideals of a nation.[25]

Mustafa Sadiq al-Rafi'i and Sayyid Qutb were two authors who attempted to set down operational principles for cultural borrowing. Rafi'i distinguished between "uncritical" and "critical" borrowing. The former amounted to no more than blindly aping the West and was to be rejected out of hand; the latter, the operative principle of which was that "the nation's moral character and temperament are not harmed," was beneficial and acceptable.[26] Sayyid Qutb made a distinction between what he termed "culture [thaqafa]" and "civilization [madaniyya]" as the categories separating unacceptable from acceptable borrowing. Culture, meaning "our religion, arts, moral systems, traditions, and our folklore," had to be maintained intact; civilization, meaning "the sciences and the applied arts," could be influenced by others.[27]

The premises of the spiritual autonomy of Eastern civilization and the impossibility of its total assimilation to the civilization of the West were perhaps best stated by Muhammad Husayn Haykal. In the 1920s, Haykal had been a proponent of the extensive Westernization of Egyptian society. He came to adopt quite a different attitude in the 1930s. As he put it in 1937, "it appeared to me at one time ... that emulating the rational as well as the spiritual life of the West would be our road to revival."[28] Now guided by a conviction of the uniqueness of the spiritual character of different civilizations, he rejected the assumption that the spiritual components of a civilization could be derived from external sources. A rigorous definition of the limits of cultural borrowing was necessary. It was the "rational material life" of the West which could be borrowed; its "spiritual ideological life," on the other hand, could not and must not be emulated.[29] There was no gainsaying the fact that "our spiritual history differs from the history of the West, and [that] our spiritual culture is not its culture."[30] While borrowing in the material realm was possible, where "spiritual life" was concerned "I think that what the West has to offer in this sphere is unsuitable for emulation."[31]

The rejection of wholesale Westernization as the framework for Egyptian modernization and the quest for an alternative Eastern mode of development was reflected in a new and more critical attitude toward Kemalist Turkey. Through the 1920s, Kemalist Turkey had served as a model of successful Westernization as well as a powerful source of inspiration for the thought and activity of many members of Egypt's intellectual elite. In the 1930s, the view of Turkey held by Egyptian intellectuals became more hostile. The Turkish experiment was now seen as embodying all the deficiencies of an attempt at modernization based totally on external borrowing with no thought for indigenous tradition. Turkey's indiscriminate emulation of the West had had appalling consequences: the brutal destruction of customary belief systems and modes of behavior; the loss of Turkey's authentic identity; and its self-effacement *vis-à-vis* an alien culture.[32]

Ahmad Hasan al-Zayyat's scathing indictment of the Turkish leader Mustafa Kemal Ataturk set the tone of the new attitude toward Turkey: "you recreated a state but executed a nation; you forged a constitution but destroyed a faith; you revived a language but buried a culture!"[33] Ahmad Amin similarly denounced the Westernizing policies of the Turks which sought "to stifle everything old and to live exclusively through the new."[34] 'Abd al-Wahhab 'Azzam maintained that, in their indiscriminate imitation of Europe, the Kemalists had brought great harm to Turkey by abandoning "many of the features of their true religion, their distinguished morals, and their glorious history."[35] It was the "organized and unrestrained war that Kemalism is waging against Islam" which drew the fire of Muhammad 'Abd Allah 'Inan.[36] What had been a constructive "reformist trend" in the 1920s a decade later had now become an open war against Islam, a systematic campaign aimed at "freeing Turkey of every hue and color of religion and painting it in all spheres, both official and unofficial, a purely secular color."[37]

Eastern-inclined intellectuals had social as well as intellectual grounds for their rejection of Turkey as a model. Muhammad Husayn Haykal is the clearest example. By the 1930s, Haykal had come to view Egypt's Westernizing experiment of the 1920s as an abject failure in terms of the meaningful transmission of its Westernizing message to its intended Egyptian audience.

In 1933, he acknowledged that modernist exponents of Westernization like himself were an elitist minority without a mass following: "those few who called for the emulation of Western civilization, like the Turks had accomplished, found only a weak echo to their preaching."[38] He was even more pessimistic in 1937: "I had tried [to transmit] to those who shared my language the intellectual culture of the West and its spiritual life, so that we might adopt them both as models and guides. However, after all my labors, I realized that I had planted seeds in barren soil. Even when the earth accepted them, it produced nothing from them."[39] The Westernizing course embodied in the Turkish model had been alien and unattractive to Egypt's lower and middle classes.[40] The result was a growing gap between Western-oriented modernists and the broader sectors of society who rejected the vision of the Westernizers: "the gap continued to widen between the masses of the Eastern peoples and those calling for our past to be brushed aside and for us to embrace the Western orientation with all our might."[41]

In place of the misconceived Turkish model of modernization, some Egyptian intellectuals found a more appropriate exemplar in Japan. Japan represented successful modernization accomplished with due regard for cultural authenticity. For Hasan al-Banna, Japan had taken "the path of wise reform," borrowing the scientific and economic features of the West while also retaining its indigenous traditions and customs.[42] Muhammad Lutfi Jum'a found "the secret of Japan's greatness and its astonishing progress" in the Japanese ability to "borrow all the tools of Western civilization and [its] progressive features while also preserving in full their religious and social traditions and their distinctive national characteristics and principles".[43] In Sayyid Qutb's view, the secret of the Japanese success in modernization lay in its rigid differentiation between the material sphere, where it had borrowed from the West, and the spiritual realm where it preserved its own culture: "Japanese culture continues to be founded on indigenous sources even though at the same time it borrows the most recent features of European civilization and even adds to them."[44] Thus Japan provided Eastern-inclined Egyptian intellectuals with an "Eastern" model of modernization, an alternative to the indiscriminate Westernization attempted by Turkey – and Egypt – in the 1920s.

East versus West

The search for an authentic Eastern path to progress and modernity had part of its basis in a more negative image of the West itself. The idealized portrait of the West common in Egyptian intellectual circles in the 1920s gradually gave way to a more apprehensive view of both the character of

Western civilization and its impact upon the East. The West was now painted in more somber colors, as an inherently aggressive "imperialist civilization" whose *raison d'être* was conquest and domination. It was the aggressive character of the West as evidenced in modern Western imperialism in particular which precluded fruitful intercultural dialogue with it. The East–West encounter was a war of survival for the East, a matter of life or death.

Various Egyptian intellectuals who in the 1920s had championed the virtues of Western civilization were taking a more negative view of the West by the 1930s. Muhammad Lutfi Jum'a had been a staunch advocate of Egyptian Westernization in the 1920s.[45] In his book *Hayat al-Sharq* (The Life of the East) of 1932, an unmistakable reorientation toward the West is visible.[46] The relationship of East and West since World War I was now portrayed in the unremittingly negative terms of an all-out war by an expansionist West against a non-aggressive Eastern civilization forced to defend its existence. Jum'a placed the blame for the antagonistic East–West relationship solely upon the West: "Europe aspires to destroy the East, to exploit and erase its vibrant sources of life, and to subjugate it to its own goals."[47] Jum'a called on the peoples of the East to unify their ranks and to fight imperialism. This was not just a matter of liberation, independence, or national honor; it was a struggle for survival itself.[48]

Mansur Fahmi's idealized image of the West of the 1920s shifted considerably in the 1930s.[49] The point of departure in his analyses of East and West written after 1930 was the belief in a basic dichotomy between "the spirituality of the East and the materialism of the West."[50] What distinguished Western civilization was its materialist emphasis. All its activities were based on the pretentious assumption that human reason could operate independently of God, discover the secrets of the universe on its own, and master natural phenomena. In addition, Western civilization was inherently aggressive and immoral.[51] In contrast to this, Fahmi presented an idealized portrait of an essentially spiritual Eastern civilization. The basis of Eastern superiority was its definition of man in terms which gave primacy to soul over body, spirit over matter, emotion over reason. Where the West focused on the temporal and the transitory, the East emphasized the eternal dimensions of humanity. Eastern civilization, despite its current material weakness *vis-à-vis* the West, was an inherently superior civilization.[52]

The early writings of the younger intellectual Hafiz Mahmud had been marked by an unabashed admiration for Western civilization.[53] By the later 1930s, Mahmud was presenting a negative image of the West. Western civilization was the progenitor of a unique form of conquest and domination which he called "materialist imperialism."[54] Whereas the imperial expansion of Eastern peoples in earlier historical eras had been "conquests of principles and beliefs" entailing the imposition of new belief systems by the conquerors upon the conquered, modern European expansion "is not in the least for the sake of the spirit but wholly for the material"; its main aim was to "bolster the material basis of European society."[55] The dichotomy between this "materialist imperialism" aiming at material aggrandizement for Western benefit and "the spirituality of the East" was intrinsic and unbridgeable.[56]

The interpretation of East–West relations as an unending historical confrontation received systematic exposition by Muhammad Husayn Haykal. In an essay entitled "East and West" of 1933, Haykal examined the historical relationship between Eastern and Western civilizations.[57] He presented the East–West relationship as "an endless struggle, a conflict whose storm has not abated for so much as a day."[58] Much of "East and West" was an historical overview of this millennial conflict. The repeated wars between Pharaonic Egypt and the Greeks, between Phoenicians and both Greece and Rome, and between Egypt under the Ptolemies and Rome in antiquity all served as early examples of the East–West struggle. The East–West confrontation became more acute with the rise of Islam and the early Arab conquests. Only then did a clear distinction between the Islamic East and the Christian West crystallize, producing the relentless and uncompromising struggle of the two civilizations "from then until today."[59] In his portrait of modern Western imperialism Haykal emphasized its materialist character. Minimizing the importance of cultural impulses, ideological motives, or strategic considerations in the development of modern imperialism, he generalized that European imperialist expansion in the modern period was "an economic conquest whose whole purpose was purely the economic exploitation of the East."[60] In his view, European imperial expansion in the modern era was to be understood in economic terms alone. It had "a purely material basis"; its leaders were motivated by "a materialist spirit"; in short, it was the natural product of "a materialist, imperialist civilization [hadara isti'mariyya maddiyya]."[61]

Despite its fundamentally materialist nature, however, the threat posed by modern European imperialism was not solely to the material resources and prosperity of the East. Materialist imperialism in time led to a more intellectual and cultural form of imperial conquest. Haykal saw modern imperialism as also leading to the conquest of Eastern minds through the devaluation and destruction of the indigenous heritage and the inculcation of alien Western ideas and customs in its place. Conquest by Europe had "undermined the East's faith in itself."[62] Imperialism had succeeded in "eroding the mental spirit of the peoples it conquered," and in so doing had "destroyed any possibility of self-reliance that these peoples may have had."[63]

Haykal's solution to the many problems posed by the current Western domination of the East was a call for the reassertion of Eastern self-awareness and the restoration of the collective self-confidence of its peoples.[64] In an indirect acknowledgment of Egypt's changing social structure and political culture by the 1930s, Haykal now argued that such a change in consciousness could not come from the top, from existing Westernized elites or Western-oriented governments which were "completely submissive to imperialist rule."[65] What was necessary was that "an organized populist movement should arise and work to strengthen this moral spirit."[66] A reversal of the current East–West relationship had to come from below.

Such a populist reaction to the Eastern loss of independence and identity was already under way when Haykal published "East and West." The views of East and West expressed by spokesmen for the Muslim Brotherhood illustrate the process of cultural convergence between elite and mass under way in Egypt after 1930. The expanding new effendiyya population of Egypt played an active role in the articulation of Egyptian Easternism and indeed in the entire complex of supra-Egyptian nationalist perspectives of the post-1930 era. Far more than had been the case previously, intensive dialogue between Egypt's intellectual elite and an expanding literate urban population eroded the previous distinction between "high" and "popular" culture, thereby forging a common Egyptian national culture.

The assumption underlying the Brotherhood's image of imperialism was that, despite local variations in colonial policy and rule, Western imperialism was a single global force. Differences were blurred; at heart, the same essential spirit animated British, French, and Italian imperialism alike.[67] This homogenization of imperialism served an obvious mobilizing function: because Western imperialism was a unitary phenomenon, it could only be confronted successfully by a united front comprising all parts of the Islamic *umma* and the East as a whole.[68]

A coda of the Brotherhood's position on Western imperialism appeared in Salih Mustafa 'Ashmawi's article "Disbelief is a Single Community and Imperialism a Single Humiliation."[69] 'Ashmawi criticized those who tried to differentiate between British, French, and Italian imperialism. "They have forgotten that disbelief is a single community and imperialism a single humiliation [*al-kufr milla wahida wa al-isti'mar dhull wahid*], and that all [European powers] have but one goal, which is the obliteration of Islam and the humiliation of the Muslims."[70] The merciless British repression of the Palestinians as they resisted British-backed Zionist efforts to "Judaize

Palestine" and to dispossess the Palestinian Arabs; France who, despite her "noble principles" of liberty, fraternity, and equality, followed no less brutal and anti-Islamic policies in her colonies; and Italy who, utterly contrary to Mussolini's absurd claim to be the "protector of Islam," was attempting to stamp out Islam in Libya – all were manifestations of the same evil force working for the destruction of Islam.[71]

Hasan al-Banna's programmatic pamphlet *Bayna al-Ams wa al-Yawm* (Between Yesterday and Today) distinguished between two different levels of European imperialist activity in the East. The most obvious was "political aggression" carried out by the armed forces of the European countries. The other level was "social oppression," in which imperialism, often aided by native allies, achieved the deeper tyranny of their materialistic civilization over Eastern peoples.[72] Even more than on the political and military level, on the social and cultural level the Great Powers acted as a unified force, working in concert to spread "materialistic life, with all its corrupting traits and its murderous germs, to overwhelm all the Islamic lands."[73] Muslim society was being destroyed by Western civilization: "they imported their half-naked women into these regions, together with their liquors, their theaters, their dance halls, their amusements, their stories, their newspapers, their novels, their caprices, their silly games and their vices."[74] Western social imperialism was "many times more dangerous than the political and military assaults" of the West, for it had led some Muslim countries to "go overboard in their admiration for this European civilization and in their dissatisfaction with their own Islamic character."[75]

The decline of the West and the revival of the East

The final major theme which assumed prominence in Egyptian Easternist thought in the 1930s was that of the impending decline of the West and the corresponding revival of the East. Influenced both by the ominous course of European history over the 1930s and by contemporary Western speculation – particularly that presented in Oswald Spengler's *The Decline of the West* – about the eclipse of Western civilization, the new view went on to predict the imminent victory of East over West in their immemorial struggle. Concepts of Western decline and Eastern revival constituted the final, predictive portion of Easternist analysis of East–West interaction over the ages. In contrast to their pessimism concerning the current dominance of West over East, their speculation about the course of the relationship in the future had a much more optimistic tone, confidently predicting that the future eclipse of the West and the revitalization of the East was inevitable. The parallel ideas of Western decline and Eastern revival provided Egyptian Easternists with a scenario for victory.

As early as 1928, Muhammad Husayn Haykal was analyzing how Western thinkers themselves were now realizing the shortcomings of the materialist civilization of the West and turning to "the East, to its beliefs and its philosophy, in the hope that in them they might discover the bond that they sought ... the simple faith in which the world in its present stage can find serenity and spiritual solace."[76] The philosophy of Henri Bergson served as powerful validation for Haykal's new expectation of Western decline and Eastern revival. Haykal viewed Bergson as the leader of "the spiritualists [al-ruhaniyun]" of Europe, those who had come to realize that science failed to provide an adequate answer to the question of the relationship of individual and cosmos and who were promoting the virtues of intuition.[77] Bergson and those like him realized that, in order to halt the deterioration of Western civilization, "there is no choice but to enlist new spiritual aid ... from the East."[78]

Buttressing its case with references to the writings of Romain Rolland and Oswald Spengler, an editorial in al-Hilal in late 1929 expounded on the ideological confusion, loss of self-confidence, and social disarray now prevailing in the West.[79] World War I in particular had written finis to Europe's illusion of indefinite progress, shattering its confidence and moral resilience while eroding its prestige in the world. Faced with the collapse of their own civilization, Europeans themselves were now seeking external sources of inspiration in the civilization of the East. Crisis in the West portended the emergence of the East, a civilization whose spiritual resources would bring salvation to humanity and deliver it from its current difficulties. In the cyclical pattern which marked the rise and fall of civilizations, it was the East which was destined to succeed the West as humanity's leading civilization in the post-Western era.[80]

Muhammad Lutfi Jum'a was also convinced that the violence which had culminated in World War I and the economic crisis manifested in the Great Depression had totally undermined Europe's claim to be the center of progress and the source of inspiration for the rest of the world.[81] The West was sick; in a state of disorientation and degeneration, it had heaped "confusion upon all mankind."[82] The cure for the present ills of the world lay in "the revival of the East," which in Jum'a's view would be neither narrowly religious, "confined to the awakening of the Islamic peoples," nor national, "confined to the resurgence of the Arab nations alone." Rather, the revival of the East would mean "a universal human revival."[83]

For Fathi Radwan writing in 1932, the brutal and violent character of Western civilization was a sure sign of its impending destruction. World War I had not ended Europe's turmoil: "another war is inevitable – another war which will destroy Western civilization, the civilization of materialism, the civilization of greed, that soulless civilization which has no aim or purpose."[84] This self-immolation of the West was bound to be followed by the rise of the East. Unlike the materialist West, the East was a spiritual civilization which had "the power and the ability to offer an antidote to Western civilization, that material and soulless civilization of greed which is drifting aimlessly."[85]

Similarly for Ahmad Husayn, "those materialist, atheistic principles [of the West], which do not recognize truth or virtue or religion or customs or traditions, shall have only one result – the destruction of Europe in the worst of destructions!"[86] His catalog of the vices found in contemporary Western civilization was a long one: "godlessness, and the desire for liberation from morality and laws, and the gratification of material lusts"; an inherent aggressiveness and "a spirit of tyrannizing over weaker peoples"; an affinity for materialist ideologies like socialism and communism.[87] Mankind's only hope for the future was to return to the spiritual truths found in Eastern civilization in general and Islam in particular.[88]

'Abd al-Wahhab 'Azzam saw a close connection between the nature of industrial society and the violent and chauvinistic impulses manifest in modern Europe. In mass society, an intensified spirit of group solidarity and self-pride had led to every people "claiming that its ancestors were the best and the first among the ancients, and [thus] that it is the master of humanity today."[89] Such feelings in turn led to "a powerful urge for war and conflict."[90] Chauvinistic tribalism and racism now dominated in Europe: "the European has become a wolf in sheep's clothing, [clothing] which he is now discarding."[91]

In Ahmad Hasan al-Zayyat's view, the materialism and violence now evident in Europe were not passing phenomena. They were the necessary result of Western civilization as it had evolved in the modern era.[92] There was no way for a decaying Europe to extricate itself from the vicious circle of violence into which its own culture had thrust it. The victim of its own values and its past, Europe was moving toward a total and catastrophic new war which would bring its extinction: "Black clouds have appeared on the horizon of the Western nations. These nations are being propelled from peace to war, hurled from life to death. This is because their iron civilization has taught them how to destroy but never how to build!"[93]

Writing in 1937, 'Abbas Mahmud al-'Aqqad saw the arms race which had become the obsession of the European powers as a direct result of the cult of science and the worship of industry in modern Europe. The tragic paradox of Western civilization was that it was now threatened by annihilation by the destructive products of the same science and industry which were the West's historical achievement.[94] Contemporary European ideologies were incapable of rescuing the West; "the socialists believe only in bread, and the fascists believe only in the dagger," while people opposed to these dominant movements "are bewildered and do not know which way to turn."[95]

Yet these apocalyptic expectations concerning the fate of modern Western civilization did not lead 'Azzam, Zayyat, or 'Aqqad to a position of utter despair. The decline of the West provided an historic opportunity for a long-suppressed East to revive and to supplant the failed civilization of the West. Thus 'Azzam called on his fellow Egyptians to understand that, rather than Westernizing their society, Egyptians needed to reassert their Eastern Islamic heritage. By reviving their culture and by rediscovering its spiritual values, they would save themselves and all mankind from the catastrophe threatened by the course being pursued by the West.[96] For Zayyat, what the world desperately needed was to recover "the humanistic potential and spiritual reservoirs of the East" in order to balance the soulless scientism of the West.[97] 'Aqqad similarly argued that humanity's best hope was for the rationalist, materialist West to absorb some of the spiritual wisdom which the East had to offer. Once reason and science acknowledged that "truth can be deduced [only] from the innermost intellect and the depths of the soul," then humanity could realize goals "far more exalted and far-reaching than those believed in by those who worship bread and follow the dagger."[98]

By the end of the 1930s, the concepts of the decline of the West and the revival of the East were finding expression across the Egyptian intellectual spectrum. At one end was the vigorous secularist Tawfiq al-Hakim, whose novel 'Usfur min al-Sharq (Bird from the East, 1938) presented an apocalyptic vision of the collapse of the West and the promise of salvation held by the East. "Europe today is in the grip of a crisis, undoubtedly the gravest it has known," one of its protagonists asserted.[99] "Europe is finished," he asserted later; "no force from within can save it ... Salvation can come only from the outside."[100] The outside was of course the East. Recourse to the deeper truths maintained in the East was mankind's only hope of salvation in view of the manifest failures of the West. "To the East! To the East! Let us go together to the East," he cried; "there, to the East, come with me to the East."[101]

At the other end of the spectrum was the portrait of Western decline and Eastern revival presented by Hasan al-Banna in the later 1930s. "The civilization of the West ... is now bankrupt and in collapse," Banna maintained;[102] the inevitable result of the hatreds now festering among the nations of Europe was bound to be "a terrible, devastating war which will tear them asunder."[103] Banna's vision of the eclipse of the West was accompanied by a firm expectation of the imminent revival of the Islamic East. In view of the manifest failures of the West, it was now again time for Islam to ascend to world dominance.[104] Indeed, the revival of the Islamic world *vis-à-vis* the West was already beginning with the struggle for independence now visible in the East. Thus the tables were turning. The trauma engendered by the imperialist onslaught was revivifying Islamic societies and impelling them to return to the divine guidance which was to be found only in Islam.[105]

Debate over East versus West: Taha Husayn and his critics, 1938–1939

These negative views of the nature, impact, and ultimate fate of Western civilization were not universally shared in the Egypt of the 1930s. Throughout the decade, other Egyptian intellectuals tried to combat and contain the anti-Western, Eastern-oriented perspective developing in the country. At the center of the defense of Westernism and resistance to an Eastern identification in the 1930s was Salama Musa and his modernist journal *al-Majalla al-Jadida*.[106] Another locus of Westernism and modernism was the cultural and literary bimonthly *Majallati*.[107] Individual writers prominent in the defense of a Western orientation for Egypt in the 1930s included Husayn Fawzi, Isma'il Ahmad Adham, Amir Buqtur, and Amin al-Khuli.[108]

The single most prominent attempt to challenge the emerging Easternist paradigm in the 1930s was Taha Husayn's controversial work *Mustaqbal al-Thaqafa fi Misr* (The Future of Culture in Egypt, 1938), the opening sections of which were a vigorous refutation of the main premises of the Easternist orientation. For Taha Husayn, Egypt was a Mediterranean nation oriented toward the north and west, not an Eastern nation looking to the east.[109] The Eastern identity being asserted by some Egyptians was a "totally illogical" assumption, a "deplorable mistake" which Husayn could neither comprehend nor accept.[110] This was especially true in "intellectual and cultural life," where Husayn maintained that "Egypt has always been a part of Europe."[111] Husayn was particularly vehement in his denial of the claim of a uniquely spiritual East. In his view, "this talk of a spiritual East" was "no good," something no Egyptian should take seriously; simultaneously it was a "dangerous" illusion which inclined the youth of Egypt toward a civilization with which they had no affinity.[112]

In the altered Egyptian discursive context of the later 1930s, Husayn's reassertion of a Western orientation for Egypt provoked an immediate and angry response from proponents of an Easternist outlook. Critical reviews of *The Future of Culture in Egypt* became something of a growth industry in 1939, as various Eastern-inclined intellectuals joined in denouncing Husayn's Westernizing perspective and in defending the validity of the

East–West distinction denied by Husayn. The convergence of perspective found in three of these reviews – those written by Husayn's old colleague Ahmad Amin, by the younger publicist Hafiz Mahmud, and by the social critic Sayyid Qutb – demonstrate the degree to which the Easternist outlook had taken hold within Egyptian intellectual circles by the end of the 1930s.

Ahmad Amin focused his review on the issue of the spiritualist East – materialist West dichotomy.[113] For Amin, that East and West possessed different mental and spiritual qualities was indisputable. A materialist outlook which reduced even non-corporeal thought processes to a material analysis prevailed in Western civilization. Genuine "spirituality [al-ruhaniyya]," on the other hand, was to be found only in Eastern civilization. To argue that a primarily spiritual worldview reigned in the East while a basically materialist one prevailed in the West was not to "deny that there is spirituality in the West and materialism in the East." Nonetheless, on the whole "while the East is essentially spiritual, the West is essentially material."

Hafiz Mahmud also attempted to demonstrate the validity of the distinction between the materialist West and the spiritual East. Like Amin, Mahmud did not claim that Western culture was totally devoid of spiritual elements. But for him, those expressions of the spiritual which could be found in Europe only represented "an individual spirituality" which had long since ceased to have an impact on the collective social life of Europe.[114] Whatever social function "spiritual" themes now possessed in Europe was utilitarian or manipulative, the cynical enlistment of transcendental motifs in the service of the political ends of the European nations. To this instrumental use of "spirit" in Europe, Mahmud contrasted the genuine spirituality found in the East. Eastern spirituality was expressed particularly in the preeminent place still occupied by religion in Eastern nations. In the East politics, society, and culture were based on religion and derived their legitimacy from religion. Only in the East did religion embrace the totality of life, thereby harmonizing between the material and the spiritual spheres of life. True spirituality was to be found "in the East alone."

A lengthy essay by Sayyid Qutb rejected Husayn's argument that, because Egyptians had already adopted so many aspects of the civilization of Europe, they necessarily possessed a European mentality.[115] For Qutb, the chief flaw in Husayn's argument was his confusion of the categories of material and spiritual. Husayn's defense of the spiritual nature of Western civilization was erroneous; what passed for spirituality in the West was an illusory spirituality always subordinated to the sphere of the material. Only the Eastern approach to life and reality, which was a felicitous synthesis between an understanding of the material world and an awareness of the realm of the spirit, constituted a true spiritual system.[116]

Conclusion

The Eastern orientation was a significant phenomenon in the evolution of Egyptian national culture. Easternism lacked both a programmatic dimension and an organizational embodiment, and as such possessed neither the ideological focus nor the political force to restructure Egypt in a more authentic/Eastern mold. But its all-inclusiveness – its focus on the "East" as a whole and its ability to subsume narrower foci of identity under an Easternist umbrella – made it an important contributor to the development and spread of more action-oriented supra-Egyptianist ideologies.

An Easternist orientation was the main conceptual conduit for numerous individuals as they moved from espousing Egyptian territorial nationalist ideas in the 1920s to the advocacy of supra-Egyptian nationalist concepts in the 1930s and 1940s. In adopting the Easternist outlook on the world, many Egyptians became receptive either to an Islamic cultural identity and/or sentiments of Islamic solidarity (Muhammad Husayn Haykal, 'Abd al-Wahhab 'Azzam, 'Abbas Mahmud al-'Aqqad, and Sayyid Qutb are diverse examples) or to an integralist nationalism which fused an Egypt-centered focus with the concept that Egypt could regain its past glory only by playing a leading role in the affairs of the Arab and Muslim worlds (such as Ahmad Husayn, Fathi Radwan, and others associated with Young Egypt). For all these, a new outlook on East and West provided an important intellectual stimulus to the development of new supra-Egyptian nationalist ideologies.

Easternist ideas played an even more crucial role in the genesis of Arab nationalism in Egypt, serving as a vital way-station for many secularly minded personalities in their passage to Arab nationalism. For Egyptian intellectuals of an essentially secular outlook such as Muhammad Lutfi Jum'a, Ibrahim 'Abd al-Qadir al-Mazini, or Mansur Fahmi, neither a primarily religious ideology nor a fusion of Egyptianism with Islam provided a satisfactory solution to the issue of national identity. Such individuals could adopt a supra-Egyptian nationalist outlook only if it was contained in a secular conceptual framework. An identification with the "East" – while a "spiritual" entity, nonetheless broader than Islam *per se* – provided such a framework. Thus the shift of secular thinkers to Egyptian Arab nationalism in part occurred through an Eastern identification.

3 "The return of Islam":[1] the new Islamic mood in Egypt

The Easternist orientation of the 1930s overlapped with a more profound cultural reorientation developing in Egypt at the same time – the return of Islam to a primary position in Egyptian intellectual discourse and public life. Even in the heyday of Western influence and Egyptian territorial nationalism in the 1920s, Islam was still the central factor in the daily life of most Egyptians. It was only in terms of the customs and ideas of the heavily Westernized elite of Egypt, and in its public life which was then in the process of organization along Western-inspired lines, that Islam can be said to have been shunted to the periphery. The new conditions of the 1930s and 1940s created a suitable environment for the return of Islamic sentiments and concepts to the center of Egyptian thought.

The return of Islam occurred on many levels. One was organizational; the emergence and rapid growth of societies with an explicitly Islamic agenda. The growth of a more Islamically oriented body of opinion within Egyptian society was paralleled by the greater political salience of Islam as manifested in the growing power of the Egyptian Palace and forces allied with it in the 1930s. Underpinning both of the above was the intellectual resurgence of Islam, the emergence of a body of new intellectual production concerned with the history, civilization, and values of Islam.

The breadth and power attained by an explicitly Islamic outlook in Egypt after 1930 must also be considered in terms of the relationship between intellectual production and consumption. As we have argued, by the 1930s the character of Egyptian intellectual production was progressively being determined from the bottom up. The emergence of the new effendiyya cohort had a definite effect on Egyptian cultural production. It was impossible for Egyptian intellectuals to disregard the inclinations and temperament of this population if they wished to remain relevant in their society. The more the creators of Egypt's intellectual products strove to reach an ever-expanding literate public, the more they were impelled to speak in terms capable of appealing to their changing audience. Given the less Western-oriented intellectual predilections of the new effendiyya on the one hand and their alienation from the existing Egyptianist order on the other, this meant speaking in more Islamic terms. Islam thus provided the basis for the new common national culture uniting elite and mass.

The new literature on Islam

In January 1937, King Faruq visited the Pharaonic sites at Luxor for the first time since his accession to the throne. His guides for part of his visit were the Director of the Department of Antiquities, Etienne Drioton, and Howard Carter, discoverer of the tomb of Tut-Ankh-Amon. In the course of their reception of the king, these experts on ancient Egypt explained the meaning of major Pharaonic totems: the ankh as "the key of life" for the ancient Egyptians, the scarab as "the key of his happiness." Faruq's response was presumably unanticipated by either of his hosts. Descending from his jeep with a copy of the Qur'an in his hand, he responded that "this is the key of happiness; it is the key of life." Kissing the sacred book, the monarch returned to his jeep and departed.[2]

When Faruq identified the Qur'an as the key of life in 1937, Egypt was in the midst of a new wave of literary production about Islam. Numerous Egyptian authors turned to writing about Muhammad, early Islamic history, or Islamic civilization after 1930. This included writers who had not addressed Islamic subjects in the past or who had previously treated Islam in a critical way. Nor was this religiously oriented literary production restricted to books. Many of the leading periodicals of the period, including some noted for the Westernizing and secularist nature of their message in the past, now gave a central place to the publication of material on Islamic themes.

Our discussion of the *Islamiyyat* phenomenon approaches the topic from three directions. The first is a survey of the range and content of the *Islamiyyat* genre, focusing in particular on the major themes and emphases found in it. The second dimension considered is the intentions and motivations of the authors of this literature – what prompted them to turn to Islamic subjects, and what they hoped to achieve through their writings on Islam. Finally, we will deal with the reception accorded the new literature on Islam – how it was received by differing segments of the Egyptian public, and what that reception says about the significance of the *Islamiyyat* phenomenon as a whole.

Historical and biographical studies on early Islam

Several historical studies of Islam appeared in Egypt in the early 1930s. 'Abd al-Wahhab al-Najjar's *Ta'rikh al-Islam: al-Khulafa' al-Rashidun* (The History of Islam: the Rashidun Caliphs, 1930); the same author's *Qisas*

al-Anbiya' (Stories of the Prophets, 1932), an overview of the lives of
pre-Islamic prophets mentioned in the Qur'an; 'Abd al-Wahhab 'Azzam's
Mudhakkirat fi Ta'rikh al-Umma al-'Arabiyya (Notes on the History of the
Arab Nation, 1932), which examined the pre-Islamic setting in which Islam
emerged, the career and message of Muhammad, and the early history of the
Muslim community; Taha Husayn's 'Ala Hamish al-Sira (On the Margin of
the Life of the Prophet, 1933), a collection of stories and tales from early
Islamic history; and Muhammad "Effendi" Rida's Muhammad Rasul Allah
(Muhammad the Messenger of God, 1934), were early contributions to the
new Islamiyyat genre. In one way or another, these works on early Islamic
history all developed themes – the liberal and modern character of Islam;
the heroic model provided by early Muslim leaders; the life of the Prophet
as a paradigm for imitation – which eventually came to characterize the
Islamic literature of the era. They were also favorably received by the
Egyptian public of the 1930s. Both Najjar's Qisas al-Anbiya' and Rida's
Muhammad Rasul Allah were reprinted in expanded editions later in the
1930s; responding to the popularity of 'Ala Hamish al-Sira, Taha Husayn
brought out a second volume in 1937 and a third in 1943. Rida himself
credited "the demand of readers" as having led him to write later studies on
the Caliphs Abu Bakr (Abu Bakr al-Siddiq, 1935), 'Umar (al-Faruq 'Umar
ibn al-Khattab, 1936), 'Uthman ('Uthman ibn 'Affan, 1937), and 'Ali (al-Imam
'Ali ibn Abi Talib, 1939).[3]

The most important biographical study of the Prophet Muhammad in the
1930s was Muhammad Husayn Haykal's Hayat Muhammad (The Life of
Muhammad, 1935).[4] More than any other example of the genre, this work is
a symbol of the entire Islamiyyat endeavor, of the attempt of Egyptian
intellectuals to enter into discourse with an expanding literate public by
responding to their outlook and values in a sympathetic manner but at the
same time to shape that popular outlook through a revised and modernized
interpretation of Islam.

The various chapters comprising the work first appeared in articles in
al-Siyasa al-Usbu'iyya in 1932–4. After appearing in book form in 1935,
Hayat Muhammad enjoyed unprecedented commercial success. The first
edition was published in March 1935, in 3,000 copies, which sold almost
immediately; another 7,000 copies were printed and sold by May. Between
1936 and 1956, six editions of 10,000 copies each were published.[5] The work
was clearly much more popular than Haykal's Egyptianist publications of
the 1920s. The number of copies printed in its first year far exceeded the
normal run of 2,000 copies realized by works of commentary in the 1930s or
the 4,000 copies of Taha Husayn's Egyptianist work The Future of Culture in
Egypt, which also was not republished for many years.[6] Haykal himself
noted that this favorable reception was a major factor in his choosing to
write on other Islamic themes.[7]

Hayat Muhammad has been the subject of intensive analysis.[8] Haykal's portrait of Muhammad was a complex and sometimes ambivalent one. On the one hand, it repeatedly emphasized the humanity of the Prophet of Islam. He was a "merely human" being who had lived "a human life."[9] In particular, Haykal's treatment of the role of the supernatural in the life of the Prophet rejected those interpretations both traditional and contemporary which attributed miraculous abilities to the Prophet. Haykal's emphasis on the purely human character of the Prophet was accomplished on the one hand by ignoring or denying some of the miracles attributed to Muhammad in the traditional sources, and on the other by rationalizing incidents which had previously been interpreted as indications of the miraculous by providing psychological or naturalistic interpretations for each.[10] Muhammad's only miracle was the "human" and "rational" miracle of the Qur'an, "the greatest miracle that God permitted."[11]

While emphasizing the humanity of Muhammad, Hayat Muhammad also stressed his greatness. The aspects of Muhammad's career so criticized in the West – his multiple marriages and role as military leader – were vehemently defended by Haykal, including at one point the assertion that great men are not subject to the rules which bind normal people.[12] Thus, while Hayat Muhammad presented the Prophet as human, it also portrayed him as a unique human. His life had "attained the zenith of exaltation to which man can attain"; he had been "the noblest son and the greatest man," and thus was "the perfect example" for other men.[13]

One other aspect of Haykal's picture of Muhammad merits attention. This is the stress placed on the rational quality of his methods and message. In Haykal's presentation, Muhammad's own methods of preaching and analysis were thoroughly rationalist. Indeed, they resembled the scientific method of the modern era based on the unbiased and objective investigation of worldly phenomena: "this scientific method is the highest point which humanity has attained in its striving for freedom of thought. However strange it may sound, this is the message of Muhammad and the foundation of his preaching."[14] For Haykal, the mission of Muhammad was a "rational" as well as a "spiritual" one.[15]

The triple emphasis on the humanity, the greatness, and the rationalism of the Prophet which permeates Haykal's biography of the Prophet played a crucial pedagogic role in Hayat Muhammad as in the Islamiyyat genre in general. Muhammad had been a perfect man, yet also a very human man. At the same time, he had combined the rational and spiritual qualities necessary to an understanding of both material reality and spiritual truth. Together, this made him an ideal model of virtue, wisdom, and insight for contemporary men to emulate.

In 1937, Haykal's Fi Manzil al-Wahy (At the Site of Revelation) was published in an edition of 10,000 copies. The focus of the work is a discussion of the sentiments aroused in Haykal while on pilgrimage and the relevance of the experience and inspiration of the Pilgrimage for contemporary Muslims.[16] Yet for all its didactic quality *Fi Manzil al-Wahy* also reiterated Haykal's commitment to Islam as a modernist, progressive faith which based religious belief on rational principles. Haykal reasserted in a forceful way his previous call to an almost unlimited *ijtihad* in which each Muslim generation could reinterpret the eternal truths of the faith according to its own needs.[17] A "genuine spiritual life" needed to be based on the integration of religion and science on the one hand and faith and intuition on the other: "there is no way but that the principles of science and the principles of intuition will combine in order to organize life."[18] Science and religion were not incompatible; rather, using science "as a means to study the verses of God is the right way to correct belief, and this is the way to genuine spiritual life."[19]

The efforts of Haykal to study early Islam with the declared aim of finding appropriate patterns for modern society continued beyond these two works. His later views on the subject were expressed primarily in his biographies of the early caliphs. In 1942 he published *al-Siddiq Abu Bakr*; in 1944, a two-volume study of *al-Faruq 'Umar*; and in 1945 he began a posthumously published study of the third Caliph 'Uthman.[20] Written during World War II, these biographies restated the position that early Islam provided contemporary humanity with a unique universal model for happiness.[21]

Other leading Egyptian intellectuals joined in the publication of works on early Islamic biography and history in the later 1930s. The first edition of Tawfiq al-Hakim's *Muhammad*, published in January 1936, sold in a few months; by March 1936 a second edition had appeared. The journal *Majallati* characterized the work as "a dazzling success of which several thousand [copies] were distributed in a matter of days."[22] Hakim's *Muhammad* sits uneasily within the *Islamiyyat* corpus. Like Haykal, Hakim emphasized the humanity of Muhammad. Although the recipient of the divine message, he was also a man who suffered from all-too-human fears, anxieties and weaknesses.[23] Yet on the whole *Muhammad* lacks the rationalist thrust found in *Islamiyyat* literature in general. Much of the play dealt with themes found in the traditional image of the Prophet, including the prodigies and miracles found in the popular accounts of his life. That an otherwise modernist author like Tawfiq al-Hakim composed a dramatized biography of Muhammad which incorporated much from the popular Muslim interpretation of his life is powerful testimony to the popularizing impulse which prompted Egyptian intellectuals to deal with Islamic subjects in the 1930s.

In 1936, 'Abd al-Rahman 'Azzam presented a series of radio talks on the life of the Prophet. It was because of listeners' requests that the talks were collected and published in 1938 as *Batal al-Abtal aw Abraz Sifat al-Nabiy Muhammad* (Hero of Heroes, or the Most Distinctive Characteristics of the Prophet Muhammad).[24] Most of *Hero of Heroes* is a popularizing description of the virtuous characteristics of Muhammad. For 'Azzam, the Prophet's personal greatness and heroism proved beyond doubt the universal applicability of his example. Muhammad's life was "an eternal life" and his message "an eternal message"; he provided the ideal model for individuals in all places and times.[25] In a similar mode, 'Azzam published a second series of radio talks on Islam a decade later. *al-Risala al-Khalida* (The Eternal Message) elaborated further on the theme of the timelessness of the example of the Prophet and the relevance of the spiritual message of Islam for a world which had just undergone the massive trauma of world war.[26]

'Abbas Mahmud al-'Aqqad entered the ranks of *Islamiyyat* writers in the early 1940s. His *'Abqariyyat Muhammad* (The Genius of Muhammad, 1942) was but the first of an ambitious series of biographies of other figures of early Islamic history produced over the next decade: *'Abqariyyat 'Umar* (1942); *'Abqariyyat al-Siddiq* and *'Abqariyyat al-Imam* (both 1943); *'Abqariyyat Khalid* (1944); *'Abqariyyat 'Amr ibn al-'As* (1944); and *'Abqariyyat 'Uthman* (1954). *'Abqariyyat Muhammad* was the most successful, going through two printings in 1942 alone; according to 'Aqqad, it was this enthusiastic response which led him to write his later works on the same theme.[27]

'Abqariyyat Muhammad was in part inspired by 'Aqqad's reading of Thomas Carlyle's essay on Muhammad, "The Hero as Prophet."[28] Like most of the other works in the genre, it presented an image of a very human Muhammad. The traditional approach to the role of miracles in the life of the Prophet was flatly rejected; "Muhammad had no need of the miraculous which reason denies."[29] It was the Prophet's rational qualities – his powers of persuasion, his ability to sway people without resort to force, his political sagacity – which were emphasized.[30] A dominant theme in the work was that the genius embodied in the Prophet Muhammad was of universal relevance. Muhammad's example was the property of all mankind, not only Muslims; all people in all times could find an appropriate model for their own edification in the career of the Prophet.[31] The same presentist perspective is found in 'Aqqad's other biographies. The entire *'Abqariyyat* series was in large part an attempt to prove the universal applicability of the model provided by the leaders of early Islam and to demonstrate their relevance for modern times.[32]

For Mahmud Taymur in his *al-Nabiy al-Insan wa Maqalat Ukhar* (The Human Prophet and Other Essays, 1945), "Muhammad was at one and the

same time a man of religion and of this world."[33] The essence of Islam was
that it was a religion which never loses sight of the basic nature of man, and
therefore that the ideal which it offered was capable of attainment by all
men. Just as the message of Islam had been realized in the person of the
Prophet, it could be realized by contemporary man through emulation of
the example of the Prophet: "the personality of Muhammad is a living
translation of the Book of God ... Muhammad should be the model for all
human beings."[34]

Less prominent Egyptian intellectuals participated in the production of
Islamiyyat works. Husayn al-Harawi's *al-Mustashriqun wa al-Islam* (The
Orientalists and Islam, 1936) is a systematic defense of the Prophet
Muhammad against the stereotypes and negative images of him which its
author perceived as pervading the Orientalist approach to Islam. Its own
portrayal of Islam was a distinctly modernist one; rather than being an
obscurantist and outmoded creed, as "Orientalist intellectual imperialism"
would have it, Islam was the most genuine expression of the modern values
of liberty, fraternity, and equality.[35] Muhammad Sa'id Lutfi's *al-Siyar* (The
Biographies, 1938) attempted to provide a concise popular account of the
formation of Islam and its cultural and political development until the early
Abbasid period.[36] Of a similar nature were several of the works produced by
spokesmen for the Young Egypt movement. In the late 1930s and early
1940s, Young Egypt sponsored an inexpensive, pocket-sized publication
series entitled "Book of the Month" ("Kitab al-Shahr") for the edification
of younger Egyptians. One set within the series was devoted to "Leaders of
Islam"; by 1945, fourteen biographies of prominent figures of Islamic
history (Muhammad; the Rashidun caliphs Abu Bakr, 'Umar, and 'Ali;
military figures such as Khalid ibn al-Walid and 'Amr ibn al-'As; and later
caliphs from Mu'awiya to Harun al-Rashid) had been published.[37]

A subgenre within the *Islamiyyat* corpus is accounts of the Islamic
Pilgrimage. Besides Haykal in *Fi Manzil al-Wahy*, several other authors –
inter alia, Ibrahim 'Abd al-Qadir al-Mazini, Muhiy al-Din Rida, 'Abd al-
Wahhab 'Azzam, and Ahmad Husayn – published works recounting their
experiences when on pilgrimage to the holy sites of Islam.[38] Where in the
1920s the intellectual fashion had been to visit the Pharaonic ruins of Upper
Egypt in order to realize one's Egyptian identity,[39] in the 1930s a new trend
took its place: that of proceeding to the Hijaz to experience personally the
full effects of participation in the *hajj*. The content of such accounts usually
combined description of the formal ceremonies of the Pilgrimage with
analysis of the social and emotional meaning of taking part in this central
event of the Muslim *umma*. Common themes included how the Pilgrimage
reinforced an awareness of the bonds linking Egyptians to other Muslims,
the communal unity of all believers, and above all the personal inspiration of

the example of the Prophet as experienced through visiting the scenes where he had lived and preached.[40]

Egyptian periodicals and the new Islamic Orientation

Egyptian periodicals also need to be considered in order to grasp the growing interest in Islamic subjects which developed in Egyptian cultural circles after 1930. Periodical literature played a major role in the *Islamiyyat* phenomenon. As P. J. Vatikiotis has observed, "between 1900 and 1950 literate Egyptians did not as a matter of course read books; they read newspapers, magazines, and periodicals."[41] In addition to periodicals serving as the forum for the initial presentation of several *Islamiyyat* works, the reviews and discussions of this literature published in the journals of the day stimulated reader interest in the works themselves and thus spread the new Islamic orientation to a wider audience.

Two publications edited by Syrian émigrés resident in Egypt were significant in the early stages of the dissemination of a more Islamic outlook in Egypt. One was the venerable *al-Manar* (1898–), which presented the often iconoclastic but always powerfully expressed opinions of its editor Muhammad Rashid Rida. The other was the weekly *al-Fath* (1926–) of Muhibb al-Din al-Khatib, a convenient and apparently widely read collage of Islamicist opinion and news about Muslim issues.

More significant in the popular spread of an Islamic orientation were the periodicals of the new Islamic movements of the 1930s and 1940s. The monthly official publications of the Society of Islamic Guidance, *Majallat al-Hidaya al-Islamiyya* (1928–) edited by Shaykh Muhammad al-Khadir Husayn, and that of the Young Men's Muslim Association, *Majallat al-Shubban al-Muslimin* (1929–) edited by Yahya Ahmad al-Dardiri, offered substantial ideological discussions of Islamic issues representative of the viewpoint of the members of each organization. Judging from the rapid growth of the movement in whose name they spoke, the various periodicals of the Muslim Brotherhood of the 1930s and early 1940s – the weeklies *Jaridat al-Ikhwan al-Muslimin* (1933–8) edited by Hasan al-Banna and Tantawi Jawhari, its successor *al-Khulud* (1938–40), the more political *al-Nadhir* (1938–40) edited by Mustafa Salih 'Ashmawi, and the bi-weekly *Majallat al-Ikhwan al-Muslimin* (1942–54) – presumably reached a larger and larger audience as time passed.

In 1931 the new official journal of al-Azhar *Nur al-Islam* (from 1935–6 *Majallat al-Azhar*) appeared with a monthly run of 10,000 copies. It is worth noting that this first official periodical of al-Azhar began publication only after several other non-official new journals had begun to disseminate the message of a reinterpreted and revived Islam. As an Azharite publication *Nur al-Islam/Majallat al-Azhar* gave considerable attention to technical Islamic subjects like *tafsir* and *fiqh*. Yet under the direction of Shaykh Muhammad al-Khadir Husayn until 1933 and the non-Azharite Muhammad Farid Wajdi thereafter, its approach largely paralleled that being developed in non-Azharite circles after 1930 – the promotion of a modernist interpretation of Islam, support for scientific inquiry in religion as well as in other spheres of life, and the selective emulation of Western culture.[42] A common Islamicist discourse was developing in Egypt, one in which new effendis and at least some older 'ulama' participated together.

Al-Hilal may have been Egypt's best-known cultural journal of the interwar era. Previously a leading forum for the dissemination of Western-inclined and positivist views, in the 1930s the journal became more Islamic-Arab in focus. While, as befitted its Christian management, the material published in *al-Hilal* in the 1930s was more Arab than Islamic in emphasis, nonetheless the historical symbiosis of Arabism and Islam meant that the journal *ipso facto* gave more attention to Islam. Numerous Arab and Islamic subjects came to be dealt with in *al-Hilal* in the 1930s. The periodical also published several special issues devoted to Arab-Islamic subjects.[43] The most impressive of such special issues was one on *al-'Arab wa al-Islam fi al-'Asr al-Hadith* (The Arabs and Islam in the Modern Age) which appeared in April 1939. The contributors to this larger than normal issue included many leading Egyptian and Arab cultural and political figures. Its appearance in 1939 was both a reflection of the penetration of the new Arab and Islamic outlook into the Egyptian establishment by the end of the 1930s, and an indication of that establishment's effort to identify itself with the new popular mood.

Egypt's other major monthly cultural journal *al-Muqtataf* had a more scientific as opposed to historical-literary emphasis, and as such gave less attention to socio-cultural subjects than did *al-Hilal*. Yet in September 1936, it published a supplement on Pharaonic Egypt, *Turath Misr al-Qadima* (The Legacy of Ancient Egypt). In 1937 *Fi Misr al-Islamiyya* (In Islamic Egypt) appeared; in 1938 *Nawahi Majida min al-Thaqafa al-Islamiyya* (Splendid Aspects of Islamic Culture) was published. According to one of its editors, *Fi Misr al-Islamiyya* was explicitly intended to balance the Pharaonic collection of the previous year by demonstrating the massive debt owed by modern Egypt to "the greatness of Islamic civilization in the Nile Valley."[44]

In the later 1920s, the weekly *al-Siyasa al-Usbu'iyya* had been the single most important Egyptian forum for Westernizing, secularizing, and Egyptianist views. Appearing only irregularly from 1931 through 1936, under the editorship of Muhammad Husayn Haykal in 1937 and Hafiz Mahmud from 1938 onwards, the periodical gave more attention to Arab and Islamic themes than it had in the 1920s. Cultural discussions appearing in its pages in the later 1930s included articles on early Islamic history, the need for an Islamic revival, and the advocacy of the selective modernization of the Islamic tradition. Politically, the burning issue of the defense of Arab Palestine received a great deal of attention. The symbolic dimension of *al-Siyasa al-Usbu'iyya*'s reorientation also deserves mention. In the 1920s, the masthead of the journal had been a Pharaonic symbol (the winged solar disk associated with the god Horus). When it resumed publication in 1937, it no longer used the symbol. According to Hafiz Mahmud, the omission was a conscious one undertaken in order for the journal to shed the Pharaonic, unIslamic, and anti-religious stigma which it had earlier acquired and to give it an Arab-Islamic character more suitable to the temper of the later 1930s.[45]

Of all Egyptian periodicals of the period, the new weekly *al-Risala* (1933–) played the leading role in the intellectual formulation as well as the popular spread of the Islamic orientation. Deriving its title from the phrase *al-risala al-muhammadiyya al-khalida* (the eternal message of Muhammad),[46] *al-Risala*'s primary subject-matter was Islam. The arts and sciences as well as the daily life and institutions of Islamic civilization received due attention in its pages. Different issues examined the work of leading Islamic cultural figures (al-Jahiz, al-Mutanabbi, al-Ma'arri, ibn Sina, and ibn Khaldun are representative examples). Special issues, often lengthier in content and larger in format than its normal production, commemorated Muslim holidays such as the beginning of the Hijri year and the birthday of the Prophet.[47]

The general thrust of most of the contributions to *al-Risala* differed from the sweeping admiration for Western culture which had been characteristic of the contents of such journals as *al-Hilal* and *al-Siyasa al-Usbu'iyya* in the 1920s. The analyses of literature appearing in *al-Risala* sought an alternative to the idea of Egyptian "national literature" which had been the literary manifestation of Egyptianism; its political commentary espoused the strengthening of Egyptian links with its Arab and Muslim neighbors. *Al-Risala*'s operating assumption was that contemporary Egyptian and Arab culture must be based primarily on the Arab and Islamic heritage. Yet *al-Risala* was not a traditionalist publication clinging to the preservation of antique forms. Established to "connect the traditional with the modern,"[48] *al-Risala*'s purpose was to reshape and reconstruct Arab and Islamic culture in a manner congruent with modern conditions by incorporating new methods of expression into traditional genres and finding new meanings in older forms. The parameters within which a reconstituted Egyptian culture was sought, however, were those of the Islamic-Arab legacy of Egypt.

Within a short time of its appearance, *al-Risala* became the most important cultural publication in Egypt. As a weekly its output of material exceeded that found in monthly publications such as *al-Hilal* or *al-Muqtataf*, while its independence of the political parties saved it from the periodic suspensions of publication which plagued more politically inclined periodicals. Most important was the range and eminence of its contributors. From 1933 to 1945, between forty and fifty prominent Egyptian and Arab intellectuals wrote for it on a regular or semi-regular basis. Its frequency of publication as well as the quality of its contributors made *al-Risala* the richest single source of serious Egyptian cultural expression during the 1930s.

The journal was a commercial as well as an intellectual success. Ni'mat Fu'ad has termed *al-Risala* a "revolution" in Egyptian publishing.[49] The journal's first issue appeared in 10,000 copies; from the second issue onwards the usual run was 15,000. Toward the end of the 1930s a figure of 20,000 printed copies of each issue was reached. Sales of 40,000 copies of special ceremonial issues were realized, and even this output was (according to the magazine's own apology to its readers) insufficient to meet popular demand.[50] The constriction of publishing during World War II reduced its average run to 4,000, but after the war it appears to have returned to its prewar circulation figures.[51] While these circulation figures did not equal those estimated in the mid-1940s for such popular illustrated weeklies as *al-Ithnayn* (90,000) or *al-Musawwar* (60,000), they exceeded those reported for the more secularist *Ruz al-Yusuf* (7,000–8,000).[52]

The weekly *al-Thaqafa* (1939–), edited by Ahmad Amin, was the journal of the Committee for the Composition, Translation, and Dissemination of Books. The journal made its appearance only in 1939, and so was more a product of the recent strengthening of the popular Islamic trend than a major contributor to it. But in the 1940s it greatly reinforced the trend. The contents of *al-Thaqafa* in many respects paralleled those of *al-Risala*. Islamic history and the Arab literary legacy were central subjects of discussion in its pages. The particular focus of many of its treatments of the Arab and Islamic past was relating the past to the present: analyzing the interaction between traditional and modern literature and art, exploring the ways of readjusting classical literary canons to modern needs, or discussing the place of religion in modern times. Like *al-Risala* before it, *al-Thaqafa* published annual special issues commemorating Muslim holidays.[53] Similar to the approach found in much of the *Islamiyyat* literature, *al-Thaqafa*'s perspective on the past was not nostalgic. Rather, it represents a clear attempt to use the traditional Islamic-Arab cultural legacy as the basis for modern Egyptian and Arab culture through reshaping it to the needs of the contemporary era.[54]

Thus Egyptian periodicals played an important role in the formulation as well as the dissemination of a more Islamic orientation. The articles in these periodicals endlessly reiterated and expanded upon the themes and concepts developed in greater detail in the *Islamiyyat* literature of the era. It was particularly through the articles, reviews, editorials, special issues, and literary debates found in Egyptian cultural journals that the perspective and values being expounded in *Islamiyyat* literature were transformed into public property and transmitted throughout literate Egyptian society.

Motives and intentions

An examination of the intentions expressed by the authors of the new Islamic literature of the period indicates three prominent sets of motivations underlying the creation of this literature. The first was the defense of Islam against its critics both internal and external. The second was the concept of the revival of the Islamic-Arab cultural legacy as the basis of modern society and culture. The third was a social motivation: the desire to appeal to new literate publics and to create a dialogue with potential consumers of intellectual production through the use of popular forms and themes of literary expression.

The defense of Islam against both internal and external threats to its integrity was perhaps the most frequently expressed motive behind Egyptian authors turning to Islamic subjects in the 1930s and 1940s. Internally the threat was the conservative attitude of the "stagnant [*jumud*]" orthodox establishment, which strove to preserve Islam in its customary forms through an adherence to traditional practices as they had crystallized in the medieval era and been maintained through the Ottoman era. In the eyes of modernist intellectuals, the orthodox version of the faith was a static one incapable of adjusting to modern reality. Their aim was to rescue Islam from the hands of reactionary orthodoxy, presenting it as a flexible creed capable of resolving the problems of the modern world.

The other enemy was the external one composed of an unholy alliance of Christian missionaries and modern Orientalists. These enemies intentionally derogated Islam, the one in an attempt to convert Muslims to Christianity, the other through the biases inherent in its basically hostile view of the faith masked under the guise of modern scientific scholarship. Both groups of external enemies gave special emphasis to the life and message of Muhammad, trying to demonstrate the flaws of the Prophet and Islam in comparison to the example of Jesus and the superiority of (depending on outlook) either Christianity or modern Western civilization. Since their ultimate goal was to erode Islam, the external foe was perceived as the more dangerous one and accordingly drew a larger share of attention in *Islamiyyat* literature.

The need for a modernist defense of Islam found frequent expression in the writings of Muhammad Husayn Haykal. The theme was clearly stated in the introduction to *Hayat Muhammad*, where he explained the motivation behind the book as an effort to "study the life of Muhammad, the bearer of the Islamic message, in order to counter the invective of the Christians on the one hand and the rigidity of conservatives among the Muslims on the other."[55] Haykal saw a close connection between missionary attacks on Islam and the distortions of Islamic conservatives. Both were patronized by modern imperialism: "this imperialism supports, in addition to the missionaries, the advocates of stagnation among the Muslims."[56] In an interview immediately after the book's publication, Haykal asserted that "the activity of Christian missionaries in Islamic nations and the support of Western policy for the spokesmen of Islamic stagnation" were the main factors leading him to write his biography of Muhammad.[57] Muslim reactionaries, in presenting an archaic image of Muhammad, were in fact providing ammunition for Western imperialists, missionaries, and others who wished to present Islam as a backward and inferior civilization.[58]

Distortions of the nature of the faith were also to be found in the work of European Orientalists. In Haykal's view there was no question that "those Orientalists who write on Muhammad and Islam are influenced in this writing by a basic motive of Christian fanaticism."[59] He also voiced the suspicion that the scientific apparatus of Orientalism was a facade for covering the "political goal" of supporting European imperialism.[60] In the final analysis, Orientalism could not extricate itself from presenting Muhammad and Islam in a fashion which would match the interests of modern imperialism, i.e., as a primitive civilization which needed to be replaced by Western civilization.

Tawfiq al-Hakim explained his motives in dealing with Muhammad and other Islamic themes in an article entitled "In Defense of Islam."[61] The spur to the writing of his play *Muhammad*, then in the process of composition, was his experience of reading Voltaire's *Fanatisme ou Mahomet le prophète* several years earlier. Overlooking the irony of Voltaire's having dedicated the work to the Pope, Hakim saw the dedication as an indication of Voltaire's residual Christian outlook and his "partisanship for his religion."[62] Voltaire proved for Hakim that the entire Western outlook on Islam had been developed in the shadow of Christianity. Most importantly, Hakim presented his turning to Islamic subjects in the larger context of cultural identity and assertion. The question for him was not that of the defense of religion alone; rather, "this is also an issue of nationality and nationalism [*jins wa qawmiyya*]" involving "the defense of our personality and our belief, in short, the defense of our life."[63]

It was Thomas Carlyle's essay on Muhammad which prompted 'Abbas

Mahmud al-'Aqqad to write his biography of Muhammad. Despite his sympathy for Carlyle's approach and his awareness of Carlyle's more favorable portrait of the Prophet, 'Aqqad nonetheless noted that "after all, Carlyle is a Western writer who does not understand Muhammad as we Muslims understand him, and who does not know Islam as we know it."[64] For 'Aqqad, the life of Muhammad should not be left to analysis by non-Muslims, however great their knowledge of the subject. In the book itself, 'Aqqad several times attacked the Orientalist perspective on Muhammad, referring to Orientalists as "slanderers of Islam."[65] A major concern of the book is an attempt to counteract the negative image of the Prophet found in Orientalist writings; two long chapters are devoted to the issues of Muhammad's attitudes to war and women, the areas where Western criticism of the Prophet had concentrated.[66]

Other authors engaged in the *Islamiyyat* endeavor also noted the defense of the faith as a reason for their Islamic writings. 'Abd al-Wahhab al-Najjar reminded his readers of his personal history as an opponent of Christian missionaries and an activist in anti-missionary organizations; it was this concern which eventually prompted him to write his historical accounts of Islam and Muhammad.[67] Terming European imperialism as "a cultural and intellectual war against Islam" and "an imperialist assault against Islam and the East,"[68] Husayn al-Harawi called for Orientalism to be fought with its own weapons, through the use of the scientific methods of the West in order to demonstrate the correct image of the Prophet and to refute the distorted Orientalist image. In Harawi's view this was "the defense of our nationalism and our minds."[69] Muhammad Rida was convinced that both the orthodox and the Western accounts of early Islamic history were ideologically motivated interpretations of the past. The state of existing historiography on early Islam demanded "the honest historian" who could present Islam correctly and without distortion. For him too the writing of the history of Islam was an act of defense against both internal and external attack.[70]

The desire to revive Islam paralleled that of its defense. For some of these writers, the idea of the Islamic-Arab heritage serving as the basis for the contemporary revival of Egypt replaced an earlier orientation to the Egyptian Pharaonic past as a source of inspiration. Now the dialogue between present and past in order to shape a better future was not between ancient and modern Egyptians; rather, it was between the early Muslim exemplars and their modern descendants.

For Muhammad Husayn Haykal, the entire concept of "revival [*ihya*']" was based on the linkage of past, present, and future. A repeated maxim found in his writings in the 1930s and 1940s was that only an understanding of the past could provide an adequate basis for satisfactory development in the present and the future. "One who has no past has no future";[71] "a nation which forgets its glorious past has no right to aspire to a glorious future";[72] "the past, the present, and the future form a unity that that can in no way be shattered. The knowledge of the past, therefore, is our tool for diagnosing the present and for arranging the picture of the future."[73]

As he explained in *Fi Manzil al-Wahy*, the source of inspiration for any civilization had to come from the values found in its own heritage. This had been true of the West, which had found "the enlightening spiritual forces" which lay at the basis of its modern revival in Greek sources; for Muslims, similar spiritual inspiration must come from the example of the Prophet. It was the contemporary example to be had from the luminous example of the Prophet that had led Haykal to undertake the writing of both *Hayat Muhammad* and *Fi Manzil al-Wahy*.[74] Haykal expressed similar views in other writings, emphasizing the revival of the "spirit" and the "high example" provided by the early Muslims as a central motivation in his writing on Islamic topics.[75]

Taha Husayn similarly presented the desire for Arab cultural revival as one of the major reasons for his writing *'Ala Hamish al-Sira*. Part of the justification for his reworking the materials presented in the work was their utility for building modern Arab culture. Nothing in the life of the ancients was worthwhile in and of itself; its entire importance was in what it could provide as inspiration for moderns. "The ancients have reality and are eternal only in as much as their views and their actions fill the hearts of later generations regardless of the passage of time."[76]

Ahmad Hasan al-Zayyat also stated the need for revival as one of the major motivations behind the publication of *al-Risala*. The various Arab terms for "revival [*ihya'*; *nahda*; *ba'th*]" were central to the discourse of *al-Risala*. The presentation of the old in *al-Risala* was never an end in itself; its importance was in what it had to offer to the present as a reservoir of material for contemporary use. In 1936, Zayyat praised the recent efforts of authors such as Ahmad Amin, Taha Husayn, and Muhammad Husayn Haykal to "build the new upon the basis of the old";[77] again in 1938, he looked back with pride on a half-decade in which the journal had fulfilled its promise to promote "the revival of old literature and the genesis of new literature."[78]

The idea that modern culture needed to be built on the foundation of the past was a common one among writers of *Islamiyyat* works. Thus 'Abd al-Rahman 'Azzam had been prompted to write about the life of the Prophet because Muhammad personified human qualities which could serve as a timeless example of "the efficient reformer" for Arabs, Muslims, and all humanity in their present difficult conditions; the recovery of this "eternal message" of Muhammad was the main motive behind his writings.[79] 'Abd al-Wahhab 'Azzam turned to the analysis of the history of early Islam in

order to reconstruct the connection between the Arab nation and its forma-
tive period, and through the Arabs to bring the message of inspiration
embedded in the example of early Islam to the entire world.[80] The reason
for Muhammad Rida's Islamic literary activity was because for today's
Muslims and Arabs "there is no way to progress save by adhering to the
ways which were the cause of the progress of their ancestors"; his works on
early Islam were an attempt to point out the lessons to be found in history,
so that "when we are aware of this history, we will be able to act today as
they acted in the past."[81]

The third major motive behind the writing of *Islamiyyat* literature was
the desire to develop an effective dialogue with the general public. Intellectuals realized that, if they wished to remain effective to their society,
reaching a larger audience was a necessity. To be influential meant to be
more populist, and the way to be more populist in the changing social
context of the 1930s and 1940s was to deal with the Islamic subjects which
were familiar and appealing to the contemporary reading public.

It was this awareness of the changing terms of intellectual discourse in
contemporary Egypt which in large part inspired Ahmad Hasan al-Zayyat
to establish *al-Risala* in the early 1930s. As he explained the premise behind
his initiative to Taha Husayn, it was the recent emergence of a "middle
group" of serious readers, culturally located between the Europeanized elite
and the masses concerned only with entertainment, which convinced Zayyat
that a cultural journal with an Arab-Islamic orientation would have more
success than that realized by now defunct Westernizing journals such as
al-Siyasa al-Usbu'iyya.[82] His editorials in the new journal reiterated that the
publication was intended to serve as the distinctive voice of a new generation of Egyptian readers. As his editorial introducing the first issue of the
new journal put it, *al-Risala* had as its inspiration "the spirit of the youth"
and was intended to be "a genuine expression of their authentic culture."[83]
Later editorials repeated the theme of *al-Risala* as the mouthpiece of the
younger generation, continuing to identify the youth of Egypt as the target
population to whom its message was directed.[84] A similar desire to commu-
nicate effectively with Egypt's new literate public was expressed in the
Islamiyyat writings of Muhammad Rida, Zaki Mubarak, and 'Abd al-
Wahhab 'Azzam.[85]

Taha Husayn's *'Ala Hamish al-Sira* was a deliberate effort to reach out to
the broader reading public in emotional rather than intellectual terms. The
stories assembled in the work were stated to be popular literature designed
for mass consumption rather than for intellectuals: "these pages were not
written for scholars or historians. I did not intend them as science or aspire
to history."[86] Husayn was aware that his approach in *'Ala Hamish al-Sira*
was capable of being interpreted as pandering to the masses. His response to

this was a defense of the sentimental dimensions of experience: "I want those [intellectuals] to know that reason is not everything, and that men have properties that need to be satisfied and nourished other than reason."[87]

In *Fi Manzil al-Wahy*, Muhammad Husayn Haykal directly connected his writings on the Islamic past with the need to shape a new kind of non-Western national ideology based on indigenous values which could be accepted as a modern framework of identity by broad sectors of society. By 1937, it was clear to him that the earlier efforts of Egypt's intellectual elite to ignore Islam in constructing a modern national culture for Egypt had failed. At the center of this failure had been a cavalier disregard for the social environment in which they were operating. The intellectual milieu of Egypt was not suitable for the wholesale reception of Western ideals. Nor had his parallel efforts to base an Egyptian revival on the ancient Pharaonic legacy been any more successful; the vital link between modern Egyptians and their Pharaonic forebears had been irreparably severed by the passage of time, with the result that the Pharaonic heritage was now incapable of serving as a source of inspiration for contemporary Egyptians.[88]

As Haykal pondered all this, he now saw that the only viable source of inspiration for a modern Egyptian revival lay in the Islamic legacy. Only Islam had sufficient resonance and meaning for contemporary Egyptians: "it is in our Islamic history alone that is embedded the seed which can bud, grow, and bear fruit, for in it there is life which moves souls and stirs and activates them."[89] Modernist ideas could be made appealing to broader sections of society only if put in an Islamic garb. Only through attention to Egypt's Islamic heritage could intellectuals continue to influence their society. He saw this as a realistic appraisal of society and an attempt to remain relevant to it, not a retreat as his critics had alleged: "what in all this is flattering the masses or following it in order to please it?"[90]

Yet Haykal's motivation, as well as that of other previously Western-oriented intellectuals who turned to Islamic subjects, cannot be reduced to "external" social factors alone. Interwoven with social considerations were the inner intellectual changes these figures were themselves experiencing by the 1930s. Responding to critics of his turn to Islamic subjects, Haykal again employed a distinction which he had used since the late 1920s – that between "rational life" and "spiritual life." He explained that, where previously he had believed that there was no essential distinction between the rational and the spiritual spheres, both of which could be modeled on the more advanced West, now a better understanding of the meaning of culture had convinced him that he had been mistaken and that the spiritual side of life needed to be based on indigenous foundations. The ideas shaping the rational dimensions of existence were universal ones capable of adaptation to all human societies, and so could be transmitted from one society to another. But the principles underpinning a community's spiritual existence were specific to different societies, and had to be inspired by that community's particular history and culture. While he continued to agree with his modernist colleagues concerning the need to emulate "the rational life of the West," he had now "reached a stage where I disagreed with them concerning the spiritual life."[91] It was now clear to him that the spiritual aspects of Egyptian life, as opposed to its science and technology, could be built only on the basis of Islam considered both as a source of values and and as a framework of collective identity.[92] Haykal's explanation encapsulates the dual "external" and "internal" motivation underlying the *Islamiyyat* genre – both the tactical motive of maintaining intellectual contact with a changing Egyptian audience, and the intellectual conviction that Islam must be taken into account in developing a modern culture for Egypt.

The public reception of *Islamiyyat* literature

The manner in which *Islamiyyat* literature was received by the Egyptian public throws considerable light on the character and significance of the new Islamic orientation. What determines the historical "result" and impact of writings on society at large is less the motivations of their authors or the intended meanings of their work; it is how these works are perceived, reinterpreted, indeed reproduced, by those who read them.[93] An examination of the sphere of reception indicates that a major change in the prevailing intellectual mood was under way in Egypt. Here we see a partial disjuncture between authorial intent and popular reception; despite the sometimes limited and tactical intentions of the writers of *Islamiyyat* works, they were often received by those who read them as portending a major shift in the world view of their authors as well as a significant turn in the direction in which Egyptian society and culture as a whole were moving.

The nature of the response of Egyptian intellectuals to the viewpoint found in the *Islamiyyat* literature can be gauged by the reception accorded the Islamic productions of Taha Husayn, Muhammad Husayn Haykal, and Tawfiq al-Hakim. Husayn's *'Ala Hamish al-Sira*, Haykal's *Hayat Muhammad* and *Fi Manzil al-Wahy*, and Hakim's *Muhammad* were among the earliest as well as the most important works in the genre, and the literary eminence of their authors assured that abundant critical attention was given to their contents.

A main point of Muhammad 'Awad Muhammad's review of *'Ala Hamish al-Sira* was to emphasize the shift from a European to an Islamic orientation which it represented. That Taha Husayn could discuss the traditional materials found in the work in a sympathetic manner indicated an unmistakable change from the position toward Islam found in Husayn's earlier controversial study of pre-Islamic poetry.[94] In this author's view, Napoleon's dictum to the effect that "if you scratch a Russian you find a Tatar" could also be applied to Taha Husayn: "in the same manner we can say that, if you rub Taha Husayn even lightly, you will find a genuine and pure Azhari in the full, virtuous, and knowledgeable meaning of the word."[95]

The popularizing manner in which Husayn had chosen to deal with Islamic religious material was seen as a particular strength of the book. A review in al-Hilal praised Husayn's approach as the proper way for Egyptian intellectuals to establish contact with youth. Husayn's method of emphasizing the emotional dimensions of Islamic history was clearly preferable to previous scholarly methods which had had the effect of confining interest in this literature to the intellectual elite.[96] Similarly, al-Risala praised Husayn's attempt to understand Muhammad "through the heart and the creation of myth."[97] For 'Abbas Mahmud al-'Aqqad, the most noteworthy literary quality of the work was Husayn's ability to reconstruct the life of his characters with an intuitive empathy with their mentality, and thereby to transform his subject-matter "from the realm of history and legend to the world of life and feelings."[98]

Both the intrinsic merits and the shift in intellectual position found in Muhammad Husayn Haykal's Islamic works of the 1930s were received with general approval by Haykal's fellow intellectuals. Tawfiq al-Hakim's commentary on Hayat Muhammad indicates the methodological breakthrough which the work was seen to represent: "the book is indisputably the first adequate biography of the Prophet which shows the development of Islamic thought in this modern age."[99] For al-Hilal, the book represented a major advance in the historical study of Islam by Muslims themselves. As a defense of Islam by a Muslim which directly refuted the distorted manner in which Western writings presented Eastern history, it was an effective response to European Orientalism and a counterattack to the Western cultural assault on the East.[100] An editorial in al-Risala evaluated the work as a noteworthy achievement both in its psychological insight which captured the personality of the Prophet in all its greatness, and in its accurate historical reconstruction of the environment in which Muhammad had lived and the Islamic community had been born. All in all, Hayat Muhammad was "a new conquest [fath jadid] in modern historical composition."[101]

The appearance of Hayat Muhammad was a public event in Egypt. In May 1935, a committee headed by the Rector of the Egyptian University Ahmad Lutfi al-Sayyid organized a public reception to honor the book and its author. Attended by dignitaries covering a range of Egyptian opinion, the ceremony was the occasion of speeches extolling Haykal and the importance of his recent book.[102] Al-Risala's account of the event noted that

Haykal's study in Europe had originally made him a transmitter of Western culture and a proponent of Egyptian territorial nationalism. Over time, however, he had been unable to escape the weight of his own cultural heritage. Thus "the Dr. Haykal who had once submitted to French and Pharaonicist influence and started with *Zaynab* has now risen to Arabism and Islamism and finished with *Hayat Muhammad*."[103] *Al-Risala*'s summation indicated the cultural importance it attributed to *Hayat Muhammad* and the viewpoint embodied in it: "It is a clear triumph for Islam, the Arabs and the East that Haykal has published this eternal spiritual book! It is the best proof that our indigenous, authentic literature is beginning to return to its source, to draw from its inspiration, and to benefit from its independence."[104]

As the symbol of an era, *Hayat Muhammad* attracted more attention than did *Fi Manzil al-Wahy*. In general, reviews of the latter viewed it as the natural continuation of Haykal's new orientation first apparent in *Hayat Muhammad*. To *al-Hilal*, the book was a reflection of Haykal's personal transformation in making early Islamic subjects the main focus of his intellectual activity.[105] The "enthusiasm for belief in Islam" absent in Haykal's earlier writing but now so apparent in this new work made Haykal a better writer and his book "a service to Islam and Muslims."[106] For Muhammad Fahmi 'Abd al-Latif, the fact of Haykal having performed the *hajj* was itself a matter of importance; it clearly demonstrated the "new spiritual life" which Haykal was experiencing.[107] *Fi Manzil al-Wahy* marked a clear departure from the earlier Western orientation of Haykal and many of his intellectual generation. Haykal now realized the cultural need for indigenous roots, and that a viable spiritual life for Egypt and the East had to be based on Islam and the Islamic spiritual legacy. Only this heritage could inspire the youth and lead them to a productive development in the future.[108]

Tawfiq al-Hakim's turn to writing on Islam and Islamic subjects in his play *Muhammad* was seen as even more of a departure than that of Taha Husayn or Muhammad Husayn Haykal. The staunch conservative Mustafa Sadiq al-Rafi'i was one of the first to express his delight over *Muhammad*. Rafi'i saw a vital need for vivid portrayals of the life of the Prophet in order for Muhammad's example to influence society; more traditional presentations had failed to achieve this kind of effect. For him the significance of *Muhammad* was hard to overestimate: "if ibn Hisham was the first to refine the biography of the Prophet in an historical way according to historical principles, then Tawfiq al-Hakim is the first to recreate it as an artistic creation according to artistic canons."[109]

Ahmad Hasan al-Zayyat's review of the play found it to be another manifestation of the sweeping and positive intellectual metamorphosis under way in Egypt. The recent literary efforts of Haykal, Husayn, and Hakim were interrelated: "where Haykal had attempted to understand divine illumination in a scientific and empirical way, and where Taha Husayn had attempted to portray it through the way of the heart and the creation of myth, Tawfiq al-Hakim has tried to represent it through intuition and the use of dialogue."[110] Hakim's drama had succeeded in reconstructing the prophetic milieu in a way that no historical account had been able to do, thereby bringing the reader into intimate contact with the realities of the beginning of Islam. In his view the play was another indication that Islamic history was now becoming a central focus of interest in contemporary Egypt.[111]

Muhammad Sa'id al-'Aryan saw *Muhammad* as a sign of the profound changes under way both among Egypt's intellectual elite and within Egyptian society as a whole. Hakim had been one of a generation of Westernized, secularist writers which had rebelled against its own heritage. Now a reorientation was under way among many of these intellectuals. Their recent writings had narrowed the gap between them and their native culture, and simultaneously made the life of the Prophet accessible to a much larger public than had been able to appreciate it in the past. The modernist and populist writings of authors like Muhammad Rida and Muhammad Husayn Haykal were enabling large groups of readers "to read the *sira* as it should be read, and to know the history of the Prophet in a way in which only the select of the *'ulama'* had known it until now."[112]

More significant from the aspect of social diffusion was the reception accorded *Islamiyyat* literature by representatives of Egypt's emerging populist movements. For Muhibb al-Din al-Khatib, spokesman of the Young Men's Muslim Association, *Hayat Muhammad* clearly demonstrated the growing desire of Muslims who until recently had derived their ideas of the Prophet from Orientalist literature to create an independent interpretation of the Muslim past. Muslims needed to write their own history: "we will never be able to understand our abilities in the present unless we know our abilities [as demonstrated] in our history."[113] In his view the new wave of works on Islamic subjects was a clear response to popular demand and manifest evidence of "a new interest in Islamic history" on the part of the Egyptian public.[114] Haykal's book was significant also for the manner in which it attempted to meet popular demand. Written in a modern style, it was appealing "to the young reader who is used to the modernist style and who can be entertained and derive benefit only from this style. Indeed, many people have observed that Haykal, when coming to write this book, thought only of this kind of reader."[115]

Hasan al-Banna of the Muslim Brotherhood also saw *Hayat Muhammad* as an indication of its author's personal intellectual evolution. Haykal's earlier secularism had been "far from the spirit of Islam."[116] This attitude had begun to change in Haykal's Easternist writings of the later 1920s and early 1930s extolling the spiritual riches of the East; these had made Banna realize that "Haykal is a different man from what people say."[117] *Hayat Muhammad* now clearly demonstrated that Haykal was closer to Islam and to the Islamic spirit than to his previous attachment to the West and secularism.[118]

A review of *Hayat Muhammad* in Young Egypt's journal *al-Sarkha* interpreted *Hayat Muhammad* as evidence of a sea-change in attitude under way in Egypt. Haykal's generation, which previously had been enchanted by Europe's intellectual as well as material charms, had forgotten that successful political action had to be based on a genuine national culture. *Hayat Muhammad* proved that the need for an authentic national culture was beginning to be appreciated by Haykal and his generation. All this was "a great triumph for Islam and Egypt."[119]

A 1939 article by a young supporter of the Brotherhood, Muhammad 'Abduh "the student," gives perhaps the clearest insight into how the Egyptian younger generation were interpreting the Islamic literature now being written by their elders:

No one could imagine that Dr. Muhammad Husayn Haykal Pasha, one of those who was indebted to the civilization of Europe ... and who assigned to themselves the task of creating an intellectual revival in Egypt which derived its teachings from the thought and philosophy of the West would make the life of the Prophet the subject of an extended study. No one could also imagine that Dr. Muhammad Husayn Haykal Pasha would go to the Holy Places on Pilgrimage ... All this no one could imagine. Yet all of it happened. Haykal wrote on the life of the Prophet ... and Haykal went on Pilgrimage to the House of God and stood in the place where Muhammad had stood, thus realizing the Islamic ideal in his soul and committing himself to strive as Muhammad and his Companions had striven.[120]

The composition of modernist biographies of the Prophet and his Companions by non-'*ulama*' intellectuals was an implicit challenge to the dominant position of the '*ulama*' as the authoritative interpreters of the Islamic heritage. Yet, as far as we can tell from their views on the first major work in the genre, Haykal's *Hayat Muhammad*, their reaction to the appearance of this new body of writing dealing with traditional subjects in a modernist fashion was by no means uniformly negative. The reformist-minded Rector of al-Azhar, Shaykh Muhammad Mustafa al-Maraghi, also a political associate of Haykal in the Liberal Constitutionalist Party, contributed a laudatory introduction to the first edition of *Hayat Muhammad*, praising it as an "honest treatment of Islam."[121] When queried in an interview of 1935 concerning the division between traditional and modern elements in Egyptian society, the Rector expressed the opinion that works like *Hayat Muhammad* were a positive step toward bridging that gap:

Take for example the book of Dr. Muhammad Husayn Haykal on Muhammad. This is an example of progressive thought and research, and there is no doubt that in a short time we will see other modernist Egyptians following his steps in examining the old and renewing it. The day on which more scholars deal with these subjects is the day when the link between al-Azhar and you [modernists] will strengthen.[122]

Maraghi himself continued to patronize the genre thereafter, speaking favorably of the new literary trend in interviews and writing an introduction for 'Azzam's *Batal al-Abtal*.[123] The editor of al-Azhar's journal *Nur al-Islam*, Muhammad Farid Wajdi, also appended favorable comments to *Hayat Muhammad*.[124] His subsequent review of the work recommended the work to his journal's readers as the start of a new era of the scientific study of early Islam.[125]

Other 'ulama' had more difficulty with *Hayat Muhammad*. A largely hostile evaluation of the book came from Shaykh Muhammad Zahran.[126] Haykal's ambition of writing a biography of Muhammad "in a new fashion in harmony with modern taste" had led him to a false presentation of the Prophet and Islam.[127] Its single most egregious error was its "rejection of all the miracles of Muhammad except the Qur'an" and Haykal's insistence that the other miracles attributed to the Prophet were "contrary to God's law."[128]

Disturbed by Haykal's challenge to the traditional image of the Prophet, a group of Egyptian 'ulama' wrote directly to the respected editor of *al-Manar*, Muhammad Rashid Rida, calling on him to respond to what they considered a mendacious portrait of the Prophet which was having a negative effect on Egyptian youth.[129] Rida's own review of *Hayat Muhammad* rejected many of the conservative criticisms directed against Haykal. In Rida's view *Hayat Muhammad* was not an atheistic tract intended to destroy Islam on the part of a modernist author. After reading it, his own impression was that the work reflected a genuine belief in Islam: "I believe that Haykal intended in this book to serve Islam and the struggle against atheism and nihilism."[130] Moreover, the book was having a positive rather than a negative impact in terms of the defense of Islam. In its rationalist portrait of the Prophet capable of appealing to modern sensibilities, "it has attracted many falsifiers back to belief in the prophecy of Muhammad, the seal of the Prophets."[131] The fact that many of its readers "viewed it as one of the most vigorous defenses of Islam" also led Rida to look favorably upon the work.[132] The calls of Zahran and other 'ulama' for the repudiation of the book were unfounded. Haykal's rationalist presentation of the life of Muhammad was as legitimate as the traditionalist interpretation of his conservative critics.[133]

A final perspective important for an understanding of the way in which the *Islamiyyat* literature was received is that provided by the opposition – by Egyptian secularists who continued to maintain a Western-influenced perspective and who rejected the values implicit in the new orientation toward Islam. The opinions of these opponents of the turn to Islamic topics confirm the popularity of the new outlook.

As early as 1935, Salama Musa offered an evaluation of the growing emphasis on Egypt's Arab heritage which *pari passu* was a critique of the increasing attention being given to Islam. The attention now given to Arabic literature in the press; the emergence of new literary journals such as *al-Risala*, the contents of which focused heavily on the Islamic-Arab literary heritage; the publication of numerous new books on Arabic literature as well as the republication of Arab classical works; the establishment of the Arab Language Academy in Cairo in the preceding year to work for the purification of foreign words from Arabic; most recently the attention given to the poet al-Mutanabbi on the thousandth *hijri* anniversary of his death: all these were part of the same ominous trend. For Musa, this emphasis on the Arab heritage was counterproductive, a threat to the continued progress of Egypt.[134]

In 1938, Musa dealt with the sectarian implications of the growing interest of Egyptian intellectuals and the reading public in Islamic subjects. As a Copt, Musa was particularly aware of the negative impact of the trend toward Islam on Copts. There was a widening gap between Muslim and Copt in contemporary Egypt: "the young Muslims are becoming zealots for their religion and are more impelled to act according to its teachings than are the Coptic youth who find no stimulus to this zeal."[135] Egypt had changed from the days of Musa's youth. Today it was popular for the young to read Islamic journals such as *al-Fath*, the leading principle of which was that "the Muslim world is one homeland."[136] What a difference between this credo and that promoted by Egyptian territorial nationalists such as Ahmad Lutfi al-Sayyid at the beginning of the century to the effect that

Egypt is the homeland of all Egyptians, Muslims, Christians, and Jews, non-believers and atheists, and there is no place for religion in patriotism. But Lutfi al-Sayyid is no longer writing. Muhibb al-Din al-Khatib is writing. Thus the new generation does not know Lutfi al-Sayyid and *al-Jarida* which Lutfi al-Sayyid published, the *al-Jarida* in which he fought the proponents of the Ottoman state and Islamic unity ... Who can guarantee that writers like Muhibb al-Din al-Khatib will not increase?[137]

Possibly the most revealing critique of the change of direction of Egyptian opinion came from the young Husayn Fawzi in the same year. In January 1938, *Majallat al-Hadith* of Aleppo conducted a poll of several intellectuals on the subject of the ways to revive Arab culture.[138] Fawzi was the only Egyptian interviewed who rejected the concept of an Arab-based revival. His response argued that there was neither the need for nor the possibility of a revival of the Arab cultural legacy in the contemporary era. In his view,

Arab culture had died after the Middle Ages, disappearing just as many other older cultures had vanished: "ancient Arab civilization has passed without a possibility of returning."[139] What is of greatest relevance is Fawzi's admission that his anti-traditionalist stance was now a minority view in Egypt and the Arab world. It was the idea of the necessity of the revival of the Islamic-Arab heritage which now dominated Egyptian public opinion. The qualification with which he began his response leaves no doubt of his belief that he and those like him believed themselves to be fighting a losing cultural battle by the late 1930s: "I have an eccentric opinion concerning ancient Arab culture. Undoubtedly it is in conflict with the sentiments of the readers of al-Hadith in their various homelands ... I am convinced that the overwhelming majority of Egyptians share in the Arab rejection of my opinion."[140] Husayn Fawzi's perception of his intellectual isolation was correct. The return of Islam to a position of importance in Egyptian social and intellectual life was indisputable by the end of the 1930s.

4   Egyptian Islamic nationalism

The new Eastern and Islamic orientations of the post-1930 era set the general mood underlying the more focused supra-Egyptian ideologies of the period. The first of these to emerge with clarity was Egyptian Islamic nationalism. Egyptian Islamic nationalism was an attempt to build a religiously based alternative to supplant the territorial nationalism which had gained ascendancy in Egypt in the 1920s. It is important to emphasize that its formulators were both Muslims *and* nationalists. By this we mean that they were the first Egyptian Muslims to undertake the task of developing a systematic nationalist doctrine whose reference point was firmly anchored in Islam.

The Islamic orthodox establishment of Egypt was not the primary force responsible for the formulation of Egyptian Islamic nationalism. This was in part because of the diversity of that establishment; Egypt's 'ulama' spanned a wide range of opinion and spoke in tones ranging from relatively liberal to quite conservative. Even in the 1930s, when *Nur al-Islam* provided the 'ulama' with their own outlet for cultural expression, their role in developing a specifically Islamic variant of nationalism was less important than that played by spokesmen for the new Islamic societies of the period. Azharite-trained *shaykh*s such as 'Abd Allah 'Afifi, Muhammad Sulayman, and Mustafa al-Rifa'i al-Lubban occasionally contributed to Islamic nationalist publications; 'alim and effendi both participated in the task of reformulating nationalism in more Islamic terms.

But on the whole Egypt's 'ulama' followed rather than led in the discourse which articulated Egyptian Islamic nationalism. The main thrust in the development of a religiously based alternative to Egyptian territorial nationalism came from the ideologues of new Islamic societies based primarily on Egypt's new effendiyya. The most important organizations responsible for the formulation of an Egyptian Islamic nationalist ideology were the Young Men's Muslim Association (1927–), the Islamic Guidance Society (1928–), and especially the Muslim Brotherhood (1928–). It was spokesmen for these organizations in particular who played the major role in the elaboration of Egyptian Islamic nationalism. The major publications in which the doctrine was expressed were journals associated with these organizations: *al-Fath* and *Majallat al-Shubban al-Muslimin* of the YMMA; *Majallat al-Hidaya al-Islamiyya*, the periodical of the Islamic Guidance Society; *Jaridat al-Ikhwan al-Muslimin*, *al-Nadhir*, *Majallat al-Ikhwan al-Muslimin*, and *al-Khulud* of the Brotherhood. The most systematic formulation of Egyptian Islamic nationalism came in the programmatic "messages [*rasa'il*]" produced by Hasan al-Banna on behalf of the Muslim Brotherhood in the 1930s.[1] Written in a didactic manner and printed in pocket-sized editions with the intention of being accessible to a wide readership, the latter provide the most comprehensive as well as the most authoritative expression of Egyptian Islamic nationalism.

Religious universalism versus national particularism

Egyptian Islamic nationalist doctrine repeatedly emphasized the universal characteristics of the Islamic faith. Islam was a universal religion. Its principles applied irrespective of geographical location, state structures, racial considerations, or class differences. Neither time nor place affected the validity of its teachings; its jurisdiction knew no boundaries. It recognized no human distinctions save righteousness; in the words of the Prophet, "the Arab has no superiority over the non-Arab save by virtue of his piety."[2] It was precisely its universal character which had allowed Islam to spread throughout the world, overcoming geographical and ethnic barriers and uniting different regions and peoples in one community. Muslims formed "one nation [*umma wahida*] bearing the banner of guidance and struggle for the good of the sake of all mankind."[3] Narrow group "partisanship ['*asabiyya*]" had been replaced with an open-ended, universal bond based on belief in God and in the message of His Prophet Muhammad.[4]

For all the conviction with which they held and voiced these beliefs, nonetheless Egyptian Islamic nationalists could not ignore the question of the relationship between Islam and nationalism. Living and writing at a time when the rival doctrine of the centrality and supremacy of the territorially defined nation-state had taken hold in Egypt and indeed in much of the Muslim world, they were forced to address the issue of how their religiously centered ideas of community related to alternative concepts of identity and loyalty. The territorial nationalist milieu in which they lived and worked compelled them to explain how the seeming particularism of nationalism could be made congruent with the universality of Islam.

The rejection of exclusivist territorial nationalism

Egyptian Islamic nationalists completely rejected the modern, Western-derived concept of the nation as the exclusive or ultimate repository of collective identity. What they termed "absolute patriotism [*al-wataniyya al-mujarrada*]" was a doctrine alien to Islam.[5] A product of Western thought, it had no place in the Islamic world.[6] The ultimate allegiance of Muslims was determined by "the bond of religion, which to us is holier than the bond of blood or of soil."[7] All other sentiments of identity and loyalty were subject to the authority of religion and existed only under its sway. An Islamic order had no space for autonomous spheres of existence:

We believe that the precepts and teachings of Islam are comprehensive, ordering the affairs of the people in this world and in the world to come. Those who think that these teachings are concerned only with spiritual or ritualistic matters are mistaken in their thinking, for Islam is a creed, a form of worship, a homeland, a nationality, a religion, and a state, spirit and deed, book and sword.[8]

The main thrust of the Islamic nationalist critique of contemporary forms of nationalism was directed against secularly derived territorial nationalism. It was the alien origins of modern territorial nationalism which drew their fire. For Muhibb al-Din al-Khatib, the various regional nationalisms now found in the Muslim world were "a bond advocated by the devil,"[9] a device introduced by the West into the East in order to divide and thereby weaken it. The adoption of the concept by Muslims had only meant that "three hundred million people who had considered themselves one nation became many small nations."[10] Mustafa Ahmad al-Rifa'i al-Lubban similarly denounced contemporary territorial nationalism as a foreign doctrine introduced into the Islamic East in order to shatter the unity of the *umma* and thus prepare the way for its subjugation by the West. By separating the Muslim peoples from each other and focusing the attention of each on its own affairs, territorial nationalism had subverted the previous bonds which linked and strengthened neighbors. The historical result of the Muslim adoption of this "lame nationalism" was the disunity and thus the foreign domination of the Muslim world.[11]

Besides being a Western plot, the nationalist idea flourishing in the modern world had inherent flaws which made it a pernicious concept. Territorial nationalism's exclusive focus on a particular people or nation often led to ethnocentrism. The self-absorption found in modern forms of nationalism all too often deteriorated into a chauvinistic "racial patriotism," "blood patriotism," or an anti-Islamic "regionalism [*al-shu'ubiyya*]" redolent with negative overtones deriving from early Islamic history.[12] Such types of group identity led in the direction of collective megalomania, the belief in one's own people as a chosen people superior to others. Assuming that man was created not in the image of God but was defined by geography or race, modern nationalism thus negated the principles of the unity of humanity and the equality of all before God. It resulted in division rather than harmony, strife rather than cooperation, a vision of the world derived from Satan rather than from God.[13]

Islamic nationalist spokesmen manifested a complex attitude toward the Egyptian variant of territorial nationalism. While they did not totally reject it, they also noted the inherent tension between it and their own sense of loyalty to Islam. Hasan al-Banna defined the fundamental difference between Egyptian Islamic and Egyptian territorial nationalists as follows:

The point of contention between us and them is that we define the limits of patriotism in terms of creed, while they define it according to territorial borders and geographical boundaries. For every region in which there is a Muslim who says "There is no God but God, and Muhammad is His Prophet," is a homeland for us, having its own inviolability and sanctity, and demanding love, sincerity, and striving for the sake of its welfare. All Muslims in these geographical regions are our people and our brothers; we are concerned about them, and we share their feelings and their sensibilities. The advocates of patriotism alone [al-wataniyya faqat] are not like this, since nothing matters to them except the affairs of that specific, narrowly delimited region of the earth.[14]

To Islamic nationalists, territorial nationalism as practiced in Egypt had serious shortcomings. In line with the anti-parliamentary, anti-party mood which developed in Egypt after 1930, the factionalism visible in the Egyptian political system was seen as a threat to the harmony and unity of the community. What Hasan al-Banna termed "the patriotism of the parties" had resulted in the division of the nation into factions engaged in "internecine fighting, mutual rancor, and attacking one another." Such divisive behavior only served the purposes of the external enemy interested in divide-and-rule.[15]

Of the entire corpus of ideas associated with Egyptian territorial nationalism, its Islamicist critics leveled their harshest criticisms at the glorification of ancient Pharaonic Egypt which was so prominent in Egyptianism. "Pharaonicism [al-fir'awniyya]" was attacked on various grounds. One was its foreign origin as but one of several artificial national identities being promoted by the West in order to destroy Muslim and Arab unity.[16] For Muhibb al-Din al-Khatib, the regional nationalisms found in the Arab East in the interwar period – Egyptian Pharaonicism; the attribution of Assyrian or Chaldean origins to Iraqis; an Aramean genealogy for Syrians or a Phoenician one for the Lebanese – were all Western inventions foisted on the Arab East in an effort to convince Arabs that they were not "one nation integrated by language, culture, and common aspirations."[17] Beyond their Western origins, their biological basis made them anachronistic in the modern age in which "nationalism is derived from culture and is not based on descent."[18]

In its content, Islamicists found Pharaonicism to be an anti-Islamic and thereby an unacceptable nationalist orientation. Historically, the Pharaonic school's claim that the people of the Nile Valley had their own unique history separate and distinct from Arab and Muslim history was an intentional denial of the unity of the Muslim community.[19] Indeed, Islamic nationalists saw Pharaonicism as the revival of paganism, the restoration of an archaic system of values which had been superseded by Islam. Hasan al-Banna was categorical in his denunciation of any "nationalism of paganism [qawmiyyat al-jahiliyya]": "If, however, what is meant by nationalism is the revival of the customs of a pagan age which have been obliterated and the reconstitution of extinct manners that have vanished ... then this meaning of nationalism is reprehensible, deleterious in its consequences and evil in its results."[20]

The alternative: supra-Egyptian Islamic nationalism

The rejection of secular territorial nationalism as well as of anti-Islamic Pharaonicism and the need to replace both with a new framework of identity which could reconcile particularist loyalties with the universal bond of Islam prompted Egyptian Islamic nationalists to formulate an alternative supra-Egyptian nationalist doctrine. In one important sense, this doctrine was more flexible and inclusive than the territorialism which it was designed to supplant. Unlike territorial nationalists who made the territorial bond the overriding determinant of group identity and whose sense of community was often exclusivist, most Islamic nationalists accepted the existence of multiple identifications and loyalties. In an equally important respect, however, the new Islamic nationalist ideology had its own rigidity. All other identifications and loyalties came after and were subordinate to a primary religious identity and allegiance.

Terminology provides the clearest indication of the Islamic nationalist outlook. Instead of employing the term "homeland [watan]" to refer to a territorial unit, they regularly applied the word to the religious community of believers in Islam. Declaring that "the people of the qibla are one person and one body," that "the Islamic world is one homeland," or that "the homeland of the Muslim is his creed," they asserted that Muslims owed their primary loyalty and allegiance to the Islamic community.[21] This commonality of homeland imposed a profound obligation of brotherhood on every Muslim: "Islamic brotherhood compels every Muslim to believe that every foot of ground in which there resides a brother who holds to the religion of the Noble Qur'an is a portion of the larger Islamic homeland, to work for the protection and prosperity of which is made incumbent by Islam on every one of its sons."[22]

Yet for most Egyptian Islamic nationalists the unquestioned centrality of the Islamic bond did not mean a total rejection of other loyalties. Hasan al-Banna accepted the legitimacy of what he termed the "patriotism of affection," meaning "love of this land, attachment to it, affection for it and sympathy for it"; positive feelings for one's country are "something anchored in the very nature of the soul, for one thing, and for another they are prescribed by Islam."[23] He also accepted what he called the "patriotism of freedom and greatness," meaning a nation's striving for independence from foreign rule and its pursuit of national glory; indeed, Islam itself placed "the greatest stress" upon this form of patriotism.[24]

In the case of the above forms of patriotism, however, it was their having been sanctioned by, and their continuing compatibility with, Islam which provided the crucial condition for their acceptance. For Islamic nationalists, neither the homeland nor loyalty to it existed independent of religion. The phrase "love of homeland is part of the faith [hubb al-watan min al-iman]"[25] was the leitmotif for Islamic nationalist analysis of the relationship between territorial patriotism and religion. What this was interpreted to mean was that the sentiment of patriotism should always be subject to the authority of religion. In order to be a true patriot, one needed to be inspired by religion. Genuine, valid patriotism existed only within religion; "no homeland save in religion" and "love of homeland is part of the religion" were characteristic formulations of the intimate relationship between patriotism and religion.[26] As 'Abd al-Hamid Sa'id, president of the YMMA, succinctly put it, "he who has no religion has no patriotism."[27]

There were two senses in which patriotism was related to religion. On the one hand, patriotism required subjection to religion to avoid degenerating into a chauvinistic and self-serving phenomenon. Only religion could transform a potentially destructive local attachment into virtuous commitment, striving, and sacrifice.[28] On the other hand, religion provided much of the emotional fuel for the sentiment of patriotism. It was religion which created the most powerful and effective bond between an individual and his homeland, instilling loyalty within him and making him willing to struggle and sacrifice for its sake.[29] As the Azharite Isma'il Shalabi Sha'afan explained the religious underpinning of patriotism, "if you say that there is no homeland without religion, you merely mean that there is nothing like religion that can stimulate man to defend it."[30] Properly construed, religion and patriotism reinforced each other. Although always above local patriotism, Islam recognized the pursuit of those patriotic goals which were congruent with its own aims. From its side, authentic patriotism drew inspiration and power from religion. Thus patriotism and religion were twins: "there is no homeland without religion and no religion without a homeland."[31]

With specific reference to Egypt, Egyptian Islamic nationalists accepted Egypt as the "specific homeland [al-watan al-khass]" of Egyptians.[32] They denied the accusations of their opponents that their religiously based concept of Egyptian nationalism would, through its focus on the Muslim world as a whole, undermine the Egyptian national struggle. Islam itself, they retorted, regarded the struggle for the independence and freedom of the entire Islamic *umma* as a sacred duty. For Hasan al-Banna, the struggles for Egyptian and Muslim liberty were overlapping and thoroughly compatible objectives: "Those who imagine that the Muslim Brothers look askance at the homeland and patriotism are wrong. The Muslim Brothers are more loyal than all other to their homeland, and readier than all others to make sacrifices in the service of the homeland."[33]

As was the case with patriotism in general, however, Egyptian patriotism should never exist in isolation from Islam or be elevated into an exclusive focus of allegiance. Loyalty to Egypt existed within the larger framework of loyalty to Islam. Egyptian patriotism was but one "specific patriotism [*al-wataniyya al-khassa*]" encompassed within the "general patriotism [*al-wataniyya al-'amma*]" represented by Islam.[34] On the practical level, the Egyptian struggle to attain Egyptian national goals such as British evacuation was part of the larger Muslim struggle for freedom; thus, "at that hour when we work for Egypt, we are serving the Arabs, the East, and Islam."[35]

Yet, despite their assertion of the compatibility of loyalty to Egypt with allegiance to Islam, it was the latter to which Islamic nationalists gave primacy. A key phrase in Islamic nationalist discourse was "all believers are brothers," a maxim which they interpreted as indicating the existence of a single, indivisible Muslim national community.[36] The mission of Muhammad had "transformed many separate nations into one nation";[37] thus all Muslims were united in "one all-embracing Islamic nationalism."[38] Sanctified by God, the unity of Muslims in their religious community was the supreme bond. Banna's conclusion to the section of his tract "Our Mission" devoted to nationalism made it clear that for him the fundamental determinant of human community was religious:

... the Muslim Brotherhood regard mankind as divided into two camps *vis-à-vis* themselves; a camp believing as they believe, in the religion of God and His Book, and in the mission of His Prophet and what he brought with him. The most sacred of bonds bind us to them, the bond of belief, which is to us holier than the bond of blood or the bond of soil. These are our closest relatives among peoples: we feel sympathy toward them, we work for their sake, we defend them and we sacrifice ourselves and our wealth for them in whatever land they may be, or from whatever origin they may spring.[39]

The other camp was non-believers in Islam, with whom Muslims wished to live in peace but nonetheless would continue to summon to Islam because "it is the best there is for all humanity."[40] If "nationalism" implies a sense of personal identification, communal intimacy, and mutual responsibility, then Islam was the nation of Muslims.

History, Islamic and Egyptian

Egyptian Islamicists saw a proper understanding of the past as a powerful instrument for the attainment of their national goals. Correctly understood, history offered indisputable proof of the centrality of the Muslim *umma* in God's design and thus in human life. The study of history also offered clear guidelines on how to return to the proper state of existence defined by God to His Prophet Muhammad and briefly realized in the early Islamic era. The Islamic past spoke, clearly and authoritatively through the words of God and the deeds of His Prophet, to the present and future concerns of man.

The unity of Islamic history

The central theme of Islamic nationalist accounts of the history of the Islamic community was the fundamental unity of Muslim history. From the time of the Prophet onwards, all Muslim peoples had formed one community sharing the same sentiments, beliefs, and customs. Islamic nationalists paid particular attention to the early phases of Muslim history, the period of the Prophet Muhammad and the "noble forefathers [*al-salaf al-salih*]" when unity had been a historical reality. By and large, the internal evolution of the *umma* thereafter was also presented as having taken the same general course whether for better or for worse. In short, the fate of Muslims everywhere over the entire Islamic era had been a common one.

Hasan al-Banna's programmatic tract *Bayna al-Ams wa al-Yawm* (Between Yesterday and Today) of 1939 provides a characteristic and authoritative example of the Islamicist approach to the history of Islam.[41] Its historical account began with the life and message of the Prophet Muhammad. This neglect of the pre-Islamic past was typical of the Islamic nationalist approach. Islamicist writings paid little attention to pre-Islamic history. Whatever their apparent differences, all periods of pre-Islamic history were similar in their essential lack of direction and guiding spirit. There was no point in dwelling on the pre-Islamic past; it had nothing to say to the present and the future.

The meaningful history of mankind began with Islam. With the hand of God now upon it, history assumed an order, harmony, and intent which it had previously lacked. History with positive value began with Muhammad. The Prophet's "universal mission was a decisive landmark for all of creation – between a dark past, a brilliant and shining future, and a happy and abundant present, as well as a clear and unambiguous announcement of a new order decreed by God, the Knowing, the Wise."[42]

In its main outlines, Banna's portrayal of the course of Islamic history was not a new one. Like earlier Islamic reformers, he regarded the time of the Prophet and the Rashidun caliphs as the seminal era of Islamic history when the true positive content of Islam as both a religious creed and a social and political order had been realized. The "superior Qur'anic social order" which was the ultimate hope of every Muslim in every age had actually existed in the early days of Islamic history.[43] The early caliphs had embodied the ideal Islamic concept of authority, uniting spiritual and secular powers and guiding the community in accord with God's instructions. Most importantly, this was the era of an undivided Muslim community, prior to the appearance of the dissension which was to plague the *umma* thereafter.[44] The historical result of this early virtue and unity was the unparalleled expansion of the faith and the state, the melding of many different peoples into one community, and the creation of a glorious civilization incorporating aspects of many existing cultures.[45]

Islamic history took a turn for the worse after its early glory. Numerous factors both internal and external – political and sectarian dissension; the enervating pleasures of civilization; "the transfer of authority and leadership to non-Arabs . . . who had never absorbed genuine Islam"; intellectual stagnation and self-sufficency – were responsible for the decline of the Islamic community after its early days of expansion and efflorescence.[46] The eventual result of internal decline was catastrophe descending from the outside. From Asia the Tatars overwhelmed the Islamic East, in the process destroying the Caliphate; from Europe the Crusaders conquered Jerusalem and threatened other Muslim lands. The Ottoman Turks temporarily succeeded in reversing the process of political decline. But this was a passing phenomenon: soon European growth and expansion which had begun with the Renaissance and the voyages of discovery paved the way for the modern Western assault upon Islam, European dismemberment of the Ottoman Empire, and by the twentieth century the subjugation of almost all Muslim lands to European domination.[47]

Two underlying features of Banna's approach to Islamic history deserve emphasis. One is the moralism of its understanding of the dynamics of history. For Hasan al-Banna, it was the moral character of men rather than the impact of structural forces which determined the evolution of history. While the tale of human weakness and moral failure visible in Islamic history was discouraging on one level, it was uplifting on another; what men had done they could undo if they had sufficient resolve and dedication. As the concluding portion of Banna's tract put it, a combination of "deep faith," "precise organization," and "continuous work" were the methods by which Muslims could reverse the course of history and regain their goal of a pure Islamic order.[48]

The other noteworthy feature of Banna's portrait is its emphasis on unity. The account relates an essentially similar history experienced by all Muslim lands and peoples. While regional variations are occasionally mentioned (Egypt's role in opposing the Crusaders and the Mongols; the different forms of imperialist domination currently being experienced by different Muslim lands), clearly what is being narrated is the history of *one* community undergoing the same vicissitudes. Furthermore, this unitary account of early Muslim unity (= glory) and later disunity (= decline) had an obvious moral to teach. The historic strength of the *umma* was in its unity. With loss of unity, deterioration and humiliation had followed. The obvious implication was that the restoration of unity would mean the recovery of the ideal order realized in the first phase of Islamic history.[49]

The Islamic nationalist narrative of Egyptian history

The territorial nationalist interpretation of Egyptian history had given great emphasis to Egypt's pre-Islamic eras, the Pharaonic period in particular, and in its treatment of the Islamic epoch had emphasized Egypt's distinct identity and its rapid reemergence as an independent entity within Islam.[50] For Islamic nationalists, this European-inspired and Pharaonically oriented interpretation of Egyptian history was false history. It was on these grounds that Islamicists periodically called for the radical revision of the curriculum of Egyptian schools. In 1932, a memorandum submitted to the Egyptian government by the Islamic Guidance Society lamented the fact that "the Muslim pupil [in Egypt] does not know the history of the Prophet as well as he knows the history of Napoleon," and called for a curricular reorientation upon Islamic history in order to lead the young Egyptian Muslim to have "pride in his religion, trust in his forefathers, and respect for the heroes of his nation."[51] A few years later, the Muslim Brothers similarly challenged the existing Egyptian educational curriculum's emphasis on ancient Egyptian history as a counterproductive one "which inevitably will increase the confusion of young pupils and which will weaken the close tie which constitutes the most important component in their national consciousness at this crucial historical time, namely the history of the Arabs."[52]

In their own accounts of Egyptian history, spokesmen for the Islamic nationalist approach drastically minimized the place of Egypt's pre-Islamic past in the Egyptian national consciousness. In some of their writings the pre-Islamic periods were simply ignored; when mentioned in others, it was in a derogatory manner. In particular, ancient Egyptian civilization was not deemed worthy of perpetuation in the Egyptian historical memory.[53]

Egypt's meaningful history only began with the entry of Islam into the Nile Valley. Islamic nationalists presented the entry of the Arabs and Islam into Egypt as a pacific and beneficial experience. During the reign of the Rashidun caliphs, the Ummayads, and the early Abbasids, Egypt had come under the benevolent sway of "a spiritual, enlightening, cultural imperialism."[54] The conquest itself was portrayed in positive terms, as a process during which Arabs and Egyptians had intermingled of their own free will. Not only did Egypt not impose its own customs and national temperament on the Arabs and Islam, as territorial nationalists assumed; instead, it willingly accepted Islamic teaching and became an integral part of the *umma*. The distinctive language, racial characteristics, and national character of Egyptians disappeared as they were totally Arabized and Islamified.[55]

Islamicists did not disavow the centrality of Egypt in Islamic history. Like Egyptian territorial nationalists, they also emphasized Egyptian primacy in Islamic affairs. The purpose of their doing so was quite different, however; where the territorial nationalists did so in order to provide legitimization for Egypt's separate existence, Islamic nationalists did so in order to prove that Egypt had an historic mission to fulfill as leader of the Arab and Muslim worlds.[56]

The concept of Egyptian primacy in Islamic history informed the Islamic nationalist narrative of the many independent Muslim dynasties which ruled Egypt from the breakdown of the centralized Caliphate in the ninth century. The long era from 868 to 1517, in which Egypt was ruled successively by the Tulunids, Ikhshidids, Fatamids, Ayyubids, and Mamluks, was viewed as undoubtedly one of political dissolution and cultural decline for the Islamic community.[57] Yet this era of crisis for the *umma* as a whole was also a time when Islamic Egypt achieved great prominence. The importance of these independent Muslim dynasties was that they had transformed Egypt into the leading Muslim state of the period, "the heart of the Islamic world and its civilization."[58] In this era Cairo had been founded and al-Azhar established; in a short time, these became the political and religious pivots of the Islamic and Arab worlds. Indeed, Egypt had been the center of Islam in the middle period of Islamic history, replacing Baghdad as the site of the Caliphate and extending its political power into Syria.[59]

Exponents of this image of Egypt as center of Islam attempted to make Egypt's role in the Muslim struggle against the Christian Crusaders and the pagan Mongols into a crucial element in the historical awareness of Egyptians. Islamicist historiography rejected the territorialist interpretation of the anti-Crusader struggle as a manifestation of the drive for Egyptian independence. In their view, it had been a thoroughly Islamic struggle, a resistance which, without the religious spirit inspiring its leaders, would never have succeeded in repelling the Crusaders. It had been an Islamic, not an Egyptian, war. Fulfilling its duty as "the protector of the East and of Islam," Egypt had led a struggle for the unity and integrity of Islam.[60] For Islamic nationalists Egypt's role as shield of Islam against the Crusaders and Mongols revealed the country's real historical destiny which could not be avoided – to be the leader of the Islamic *umma*.

The Ottoman era of Egyptian Islamic history was generally treated briefly and negatively by Islamic nationalists. It had been "a period of stagnation in our history from which we derive no pride, nor which we deem worthy of special mention."[61] The Ottoman significance in Egyptian history had been to preside over Egyptian decline from its level of pre-Ottoman strength and importance, and thus to pave the way for the eventual conquest of the country by imperialism.[62]

Contemporary Muslim struggles against Western imperialism received a decidedly Islamic emphasis in the accounts of Egyptian Islamic nationalists. With specific reference to Egypt, the nationalist Revolution of 1919 was not interpreted as having been inspired by local, territorial nationalist impulses; rather, it was but one expression of a general Muslim revolution against the West occurring in the world today, a parallel event to other revolts in Iraq, Syria, Palestine, North Africa, and elsewhere. The *umma* as a whole was rising to throw off the Western yoke, to recover its lost independence, and to return to a golden age of unity and splendor similar to that which had obtained at the start of its history. In view of their country's long history as a member and a leader of that community, the role of Egyptians today was clearly to join other Muslims in the struggle to "liberate the Islamic homeland from all foreign domination" and to "establish of a free Islamic state in this free homeland."[63]

Thus the Islamic nationalist image of Egypt's place in Islamic history restructured Egyptian history in Islamic terms. Since the birth and expansion of Islam, Egypt was but one segment of a larger picture, one element in a unified historical pattern. This image of Egypt negated the concept of a separate Egyptian history within Islam. The history of the people of the Nile Valley for well over a thousand years had been intimately, inextricably interwoven with the history of Islam.

Islam and Arabism

Two processes were at work in Islamic nationalist discussions of the relationship between "Arabism [*al-'uruba*]" and Islam. One was an effort to Arabize Islam. Through stressing the numerous Arab components of Islam, Egyptian Islamic nationalists attempted to define Islam as a primarily Arab phenomenon. Simultaneously, their endeavors aimed at the Islamization of Arabism. This meant demonstrating that the contents of Arabism were largely religious rather than secular in character. Together, their parallel emphases on the Arabness of Islam and the Islamic character of Arabism forged an unbreakable connection between the religious phenomenon of

Islam and the ethnic community of the Arabs. Arabism was not something distinct from Islam; the two phenomena existed in symbiosis.

The unique place of the Arabs in Islam

"Despite the abhorrence of the hypocrites, Islam and Arabism are interlocked in an indissoluble bond. The life of the one is bound to the life of the other. There is no survival for Islam except in Arabism, and no survival for Arabism except in Islam. They are like the two wings of a bird; if one wing is broken, the other drops."[64]

This belief in an organic relationship between Islam and Arabism was a central tenet of Islamic nationalist ideology. An Arab character was inherent in Islam from the moment of its birth as a religious community fashioned from Arab materials. Islam had been marked by "the Arab mentality" and "the Arab spirit"; it was "the Arab religion."[65] The Prophet himself had recognized the integral connection between Islam and the Arabs when he said "If the Arabs are humiliated, then Islam is humiliated, and if the Arabs are strengthened, then Islam is strengthened."[66] Indeed, due to the fact that the Messenger of God had been an Arab, "every Muslim is half Arab because the Muslims are the people of Muhammad and Muhammad was an Arab."[67]

Two different emphases can be found in Egyptian Islamic nationalist presentations concerning the relationship between Islam and Arabism. One was to point out the innate qualities of the Arabs which led to their selection as the vehicle of Islam. From this perspective, the delivery of the Qur'an to the Arabs in the Arabic language was viewed as divine recognition of the special spiritual virtues of the Arabs. For some, the innate spiritual strength and moral character of the Arabs were why God chose them of all peoples to bring His message to mankind. The strengths of its Arab character were one factor responsible for the historic successes of Islam; without the leadership of the Arabs, Islam would not have flourished.[68]

The other line of argument was to emphasize the contribution of Islam to the formation of the Arab collective. What was stressed here was that the Arabs owed their historical greatness to Islam. This approach focused on the Arab lack of achievement prior to the emergence of Islam. Unruly, quarrelsome, and divided, they had been immersed in the darkness of the Jahiliyya. Without Islam, the Arabs would have remained a marginal people living on the periphery of history. What a difference with Islam! Islam had purified the Arabs of the abominations of the Jahiliyya, delivered them from their ignorance, taught them the way of morality, and perhaps most importantly unified them into a single people capable of playing a leading role on the world stage. In place of their previous isolation on the edges of civilization, the Arabs now became a world-historic people.[69]

This insistence on the close connection between Islam and Arabism had important implications for the Islamic nationalist view of Egypt. Egyptian Islamicists implicitly rejected the territorial nationalist postulate of the existence of a unique Egyptian national personality. Their writings focused on the existence and characteristics of another national collectivity – the Arab nation. Rather than the territorial nationalist exploration of the distinctive characteristics of Egyptians, they expounded on the "distinctive qualities of Arabism [khuwwas al-'uruba]" such as bravery, dignity, trustworthiness, hospitality, or determination which distinguished the Arabs above all others and made them a people uniquely qualified for world leadership.[70] Since the Arabs possessed "the fullest and most abundant share" of "virtues and moral character" among all the peoples of the world, it was their special responsibility to lead the way to "the revival of humanity."[71] Islam had united and inspired the Arabs not for their own sake, but so that they might serve the higher purpose of "bringing the message of monotheism to all nations and making the world one nation."[72] In this sense, the Arabs were a universal nation.

The sanctity and significance of the Arabic language

Egyptian Islamic nationalist analysis placed enormous emphasis on the importance of the Arabic language for Islam. The Arabic language shared in the miraculous aura which surrounded the Qur'an. As the medium of revelation, Arabic was "an eternal language."[73] It was also the irreplaceable vehicle of the faith: a thorough knowledge of Arabic was an essential prerequisite for a full understanding of the principles of Islam as well as the key to the comprehension of Islamic Law.[74] As Muhammad Sa'id al-'Urfi summarized the centrality of Arabic in Islam, "the language of the Qur'an is the language which unites the Muslim peoples and brings them together in understanding one another. The Arabic language is the language of Islam."[75]

From this premise Egyptian Islamicists drew the practical conclusion that the revival and rehabilitation of Islam demanded the strengthening of the position of both the Arabic language and the culture of the Arabs in contemporary Islamic society. Only the revival of the Arabic language and Arabic literature could serve as the vehicles for an Islamic cultural renaissance. Just as "the neglect of classical Arabic was one of the main reasons for the decline of the Islamic umma" in the past, so the revival of literary Arabic was necessary for "the revival and renewal of the whole Islamic community in the modern era."[76]

An important consequence of the assertion of the centrality of the Arabic language in Islam related to the definition of who was an Arab. By emphasizing the importance of Arabic, Egyptian Islamic nationalists made language the main determinant of national identity. All speakers of Arabic, including Egyptians, were Arabs. From the moment when Egyptians had adopted Arabic, they absorbed the unique characteristics of the Arabs, becoming Arabs themselves.[77] Hasan al-Banna offered an explanation of the role of language in the definition of community which mirrored that being expounded by secular Arab nationalists: "Sociologists have determined that language is the strongest bond between nations and peoples ... Islam perceived this truth and imposed Arabic upon the believers for their prayer and worship, granting Arabic nationality [al-jinsiyya al-'arabiyya] to everyone who speaks the language of the Arabs. ... Thus everyone who speaks Arabic is an Arab."[78]

To be sure, Egyptian Islamic nationalists did not consciously accord the Arabic language an autonomous identity and importance. For them, the significance of Arabic was firmly anchored in its unique position in Islam. Nonetheless, in taking the most obvious objective characteristic which linked Egypt to the Arab world and infusing it with subjective significance, they made the Arabic language and culture the point of departure for defining the communal identity of Egyptians. In doing so, they unintentionally contributed to the development of an ethnic-linguistic concept of nationalism in Egypt.

Islamic redemption and Arab unity

Much Egyptian Islamicist writing had a decidedly messianic flavor. A predominant theme was the expectation of the impending redemption of Islam through a return to the true character of the faith as it had manifested itself in the lifetime of the Prophet and the golden age of the *salaf*. Moreover, the revivification of the *umma* would be an event of momentous significance for the world as a whole. A revived Islam would be a guide for all people, "the bearer of light and the path of righteousness for all men."[79]

The Arabs were central to this redemption of Islam. Just as they had been responsible for the golden age at the birth of Islam, so they would lead the way to the future revitalization of the faith. Without the return of the Arabs to their prior position of leadership within Islam, there was no possibility of Islamic revival: "the magnificence of Islam is built upon the glory of the Arabs, and its redemption is dependent on their redemption."[80] The fate of the Arabs and Islam were one and the same.[81]

How were the Arabs to fulfill their role as the redeemers of Islam? The indispensable condition for the Arabs leading the way to Islamic revival was

Arab unity. An anonymous letter protesting Shaykh Mustafa al-Maraghi's hostility to Arab unity made the connection explicit: "if Islam is to have a revival, if Islam is to awaken after slumber, that can be only by the road of the Arabs."[82] History proved the point: since the Prophet's uniting of the Arab tribes at the dawn of Islam had been the precursor to Islamic expansion and greatness, so future Arab unity would serve as the catalyst for subsequent Islamic revival, unity, and glory.[83] On a personal level, this importance of the Arabs for the future of Islam also meant that commitment to Islam simultaneously demanded loyalty to Arabism and Arab nationalism.[84] Since Arab unity would benefit Islam, it was incumbent on all Muslims to support the movement toward Arab unity. "The unity of the Arabs," Hasan al-Banna stated in 1938, "is an inevitable condition for the restoration of the glory of [Islamic] revival, the establishment of its state, and the strengthening of its power. For this reason it is the duty of every Muslim to strive for the revival of Arab unity, to support it, and to defend it."[85]

The favorable attitude of Egyptian Islamic nationalists toward the goal of Arab unity had unintended consequences for the development of Arab nationalism in Egypt. By presenting the revival of Islam as contingent on Arab unity, Egyptian Islamic nationalists reinforced the concept of the value of Arab solidarity and cooperation which was emerging in more secular circles at the same time. By validating the legitimacy of the goals of Arab revival and unity in religious terms, they helped pave the way for Arab nationalism to become an alternative focus of Egyptian national identity.

Conclusion: the circles of supra-Egyptian national identity

The non-exclusive nature of Egyptian Islamic nationalist doctrine received its most concrete expression in the concept that Egyptians owed allegiance to several "circles [halaqat]" of national identity. The concept saw no conflict between loyalty to several communities. Rather, the circles identified formed an overlapping and mutually reinforcing network of allegiances; properly construed, loyalty to one served the others as well. What was erroneous was to view any one circle as an exclusive sphere of identity, as territorial nationalists conceived of Egypt or as secular Arab nationalists viewed the Arabs. All were interrelated units in an integrated network of loyalties.

Hasan al-Banna's address to the Congress of the Muslim Brotherhood in 1938 enumerated the conventional set of four ascending circles of allegiance – Egypt, the Arabs, Islam, and mankind:

The Muslim Brothers honor their particular nationalism, considering it as the prime basis for the desired revival. They see nothing amiss in every man working for his homeland and giving it preference above other homelands. Furthermore, they uphold Arab unity [*al-wahda al-'arabiyya*], considering it as the second circle in this revival. Then they work for Islamic unity [*al-jami'a al-islamiyya*], viewing it as the complete extent of the general Islamic homeland. After all this, I have to add that the Brothers seek the good of the entire world in that they call for world unity, because this is, after all, the aim and purpose of Islam.[86]

Loyalty to Egypt formed the first circle of identity. The Egyptian nation was a valid object of Egyptian Muslim loyalty and commitment. Indeed, Islam enjoined Egyptians to struggle for the legitimate national goals of Egypt – national solidarity, the liberation of the country from foreign rule, the unity of the Nile Valley. To be sure, loyalty to the Egyptian nation was always viewed as a stage in the realization of higher goals rather than as an end in itself, as territorial nationalists posited. The Egyptian homeland was part and parcel of a larger Arab nation, and through that was a unit in the greater Islamic community. Thus effort on behalf of Egyptian nationalism was also of utility to the other referents for Egyptian loyalty: "when we work for Egypt, we work for Arabism, the East, and for Islam."[87] The genius and talents of the Egyptian nation could only find full expression within the wider Arab, Islamic, and Eastern circles.[88]

The important place occupied by Egypt in the Islamic nationalist theory of circles deserves emphasis. Egyptian Islamicist spokesmen were not totally lacking in the sense of Egyptian distinctiveness which was the hallmark of Egyptian territorial nationalism. They too saw Egypt as the natural leader of the Arab and Muslim worlds, and called upon their country to assume the role of regional leadership for which it was uniquely suited.[89] For Hasan al-Banna, Egypt's location, its faithfulness to Islam, and its stature among contemporary Muslim lands made it more qualified than any other "specific [Muslim] nation" to be "the leader of Islam and the Muslims."[90]

Arabism and the Arab nation constituted the second circle of national identity for Muslim Arab Egyptians. Arab unity was viewed as the indispensable prerequisite for the revival of the Islamic *umma*. As with Egyptian nationalism, the Arab striving for unity was also presented as an action which would ultimately serve Islam. Therefore, Arab unity was the concern of all Muslims throughout the world.[91]

The third circle of loyalty was the most important one. While identification with Egypt and the Arabs were regarded as acceptable in Egyptian Islamic nationalist teaching, the ultimate goal of Egyptian Muslims was of course the realization of Islamic unity and the restoration of an Islamic order. Only Islamic unity could create the conditions for the full revival of Islam in the modern world.[92] As for Egypt, "Egypt has no value as an entity in and of itself. Rather, its value is in its leadership of the Islamic world and its defense of every inch of land of this unified homeland."[93] From this perspective the responsibility of the Muslim Brotherhood was to work for "the realization of Islamic unity [*al-wahda al-islamiyya*]."[94]

The achievement of Islamic unity in turn had world-wide implications for Egyptian Islamic nationalists. As God's final and most complete revelation to mankind, Islam was a universal faith. Thus the consequences of the realization of Islamic unity would not be limited to Muslims alone. Islamic unity indeed meant world unity, since a united Muslim community would have the ability to resume the dissemination of the faith throughout the world. This was "the seal of the circles [*khitam al-halaqat*]," in which Islam became the universal faith of all mankind.[95] Islamic unity was thus the prerequisite for "the word of God becoming supreme" throughout the world.[96]

5   Integral Egyptian nationalism

The supra-Egyptian nationalist doctrines which developed in Egypt after 1930 did not all have an external referent, such as the Islamic or Arab communities, as their point of departure. There was also a nationalist ideology which, while possessing a supra-Egyptian dimension, nonetheless kept Egypt as its central focus. Unlike the other supra-Egyptian ideologies, its external dimensions were tactical rather than strategic, instrumental rather than fundamental. Egypt remained its primary concern, with an Egyptian external identification and role seen as the necessary mechanisms for the achievement of specifically Egyptian national purposes. Although sharing many of the supra-Egyptian elements found in the Egyptian Islamic and Egyptian Arab nationalist approaches, it retained an Egypt-centered core.

We have termed this approach integral Egyptian nationalism. The term "integral nationalism" was coined by Charles Maurras to refer to the variant of late nineteenth to early twentieth-century European nationalist doctrine which was distinguished by "the exclusive pursuit of national policies, the absolute maintenance of national integrity, and the steady increase of national power."[1] The generic feature of integral nationalism is the absoluteness of the nation: "integral nationalism defines the one nation as the Absolute. It is not justified by its followers in terms of service to a higher cause; the cult of the nation becomes an end in itself."[2] Internally integral nationalism was usually illiberal, subordinating considerations of individual liberty to the demands of national strength; externally it was expansionist and militarist, assuming the inevitability of the need for force in international relations. Its ethos was "deliberately irrational": "Nationalists should cast logic aside and all barren intellectualism. They should judge everything in relationship to the nation as it is. Above all, they should be guided by sentiment and should be driven by national feeling as by a tempest."[3]

The leading participants in the intellectual formulation of integralist conceptions within the Egyptian context were mainly younger Egyptians who became prominent in the 1930s, such as Fathi Radwan, Ibrahim Jum'a,

Husayn Mu'nis, Mahmud Kamil, Fikri Abaza, Mahmud al-Manjuri, and Sulayman Huzayyin. Most important in the ideological articulation and popular dissemination of integral Egyptian nationalism was the colorful and controversial figure of Ahmad Husayn and the "Young Egypt [*misr al-fatah*]" movement which he led. The new effendiyya associated with Young Egypt were the key group in the development of integral nationalism in Egypt, and the movement's journals – *al-Sarkha*; *Wadi al-Nil*; *al-Thughr*; *Jaridat Misr al-Fatah* – served as the main medium for the dissemination of the doctrine of the movement.

From territorial to integral nationalism

Integral Egyptian nationalism can best be introduced in relation to the earlier Egyptian territorial nationalism out of which it emerged. The general thrust of Egyptian territorial nationalism was liberal and polycentric. Its formulators assumed the natural division of humanity into parallel nations, each with the same basic rights to national independence and acceptance as equal members of the family of nations. It was basically Western-oriented, in large part inspired by nineteenth-century European liberal thought, and was rationalist and utilitarian in its definition of Egyptian national goals in the pragmatic terms of economic growth, political and social emancipation, and cultural and educational enlightenment.

Integralist Egyptian nationalism abandoned the rationalist and universalist character of its territorialist parent and in its place inserted irrational and chauvinistic elements. The integralist approach drew much of its inspiration from more pessimistic schools of modern European thought, particularly from the Italian and German versions of contemporary fascism. It was also a vehemently anti-Western ideology which aimed at eradicating the Western-derived symbols, values, and institutions which it held were in large part responsible for Egypt's current abysmal condition. Above all, integralist Egyptian nationalism was ethnocentric. In place of the belief in a polycentric family of nations of which Egypt was no more than an equal member, its ideologues viewed the Egyptian nation as a special one destined for world leadership and greatness. The substantive corollary of this sense of Egyptian superiority was an emphasis on the need for Egyptian strength and power as the prime requirements for Egypt to manifest the inherent capabilities of this superiority. The pursuit of strength and the cult of power – elements foreign to the earlier Egyptian territorial nationalism – were central attributes of its integralist offspring.

The organization and mobilization of the citizenry for the purpose of serving the nation was a central objective of integral nationalism. As Young Egypt summarized its own activities in a petition to the king of 1937, the movement's goal was "spreading the military spirit everywhere and making the entire nation a mobilized nation."[4] Integral nationalists viewed all spheres of Egyptian life in terms of the need for organization, strength, and power. For Fathi Radwan, Egyptian education needed to be inspired by "a strong spirit" and to aim at the inculcation of "strong morals" such as "order, obedience, self-control, and the ability to bear adversity" in Egyptian youth.[5] Mahmud al-Manjuri extended the desire for national strength to the literary sphere, perceiving a need for "strong literature" and calling on Egyptian intellectuals "continually to recite the verses of the literature of strength."[6]

The precedence of national over individual needs was another axiom of integralism. The natural order was a mosaic of nations rather than an assemblage of individuals. Human reality was national reality; individuals existed only within the context of the collectivity, acquiring meaning only through it. The individual existed to serve the nation; as Mahmud Kamil put it, "it is just and even necessary to sacrifice individual rights on the altar of the national collective."[7] Thus integralist appeals called on the individual to "place his efforts, his life, and his wealth at the service of society" and to be prepared to "sacrifice himself and all that he possesses for the sake of God, Homeland, and King."[8]

Egyptian integral nationalists were not noted for a restrained use of language. Integralist rhetoric emphasized such qualities as "faith" and "will," "determination" and "confidence," and was studded with passionate summonses to "action," "sacrifice," and "struggle." Most of the emotional qualities emphasized in integralist discourse are visible in the following passage of a speech by Ahmad Husayn:

We wish to restore spirit to Egyptian youth, so that they will be filled with faith and determination, will venerate manliness and virtue, will consider themselves chivalrous and courageous. We wish to produce a generation full of confidence in itself, glorifying its country and taking pride in its history. We wish to fill souls with boldness, daring, and the will to sacrifice.[9]

In the words of Husayn's closest associate Fathi Radwan, what Egyptians needed was "a spirit which will increase their confidence in themselves and their pride in their country, which will strengthen their hope in life and make them understand that they are the masters of the world [sadat al-dunya]."[10]

Integral Egyptian nationalists worshiped power. In their view a nation was nothing if it lacked the capabilities to enforce its will upon the world. National strength defined in both spiritual and physical terms was the indispensable requirement for Egypt to regain the greatness and glory which it so richly deserved; correspondingly, the enhancement of the power of Egypt was a fundamental aim of integral nationalism.[11] The integralist cult of power is most visible in the slogans and activities of the main integralist movement of the 1930s, Young Egypt. The concept of "struggle [*jihad*]" suffused the vocabulary of the movement. Its program defined its goals in terms of "our economic struggle" or "our social struggle"; its name for its members was "struggler [*mujahid*]"; their distinctive green shirt was termed "the emblem of the struggle."[12] The Social-Darwinist concepts of life as a perpetual struggle and the survival of the fittest reverberate through the speeches and writings of the movement's leader Ahmad Husayn. Perhaps his fullest statement of his "life as struggle" came in a speech of 1935:

There is no way for us to achieve all that [Young Egypt's goals] except by strength, physical strength. Indeed, nature teaches us that there can be no agreement between the ruler and the ruled nor between the strong and the weak. Accord can only be reached by struggle and strife. The conqueror is the worthy one, because he continues to exist; the conquered is weak, and is exterminated. Life knows no restraint or leniency. He who is strong, lives; he who is weak, dies.

In vain does a weak people imagine that they can ever reach an amicable accord with a strong people. For that is an "accord" like the accord of the wolf and the lamb, which always ends with the wolf eating the lamb. This is life. So, if you desire your freedom, dream of it and want to achieve it, there is but one path before you – to be strong, to be strong first and last.[13]

"The pages of history" offered proof of the necessity of power in human relations. No nation had ever attained its independence without strength; indeed, no idea or religion had triumphed "save through strength, physical strength."[14] For Husayn, "strength is everything: it is the law of life in every age and epoch."[15]

What accounts for the differences between the polycentric and utilitarian Egyptian territorial nationalism of the 1920s and the ethnocentric and vitalist integralism of the 1930s? Egyptian territorial nationalism was the outgrowth of two historical processes; the adoption of the liberal and progressive world view of nineteenth-century Europe by the educated elite of Egypt in the late nineteenth and early twentieth centuries, and the Egyptian Revolution of 1919 which had enshrined the territorialist outlook in public discourse and the institutions of the new Egyptian nation-state. Inspired by an optimistic *Zeitgeist*, territorial nationalism in Egypt reflected a general attitude of confidence and hope. It was a fundamentally optimistic outlook which assumed that the progress which had marked Egyptian and world development in the recent past could and would continue into the future, and that Egypt was well on its way to becoming part of the modern community of nations.

Integral Egyptian nationalism, on the other hand, emerged in a decade of crisis and strain. The creation not of the Westernized elite of the older generation but of a younger generation coming to political maturity in the difficult circumstances of the 1930s, it was an angry movement of rebellion and reaction against the values and institutions of a flawed territorialist and parliamentary order which by then was seen to have failed. While it accepted many of the premises of Egyptianism concerning the Egyptian people and nation, it augmented them with additional qualities which Egyptianism lacked and which were seen as possessing the potential to rectify its failures – an insistence on cultural authenticity and pride rooted in Egypt's native Arab-Islamic customs and traditions; a demand for Egyptian strength and power; a call for Egypt to increase its capabilities and realize its destiny through regional assertion. Egyptian integral nationalism was territorialism influenced by and readjusted to the darker world of the 1930s and 1940s.

Egyptian history – a continuous display of national greatness

While all schools of Egyptian nationalist thought reached into history to find justification for their positions, few relied on it more heavily than did integral nationalism. The younger ideologues responsible for the articulation of the integralist approach possessed an acute intellectual awareness as well as a personal sense of anguish over the vivid contrast between the glories of the Egyptian past and the miseries of the Egyptian present. For them, the repeated examples of national greatness to be found in Egyptian history simultaneously offered compensation for their despair over Egypt's current conditions and indisputable proof that Egypt could become great once again. As Ahmad Husayn expressed the premise, "only one thing – ignorance, ignorance of our country, ignorance of our history, ignorance of ourselves, ignorance of our capabilities" – was responsible for Egypt's current retardation.[16] The study of history offered both refuge from the pains of the present and manifest evidence that Egypt had the capability to realize a better future.

Many of the specifics of the integralist image of the Egyptian past were drawn from earlier Egyptian territorial nationalist thought. This was particularly true of their portrayal of the long Pharaonic epoch. Integralists also took pride in Egypt's precedence among the nations of the world, its splendid cultural as well as material achievements, and its position as the source of inspiration for other ancient peoples. As with territorialists, emphasis was placed on the continuity between ancient and modern Egypt. The Pharaonic period had not been unique, but had defined what they regarded as Egypt's enduring character and world role. Internally, the foundations of Egyptian spiritual and material superiority had been laid down in ancient Egypt; externally, the Egyptians of the Pharaonic age had defined Egypt's universal mission of bearing enlightenment and wisdom to others. The ancient Egyptians had been the creators of the first Egyptian empire, expanding Egyptian dominion beyond the confines of the Nile Valley; they had also been the first Egyptian freedom fighters, repelling the Hyksos and Persian attempts to conquer Egypt. In all this, the ancient Egyptians had set the standards for subsequent Egyptian behavior.[17] The lesson to be drawn from the study of Pharaonic Egypt is what mattered most to integral nationalists. Contemporary Egyptians needed to realize that

the magnificence which surrounds you is not foreign to you. Those who built all this passed on their determination and their power to you. It is necessary that the Egypt which has carried the banner of humanity in past ages revive again, returning to its place of primacy ... It is necessary that we strive and strive until we return Egypt to all its power, to all its majesty, to all its magnificence.[18]

What stood out in integralist accounts of post-Pharaonic Egyptian history were the repeated manifestations of national greatness and world leadership visible throughout virtually all of Egyptian history. Central to the integralist perspective was the firm conviction that Egypt's splendor and world influence had not been restricted to the Pharaonic period, but had reverberated through post-Pharaonic history as well. As Ahmad Husayn phrased the point,

I used to believe, as all students and all Egyptians believe about the past, that civilization in Egypt, in other words the golden age in Egypt, was limited to the Pharaonic age ... Suddenly I became aware of my mistake, the mistake of every Egyptian who thought this way. The golden age has repeated itself two and three and four times. Indeed, Egypt through most of the phases of its history has always been as it was in the age of the Pharaohs, the home of science, knowledge, and religions.[19]

The first post-Pharaonic era, that of the Ptolemies, was clearly one of Egyptian glory for integral Egyptian nationalists. Politically, the Ptolemies had expanded the sway of Egypt, creating an Egyptian empire reaching into the Fertile Crescent and the Mediterranean Basin; culturally, the Hellenistic period was one of Egyptian internal efflorescence and external leadership through its magnificent cultural centers at 'Ayn Shams and Alexandria, from whence Egyptian influence had radiated throughout the entire world. In the Ptolemaic era, Egypt had been "the primary pivot among the states of the world."[20]

Egypt had also maintained a world role through the long era of Roman domination. Its contribution at that time had been primarily spiritual, as the torchbearer of the message of Christianity. Egypt had been the refuge of Christianity, nurturing it in the face of Roman persecution. Eventually it triumphed in its spiritual struggle on behalf of Christianity, spreading its teachings through the rest of the Roman Empire and eventually the entire world. Egypt had indeed been the historic agent of the transformation of Christianity from a small and persecuted faith to a universal religion.[21]

The integral nationalist interpretation of history diverged from its territorialist parent when it reached the Islamic-Arab era. Where territorialists had presented the Arabs as foreign conquerors, integralists saw more symbiosis between Arabs/Muslims on the one hand and Egyptians on the other. The Muslim Arab entry into Egypt was presented as a pacific one; already attuned to the monotheistic message through their prior adoption of Christianity, "Egyptians welcomed the new conqueror who raised the word of God and preached monotheism."[22] Ibrahim Jum'a stressed the synergic effects of the Arab conquest, presenting the Arab-Muslim entry into Egypt as the agency of the blending of Egyptians into Arab-Islamic civilization and the creation of a new, composite, "Islamic Arab Egyptian nation" along the banks of the Nile: "after the first three *hijri* centuries had passed, an Islamic Arab Egyptian nation [*umma misriyya 'arabiyya Islamiyya*] emerged. [It] shared united goals, was a well-defined political entity, and had a distinct personality within the greater Islamic state."[23]

What received most attention in the integralist account of Egyptian history under Islam was Egypt's continuing greatness and leadership of the Muslim *umma*. Ahmad Husayn saw Egypt beginning to play a leading role in Islamic history as early as the Rashidun era, when rebels from Egypt had taken the lead in the murder of the Caliph 'Uthman.[24] Egypt's primacy in the Muslim world was unquestioned under the string of independent dynasties which ruled Egypt from the Tulunids to the Mamluks. Under these dynasties Egypt became a leader of Islam. The establishment of al-Azhar under the Fatamids reasserted the tradition begun with Alexandria and 'Ayn Shams, that of Egypt as the teacher of neighboring peoples. Egypt had been the shield and defender of Islam through much of the Islamic era, serving as a secure refuge for Muslim thinkers as the Islamic East fell into turmoil and as a physical barrier against both Crusader and Mongol expansion. Egyptian military success against Crusaders and Mongols was but a demonstration of Egypt's inherent ability to overcome all her enemies. Thus the Islamic era bore witness to the same truth apparent in other epochs of the long Egyptian past: "Egypt has always been the beating heart of the world, the source of its learning and its culture in most periods."[25]

Egypt's Islamic golden age came to a close with the Ottoman conquest. The three centuries of Ottoman domination were viewed as a period of Egyptian decline, and accordingly they received little attention from integral nationalists.[26] From the late eighteenth century, however, a process of revival began. The reign and achievements of the founder of Egypt's ruling dynasty, Muhammad 'Ali, were a major subject of discussion in the integralist historical narrative. After a long period of national decline, Egypt again surged forward in all walks of life. A new political, economic, and social order had emerged in Egypt in the early nineteenth century, providing the framework for rapid modernization in agriculture and industry, governmental administration, and education. Perhaps most important from the integralist perspective were Muhammad 'Ali's creation of a mighty Egyptian army and navy and his subsequent regional ascendancy which again made Egypt a world power.[27]

But Egypt's time of glory was a brief one. Fearful and jealous of Egypt, a coalition of European powers led by Great Britain took up arms against Muhammad 'Ali. They were successful. Under European pressure, Egypt's latest golden age came to an end. The Egyptian empire collapsed, and Egypt soon came under the control of the rapacious foreigner. The villain in the story of the termination of Egypt's most recent period of greatness was the same Great Britain which today occupied Egypt: "were it not for England, the mortal enemy of Egypt, today we would be living in the mightiest empire."[28]

The vivid contrast between Egypt's glorious past and oppressive present generated the prevalent integral nationalist mood of bitterness and anger. Yet Egypt's current phase of decline was not assumed to be irreversible. On the contrary, the dialectics of Egyptian history – the repeated revivals and return to world greatness demonstrated over its long history – produced an expectation of a new golden age on the horizon. What was necessary to realize it was first a proper awareness of the character of Egypt as manifested in its history, then a commitment to work for the revival of Egyptian greatness.[29] For all its anguish over the current state of Egypt, the tone of the program of the main integralist movement concerning the Egyptian future was triumphant: "it [Egypt] shall never die, indeed it shall revive again, returning to its original position as a beacon to the world, a crown for the East, and a leader of Islam."[30]

Egypt over all

Since Egypt rather than the Arabs, Islam, or the East was the central focus of integral Egyptian nationalism, the doctrine's position on Egypt must be examined before its supra-Egyptian aspects are addressed. Two interrelated concepts lie at the heart of the integralist image of Egypt. First and foremost was the conviction of the innate superiority of the Egyptian nation over other national communities. Along with this went the belief that it was Egypt's destiny to be a regional as well as a world leader in the future. Because of its inherent qualities of superiority, Egypt possessed a unique mission to other Eastern, Arab, and Muslim peoples in particular as well as to mankind in general.

The ideologues of integral Egyptian nationalism repeatedly asserted the superiority of Egypt to other national communities. Egypt had been selected by God and shaped by nature to play a unique role in human affairs. The uniqueness of Egypt among the nations was an objective fact clearly demonstrated in history, which offered repeated evidence of the unique achievements of Egypt.[31] The motto of the Young Egypt Society, "Egypt Over All [misr fawqa al-jami']," is the most famous phrase expressing the axiom of the absoluteness of the nation.

Integralist portrayals of Egypt typically characterized it as the "spring," "cradle," or "mother" of human culture, the source from which the arts and sciences of civilization had radiated throughout the rest of the world.[32] Many of the basic arts and sciences characteristic of civilization had had an Egyptian origin. Equally significant was Egypt's historic role as the birthplace of monotheism in the Pharaonic era and as the refuge of Judaism, Christianity, and Islam alike in subsequent epochs.[33] Particularly meaningful in the integralist vision was the belief in Egypt's temporal precedence over other nations, especially those of Europe, in the achievement of civilization. Egypt had been "the master of the world in the sciences and arts, philosophy and politics ... at a time when others lived in caves and forests";[34] it had been Egypt which had carried the torch of civilization at the time when "Europe was living in the dark ages."[35] Nor had Egyptian precociousness manifested itself only in more remote historical epochs; in the nineteenth century, Muhammad 'Ali had modernized the country and made it a world power "at a time when Japan had not yet entered the arena of struggle, when the United States had not yet unified its ranks, and when modern Germany and modern Italy had not yet come into existence as independent, unified nations."[36]

Overall, Egypt's many achievements were the continual unfolding of an inherent "Egyptian genius."[37] The "boasts [mafakhir]" of Young Egypt capture the range of religious and cultural, political and military, Egyptian accomplishments in which integral nationalists took pride:

> Egypt is the center of the world, the teacher of humanity, the mother of civilizations;
>
> [it] is the source of wisdom and the refuge of all religions – from it issued forth the Mosaic religion, and in it Christianity was given shelter;
>
> [it] was it which raised the banner of Islam on high, and produced the university of al-Azhar;
>
> [it] was it which fought Crusading Europe, defeated it, and held its kings at ransom;

[it] was it which rescued the world from the evil of the criminal
Tatars;

[it] was it which annihilated its enemies, conquered them, and has
remained alive forever;

[it] was it which threw the English army into the sea [in 1807];

[it] was it which sent its armies to the gates of Europe, and whose
fleet frightened the fleets of Europe in the days of Muhammad
'Ali;

[it] is it which extends until the Equator at the furthermost limits of
the Sudan;

[it] is it which leads Islam today, and which will be responsible for
the leadership of it [in the future];

[it] is it which will become over all in defiance of all.[38]

Egypt's superiority over other nations rested in the first instance on its
historical antiquity and stability. Egypt had been the first nation to crystallize as an entity; its people were "the first people in the world."[39] From its
formation as a collective until the present, Egypt had maintained its national
character and integrity. The vicissitudes of time had not affected the
country's essential nature, which had remained the same over the millennia.[40] Egypt's perdurability was particularly apparent in comparison to the
historical experience of other peoples. From its birth in the Pharaonic era,
"Egypt has remained a nation with civilization and culture although many
other peoples have died in the meantime."[41] To be sure, Egypt had witnessed many invaders coming from the outside; but it had always been able
to "destroy them and defeat them in the end, and that by transforming them
into Egyptians in blood, flesh, and mentality."[42] Thus "eternal Egypt [*misr
al-khalida*]" was a meta-historical phenomenon, a nation immune to the
ravages of history and of time.[43]

Secondly, integralist thinkers attributed Egyptian superiority to the
country's unusual geographic situation. Egypt was blessed with geographic
advantages unparalleled in any other country. The most obvious and important was the Nile itself, the life source of Egyptian civilization. To this were
added the country's temperate and benign climate, its fertile soil, and its
predictable seasons, all of which buffered Egypt from the wild and destructive swings of nature experienced elsewhere. Above all, Egypt's geographical position was responsible for the country becoming an international crossroads, the center of the world connecting Africa to Asia and
West to East.[44]

Integral nationalists also identified a human element contributing to
Egyptian superiority. The living reservoir of Egyptian greatness was its
common people. Earlier Egyptian territorial nationalism had idealized the
Egyptian peasantry.[45] Integral nationalism heightened the idealization of

the *fallahin*. The qualities of faith and confidence so necessary for Egypt to rediscover if it wished to regain its proper place in the world were not to be found in its Westernized elite or its intellectuals, who saw only the current subjugation and humiliation of Egypt; rather, they had continued to exist only in the mentality of "the simple peasant," who retained an instinctive awareness of the greatness of Egypt and that "Egypt is the mother of the world."[46] It was the firm belief of the Young Egypt movement "that the *fallah* is the crown of Egypt and the secret of its strength, and that the one truth which had not changed in the world in six thousand years is that he is the one thing that has kept Egypt vibrant and strong until today."[47]

Integral nationalism in Egypt had a decidedly populist tone. The litany of virtues integralists attributed to the peasantry was a long one. Their fortitude and habits of work were superior to those of other peoples: "when I looked at the European peasant and compared him to the Egyptian peasant, I saw in this comparison that the Egyptian *fallah* is stronger and more patient in his work."[48] The *fallahin* embodied the primordial and authentic qualities of the nation, retaining a dedication to and love of the land which other Egyptians had lost. Aware of the traditions of their forefathers and therefore firm in an understanding of who they were, they faced hardship with fortitude and bravery. Indeed, the way to appreciate Egyptian greatness was to go to the peasantry and observe the genuine Egyptian qualities which they preserved. They held the answers to Egyptian rebirth.[49]

Belief in a continuing mission for Egypt was the natural corollary of the integralist conviction of the country's inherent superiority. Integral nationalists envisaged a future role of leadership as an organic component of the country's national character and personality. The country's playing a major role in world affairs was not a matter of choice, but an obligation imposed on it by its essential nature.[50] In the ringing prose of Ahmad Husayn, "the greatness of this country is a preordained affair towards which it is proceeding with clear steps, world events being no more than a prologue to this greatness."[51]

Integral Egyptian nationalists projected an air of confidence about Egypt regaining its position of world superiority and leadership. Through the 1930s, Ahmad Husayn repeatedly asserted that Egypt had the capability to equal or surpass the achievements of modern France, Italy, or Germany, provided Egyptians recovered the determination, confidence, and faith which they presently lacked.[52] The program of Young Egypt, with its vehement affirmation that "it [Egypt] shall never die, indeed it shall revive again, returning to its original position as a beacon for the world, a crown for the East, and a leader for Islam,"[53] codified the integralist expectation of Egyptian mission.

Ultimately, Egypt's cultural mission was a global one. Sulayman

Huzayyin offered one of the fullest statements of how Egypt's position invested it with a world role. In the present world, Egypt had no less a mission as "a connecting-link between East and West" than she had possessed in the past.[54] Because Egypt had been in touch with both East and West for millennia, she was "perhaps the only country where Easterners and Westerners alike could find in her culture and cultural heritage something familiar to them and with which they can feel at home."[55] Egypt needed to blend Western culture with the best of her own heritage whether Pharaonic, Hellenistic, Arab, or Islamic; in so doing, the country would again give "the Eastern and the Western world alike new fruits of the mind bearing the contribution of a reviving Egypt to the growth of a new world culture."[56]

The integral nationalist concepts of Egyptian superiority and mission had their origins in several interlocking influences. One was the emphasis on Egyptian uniqueness present from the start in Egyptian territorial nationalism. Another was the idiom of nationalist discourse in general, with its assumptions of specific national qualities and capabilities. Heightened in time by widely shared premises about race, such speculation naturally led nationalists to search for their own nation's particular "genius" and universal mission. An aggressive chauvinism similar to and undoubtedly influenced by contemporary European fascism is obvious in the rhetoric of Young Egypt in particular. But perhaps the most important influence was the immediate Egyptian intellectual context of the 1930s. The widespread Eastern and Islamic orientations of the period, with their assumptions of decline of the West and the dawning of the East and/or Islam, encouraged integral Egyptian nationalists to view their own country, with its glorious historical legacy, as the obvious leader of Islamic revival, Eastern renaissance, and ultimately universal regeneration.

Islam and the Arabs in integral Egyptian nationalism

In contrast to the territorial nationalism from which it emerged, the integral nationalist concept of Egypt was a non-exclusive one. That Egypt was more than just Egypt was a fundamental principle of the integralist approach. On the one hand, Islam and the Arabic language were seen as inseparable parts of the Egyptian national makeup and heritage; on the other, the Muslim and particularly the Arab worlds were presented as spheres of Egyptian influence and arenas for the realization of the greatness and glory which Egypt so richly deserved. The goals of Egyptian nationalism which were the object of all Egyptian nationalists would be realized within an Arab and Muslim context, not in isolation from it.

At the same time as rejecting the exclusivism found in territorial nationalism, integral nationalism simultaneously inverted the hierarchy of loyalties found in Egyptian Islamic nationalism. Where Islamic nationalist writings considered the struggle for Egyptian national goals to be only a stage in the realization of wider Islamic ends, integral nationalists discussed Arab and Islamic cooperation primarily in terms of their contribution to the achievement of Egyptian purposes. The ultimate measure of significance in integral nationalist doctrine was the needs and requirements of Egypt, not those of the larger linguistic and religious communities with which Egypt was linked. Egypt's relationship to the Islamic *umma* in integralism was ultimately viewed as a springboard – indispensable, but nonetheless primarily instrumental – to the realization of Egyptian aims. What was an end in the one approach was a means in the other.

Integral Egyptian nationalism was not a static phenomenon through the 1930s and 1940s. In the initial phase of the formulation of the doctrine, its Nile Valley focus and its hegemonic approach to Egypt's role in the world around it were the most prominent features of the integralist outlook. The fundamental aim of the Young Egypt Society's program of 1933 – "that Egypt ascend over all other states, becoming a mighty empire comprised of Egypt and the Sudan, allied with the Arab states, and leading Islam" – clearly indicates the Egyptocentric orientation of Young Egypt at its inception.[57] Over time, however, integralist thought took on a more Arab and Islamic coloration. The progression was one of weaving Arabism and Islam more and more intimately into the fabric of Egyptian national identity. Under the impact of the emergence of the parallel Egyptian Islamic and Arab nationalist doctrines of the period, a greater awareness of the Arab-Islamic aspects of Egyptian identity as well as a greater insistence on increased Egyptian interaction with its Arab and Muslim neighbors became evident in integralist speculation.

Egyptianism versus Islam and Arabism – denying any contradiction

Integral Egyptian nationalists refused to acknowledge any incompatibility between a distinctive Egyptian national identity with its roots in the Pharaonic heritage and a supra-Egyptian affiliation with the Arab and Muslim communities. They regarded the periodic debates over Egyptianism and/or Pharaonicism versus Arabism and/or Islam of the 1930s as pointless exercises at best, and at worst as a dangerous form of speculation which distorted the unity of Egyptian national outlook and purpose. As Fathi Radwan observed in 1933, the debate of Pharaonicism versus Arabism then raging in the daily press was "a shame and a disgrace"; it benefited only the imperialists to "divide the history of Egypt into two parts and thus corrupt the unity of the history of this great nation."[58]

The integralists' denial of a contradiction between Egyptian and supra-Egyptian loyalties was based on two considerations. The first was the cosmopolitan nature of Egypt itself. In their view, much of Egypt's greatness derived from its unique role as an international crossroads where different world traditions and cultures had met and been mutually influenced by each other. The result of Egypt's role in fostering cultural cross-fertilization between peoples and cultures had been the internationalization of her own tradition, as the country absorbed what was beneficial from others and folded it into its own culture. Egypt's heritage was not one-dimensional, restricted to influences originating in one or another of the many different eras of her history. On the contrary, Egypt was a synthesis of various historical influences, what Fathi Radwan once termed a uniquely "universal land [ard insaniyya]."[59]

The other line of approach was to emphasize the constant interaction between Egypt and its neighbors throughout history. Egyptians had never been isolated from neighboring ancient peoples and civilizations like the Sumerians, Babylonians, Phoenicians, or Assyrians. All had developed from common origins and in constant cultural proximity. Ahmad Husayn maintained that it did "violence to history" to think that Islam had ushered in Arab unity, as some Islamic nationalists asserted; historically, "Pharaonic Egypt was contemporary with the Phoenician state in Syria and the Assyrian and Babylonian state in Iraq, and there were strong ties uniting these ancient countries and shaping them into a living body with interacting and mutually supporting parts."[60]

Integralists emphasized the open-ended nature of Pharaonic Egypt. The Pharaonic legacy was viewed as the common heritage of all Arabs, not just the property of Egyptians, and all Arabs could learn from the wisdom to be found in it. Indeed, other Arabs owed a debt of thanks to Egypt for having investigated their Egyptian past and, in so doing, for having contributed to the strengthening of the collective Arab heritage.[61] This also led integralists to criticize those anti-Pharaonicists who attacked the Pharaonic approach in the belief that it worked against Arab solidarity; to attack Egypt's Pharaonic legacy was indirectly to attack the historical heritage of all Arab peoples, of which Pharaonic Egypt was an integral part.[62]

The integralist conclusion from all this was that there was no contradiction between Egyptianness and a supra-Egyptian identity. Egypt had never existed in isolation from its neighbors. At the same time as it had taught to others, it had absorbed from others. With specific reference to the Arab nation, the achievements of ancient Egypt belonged to all Arabs, anchoring their prominence in antiquity. Egypt was more than Egypt.

The unity of the Nile Valley

A consistent demand of Egyptian nationalists of all stripes through the first half of the twentieth century was Egyptian sovereignty over the Sudan. The legitimacy of the *de facto* separation of Egypt and the Sudan enforced by Great Britain after the Sudan's reconquest in 1896–8 was a repeated subject of Anglo-Egyptian contention until Sudanese independence in the 1950s. For territorialist and supra-Egyptianist spokesmen alike, the unity of the Nile Valley was a given.

Each variety of supra-Egyptian nationalism, however, approached the issue of Nile Valley unity somewhat differently. Egyptian Islamic nationalist spokesmen gave primary attention to the Islamic world as Egypt's main sphere of affiliation and fulfillment. Egypt's universe of action extended far beyond the confines of the Nile Valley; in their writings the Sudan had no more significance than any other part of the *umma*.[63] For integralists, the issue of the Sudan was somewhat more important. The recreation of a mighty empire "composed of Egypt and the Sudan" was a consistent demand in all of Young's Egypt's programmatic statements of the 1930s; often this was coupled with the assertion that the two halves of the Nile Valley "cannot be separated or divided."[64] When the movement optimistically appointed a set of shadow ministers in 1938, one bureau was concerned with Sudanese affairs.[65] The movement's new program of 1940 was quite detailed about Egyptian–Sudanese unity, putting forth several concrete suggestions for measures which would have resulted in the equality of Egyptians and Sudanese in government, administration, and public life.[66]

The above notwithstanding, Young Egypt was an *Egyptian* movement. The demand for Egyptian–Sudanese unity in its programmatic statements never stood alone, but was coupled with the other external goals of Egyptian leadership of the neighboring Arab and Islamic regions.[67] Its publications gave relatively little attention to Sudanese issues; it does not appear to have had any branches in the Sudan. Its leader Ahmad Husayn paid his first visit to the Sudan only in December 1938.[68] A year later, he acknowledged that it was only after that trip that he had come to "the firm belief that Egypt and the Sudan are one unit, created so by God."[69] Finally, Young Egypt's vision of African lands which it wished united with Egypt sometimes reached well beyond the Sudan itself; a map of the "glorious Egyptian empire" the movement wished to create reached well beyond the Sudan, stretching beyond the great lakes of east Africa into the southern part of the continent.[70] On the whole, the Sudan for Young Egypt was treated in the same hegemonic terms in which the movement treated the Arab and Islamic worlds – in terms of what it meant for Egyptian greatness and glory.

Islam in the service of Egypt

The integral Egyptian nationalist perspective on Islam differed significantly from that prevalent in both Egyptian territorial and Egyptian Islamic nationalism. The difference between territorial and integral Egyptian nationalism was the more fundamental one. For most territorial nationalists, there was a basic contradiction between religion – any religion – and modern nationalism. In the integralist view, on the other hand, Islam's status as the religion and value system of the vast majority of Egyptians made it an inseparable part of the Egyptian national makeup. Whereas territorialist theory explicitly placed Islam outside the framework of Egyptian national identity, integralist doctrine viewed it as a vital part of that identity.

The distinction between the Islamic nationalist and integralist view of Islam was not as basic, but nonetheless was appreciable. While the ideologues of both approaches often saw Islam as the fundamental source of instruction and guidance for modern Egyptian life, the place of Islam in the Islamic nationalist versus the integralist hierarchy of values was different. For Egyptian Islamic nationalists, Islam was the ultimate and most important repository of Muslim Egyptian identity and allegiance. It is questionable if the same was true of most integral Egyptian nationalists. They viewed Islam through a nationalist prism which made the Egyptian nation their primary concern. In their writings, what Islam had to contribute to the achievement of the specifically Egyptian national goals of revival, power, and greatness often bulked larger than the spiritual ends of Islam itself.

The theoretical incorporation of Islam into integral Egyptian nationalism occurred through their acceptance of religion as a basis for national identity. Where Egyptian territorial nationalists had seen religion as an anachronistic principle of communal loyalty, their integralist offspring had no such qualms. For Mahmud al-Manjuri, the Islamic religion had been the sole external influence which had significantly altered the essential nature of the eternal "Egyptian mind," totally remolding it in accord with its own ideals and values; the coming of Islam to Egypt was indeed "the decisive historical event in our intellectual transformation."[71] In view of this, Manjuri saw dual sources of spiritual inspiration for modern Egyptians; the perduring "spirit of the Egyptian nation" on the one hand, "the spirit of religion" on the other.[72] In the rhetoric of Ahmad Husayn, the struggles for national and religious goals were often indistinguishable: "one who is not fighting for the sake of God is not fighting for the sake of the homeland" and "your patriotic struggle is part of your struggle for the sake of God" were typical formulations.[73]

Yet, beyond such generalizations, the programmatic Islamic dimension was left largely undeveloped in integral nationalist doctrine. While the successive programs of Young Egypt consistently advocated that Egypt assume a leading role in the Muslim world, just what that meant in actuality was left nebulous. The movement's program of 1933 contained no specific provisions concerning an Islamic policy for Egypt in the external arena beyond the vague exhortation for al-Azhar to be reinvigorated and to "regain its old position."[74] Even the movement's adoption of an explicitly Islamic orientation by 1940 – its change of name to the Islamic Nationalist Party and its drafting of a new program – did not result in significantly greater specificity as to what Egyptian leadership of Islam meant in practical terms. Its goals in the Islamic arena consisted merely of a call for "fighting imperialism over the Islamic nations in all parts of the world and achieving the complete liberation of the Islamic world," which in turn was to be followed by "the realization of spiritual Islamic unity, the revival of the glory of Islam, and the dissemination of its message throughout the world."[75]

What integral nationalists did discuss in detail were the ways in which Islam had contributed to Egyptian purposes. Historically, Islam was seen to have rescued Egypt from a condition of listlessness and torpor, supplanting an exhausted "ancient Egyptian nationalism" with a more vigorous "Islamic Egyptian nationalism." This new sense of nationalism had imbued Egyptians with fresh energy and set them on the path to new glory under the banner of Islam. The leadership potential inherent in the Egyptian nation was thus provided with a new impetus under the aegis of Islam.[76]

In the social sphere, the integralist emphasis was upon Islam as offering a system of values which provided for the Egyptian nation's social requirements. Virtually all the good qualities which Young Egypt wished to see obtain in Egypt were to be found in Islam: "it [Islam] is that which teaches us the means of ruling, of consultation, democracy, equality, freedom, and brotherhood. It is that which teaches us the systematic and beneficial socialism of the *zakat*."[77] The egalitarian nature of Islam, "a code that makes people as equal as the teeth of a comb," was presented as the inspiration of the social reforms which Young Egypt advocated for Egyptian society.[78]

Perhaps most important for integral Egyptian nationalists was what Islam had to offer to Egypt in the way of strength. For Ahmad Husayn in particular, Islam was a religion of power capable of supplying Egypt with the national strength demanded for its continued advance toward greatness.[79] "Power [*quwwa*]" was "of the essence of Islam and its religion" in Husayn's view.[80] Its organized and disciplined nature was the source of much of its strength, and was visible in such central ceremonies as the Friday prayer, with its orderly rows of believers praying with "one voice, one heart, and one spirit," and the annual pilgrimage where believers from all over the world assembled to perform the same religious rituals dressed in the same fashion.[81] Islam was thus "the religion of God's unity and of solidarity, the religion of order and leadership."[82] According to Husayn, Young Egypt's own paramilitary character derived from Islam rather than from contemporary European models: "how often have I said to you that this military system and unity of dress is only a product of Islam."[83]

The nationalist lens through which integralists viewed religion appears most clearly in a speech delivered by Ahmad Husayn before the Young Men's Muslim Association in December 1933.[84] The central thesis of his presentation was that Egypt and its people possessed an inherently religious nature: "Egypt, gentlemen, was, is, and always will be the refuge and protector of religions ... This is because it is a religious country before all else, living religion and believing in it."[85] The tone of Husayn's summons to a return to religion was fully as Egyptian nationalist as Muslim:

Since the creation of the world, Egypt was the carrier of civilization everywhere. Egypt was a leader, a guide, a master. Egypt was the leader of Islam and of the Muslims. So let us rush to regain our religious leadership. Let us rush to raise the banner [of religion] before the Near and the Far East. Let us rush to take up our position in the sun, above all others.[86]

Unlike the customary Muslim perspective which viewed Islam as replacing ignorance with enlightenment, from Husayn's perspective the Egyptian adoption of Islam was merely another phase in the immemorial unfolding of the uniquely religious nature of the Egyptian people. Islam was congruent with the Egyptian character, not a transformation of it.

Egypt as leader of the Arab nation

The primary basis upon which integral Egyptian nationalists based Egypt's affiliation with the neighboring Arab world was language. Ahmad Husayn specified language as "the first factor constituting the nation," and called for Egypt to assume the role which Prussia had played in regard to German nationalism in order to realize the political unity of the Arab linguistic group.[87] Mahmud Kamil cited both Germany and Italy, with their primarily linguistic bases for nation-building, as appropriate models for the Arabs to follow.[88]

A shared history and common interests were additional factors uniting Egypt with the Arab world. Integralists acknowledged that Egypt and its Arab neighbors had existed in close and continuous interaction throughout history. It was inconceivable to consider Egyptian history in isolation from its Arab neighbors. Egyptian rulers from the Pharaohs and the Ptolemies to Islamic states such as those of the Fatamids and the Mamluks had all considered the Arab lands as a legitimate sphere of Egyptian concern. This was particularly true in the modern era. The successes of Muhammad 'Ali in taking control of the Sudan, greater Syria, and much of the Arabian Peninsula and integrating them into a greater Egyptian empire in the early nineteenth century were presented as the model which should inspire contemporary Egyptian policy.[89] Common political interests also tied the Arabs together, at no time more than in the present era when all faced the same imperialist threat and the same needs for independence, liberty, and progress.[90] The range of elements linking Egypt to the Arab world, and their practical implications, were clearly stated by Ahmad Husayn in 1938:

you must realize that the unity of any people is based on five factors: language, religion, culture, a shared past, and common aspirations, that is, interests. These factors are all found in their entirety in the Arab states, in Egypt, Syria, and Iraq, and the day will soon come, without a doubt, when this unity will be realized and ties forged [between them].[91]

The logical conclusion of the language, religion, history and interests shared by Egypt and the Arabs meant Egypt had to be regarded as an Arab country whose political destiny was linked to that of the Arab world. As early as 1935, 'Abd al-Hamid Muhammad al-Mashhadi was declaring that all the Arab states, Egypt included, formed "one nation [umma wahida]."[92] For Mashhadi, an Arab nationalist was one who believed that "the Arab nation is one nation" and that "the Arab homeland in its entirety is his homeland," and who aspired to "the establishment of an independent Arab political and civilizational entity."[93] Mashhadi anticipated many of his colleagues in Young Egypt in his insistence that "the [Arab] national movement is one movement which must have one common program and one supreme organization throughout the Arab nation," and in his call for "the formation of a front for struggle and nationalist action throughout the Arab homeland."[94]

The most detailed integralist statement of what Egyptian integration with its Arab neighbors should mean in specific terms came in the new program of the Islamic Nationalist Party of March 1940. Other than its opening call for Egypt to become "allied with the Arab states," Young Egypt's original program of 1933 had said little about Egypt's role among its Arab neighbors.[95] The program of the Islamic Nationalist Party of March 1940 was much more specific. One of the fundamental goals of the newly named party was "to realize Arab unity [al-wahda al-'arabiyya] among all the Arab states through uniting their foreign policies, their national defense, and their general culture, and through decreasing customs duties between them, finally eliminating them entirely."[96] A call for common Arab efforts in six specific spheres formed the substance of its concept of Arab unity: "fighting imperialism, in all its forms, in all parts of the Arab lands"; the progressive lowering and eventually the total abolition of customs duties between the Arab states as well as the elimination of visas for inter-Arab travel; the conclusion of preferential trade agreements; the coordination of educational policies in order to produce a common Arab culture; agreement on "a unification of fundamental laws, based on the Islamic *shari'a*"; and the conclusion of a mutual defense treaty as well as the unification of foreign policy between the Arab states.[97]

These proposals for Arab economic, cultural, and political cooperation were certainly less ambitious than the Fichtean vision of the total fusion of all Arab lands into one Arab state being developed by Fertile Crescent Arab nationalists by the 1940s. But they were in many ways more ambitious than those embodied in the provisions of the new League of Arab States created a few years later. They also represent a sea change in outlook from the Egyptian isolationism which had previously prevailed in Egyptian territorial nationalism.

6   Egyptian Arab nationalism

The third supra-Egyptian nationalist ideology to develop in Egypt in the 1930s and 1940s was Egyptian Arab nationalism. Like Islamic nationalism and integral nationalism, it too rejected the exclusivist territorial nationalism of the past and in its place postulated an Egyptian identification with a larger entity – in this case, the Arab nation. Its specifics in part overlapped with Islamic nationalism which accepted the Arabness of Egypt as a part of Egypt's Muslim identity, and with integral nationalism which viewed the Arab world as the most immediate arena of Egyptian leadership and greatness.

But Egyptian Arab nationalism had its own character which made it quite distinct from its rivals. The most significant difference was in breadth. The Arabist outlook was less parochial than Islamic nationalism, which because of its religious focus, had little appeal to non-Muslims or those of a secular inclination. It was also less solipsistic than integral nationalism, whose aggressive nature alienated many Egyptians. Belief in Egypt as part of the Arab nation possessed a greater scope of attraction than either the Islamic or the integralist approach. In terms of production, a larger pool of intellectuals participated in its articulation; in terms of reception, it ultimately appealed to a wider range of public opinion. Its content incorporated elements of both Islamicism and integralism as well as of earlier territorial nationalism, but reshaped to fit its particularly Arab perspective. As a result of its synthetic character, it became the most widespread supra-Egyptian ideology of the era.

Egyptian Arab nationalism emerged parallel to, but by no means in isolation from, the ideological doctrines of Pan-Arabism developing in Western Asia at the same time.[1] Although there were certainly theoretical similarities as well as reciprocal influences between Fertile Crescent and Egyptian Arab nationalism, the latter was not simply a branch or subset of the former. Its development cannot be explained simply as the outcome of the diffusion of Pan-Arabist thought into Egypt. It was primarily an Egyptian response to Egyptian stimuli both "objective" – the impact of specific Egyptian conditions of the 1930s and 1940s – and "subjective" – the influence of other nationalist perspectives including Egyptian Islamic nationalism and integral nationalism. Its formation in the unique political and social context of the era as well as its perpetual dialogue with other schools of thought gave Egyptian Arab nationalism a uniquely Egyptian flavor.

Numerous Egyptian intellectuals and intellectual groupings joined in the discourse shaping Egyptian Arab nationalism. Ideologues of both Islamic and integral nationalism entered into the discussion of Egypt's relationship to the Arab world; although less intimately, so did spokesmen for the older territorial nationalist outlook. The range of social and political strata participating in Egyptian Arab nationalist discourse was equally broad. Native Egyptians and Arab émigrés living in Egypt; Christians and Muslims; established politicians and radicals from the new extraparliamentary movements; older figures and the new effendiyya emerging in the 1930s and 1940s; Wafdists and Liberals; Palace and 'ulama': members of all these social groups and political persuasions were involved in the intellectual construction and social dissemination of Egyptian Arab nationalism.

Redefining the nation: the Arab character of Egypt

Language and culture as the basis of the nation

Exponents of Egyptian Arab nationalism approached the issue of national identity primarily in cultural terms. Language in particular was central to Egyptian Arabists. They viewed the Arabic language as an absolute, possessing a reality independent of those who spoke it. Man was the product of language, not its creator. Language was "a living entity [ka'in hayy]" which stood above the processes of history and exerted an autonomous power over human affairs.[2]

In many ways, the Arabic language performed the same function in Egyptian Arabist doctrine which the Egyptian environment had had in territorial nationalism. It was language which created and molded nations; other factors such as geography, race, or religion paled in comparison with the power of language. Language determined both the boundaries and the character of national communities. The fundamental divisions among humanity were linguistic. A common language shaped a distinctive mentality, a collective personality, all in all a unique "national spirit" for its speakers.[3] Because languages were different, nations were different. No one stated the linguistic determinism of Egyptian Arab nationalism better than Ibrahim 'Abd al-Qadir al-Mazini:

nationalism [al-qawmiyya] is nothing but language. Whatever the nature of a country may be, and however deeply embedded in antiquity its origins may be, as long as peoples have one language, they are one people. For man is unable to think – at least until now – save through words. They alone are the tools of thought, and there is no path to it except through them. It is impossible for us now to postulate meaning apart from the words which express it. Every language has its own modes and methods, modes of thought and methods of conception ... In this regard, the sons of each language conform to and resemble each other and are distinguished from the sons of every other language.[4]

Language both created and demonstrated the social nature of man. A common language bound people together, converting them from isolated monads into social beings aware of their existence within a larger collective framework. Languages molded each generation as it emerged, transmitting the inherited understandings and values of the collectivity from generation to generation.[5] Language was the cement of society on two levels: one was that of binding an assemblage of individuals into a cohesive community; the other was that of linking a given generation to its predecessors and its successors. The fate of a nation depended in good part on the state of its language: "All nations undergo the fate of their language, be it weakness or strength, humiliation or dignity. As long as the instrument of its expression and understanding and comprehension is in good order, the nation prospers. For it is this instrument which unifies a nation's attitudes, correlates its aims, and strengthens the ties between its past, present, and future."[6]

The derivation of national identity from language was of the utmost consequence for Egypt. Since Arabic was "the main bond which unites the Arab peoples" and "the primary trait which distinguishes an Arab,"[7] Egyptian use of the Arabic language was all that was needed to define Egyptians as Arabs. Egyptian membership in the Arab nation stemmed directly from their being speakers of Arabic. As Muhibb al-Din al-Khatib phrased the premise, "Egypt has been speaking the language of the Qur'an for fourteen centuries, knowing no other language besides this. Is this not enough to render Egypt Arab?!"[8] Because of Arabic, Egypt possessed an "Arab personality [al-shakhsiyya al-'arabiyya]."[9]

Egyptian Arabists attributed the superiority of Arabic over other factors of national cohesion to the non-material nature of language. Whereas determinants such as environment or kinship were material in nature and thus at variance with the inner qualities of man, language reflected the spiritual essence of humanity. It was the possession of the attribute of language which distinguished man from other creatures. Language was the indispensable vehicle for the manifestation of the uniquely human traits of intellect and reason, and simultaneously was the medium for the expression of human emotion and feeling. An ideology such as Egyptian territorial nationalism which sought to root identity in a material factor such as environment reduced man to the level of the animals; the linguistic concept of identity, on the other hand, based identity and community on what was special in man.[10]

The Arabist emphasis on the primacy of language originated in part from a desire to free national identity from territorial and racial foundations, both of which were viewed as material in nature and therefore unworthy of consideration as the basis of a spiritual phenomenon like national identity. "Geographical unity" was seen as providing the "stage" for human communities to coalesce, but in and of itself did not determine the nature of communal bonds; "what is the value of a stage, however imposing and beautiful, if it is devoid of actors?"[11] Similarly, race was too vague and unsubstantiated a concept to define a nation. Whereas the racial composition of a people was undefinable with any precision, its language was a manifest reality whose massive importance could be empirically demonstrated.[12]

With specific reference to Egypt, the Nile Valley had not sustained a pure, isolated Egyptian race. Over its long history Egypt had been a melting-pot for various ethnic groups; as a result, it was impossible to determine the precise racial composition of the Egyptian people.[13] For 'Abd al-Rahman 'Azzam, it was "totally absurd" to talk in terms of the racial origin of the Egyptian nation; "anyone who dwells in our country, associates with us, and learns our language perfectly is *ipso facto* an Arab like us."[14] Egyptians were not members of a Pharaonic race originating in antiquity, Muhammad 'Ali 'Alluba maintained; "Pharaonic" defined an historical epoch, not a racial group. Even if there was some racial basis for Egyptian national identity, it was insignificant in comparison to the power of "a shared language, shared traditions, shared customs, and the same pains and hopes."[15]

The historical unity of the Arab nation

A shared history was the second component defining the Arab nation. The parameters of Arab history as presented by Egyptian Arabists were identical with those of the Arabic language. The multifarious details of the long past of the many Arab lands were squeezed into a unified pattern shaped by the presupposition of the historical unity of all speakers of Arabic. The division of Arab history into Egyptian, Iraqi, Syrian, or other categories was for Arabists the result of the recent arbitrary fragmentation of the Arab nation achieved by imperialism. In their view, all Arab regions had shared the same historical destiny.

Egyptian Arab nationalist treatments of ancient history stressed the antiquity and unity of the Arab national community. The seed of the Arab nation was the Semitic-speaking population living in the Arabian Peninsula thousands of years ago. The historical Arab nation was formed out of successive waves of migration of this Semitic nucleus through much of the ancient Near East, where they mixed with other linguistic groups to form a single Arabic-speaking population. Already in antiquity, these processes of migration and intermixture had resulted in the creation of a unified Arab national entity.[16] The numerous peoples found in the Near East in historical times – unquestionably Semitic ones such as the Babylonians, Canaanites, Hebrews, Phoenicians, and the Arabs of the peninsula, as well as more dubiously Semitic ones like the ancient Egyptians, Sumerians, and Hittites – were sometimes lumped together as local variants of the same Arab racial community. The Arab region had served as the birthplace and homeland of several great civilizations, among them the Pharaonic, the Babylonian, the Phoenician, and the Carthaginian in antiquity and of course Islamic civilization in a more recent epoch.[17] The great monotheistic religions of the ancient Near East were also presented as products of the Arab national genius. Moses, Jesus, and Muhammad were all Arab national figures.[18]

This long record of Arab existence and interaction since the formation of the Arab nation in antiquity was a powerful weapon in the contemporary struggle against imperialism. The discovery of the Arab character of ancient Near Eastern history refuted the possibility of the modern Arab world crystallizing into separate nations along the lines of recent imperialist divisions. The imperialist-inspired effort to invoke ancient Egypt, Assyria, Phoenicia, or Carthage as foci of distinctive national loyalty was demolished by the knowledge that all these ancient peoples had been Arabs.[19]

Arabist ideologues maintained that Egypt had long been part of the historical Arab nation. From the dawn of history, the fertile Nile Valley had been a magnet attracting migration from the Arab region. In Makram 'Ubayd's view, the people of Egypt had their origins in "the Semitic stock which immigrated to our land from the Arabian Peninsula."[20] That "Egyptians are Arabs [was] proven by history. We, the Egyptian community, came from Asia. Since antiquity we have been closely related to the Arabs in regard to color, language, Semitic character traits, and nationalism."[21] 'Abd al-Rahman 'Azzam went as far as to assert the "racial unity [wahda 'unsuriyya]" of Egyptians and Arabs; the Arabic-speaking peoples had so intermingled with each other over the millennia that "it is virtually impossible to separate them racially."[22] Thus the Arabist rejection of the concept of an Egyptian race was not paralleled by a similar rejection of Arab racial unity.

From the Arab nationalist perspective, the birth and spread of Islam was but the final stage of a long process of Arab movement into the Nile Valley.[23] The proof that the Arab Muslims who entered Egypt in the seventh century had not been foreign invaders like the Persians or Romans before them and the Turks and British afterwards lay in the massive

Egyptian adoption of the language, religion, culture, and customs of the newcomers, which would have been impossible were it not for the network of ties linking Egypt and the Arabs since antiquity.[24]

The emphasis of Arab nationalist accounts of Egyptian history in the long Arab-Islamic epoch was on the place of Egypt within the larger Arab tapestry. Ahmad Ramzi summarized the various ways in which "we the people of Egypt have a long history of service to Arabism."[25] Intellectually, Egyptians made important contributions to Arab culture and Arab intellectual life through much of Arab-Islamic history, "all of which show that Arabism and the Egyptian personality are an inseparable pair." Politically, Ramzi found Egypt's main contribution to the history of Islam to have occurred in the same era as that singled out by other Egyptian nationalist approaches, in the long era of fragmentation after the breakdown of the Abbasid Caliphate when independent Muslim dynasties based on Egypt "served Arabism for eight centuries." Throughout the Islamic era, "Egypt has been the heart of the Arab world and its pulsating center, the true home of Arab movements, religious consciousness, and awareness."[26]

The Arabist interpretation of modern history also presented Egypt as playing an integral role in the recent historical evolution of the Arab nation. The internal reforms of Muhammad 'Ali were viewed in Arab nationalist terms, as marking the restoration of Arab confidence and setting an example for Arab revival elsewhere. In the regional arena, Muhammad 'Ali and his son Ibrahim were presented as the founders of the modern Arab nationalist movement, fighters for Arab liberation from the Ottoman yoke, and their campaigns of conquest in the Sudan, Arabia, and the Fertile Crescent portrayed as a daring effort to unite the shattered Arab nation under one rule.[27]

Egyptian Arab nationalists emphasized Egypt's important place in the Arab cultural revival or *nahda* of the later nineteenth and early twentieth centuries. Not only had Egyptian thinkers, most notably the great Muhammad 'Abduh, played a central role in the development of modern Arab thought; in addition, Egypt had served as a place of refuge where numerous Arab intellectuals from other regions had been able to function in relative freedom and to contribute to the *nahda*.[28] For Zaki Mubarak, Egypt was indeed "the homeland of Arabism [*watan al-'uruba*]," the center of Arab intellectual life since the nineteenth century.[29]

In the Arabist narrative, the exclusivist nature of Egyptian territorial nationalism and the Revolution of 1919 was an aberration. For Ibrahim 'Abd al-Qadir al-Mazini, the shortcomings of the Revolution of 1919 were in part due to Egyptians having "confined our nationalism behind the equivalent of the [Great] Wall of China," working in isolation from, rather than in cooperation with, their fellow Arabs also struggling against imperialism at the same time.[30] But Egyptian Arab nationalists also maintained that, despite its separatist character, the Revolution of 1919 had been an important exemplar for other Arabs in the common struggle against imperialism, and that the new Egyptian state had offered a valuable model to other Arab lands on how to consolidate political independence in the contemporary era.[31]

The Arabness of the Nile valley

The cultural as opposed to territorial emphasis of Egyptian Arab nationalism appears in the manner in which Egyptian Arabists treated the issue of Nile Valley unity. For Egyptian territorial nationalists, the factors making Egypt and the Sudan one indivisible unit were largely geographical and environmental.[32] Egyptian Arab nationalists, on the other hand, viewed Egypt and the Sudan as a unit because of their shared culture. When Ahmad Ramzi, for one, discussed the "Kingdom of the Nile Valley," the reality of that entity was not premised primarily on the geographical unity of Egypt and the Sudan; rather, its basis was "the Arabness of the Nile Valley."[33] Similarly Sulayman Huzayyin, although not denying the territorial connection between Egypt and the Sudan, emphasized that since the Arab-Muslim conquest in the seventh century the unity of the Nile Valley was based on their common possession of an imported culture deriving from the Arabic language and Islam. While the "natural bond" based on geography had existed for millennia, it was the spread of Arabic and Islam which "forged an organic, spiritual, and historical union between the component parts of the Nile Valley."[34] The coming of the Arabs and Islam "opened a new era in the relationship between Egypt and the Sudan," one based now on "cultural bonds."[35] In Huzayyin's view the Nile Valley was not an isolate, as territorialists would have it; because of their common language and religion, all of Arab northern Africa and Western Asia were one geographic region.[36]

Both Ramzi and Huzayyin went on to make the Arabness of the Nile Valley the legitimizing factor for Egyptian leadership of the Arab world. Ramzi viewed the Nile Valley as "the heart of the Arab world," the motor of Arab history and culture in the Islamic era.[37] Huzayyin went further. Once Arabized and Islamified, the Nile Valley "suckled and nurtured the new religion and the new culture, thereby elevating Arabic civilization and Islam to new heights."[38] The adoption of Arabic and Islam by the population of the Nile Valley gave them new significance in the world. For Huzayyin, the unity of the Nile Valley – goal of Egyptian nationalists of all stripes – lay in the Arab mission of the Arab-Muslim people of the Nile Valley.[39] Thus an earlier territorial bond between Egypt and the Sudan whose implications were Egyptianist was transformed by Egyptian Arabists into a cultural link with supra-Egyptianist connotations.

Islam, Arab culture, and Arab nationalism

There were varying views in Egyptian Arab nationalist discourse concerning the relationship of the Islamic religion to the Arab nation. Some accepted Islam as a nation-building factor almost equal with language and history; others accorded it only a secondary status; yet others viewed religion as a divisive element in Arab nationalism. What is most interesting is the nationalist framework within which Islam was considered by Arabist ideologues. Often their primary concern was Islam as a reflection of the Arab national genius and as an instrument for the realization of Arab national goals.

Egyptian Arab nationalists sometimes treated Islam as a secondary component in the bundle of elements constituting the substance of the nation. Such a perspective on Islam was in part rooted in the primacy accorded the Arab language in Egyptian Arab nationalism. Temporally, religion was viewed as a more recent, and thereby less fundamental, factor than language. Already forming during the prehistoric epoch, language was older than religion, which had its origins in historic time. The implication of this view was that language was a stronger and more durable force than religion. In the view of Mustafa Fahmi, "ties of language are stronger than those of religion";[40] for Muhammad Lutfi Jum'a, "language is the most important bond forming the social collective of the nation and its civilization."[41] Other Egyptian Arabists went further, denying religion as a component in national formation. Such a view was implicit in Mazini's assertion that "nationalism is nothing but language";[42] it was made explicit by Zaki Mubarak when he stated "Arabism is language, not race or religion."[43]

Equally important was the Arabist tendency to treat Islam as an Arab product. For 'Ali al-'Inani, the Prophet Muhammad was but one of a chain of "Arab prophets" stretching back to Abraham.[44] Similarly for Muhammad Lutfi Jum'a, Islam was not a unique phenomenon in Arab history; seen within the sweep of Arab history, it was but one of several manifestations of the Arab genius which had contributed a chain of great civilizations to humanity. Arab collective existence antedated Islam; the latter was but the most recent and brilliant unfolding of the Arab national character.[45] While Zaki Mubarak saw Islam as "the most authentic and genuine product of the Arabs," it was not the only Arab religion: "Christianity and Judaism are both Arab religions, for Islam, Christianity and Judaism share the same stage, namely the land of the Arabs." It was "Arab spirituality" which had first manifested itself in Moses, then in Jesus, then in Muhammad; the religions associated with each were all branches of the same monotheistic root.[46] Thus Mubarak folded Islam into Arabism, also presenting it as the latest manifestation of the Arab religious genius.

Not all Egyptian Arab nationalists accepted Islam as a component of the Arab nation. Some saw Islam as a potentially disruptive factor for Arab nationalism, one which would endanger Arab cohesion by undermining coexistence and collaboration between Muslim and non-Muslim Arabs. Ibrahim 'Abd al-Qadir al-Mazini, for one, insisted that "the national idea" which he was advocating "does not distinguish between religions, and will not allow [religious] differences to interfere or influence the development of the Arab question."[47] For 'Abd al-Hamid Sulayman, Arab unity was attainable only if it was "separate from any religious concept."[48] Fu'ad Abaza also saw "the linguistic bond" alone as the basis of the Arab nation; "the religious bond" in his view had no relevance for Arab nationalism.[49] In Mahmud 'Azmi's view, the presence of Islam as an element in Arab nationalism worked against efforts aimed at increasing Arab political cooperation. The religious orientation and systems found in several Arab regions were inhibiting efforts toward Arab political cooperation by alienating Christian Arabs from full participation in the Arab nationalist movement. More generally, 'Azmi's position was that "it has been proven by practical experience that the intrusion of religion into the general political and social affairs of a country in which there are various religions among its inhabitants, and whose prevailing religion itself calls for religious pluralism, can have the gravest consequences for national existence."[50]

The denial of territorial and Pharaonic nationalism

Considerable Egyptian Arab nationalist attention was given to a critique of the territorialist glorification of Egypt's ancient legacy as the essential model for the contemporary revival of Egypt. The basic point in this critique was the belief that Pharaonic civilization was extinct and as such could not possibly serve as the inspiration for modern Egypt. For Muhammad 'Ali 'Alluba, the Egyptianist effort to revive Egypt's ancient heritage was an effort to "resurrect the dead and blow life into ghosts"; in his view, "it is better for the Egyptian to leave off caring for the dead and to start looking after the living."[51] In the opinion of Muhammad Lutfi Jum'a, the Pharaonic legacy was "buried in its final resting place in the bowels of the earth; it will not be revived except on the lips of historians and in the pages of books."[52] Mahmud Muhammad Shakir decried Mahmud Mukhtar's Pharaonic sculpture *The Revival of Egypt*, a prime symbol of the territorial nationalism of the 1920s, as "only a bad imitation of the remains of a civilization which has become extinct and passed away and which cannot be resurrected a second time in the land of Egypt."[53] The Pharaonic heritage possessed no emotional meaning for 'Abd al-Wahhab 'Azzam: "when I was a student I did not feel that there was a Pharaonic movement. Rather, I grew up on love of the Arabs and reverence for their literature and history."[54] For 'Abd al-Rahman 'Azzam, Pharaonic Egypt, Phoenicia, and Assyria were now "extinct nations," all of the traits of which had been "swept away by the Arabic language, so much so that nothing remains in all these countries but what is Arab."[55] As Lutfi Jum'a put it, looking to the Pharaonic past for inspiration was "chasing after a mirage in which there cannot possibly be water."[56]

The substantive aspect of the Egyptian Arab nationalist attack on the Pharaonic tendency related to its inherent flaws which made it an undesirable model for modern Egyptian national life. For Jum'a, ancient Egypt was a symbol of ruthless oppression, a tyrannical regime which had harnessed all the resources of the Land of the Nile, including the labor of its people, for the purpose of serving and glorifying its rulers.[57] As portrayed in Ahmad Sabri's journal al-Ansar in the early 1940s, the Pharaonic period had been one of massive social inequality and political domination of the majority by "a tyrannical Pharaonic government."[58] Given the reactionary character of Pharaonic Egypt, the Pharaonicist call for Egyptians to turn to their ancient past for guidance meant a retrogressive "return to the times of darkness and oppression."[59] In terms of its practical implications Pharaonicism was denounced as a separatist trend which, by isolating Egypt from other Arabs, would prevent beneficial efforts at Arab cooperation.[60] Finally, Pharaonicism was presented as an ineffective national ideal whose appeal was limited to a very small circle of educated Egyptians. For 'Abd al-Rahman 'Azzam, ancient regional identities such as the Pharaonic, the Phoenician, and the Assyrian had long since been superseded by an affiliation with the greater Arab nation. Where the proponents of Pharaonicism and Phoenicianism were engaged in a futile exercise capable of "reviving only one village," in contrast "the call to Arabism will revive seventy million people in Asia and Africa."[61]

A specific target of anti-territorialist attack by Egyptian Arabists at the end of the 1930s was Taha Husayn's controversial book The Future of Culture in Egypt. Husayn's Arabist critics charged that its theory of a Mediterranean, and by extension a European, civilization to which Egypt was intimately linked ignored the tremendous influence of the Arabic language as well as that of Islam on the Egyptian national character. Egypt had been thoroughly Arabized and Islamified for a thousand years; it was these forces, rather than a more tangential linkage with the West, which were the determinants of Egyptian national culture and collective self-image. There was no objective basis for Husayn's claim of the similarity of the Egyptian and the Western mentalities, or that of their common origin in the Greek mentality. The Egyptian character, national personality, and spirit were all derived from "the Arab-Islamic mentality" which was the only mentality now possessed by the people of the Nile Valley.[62]

Language and literature in Egyptian Arab nationalist discourse

The Arabness of Egyptian culture and literature

In place of the earlier territorial nationalist concept of an Egyptian "national literature" shaped by the environment of the Nile Valley and specific to Egypt alone,[63] Arabist intellectuals attempted to demonstrate that Egyptian literature was part of a larger Arab culture shared by all speakers of Arabic. Their view was that the Arabic language and Arab culture were the primary determinants of both the form and the content of Egyptian literature. Because its medium of expression was Arabic, Egyptian literature inevitably possessed an Arab character. One could not speak of a self-contained Egyptian cultural and literary heritage, but only of an Egyptian regional variant existing within a larger Arab culture.[64]

Thus there was no basis for the territorialist belief in the existence of an autonomous Egyptian national literature independent of Arab culture. The attempt to revive Pharaonic culture and to develop a local literature was decried as an unnatural enterprise which both ignored the linguistic basis of culture and would have the negative practical effect of undermining Egyptian leadership in the Arab cultural sphere. For Ahmad Hasan al-Zayyat, the concept of Egyptian national literature meant the production of a "chatterbox literature [*adab tharthara*]," a disoriented literature uprooted from its cultural roots and consequently devoid of any real meaning.[65] The idea of a specifically Egyptian literature was an artificial one which attempted to create a literature in isolation from the tradition necessary to nurture it; it was also an imperialist, politically inspired endeavor which wished to divide a unified Arab world.[66]

Belief in the essentially Arab character of Egyptian literature found expression even by intellectuals who were not otherwise Arabist in outlook. Taha Husayn – widely criticized for the presumably anti-Arab tone of *The Future of Culture in Egypt* – elsewhere staunchly defended both the Arabic language and the Arabic cultural heritage against territorial nationalist criticisms. For him, the Egyptianist attack on Arabic and the Arab literary legacy as an archaic, primitive tradition, the product of uncivilized nomads, represented a new Shu'ubiyya movement similar to the anti-Arab school of thought which had existed a thousand years earlier. His own view on the

Arab nature of Egyptian culture was forthright: "whatever we do or try, today we live in an Arab culture."[67] Egyptians could not deny their Arab heritage: "try as we may, we can never rid ourselves of it, nor weaken it, nor diminish its influence on our lives ... The Arabic language is not a foreign language for us. It is our language. It is a thousand and one times closer to us than the language of the ancient Egyptians."[68]

Amin al-Khuli's view of the nature of Egyptian literature gave somewhat more weight to the role of environment in the formation of culture and literature.[69] Nonetheless, he also rejected the claim that Egyptian literature was something other than Arab. The local literary traditions of the various Arab lands existed in symbiosis with a larger Arab culture shared by all speakers of Arabic. While each Arab region possessed a local culture influenced by its particular environment, their common use of the Arabic language also created a single Arabic cultural whole. As Khuli put it, "the Arabic language is the source and origin of these regional literatures in all their forms"; Arabic was "the nucleus and germ of them all."[70] Khuli saw no contradiction between a regional quality in Egyptian literature and its Arab character; both local and wider Arab influences played a role in determining the nature of Egyptian cultural expression.

In this atmosphere in which even the less committed espoused such ideas, true believers tended to express their faith in the Arabness of Egyptian culture in rhapsodic terms. 'Abd al-Wahhab 'Azzam, for one, portrayed Egyptian literature as almost exclusively Arab in character. 'Azzam asserted that the Arabic compositions of Egyptians all possessed an unmistakably Arab character, resembling other Arabic writings of the same genre and dealing the same topics addressed in Arab literary productions written elsewhere. As it had in the past, modern Egyptian literature continued to draw its sustenance from the Arab literary tradition. Egyptians could not escape the emotional pull of the literature written in their native Arabic:

The literature that we read, study, and commit to memory; [the literature] that we cherish and which refreshes our spirits; [the literature] on which we raise our children and with which we inculcate feeling, imagination, and morals; [the literature] whose lofty morals set an example for us and whose faults dishonor us; [the literature] which we enjoy and appreciate, in which we find our repose, from whose gravity we benefit, and whose humor delights us; [the literature] whose origins we know and to which we have recourse in our joys and sorrows; [the literature] whose proverbs we quote, whose stories we retell and copy as if we were contemporary to them – all this, I say, is indisputably Arabic literature.[71]

In defense of classical Arabic

The issue of language had been a matter of frequent discussion among Egyptian intellectuals since the late nineteenth century. In the 1930s, debate over language took on a more conservative tone. A few radical Westernizers such as Salama Musa and Isma'il Adham continued to advocate the sweeping Egyptianization of literary expression through the use of the colloquial dialect in place of classical Arabic.[72] But most of those who discussed the issue of language after 1930 defended the centrality of literary Arabic in Egyptian cultural life. The Egyptian Arab nationalist premise of the centrality of language in the formation of national identity meant that Arabic was no longer perceived in the strictly instrumental terms of its suitability as a means of communication. Now viewed as the crucial component of collective identity, the Arabic language became a national asset to be defended and preserved.

Thus in the 1930s the prevailing position on the desirability of significant change in the Arabic language was a cautious one. Earlier Egyptianist suggestions for the greater use of ancient Pharaonic terminology were rejected as "an attempt at resurrecting the dead."[73] Opposition to the use of the colloquial language was often justified in terms of the Arab and Islamic identity of Egypt. Taha Husayn referred to Arabic as "our national language" and "a component shaping our patriotism and our national personality";[74] Ahmad Ahmad Badawi saw the use of colloquial Arab dialects as a threat to the linguistic bond linking all Arabs and thus something which would "harm Arab unity";[75] and Mahmud Taymur asserted that "our duty as the offspring of the Arabs is to preserve their legacy and defend their language, which is the firm bond between the Arab countries."[76]

The central demand of Egyptian Arab nationalists in the linguistic arena was for the selective modernization and the standardization of usage of classical Arabic. Their goal was to reduce the differences in the language employed in different Arab regions through greater use of the shared literary language.[77] Selective modernization and unification of Arabic scientific and technical terminology was also advocated, within the framework of the maintenance of the existing structure and principles of classical Arabic.[78] In place of the earlier concept of the "Egyptianization" of Arabic, linguistic debate now focused more on the issue of "Arabization" – how to absorb foreign terms into Arabic in a controlled manner which would not undermine the integrity of the literary language.[79] One specific suggestion was for the production of a new, comprehensive Arab dictionary and encyclopedia, to be compiled through the joint efforts of intellectuals from all Arab countries.[80]

This solicitousness for the fate of classical Arabic received official sanction from the early 1930s onwards. Thanks to royal patronage, the Arab Language Academy (Majma' al-Lugha al-'Arabiyya) was established in Cairo in 1932. Under the auspices of the Ministry of Education, its declared purposes were the preservation of the integrity of literary Arabic as well as its adaptation to modern usage and needs, the replacement of colloquial usages by phrases taken from literary Arabic, and the development of Arabic scientific terminology. With its membership composed of leading Egyptian intellectuals and cultural luminaries from other Arab countries, the Academy in time became both a major agency in the effort at revivifying classical Arabic and another forum in which Egypt asserted Arab cultural leadership.[81]

The renewed emphasis on the literary use of classical Arabic in the post-1930 years was also reflected in the form of Arabic used by two of Egypt's most notable literary figures. The change is most apparent in the work of Mahmud Taymur. Taymur's use of the Egyptian colloquial dialect for both narrative and dialogue in his short stories of the 1920s was a prime example of the concept of a distinctively Egyptian national literature. From the 1930s onwards, however, Taymur became a staunch supporter of the literary use of the classical form of Arabic. Some of his earlier stories were rewritten in more formal language; new compositions either were written in the classical language or sometimes were composed in two parallel versions, one in literary Arabic, the other in the colloquial.[82] The case of Tawfiq al-Hakim was similar. Most of Hakim's early work had employed colloquial Egyptian for dialogue. In part because of their subject-matter, his intellectual dramas of the 1930s made greater use of the classical language. By the 1940s, his plays and narrative prose works were being composed in formal literary Arabic devoid of colloquial forms and terms.[83]

Arab themes in Egyptian literary production

The fiction produced by Egyptians through most of the interwar period clearly reflected the territorial nationalist orientation which had developed in the wake of the Revolution of 1919. Realistic in approach, generally contemporary rather than historical in setting, and dealing with Egyptian problems, it had little to say about the Arab-Islamic legacy of Egypt.[84] It was only from the second half of the 1930s onwards that a sizable corpus of Egyptian creative literature dealing with Arab and Islamic historical themes developed. This literature did not totally eclipse territorialist historical fiction; novels dealing with Pharaonic Egypt by such authors as Muhammad 'Awad Muhammad, 'Adil Kamil, and the young Najib Mahfuz continued to be produced into the 1940s.[85] But the fact that several Egyptian novelists now turned their attention to Arab and Islamic history attests both to their growing interest in Egypt's Arab-Islamic legacy and to an increasing popular receptivity to such subject-matter.

Ibrahim Ramzi's *Bab al-Qamar* (The Gate of the Moon, 1936) may have been the first Egyptian-written historical novel of an Arabist nature. A panoramic fictional account of pre-Islamic Arabia, its author's supra-Egyptian outlook is indicated by its introductory summons to "Arab unity" and call for the formation of a league of Arab and Muslim states.[86] A more prolific author of Arab-Islamic historical novels was Muhammad Farid Abu Hadid. Between 1939 and 1945, Abu Hadid produced several works focusing on pre-Islamic Arab history: *al-Muhalhil Sayyid Rabi'a* (al-Muhalhil The Chief of Rabi'a), an account of the Basus War; *al-Malik al-Dillil* (The Straying King), on the life of the poet-prince Imru' al-Qays; *Zinubiya al-Malikat Tadmur* (Zenobia the Queen of Palmyra), a fictionalized account of the famous Arab queen of Palmyra and her conflict with the Roman Empire; and *Abu al-Fawaris 'Antara ibn Shaddad* (The Greatest of Knights, 'Antara ibn Shaddad), on the adventures of the black slave whose military exploits earned him glory. The latter three, presented as stories of heroes in a pre-Islamic Arab struggle against foreign oppression, carried the implicit nationalist message of the need for contemporary Arabs to struggle for national liberation and the realization of their national goals.[87]

Several other Egyptian authors produced historical novels about Arab or Islamic subjects in the 1940s. One was Muhammad Sa'id al-'Aryan, whose novels *Qatr al-Nada* (Drops of Dew, 1945), *Shajarat al-Durr* (Shajarat al-Durr, 1947), and *'Ala Bab Zuwayla* (On the Zuwayla Gate, 1947), deal with Egypt during the Tulunid, Ayyubid, and Mamluk periods respectively.[88] The poet 'Ali al-Jarim produced fictional accounts of the lives of the Arab poets al-Mu'tamid (d. 1091) (*Sha'ir Malik*), Abu Firas (d. 967) (*Faris Bani Hamdan*), al-Mutanabbi (d. 965) (*al-Sha'ir al-Tamuh* and *Khatimat al-Mataf*), al-Walid ibn Yazid (*Marah al-Walid*), and 'Umara al-Yamani (*Sayyidat al-Qusur*) in the mid- and late 1940s.[89] 'Ali Ahmad Bakathir, of Hadramauti descent but resident in Egypt and active on the Egyptian literary scene, contributed *Salamat al-Qass* (Salama the Priest, 1943), set in pre-Islamic Arabia, and *Wa' Islamah* (Oh For Islam!, 1945), glorifying the Mamluk victory over the Mongols at the battle of 'Ayn Jalut in 1260.[90]

The novels of Ramzi, Abu Hadid, 'Aryan, Jarim, and Bakathir on the one hand reflected, on the other supported and helped to legitimize, the growing Arab-Islamic historical awareness developing in Egypt. Through the presentation of Arab and Islamic history in fictional form, quite a different collective memory was disseminated from that which had been promoted by Egyptianist writers in the 1920s.

The dominant poetic tendency in the Arab world in the 1930s and 1940s was romanticism. The leading poetic school of the era was the Apollo group, the name of both a new Apollo Society (Jam'iyyat Apulu) founded by Ahmad Zaki Abu Shadi in Egypt in 1932 and its short-lived journal *Apollo* (Ar. *Apulu*) which operated from 1932 to 1934. Poets from various Arab countries contributed to *Apollo*, participating in the development of the romantic outlook characteristic of the school. The Apollo poets viewed the Arabic-speaking world as one community of discourse as well as the intended audience for their poetry. The group emphasized Egypt's special place in Arab cultural life, assuming Egyptian leadership of the Arab cultural community and Egyptian responsibility to promote creative expression in other Arab regions.[91]

While romantic poetry was generally apolitical, Egyptian poets occasionally did address Arab and/or Islamic issues and express sympathy with Arab-Islamic causes. Poetry in support of the Palestinian Arab cause, eulogizing the late King Faysal of Iraq, and decrying the Pharaonicist approach appeared in Egyptian journals in the early and mid-1930s.[92] 'Ali Muhammad Shakir's "Nahnu 'Arab" ("We are Arabs"), written in the context of the debate over Egypt's national character of late 1933, unambiguously voiced the changing mood: "if you say Egypt, you say Arab as well / if you say Arab, it is Egypt of which you speak."[93] In the later 1930s the crisis in Palestine stimulated emotional declarations of admiration, solidarity, and support for the Palestinian Arab cause from Egyptian poets.[94] Poetry written in praise of Arab leaders or in support of specific Arab causes continued to appear through World War II;[95] the end of the war, the creation of the Arab League, and the reemergence of the Palestine question as an issue after the war all served to stimulate considerable poetic concern with Arab issues in the immediate postwar period.[96]

'Ali Mahmud Taha (1901–49) was the most famous Egyptian poet of the 1930s and 1940s.[97] A growing Arabist orientation is clearly visible in Taha's poetry.[98] The works in his first collection of poems, al-Mallah al-Ta'ih (The Wandering Mariner, 1934) were romantic in nature and evinced little interest in political topics. His poetic works of the early 1940s – Layali al-Mallah al-Ta'ih (Nights of the Wandering Mariner, 1940); Zahr wa Khamr (Spirits and Shades, 1942); and al-Shawq al-'A'id (Recurrent Longing, 1945) – contained only occasional pieces on Arab themes. The contributions in Taha's Sharq wa Gharb (East and West, 1947) are more political in character, showing the poet in what Anwar al-Ma'addawi has characterized as the poet's phase of "nationalist realism."[99] Several of the poems in East and West addressed Arab and Muslim issues such as recent or current anti-imperialist struggles in Palestine, Syria, Morocco, and Indonesia.[100] Taha's Arab nationalist views appear best in a poem of 1946, "Liqa' wa Du'a" (A Meeting and a Call), composed to honor the visit of King 'Abd al-'Aziz ibn Sa'ud to Egypt:

> Egypt is nothing but your second homeland.
> She is nothing but the Arab nation
> United in thought and tongue.[101]

Arab unity, Arab revival, Arab reality

"Unity [*wahda*]" carried many meanings in Egyptian Arab nationalist discourse. Depending on time and individual it was conceptualized variously in cultural, economic, or political terms, and encompassed specific proposals ranging from occasional cooperation to institutional integration. But it sometimes had connotations which transcended its practical programmatic specifics. As an abstract concept, unity was viewed as the natural state of Arab existence as well as the indispensable requirement for Arab success in all spheres of life.

The centrality of unity in Egyptian Arab nationalist discourse in part derived from its perceived relationship to Arab national revival. The concept of "revival [*nahda*]" suffused all varieties of Egyptian Arab nationalist thought. Egyptian Arabists repeatedly called for a return to the state of political and cultural greatness which had characterized the Arab nation in the past. The only path to such a revival was through unity. It had been when it was unified in the early Islamic period that the Arab nation had experienced its greatest moments; correspondingly it was the rupturing of unity which ushered in the long era of Arab decline. Given this record of unity = greatness and disunity = weakness, it was assumed that a return of unity was the prerequisite for Arab political recovery, cultural renaissance, and a return to a position as a great nation among the nations of the world.[102] As Mahmud Sulayman stated the link between unity and revival, "there is no way to revive Arabic civilization and to return it to its ancient status save through striving for Arab unity."[103]

But Arab unity had more than instrumental value for the most committed Egyptian Arabists. Unity was the natural and true condition of the Arab nation; it was Arab "reality [*haqiqa*]."[104] The current division of the Arab world into numerous political entities was an artificial situation, an unnatural state imposed on the Arab nation by Western imperialism. In this sense unity implied more than just revival; it was a return to the proper condition of Arab existence. It was for this reason that Egyptian Arabists repeatedly denied that Arab unity was an impossible goal or a "utopian dream," maintaining instead that it was a condition whose eventual realization was inevitable.[105] As early as 1934 'Abd al-Rahman 'Azzam was asserting that "the call for an Arab empire is not a dream spawned by a far-reaching imagination, but is based on historical reality and present necessity. The economic, social, and political life of the Arab peoples requires this empire. It is the sole assurance of the independence, freedom, and internal as well as external peace of these peoples."[106] For his nephew 'Abd al-Wahhab 'Azzam, "Arab unity is neither an imaginary nor an artificial matter. It is an existing reality whether or not we think about it or work for it."[107] Ahmad Husayn was more vehement; for him, Arab unity was "a tangible reality that can only be denied by one who denies the sunrise."[108]

Egyptian Arabists did not legitimize the concept of Arab unity in Arab terms alone. The most committed of them also maintained that the justification for Arab unity derived from its global implications. The Arabs had a universal mission unparalleled among nations. Through unity the Arabs would be able to disseminate their own national virtues such as justice, equality, and fraternity to all mankind, as well as to lead humanity to a state of freedom, peace, and universal brotherhood.[109] 'Abd al-Rahman 'Azzam presented Arab unity and mission as two sides of the same coin; just as "there is no doubt about the Arab need for unity, so the need of the world for the Arabs is not in doubt."[110] As 'Abd al-Wahhab 'Azzam stated the premise, "the purpose of Arab unity and Arab revival . . . is the happiness of all mankind."[111] In this vision of the Arab future, the Arabs had a "universal mission" or a "world mission";[112] the ultimate goal of Arab unity was "world unity" or the "unity of mankind."[113] All in all, in an oft-repeated phrase apparently introduced into Arabist discourse by 'Abd al-Rahman 'Azzam, the Arabs were "the nation of the future [ummat al-mustaqbal]."[114]

The practical dimensions of Arab unity

The need for Arab cultural cooperation

While Egyptian Arab nationalist discourse sometimes demonstrated a utopian tendency to attribute mythic meanings to the idea of unity, its practical implications received greater emphasis. The course of progress toward Arab unity generally envisaged by Egyptian Arabists was that cultural and economic cooperation and integration had to precede political collaboration and unity. "The unity of Arab culture" was a primary objective of Egyptian Arab nationalists.[115] Cultural unity, Muhammad Husayn Haykal argued in 1939, "is the primary foundation and the solid basis on which to rest the creation of the union they [the Arabs] desire. Because cultural unity is a basic matter in the life of any nation, the unification of culture among the various [Arab] peoples is what leads to their being bound together by the strongest ties."[116] Naturally it was Egypt, with its present cultural primacy within the Arab world, which was seen as the leader of the effort to unify Arab culture; in the words of Muhammad 'Abd Allah al-'Arabi, "strengthening, organizing, and institutionalizing our cultural ties with the Arab nations is one of the first obligations of modern Egypt."[117]

Cultural unity was also viewed as an indispensable weapon in the common Arab struggle against Western cultural imperialism. The West was a cultural as well as a political threat to the independence and integrity of the Arabs; indeed, the deeper menace was on the cultural level. For years Westerners had criticized Egypt's indigenous Arab heritage as backward, unprogressive, and sterile. Egyptian Arabists viewed such criticisms as a Western plot to undermine the independent foundations of Arab cultural life. In these circumstances, the success of the national cause depended not only on political resources and commitment but also on the Arab ability to use the spiritual armor and cultural ammunition to be found in the arsenal of the Arab legacy.[118]

The benefits of Arab economic integration

Economics was seldom ignored in Egyptian discussions of Arab unity. References to economic cooperation as "the foundation stone of Arab unity" or assertions that "there is no hope of political unity save in economic unity" were truisms in Egyptian Arab nationalist discourse by the 1930s.[119] On the whole, however, the details of the Arab economic relationship received less attention than did Arab cultural and political cooperation.

The basic outlines of the Arabist case for greater Arab economic integration were set down by 'Abd al-Rahman 'Azzam and Ibrahim 'Abd al-Qadir al-Mazini in the mid-1930s. For the former, Arab unity was an economic necessity imposed by the nature of the modern world. "We live in an age of cartels and consolidation," he proclaimed, in which the only way to success was by forming larger and larger units; the natural economic unit for Arabs was of course the Arab nation.[120] Mazini went into more detail. While he believed that both Egypt and the Arab world as a whole would benefit from Arab economic integration, he asserted that it was Egypt which would "reap the greatest benefits" from Arab economic unity.[121] Egypt had the most highly developed Arab economy and the most advanced commercial and financial institutions; as such, it was only natural that the rest of the Arab world should be an Egyptian-led economic zone.[122] Mazini saw the Arab world as particularly important as a market for Egypt's industry. Egypt could not compete in Western industrial circles; in the Arab world, on the other hand, it possessed a considerable competitive advantage. Thus "our industry will increase in size if it finds an outlet to the East, by which we mean the countries of the Arab East."[123]

Other Egyptian Arabists echoed these arguments. Writing in 1936, 'Abd al-Qadir Hamza saw the markets of the Arab world as vital to successful industrialization; the Arab lands offered "natural markets" for Egyptian industrial exports.[124] Tal'at Harb similarly advocated the improvement of inter-Arab communications and the fostering of Arab commercial connections as essential to Arab growth and progress.[125] The case for greater

inter-Arab economic cooperation was often presented in primarily instrumental terms – as a vehicle for advancing the economic interests of Egypt
itself. The logical result of this Egyptocentric perspective on Arab economic
coordination was stated by Muhammad 'Ali 'Alluba in 1942; in his view, the
surrounding Arab world was "our legitimate living space [*majaluna al-
hayawi al-shar'i*]," unity with which would "guarantee the acquisition of
raw materials and the opening of commercial markets vital for industrial
development."[126]

Arab unity as a political imperative

Various arguments for Arab political unity appeared in Egyptian Arabist
discourse. By far the most common practical argument for Arab political
unity was the utility – indeed the indispensability – of Arab solidarity and
cooperation in the common struggle against imperialism. 'Abd al-Rahman
'Azzam stated the outlines of the utilitarian argument for Arab political unity
as early as 1932:

In the absence of unity the separate [Arab] lands will remain weak and unable to
preserve their independence without allies or protectors from outside the Arab race
... It follows that Arab unity is an essential goal for all Arab countries in order to
perfect the means of self-defense and the defense of liberty.[127]

The basic anti-imperialist and strategic justifications for Arab unity
appear clearly in the writings of Ibrahim 'Abd al-Qadir Mazini during the
mid-1930s. Mazini viewed the various local nationalisms found in the Arab
world in the interwar period as artificial, the result of imperialist efforts to
destroy the natural unity of the Arab world and thereby to weaken their
ability to resist the West.[128] He wrote numerous articles attempting to
convince the Egyptian public that an isolated Egyptian effort against
Western imperialism was an ineffective national policy. In his view, an
"Arab policy" was "the only policy which Egypt can adopt, embrace, and
strive for in order to feel confident and assured about its future."[129] The
world was now in "an age of alliances"; in view of this global trend, "there is
no hope for Egypt nor for any of the Arab countries in terms of their security
and tranquillity if each of these countries continues alone in its actions,
regarding itself as self-sufficient from its neighbors."[130] Given present
conditions, the complete liberation of the Nile Valley and the realization of
the full national aspirations of the Egyptian people could be achieved only
through close cooperation with other Arab nationalists engaged in the same
endeavor. A united Arab nationalist movement was an existential necessity
for Egypt as well as the Arabs:

Even if this Arab nationalism were nothing but a delusion with no basis in the
realities of life and history, it would be necessary for us to create it. For what hope

have little nations of a secure life? What good is a nation of a million people? . . . But if the million in Palestine are added to the million in Syria and the millions in Egypt and Iraq for example, they become something to reckon with.[131]

Mazini viewed the Arab world as Egypt's "security zone," Egypt's advance line of defense vital to the maintenance of its future safety and independence.[132] Arab security lay in Arab solidarity; "if they [the Arabs] could make one nation of their peoples, standing in one rank in defense of their common life, then the strongest of nations would not challenge them."[133] Egyptians needed to realize that "Egypt can never enjoy a secure future except with the support of the Arab nations."[134] Egyptian involvement in the Arab nationalist movement was a policy imposed on the country by its own vital interests.

Other Egyptian Arabists echoed Mazini's arguments. British and French imperialism were but two facets of the same reality, one enemy whose defeat could not be accomplished without cooperating in a united "Arab front."[135] The historical examples invoked to prove the necessity of unity in order to attain independence were Italy and Germany; the experience of both nations demonstrated that unity was the path to power.[136] Participation in this common Arab effort was thus a matter of life or death for Egypt; Egypt's national aspirations could be realized only through a united all-Arab effort against imperialism. The moral was captured by 'Abd al-Mun'im Muhammad Khalaf's characterization of the twentieth century as the age of "great nationalism [al-qawmiyya al-kubra]"; small nations such as the existing Arab states had little prospect for success in the modern era without unity.[137]

In the 1930s and early 1940s, the majority of Egyptians who addressed the subject of Arab unity were not thinking in terms of the total elimination of existing Arab states. The prevalent Egyptian attitude toward Arab political cooperation was one of support for the concept in principle, yet tempered by an acceptance of the continued political independence of existing Arab regimes.[138] 'Abd al-Qadir Hamza explained the primary reason why an Arab "empire" was not a realistic option in the 1930s: "the word Empire is the name of a specific kind of political regime whose formation the present circumstances of the Arab countries does not allow, since they are independent political units which have established their own regimes and specific existence."[139]

The form of Arab political integration which gained by far the greatest degree of support in Egyptian Arab nationalist discourse was that of institutionalized cooperation among existing Arab countries. The substantive proposals propounded by Egyptian Arabists usually envisaged Arab "unity" as the formal association of Arab regimes in a new federalist structure. The terms used were variously "the Arab alliance [al-hilf al-'arabi]," "the Arab bloc [al-kutla al-'arabiyya]," "the league of Arab nations ['usbat al-umam al-'arabiyya]," "the Arab union [al-ittihad

Supra-Egyptian orientations and ideologies

al-'arabi]," or "the Arab league [*al-jami'a al-'arabiyya*]."[140] Specific proposals for Arab federation generally accepted the internal political autonomy of the separate Arab states, each of which would retain the exclusive right to determine its own domestic policies. The sphere of authority of the league, alliance, or federation was usually defined in terms of interstate cooperation in such non-political areas as finance, commerce, legal matters, and education, the coordination of foreign policy, and the negotiation of inter-Arab defense arrangements. Possible models for the Arabs to consider included the British Commonwealth or a federal structure analogous to that attributed to the United States of America.[141] Some Egyptian Arabists occasionally called for "comprehensive Arab unity beginning at the Persian Gulf and ending at the Atlantic Ocean" or for "the formation of a greater united Arab nation";[142] but such summons to complete Arab unity represented a minority view in Egypt in the 1930s and 1940s. While Arab "unity" was an emotionally resonant concept for Egyptian Arabists, it was also seen by them as a functional unity aimed at the revival of an Arab nation whose present division into separate units was a reality which had to be accepted.

Egyptian distinctiveness and primacy in the Arab world

Most Egyptian Arabists accepted the existence of multiple loyalties. All Arabs had two identities – a regional one shaped by local factors, and a more general Arab one determined by language and culture. As Zaki Mubarak put it in a speech in Iraq in 1938, "we [Egyptians] are Arabs; nevertheless we are Egyptians. And you [Iraqis] are Arabs, yet you are Iraqis. The inhabitants of the Arab Peninsula are Arabs, yet even so they are Hijazis or Yemenis."[143] In 1939, Makram 'Ubayd expounded on what he called "the theory of related patriotisms."[144] Human beings existed within a hierarchy of identities and loyalties; "man lives for himself and then for his family and region. Simultaneously he lives for his homeland and the homelands that are tied to his homeland by an inseparable bond."[145] In the case of Egypt itself, this pluralist outlook held that Egyptians possessed two primary allegiances – the loyalty they owed to Egypt, their "specific homeland" or "first homeland," and their allegiance to the larger Arab nation, their "general homeland" or "second homeland."[146] In the view of Ibrahim 'Abd al-Qadir al-Mazini, the several Arab states were as real as the greater Arab nation in which he also believed: "Our Arab nation is made up of different states. There is nothing wrong in that. Unity of origin, culture, historical legacy, language, and religion do not prevent any of the Arab nations in their particular homeland from possessing their own distinctive traits which they may cultivate and make use of."[147] While he hoped that in the long run "the Arab countries shall become 'united states' like America and Switzerland,

and not just states," nonetheless "I would not go so far as to recommend a complete merger. This is not for political reasons, but because I believe that a merger would obliterate the discrete national traits of our Arab peoples."[148]

Egyptian Arab nationalists asserted that there was no contradiction between an Egyptian's sense of "local patriotism" and his "general Arab nationalism."[149] Arab unity was not a threat to Egyptian distinctiveness; on the contrary, Arab nationalism recognized regional diversity and aimed at harmonizing local with more general needs and aspirations. Perhaps the most common metaphor for the relationship between the separate Arab lands was that of the several Arab countries as "brothers" or "sisters," members of "one family" who had the same sort of ties and obligations as linked the kinship group.[150] As Muhammad 'Ali 'Alluba put it, "the unity I would like to see realized is for every Arab nation to believe itself to be a member of the larger Arab community, each one coming to the aid of its brother when in distress. Between these nations there should be special ties like the ties between members of one family."[151]

Equally as common as the desire to respect regional diversity on the part of proponents of a greater Egyptian role in the Arab world was their belief in Egypt occupying a position of primacy within the body of the Arab nation. Egyptian Arab nationalists stressed Egypt's status as the most developed and important country in the Arab world. Egypt was the "big brother" or "big sister" of the other Arab regions, with all the responsibilities possessed by an elder sibling toward his or her younger kin.[152]

Egyptian Arab nationalists based Egyptian leadership of the Arabs in the first instance on cultural grounds. Contemporary Egypt was the center of Arab cultural life, "the ka'ba of Arabic literature."[153] Egypt's destiny as the cultural leader of the Arab world was self-evident to Taha Husayn: "something which no one can doubt is that God has bestowed upon Egypt the power to revive and spread culture such as has not been granted to any other Arab nation."[154] For Zaki Mubarak, Cairo now held the position of Arab cultural center occupied by Baghdad a thousand years earlier; it also bore the same responsibilities of cultural leadership once borne by Baghdad under the Abbasids.[155] In view of the country's cultural hegemony over the Arab world, only Egypt was capable of leading the way to the revival of Arab cultural life.[156] Furthermore, other Arabs acknowledged Egypt's primacy and were calling on Egypt to assume its position of cultural leadership. Given all this, Egypt had a "noble mission" of serving as the cultural guide for other Arabs.[157]

Egypt's cultural hegemony was paralleled by its economic and political advantages. Its existing economic facilities – an industrial base far larger than that of any Arab country, a well-developed corporate network, and the presence of Bank Misr, the largest and most important Arab financial institution – made Egypt the economic as well as the geographic center of the Arab world. Bank Misr's role in replacing foreign with indigenous economic leadership was noted with pride; the bank was already assisting other Arab lands to overthrow European economic domination of their economies, and would continue to do so in the future.[158] Egypt had international economic connections unlike those found in any other Arab country, and thus was the logical center for the expansion of Arab trade and economic activity in the wider world. Given these manifold economic advantages, it was high time for Egypt to develop an "active policy" aimed at promoting Egyptian economic leadership of the Arab world.[159]

Egypt occupied a similar position of Arab political leadership. In the first instance, Egypt's leading role in Arab politics was demonstrated by history; from Saladin's defense of the Arabs and Islam to Egypt's current role as a model and exemplar for other Arabs in their common struggle for national independence, Egypt had repeatedly performed "its historic mission ... of service to the Arabs and the Islamic East."[160] Egyptian precedence in anti-imperialist struggle in the recent past, its well-developed and relatively liberal political institutions, and its burgeoning civil society all made Egypt "the metropole of the Arabs and the East" or "the vanguard of the Arab nations."[161] All this made it imperative that "strengthening the place of Egypt [in the Arab world] must become a part of national policy."[162] Given this Egyptian position of cultural, economic, and political primacy, regional leadership was a sacred responsibility of Egypt:

Egypt must always remember that she bears special responsibilities vis-à-vis Arabism and Islam. She carries the message of Arab culture. The eyes of the Arab nations are turned toward her, to follow her example and cooperate with her in the revival of Arab culture. Furthermore, she bears the religious and social leadership of Islam. The eyes of the Islamic nations are turned toward her to cooperate with her in the protection of their common Islamic heritage. The solidarity of Egypt with the Arab and Islamic nations in all ways possible is a force which should not be taken lightly. The special position which Egypt occupies among the Arab and Islamic nations enjoins her to be a model of beneficial mutual understanding among those sister nations, who rally around and embrace her with their affection and esteem.[163]

Thus the Egyptian Arab nationalist vision of Egypt's proper relationship to the Arab nation and Arab nationalism was a distinctly non-egalitarian one. The several Arab regions were all brothers, members of the same family; but Egypt was big brother. This was a hegemonic concept of Arab nationalism in which the terms of Egyptian membership in the larger Arab nation and its participation in the Arab nationalist movement were that

Egypt would enjoy a position of supremacy and leadership. At least in this sense, Egyptian Arab nationalism retained some of the Egyptianist flavor which had characterized Egyptian territorial nationalism.

Conclusion

Of the various supra-Egyptian ideologies which emerged in the post-1930 era, Egyptian Arab nationalism eventually became the most widely articulated and important. The cultural-linguistic emphasis of Egyptian Arab nationalism gave it a deeper and more meaningful appeal than an integral Egyptian nationalism in large part rooted in less tangible and immediate sources deriving from territory and the remote legacy of the Pharaonic past. The relatively secular and more manifestly modernist nature of Arab nationalism may have given it a similar advantage over Islamic nationalism. The religious tenor of Islamic nationalism and the obvious chauvinism of integral nationalism were significant barriers to their wholehearted acceptance by the consumers of nationalist ideas, many of whom had adopted a partially secular and in many respects a liberal world view. Another reason for the broad appeal of Egyptian Arab nationalism was the inability of Egypt's Copts to participate in either Egyptian Islamic nationalism with its inherently Muslim focus, or in Egyptian integral nationalism, which took on a more Islamic coloring over time. For Copts only Arabism, with its stress on a language and a culture which they shared, could provide a supra-Egyptian option.

Equally important was the breadth of the appeal of the Arabist perspective and its ability to absorb both Islam and Egypt into itself. The bulk of Egyptian Arab nationalist ideologues recognized the Islamic heritage as a legitimate component of Arab national identity. By emphasizing Arab culture which was also in large part Muslim culture, Arab nationalist doctrine was not incompatible with the powerful identification of Muslim Egyptians with Islam. Egyptian Arabists also accepted the integralist axiom of Egyptian leadership of the Arab nation and offered a vision of Egyptian primacy in the Arab world which came close to that of integral nationalism. Thus Arabism was able to present itself as congruent with both feelings of Islamic identity and with the integralist desire for Egyptian regional hegemony.

Egyptian Arab nationalism was also the most practical variant of supra-Egyptianism. Arab cooperation and unity were more feasible than ideas of Egyptian religious leadership of the Muslim world which encountered insuperable barriers imposed by geography, existing political realities, and an awareness that the Caliphate was an archaic institution. At the same time, the Egyptian leadership of the Arab world satisfied the integralist desire for a larger Egyptian place in the surrounding world. Arab nationalism matched the conditions of the era – both the desire of Arab elites for cooperation which had been developing through the 1930s and the concepts of regional integration which gained currency during World War II. In short, only Egyptian Arab nationalism gave tangible expression to the sense of Egyptian hegemony and mission found in all forms of supra-Egyptianism.

Part II

Supra-Egyptianism in Egyptian politics

7   Egypt, Arab alliance, and Islamic Caliphate, 1930–1939

The relationship between the new supra-Egyptian orientations and ideologies of the post-1930 period and the positions taken by the various political forces operating in Egyptian public life was a complex one. Through the period under consideration in this study, there was a sizable gap between ideological development and political evolution. On most issues, the demands of supra-Egyptian ideologues and movements exceeded what Egypt's political parties and leadership were willing or able to do in the way of the tangible expansion of Egyptian involvement in Arab and Muslim affairs. Nonetheless, over time a definite trend in the direction of Egypt playing a more assertive role in Arab and Muslim international politics is visible.

The political adjustment to a more supra-Egyptianist position passed through three phases in the period from 1930 to 1945. In the first half of the 1930s, Egyptian political involvement in Arab and Muslim politics remained much as it had been in the 1920s: intermittent and largely reactive. In the later 1930s, prompted especially by the intensifying crisis in Palestine, Egypt's regional policy for the first time became a major issue in Egyptian public life. After a hiatus in the formulation of new initiatives in Egyptian foreign policy during the early years of World War II, the expansion of Egypt's regional role entered its third phase in 1943–5 when the Egyptian government took the lead in the diplomatic negotiations which eventually resulted in the formation of the League of Arab States.

The following three chapters examine this gradual movement in the direction of a more active regional role by the Egyptian government between 1930 and 1945. This chapter deals with several regional issues which became matters of political attention and/or controversy in Egyptian public life over the course of the 1930s. The following chapter discusses Egypt's growing involvement in the Palestine issue in the later 1930s. The final chapter of this section deals with Egyptian regional policy during World War II, focusing particularly on Egyptian state leadership of the movement toward Arab federation which occurred during the later years of the war.

Iraq and Arab alliance, 1930–1931

At the start of the 1930s, both the Egyptian government and the public still demonstrated little receptiveness to the idea of Egyptian involvement in regional politics. This appears clearly in the tepid Egyptian response to Iraq's efforts to promote a greater measure of cooperation among Arab states in the early 1930s. From the conclusion of the Anglo-Iraqi Treaty of Alliance of June 1930, which set the terms for Iraqi independence, until his death in September 1933, King Faysal of Iraq undertook a variety of initiatives aimed at improving inter-Arab cooperation. These included visits by Iraqi diplomats as well as the king himself to other Arab lands in 1930–1 in order to promote an "Arab alliance [al-hilf al-'arabi]"; the conclusion of individual treaties of friendship, extradition, and/or bon voisinage with Transjordan, Sa'udi Arabia, and Egypt in 1931; confidential negotiations with the French in the same year in the hope of Faysal regaining the Syrian throne which he had lost in 1920; and in 1932–3 the sponsorship of the idea of a popular Arab congress to promote greater inter-Arab cultural and political cooperation.[1]

Within Egypt, the idea of greater Arab political cooperation being promoted by the Iraqi government kindled no significant Egyptian response in 1930–1. Egyptian press commentary on the Anglo-Iraqi Treaty of June 1930, while generally favorable to this step toward Iraqi independence, viewed the treaty as a matter extraneous to Egypt.[2] Even advocates of improving Egyptian cultural and economic linkages with its neighbors did not go as far as to suggest Egyptian political involvement in Arab affairs in the early 1930s. Muhammad 'Ali 'Alluba, who in 1930 was calling on Egypt to "lead the way for the Arab nations, assume the banner of their culture, and consolidate relations among these sisterly states," nonetheless favored only forms of Arab cooperation "far removed from politics."[3] Similarly Mahmud 'Azmi, whose advocacy of Arab economic cooperation went back to the late 1920s, in 1930 limited his promotion of Arab interaction to non-political spheres since "the political conditions existing in some of these [Arab] lands are not conducive to the creation of bonds of a political nature."[4] The Syrian-born editor of al-Muqattam, Karim Thabit, at the same time as extolling the virtues of improving bilateral Egyptian–Iraqi relations, explicitly limited such cooperation to areas "outside the realm of politics."[5]

Responses to the notion of an Arab alliance in official Egyptian circles were equally negative. King Fu'ad is reported to have been hostile to any Egyptian involvement in an Arab alliance system.[6] When asked about recent movement toward greater Arab cooperation in early 1931, Prime Minister Isma'il Sidqi offered only a bland endorsement of Arab social and cultural interaction.[7] The Treaty of Friendship and Bon Voisinage concluded between Egypt and Iraq in April 1931 was Egypt's first diplomatic agreement with a fellow-Arab state; but it was unaccompanied by any further measures of diplomatic linkage between Egypt and its Arab neighbors for several years.[8] As a British report of 1931 evaluated the initial Egyptian reaction to ideas of greater Arab political cooperation in 1930–1, "Egypt is so isolated from the Arab world that it is not easily drawn into movements [of Arab cooperation]."[9]

The Wafd and Arab solidarity

The Wafd had evinced little concern with events in the Arab world in the 1920s.[10] This aloofness from regional politics was shifting by the early 1930s. The Wafdist leaders Bahiy al-Din Barakat and Makram 'Ubayd paid well-publicized visits to the Fertile Crescent in 1931. Barakat did not hesitate to express the sympathy of Egyptians for the Palestinian Arab cause and to commend the recent Iraqi initiatives directed at promoting Arab unity.[11] For his part Makram took pains to emphasize the common origins of Egyptians and other Arab peoples, to stress the Arabness of the Coptic minority to which he belonged, and to warn that the effort to establish a Jewish state in Palestine would be met with resistance throughout the region.[12]

Most indicative of the direction in which the views of Wafdist leaders about Egypt's relationship with the Arab world were moving were Makram's views on the subject of "Arab brotherhood" as developed in a speech in Sofar (Lebanon).[13] While acknowledging the bonds of blood, language, history, and religion uniting the Arabs, the main thrust of his remarks was that there was another link "more powerful than these; it is the bond of suffering." All Arabs were students in "the school of suffering," his euphemism for Western imperialism in the contemporary era. Since imperialism had treated all Arabs alike, it was incumbent on the Arabs to "exploit this unity for the sake of buttressing our sovereignty and our independence." Although rejecting the creation of "one state" which would unite all Arabs, he nonetheless enjoined his listeners to work for what he termed "political-economic unity"; practical collaboration which would strengthen each individual Arab country. This meant the adoption of "one aim and one goal" by all Arabs. Makram's sense of Arab solidarity as manifested in this speech was a highly contingent one deriving primarily from the specific circumstances of the contemporary era of imperialist domination.[14]

Makram did not restrict his advocacy of Arab cooperation to Fertile Crescent audiences. In an interview upon returning to Egypt,[15] he reiterated that a "bond of shared suffering" united all Arabs and stated that "the best way to achieve our patriotic aspirations is [through] solidarity and mutual aid between Egypt and all Arabic-speaking peoples." He hastened to assure Egyptians that there was no incompatibility between such a "political bond" based on the common needs of all Arab peoples and their individual national movements.

Makram 'Ubayd's trip and the views he expressed have been credited with helping to make the subject of Arab solidarity a legitimate topic of discussion in Egypt. By themselves Makram's views did not herald the "astounding change which has taken place in Wafdist circles in relation to the Arab idea," or the birth of "a new spirit and a remarkable revolution in [Egyptian] attitudes" toward inter-Arab cooperation, as it was sometimes viewed by Arabs elsewhere.[16] But they do indicate the seed of a more open attitude toward regional affairs emerging on the part of Egypt's premier nationalist movement.

Egypt and the general Islamic Congress at Jerusalem, 1931

A major event in Arab and Muslim politics in the early 1930s was the international Islamic Congress which convened in Jerusalem in December 1931. The reaction of the Egyptian government and the country's political parties to the call for an Islamic Congress offers perhaps the best example of how a regional political initiative could reverberate within Egyptian domestic politics in the early 1930s.

The response in Egyptian religious and official circles to the invitation from the Congress's organizers (Mawlana Shawkat 'Ali of India and the Mufti of Jerusalem, Hajj Amin al-Husayni) for the Egyptian government to send a delegation to the Congress was a negative one. To the Egyptian religious hierarchy of al-Azhar, the possibility that the gathering might establish a rival Muslim university in neighboring Palestine was not appealing: Azharite leaders spoke publicly against the convening of the Congress, criticized the idea of creating a new Islamic university in Jerusalem, and encouraged student demonstrations protesting the entire initiative.[17] The reaction of King Fu'ad and the Sidqi ministry was equally hostile. The possibility of the Congress discussing the subject of the restoration of the Caliphate obviously represented a threat to whatever caliphal ambitions Fu'ad may still have had. The attitude of the Egyptian government was that "it was intolerable that a rival university should be established a few hours' train-journey away," as Sidqi angrily informed the British.[18] In order to prevent the Congress from materializing, the Egyptian government intervened with the British, expressing its disquiet over the Congress in the apparent hope of prompting British action against an assembly which, as the Egyptian ambassador in London put it, was "vague and impracticable in the highest degree."[19]

In November 1931, Hajj Amin al-Husayni visited Egypt in an effort to win Egyptian support for the Congress. He repeatedly denied that the assembly would consider the Caliphate question, stating that its agenda would be confined to the three subjects of the defense of the Holy Places in Jerusalem, the restoration of the Hijaz Railway, and Muslim cultural cooperation.[20] In a meeting with Prime Minister Sidqi, he reiterated his declaimer about the Caliphate as well as offering assurances that he would not allow the Congress to become a forum for anti-regime propaganda by the ministry's opponents.[21]

The main support for the Islamic Congress in Egypt in 1931 came from the Egyptian opposition. The Wafd presumably saw the same opportunities for anti-Sidqi capital in the affair which Sidqi himself feared. The Wafdist press defended the Congress and its organizers against their Egyptian critics, and a Wafdist delegation led by the head of the Wafd, Mustafa al-Nahhas, visited Hajj Amin during his visit to Cairo to assure him of Wafdist support for the Congress.[22]

The contacts of the Mufti with the Egyptian opposition had an immediate negative effect upon the Egyptian government. A projected meeting of Hajj Amin with King Fu'ad was cancelled, and the government press again resumed attacks on the idea of the Congress.[23] Although the Egyptian government could not prohibit Egyptian attendance at the Congress when it did convene, it sent no official representatives and discouraged both Egyptian civil servants and Egyptian 'ulama' from participating.[24]

The Islamic Congress met in Jerusalem from 6 through 17 December 1931. Somewhere between 133 and 145 delegates from over twenty Muslim countries attended the sessions.[25] The organizers of the event claimed twenty-one Egyptians in attendance; a British report put the number at twenty-five.[26] There was no official representation of either the government of Egypt or the Egyptian corps of 'ulama'. The only organized Egyptian delegation was a group of notables representing the Young Men's Muslim Association.[27]

The organizers of the Congress made every effort to involve the more prominent delegates from Egypt in its deliberations. Three of the delegates from Egypt (Muhammad 'Ali 'Alluba, 'Abd al-Rahman 'Azzam, and Muhammad Rashid Rida) were selected to the Executive Committee of the Congress; Egyptians also sat on several of the eight committees which examined the specific concerns addressed by the assembly.[28] The Liberal leader 'Alluba played a particularly prominent role in the Congress; in addition to his being selected first as vice-president and later as treasurer of the secretariat of the Congress, he also chaired the committee which considered the question of the Holy Places in Jerusalem.[29]

The most visible Egyptian in the proceedings of the Islamic Congress was 'Abd al-Rahman 'Azzam of the Wafd. His speech on the first day of the Congress conveying the good wishes of the Wafd and "all Egyptians" to the delegates drew an immediate verbal protest from the anti-Wafdist journalists Sulayman Fawzi and Muhammad al-Subahi, who decried the assumption that the Wafd spoke for all Egyptians; to the accompaniment of cries of "long live Sa'd, Nahhas Pasha, and the Wafd," both were assaulted and mauled by those in attendance for their denial of the Wafd = Egypt equation.[30] 'Azzam's later addresses to the Congress carried ringing denunciations of the artificial barriers imposed by imperialism between the Arab peoples and equally vehement affirmations of the inevitability of the realization of Arab unity in the future.[31] 'Azzam was the only Egyptian delegate to the Islamic Congress who attended the one-day meeting, organized by the Palestinian leader 'Awni 'Abd al-Hadi, which considered the question of Arab nationalism and resulted in the passage of resolutions affirming the indivisibility of the Arab countries and their united opposition to imperialism. This Arab National Congress of 1931 was one of the first instances in which Arab nationalists included Egypt as a part of the Arab nation.[32]

'Azzam's most dramatic contribution to the Islamic Congress came in an emotional speech of 15 December in which he denounced recent Italian repression in Libya and proposed that the Congress pass a resolution calling for a Muslim boycott of Italy.[33] The speech drew an immediate protest from the Italian consul in Palestine and led the British authorities to deport 'Azzam from Palestine. 'Azzam's departure from the Mandate by auto through Gaza to the Egyptian border resembled a triumphal procession, as sympathetic Palestinians held demonstrations along the route to hail this Egyptian champion of Arab rights.[34]

Within Egypt, press reaction to the Islamic Congress of 1931 split along partisan lines. The government and pro-Palace press were predictably hostile. Sidqi's mouthpiece al-Sha'b referred to the conclave as "the so-called Islamic Congress," belittling it as a "joke" whose activities were meaningless, and attacked 'Azzam for attempting to make political capital for the Wafd at what was ostensibly a religious gathering.[35] The Liberal al-Siyasa adopted a more positive stance, acknowledging the potential benefits such a meeting might possess for Muslim cultural interaction.[36] While al-Siyasa did not look favorably at the establishment of an Islamic university in Jerusalem which might threaten Egypt's "intellectual leadership among the Islamic nations," it nonetheless used the issue to criticize the torpor and stagnation which in its view prevailed at al-Azhar.[37] The

Wafdist *al-Balagh* was an enthusiastic supporter of the Islamic Congress. It gave front-page coverage to Congress sessions, particularly to the activities of the Wafd's own 'Azzam in the proceedings, and praised both the Congress's attempt at "protecting the common heritage" of Muslims and its efforts at fostering Muslim "intellectual unity" as worthwhile endeavors.[38]

Partisan differences apart, there were also commonalities in Egyptian coverage of the Islamic Congress in late 1931. From our perspective, the most important of these was the desire of Egyptian commentators to see the Congress address cultural matters only and to avoid the subject of Muslim political cooperation. Thus *al-Sha'b* repeatedly denounced the political overtones of the Congress;[39] *al-Siyasa* called for it to avoid the politically-divisive Caliphate issue and to concentrate on matters of cultural collaboration;[40] and *al-Balagh*, while viewing the subject of Palestine as a legitimate matter of concern of the Congress, nonetheless placed that issue within the framework of the preservation of the Muslim cultural heritage rather than in an explicitly political context.[41]

Egyptian involvement in the Islamic Congress at Jerusalem in 1931 may be evaluated in both a positive and a negative light. On the one hand, the attitudes of Egyptians toward the event and the behavior of those who attended it certainly reflected the imperatives of Egyptian domestic politics. But it is also necessary to note the unprecedented aspects of the Egyptian participation in the Congress. The important role played by Egyptians at the Islamic Congress had had no parallels in the 1920s. This is especially true of the Wafd, for which 'Azzam's participation, visible role, and confident predictions of eventual Arab unity were in marked contrast to his mentor Sa'd Zaghlul's contemptuous dismissal of the Arabs as "zeroes" in the mid-1920s.[42]

Prime Minister Sidqi in Palestine, 1932

The participation of both Wafdist and Liberal leaders in the Islamic Congress in December 1931 was undoubtedly a factor behind one of the few regional initiatives undertaken by the Sidqi ministry during its tenure in office. In February 1932, the Egyptian premier made an official visit to Palestine and Lebanon. Little of substance seems to have occurred during or as a result of the visit, Sidqi reportedly rejecting an appeal by Palestinian and Lebanese merchants for reducing tariffs on their agricultural exports to Egypt on the impeccably Egyptianist grounds that Egypt's tariffs were designed "first and foremost to protect her [Egyptian] interests and requirements."[43]

But the trip's symbolic significance should not be ignored. That an incumbent Egyptian prime minister for the first time since the achievement of formal Egyptian independence a decade earlier paid a state visit to a neighboring Arab region is itself an indication of an evolving Egyptian relationship with the Arab world by the early 1930s. This is particularly the case with Isma'il Sidqi, who throughout his political career had been and would continue to be one of the most Egypt-oriented of Egyptian politicians. The verbal expressions of Arab solidarity offered by Sidqi while he was in Palestine differed little from those of more Arabist spokesmen; in public receptions, he repeatedly expressed his support for improving Egyptian–Palestinian relations, referred to the bonds of language, religion, and even "kinship" linking the peoples of the two countries, and spoke of the numerous ties between Palestine and Egypt which made the two lands part of "a single region [qutr wahid]".[44]

Egypt and an Arab congress, 1932–1933

The last initiative in the Iraqi campaign for increasing inter-Arab cooperation of the early 1930s was its support for the convening of an Arab congress to discuss inter-Arab collaboration in 1932–3. When discussions concerning the convening of an Arab congress in Baghdad under the sponsorship of King Faysal took place among Fertile Crescent Arab nationalists in late 1932–early 1933, its proponents attempted to involve Egypt as a participant.

The Egyptian response was again a reserved one. According to British evaluations, both the king and the Egyptian government opposed any Egyptian participation in such a gathering.[45] The position of the Wafd was more complex. The organizers of the congress appointed two leading Wafdists known for their pro-Arab sympathies, Hamid al-Basil and 'Abd al-Rahman 'Azzam, on the Preparatory Committee for the congress.[46] But a split in the Wafd itself almost immediately nullified this attempt to involve the Wafd in the nascent movement toward Arab unity. Both Basil and 'Azzam were among the group of party leaders who broke with Nahhas and with the Wafd in the autumn of 1932. Their putative involvement in the congress thus led to their opponents in control of the Wafd soon adopting a detached attitude toward the event. By the end of 1932 Nahhas is reported to have counselled the Iraqis to postpone the congress, and by early 1933 the Iraqis themselves had abandoned the hope of Wafdist participation in the gathering.[47] Postponed in March by King Faysal until an unspecified date later in 1933, in the end British pressure dissuaded the king from sponsoring the congress.[48]

King Faysal's death in September 1933 wrote finis to the idea of an Arab congress, and halted the other Iraqi initiatives aimed at fostering Arab political cooperation. The impact of these efforts on Egypt is problematic.

On the whole the Egyptian reaction to the Iraqi attempt to promote Arab political cooperation in the early 1930s had been a reserved one. Perhaps the best testimony to the aloofness of Egypt from Arab political affairs at the time comes in the content of a lengthy British report on the subject of Arab unity prepared by George Rendel of the Foreign Office in late 1933; its definition of the region where Arab unity was becoming an issue excluded Egypt, and its analysis made no mention of Egypt in relation to the subject.[49]

'Ali Mahir and the Arabs

The first Egyptian government of the 1930s to which a more assertive regional policy has sometimes been attributed is the caretaker ministry headed by 'Ali Mahir which governed Egypt from January through May 1936.[50] This is a questionable intepretation. Recent studies by Ralph Coury and Thomas Mayer have noted various reasons, including Mahir's personal reservations about Egyptian efforts to obtain the Caliphate, his relatively conciliatory attitude in regard to the Palestine question, and the later testimony of his associate 'Abd al-Rahman 'Azzam to the effect that 'Azzam's own arguments in favor of Egypt's pursuing an Arab policy had at best a limited impact upon Mahir, for questioning whether 'Ali Mahir can be characterized as an advocate of greater Egyptian regional involvement in the 1930s.[51]

Only two of the actions undertaken by the Mahir ministry of 1936 merit consideration as new regional initiatives. The first is the appointment of the pro-Arab spokesman 'Abd al-Rahman 'Azzam as Egyptian Minister to Iraq and Iran in April 1936. Upon the death of King Fu'ad and the accession of his son Faruq in the following month, Mahir is also reported to have instructed 'Azzam to make regular reports on regional affairs for the edification of the young king.[52] While the appointment does indicate a growing attentiveness to Middle Eastern affairs in Egyptian policy-making circles, the composite nature of 'Azzam's brief – Egyptian Minister to *both* Iraq and Iran – also indicates that this increased concern for regional relations was general rather than focused on the Arab lands alone.

The second initiative of the Mahir ministry concerning the Middle East in early 1936 was the inauguration of formal diplomatic relations with Sa'udi Arabia. Due primarily to King Fu'ad's personal animosity for King 'Abd al-'Aziz ibn Sa'ud, Egypt had neither recognized nor had formal diplomatic relations with the new Sa'udi state since its consolidation of authority over most of the Arabian Peninsula in the mid-1920s. This hostility to Sa'udi Arabia was not shared by most other Egyptian policy-makers, who through the later 1920s and early 1930s had tried to normalize Egyptian–Sa'udi diplomatic relations but were prevented from doing so by King Fu'ad. Only in 1936 was the logjam broken. The immediate stimulus to an Egyptian–Sa'udi *rapprochement* at that time came from the Sa'udi side. A desire for closer interaction with other Arab regimes was being demonstrated by King 'Abd al-'Aziz ibn Sa'ud by the mid-1930s.[53] The first fruit of this new Sa'udi openness to inter-Arab cooperation was the conclusion early in 1936 of a Sa'udi–Iraqi Treaty of Arab Brotherhood and Alliance which called for "unifying the Islamic and Arab culture and the military systems of the two countries" and invited "any other independent Arab State" to accede to its terms.[54] In an interview with *al-Ahram*, ibn Sa'ud repeated the invitation for other Arab countries to adhere to the treaty.[55]

On 8 April 1936, Mahir informed the British that "he had at last persuaded King Fuad that relations between Egypt and the Hijaz ought to be regularized."[56] Formal negotiations with the Sa'udi envoy Fu'ad Hamza began on 20 April. The main issues between the two countries were religious in nature; first the issue of the dispatch of the ceremonial Mahmal and Kiswa from Egypt to Mecca which had been halted after an Egyptian–Sa'udi incident of violence in 1926, and the parallel question of Egyptian support for religious endowments in the Hijaz which had been suspended since the Sa'udi conquest of the region in the mid-1920s.[57] Agreement on these residual issues was not arrived at in April 1936: rather, the negotiators deferred them for later resolution while agreeing to the purely political act of the conclusion of a treaty regularizing relations between the two countries.

King Fu'ad, the main opponent of Egyptian recognition of Sa'udi Arabia, died on 28 April 1936. Perhaps not coincidentally, the Egyptian–Sa'udi Treaty of Friendship was finalized on 7 May 1936.[58] Its first article was the most important one; in it Egypt at last recognized Sa'udi Arabia as "a free and independent state." Other articles provided for "perpetual peace and friendship" as well as the amicable resolution of differences between the two parties, the exchange of diplomatic and consular representatives, and Egyptian assistance in improving pilgrim facilities in the Hijaz.

Contemporary Egyptian reaction to the Egyptian-Sa'udi Treaty of May 1936 seems to have been uniformly favorable. During the negotiations, the Arabist-inclined *al-Ahram* predicted that a treaty between the two countries would be the harbinger of a new "Arab Eastern policy" on the part of the Egyptian state.[59] To *al-Muqattam* the treaty was the latest example of "the clear tendency and desire in all the Arab lands now towards mutual cooperation and interconnection"; the Muslim Brotherhood's journal hailed it as "a blessed step on the path to Arab unity."[60] *Al-Siyasa* linked the treaty to the new threat to all Arab countries now posed by Italy, and concluded its analysis with the hope that it would mark the beginning of an era of closer relations between the states of the region.[61] An editorial which appeared in Isma'il Sidqi's outlet *al-Sha'b* on the eve of the conclusion of the agreement demonstrated the effect which changing international conditions were having on Egyptian perceptions by 1936: "if the Arab nations were in need of literary, cultural, and *political unity* in the years following the great European war, the need has become more prominent and urgent after the turn which international developments have taken."[62] A British evaluation by Sir Walter Smart paralleled the analysis found in *al-Siyasa* and *al-Sha'b*: "[r]ecent developments between Arabian countries have shown that the religious issue is giving way before the necessity of political cooperation."[63]

The Wafdist ministry of 1936–1937

After elections in May 1936, the Mahir ministry was succeeded by a Wafdist government headed by Mustafa al-Nahhas. Since the Revolution of 1919, the Wafd had been Egypt's dominant political movement. It had also been the most consistent and important organization promoting the Egyptianist *Weltanschauung* spawned by the Revolution. The Wafd was not a static entity, however. By the later 1930s, the Wafd was losing its preeminent stature in Egyptian public life. Although it was still the single most important political party in Egypt, it now faced more and more powerful rivals, and was increasingly being seen as one of several competitors on the Egyptian political scene rather than as the embodiment of the nation in its struggle for national independence.[64]

Wafdist ministries ruled Egypt from May 1936 to the end of 1937. The major development in Egyptian foreign policy with which the Wafd is associated was the conclusion of the long-awaited Anglo-Egyptian Treaty of Alliance of August 1936. Although this agreement did not relate directly to Egypt's regional position, the treaty's formalization of Egyptian independence and its provision for Egyptian entry into the League of Nations had indirect consequences for Egypt's relations with its neighbors. Egyptian commentary on the treaty often viewed it as a liberating development which would allow a now-independent Egypt to play a greater role in the world around it. For Emile Zaydan of *al-Hilal*, the treaty opened "new horizons" for Egypt and the opportunity to consolidate its ties with other Arab, Muslim, and Eastern peoples.[65] Taha Husayn saw it as the start of a "new era" of greater international responsibilities for Egypt, including the obligation to spread the benefits of its more advanced culture to its more backward neighbors.[66] Muhammad Husayn Haykal phrased this expectation of new external opportunities for Egypt more precisely in his remarks in parliament during the debate over ratification of the treaty; as he saw it, Egypt was now free to develop a new "Arab or Eastern or Islamic policy," something it had not been able to do prior to the conclusion of the treaty of 1936.[67]

This sense of new regional opportunities was shared by the Wafdist government. The Nahhas ministries of 1936–7 did more to promote official Egyptian involvement in regional affairs than had any of their predecessors save possibly the ministry of 'Ali Mahir. They continued the process of *rapprochement* with Sa'udi Arabia begun by the Mahir ministry, enlarging 'Abd al-Rahman 'Azzam's diplomatic assignment to include that of serving as Egyptian Minister to Sa'udi Arabia.[68] In November 1936, an exchange of letters between Nahhas and the Sa'udi negotiator Fu'ad Hamza finalized agreement on the dispatch of the Mahmal and Kiswa to the Holy Cities as well as the resumption of Egyptian financial support for religious endowments in Sa'udi Arabia.[69] Administratively, new sections for supervising regional affairs were established in the Ministry of Foreign Affairs and the Publications Department by late 1936. Practical efforts by the Wafdist government to foster Egypt's regional economic position included the creation of a committee in the Ministry of Finance to examine the Egyptian commercial position in the Middle East, South Asia, and Africa in the hope of "opening new markets" for Egyptian exports to these regions, an agreement with Iraq reducing tariff rates between the two countries, and a new commercial agreement with the government of Palestine.[70]

Yet in contrast to its promotion of Egypt's cultural and economic position in the region, the Wafd's attitude toward extending Egypt's involvement in regional politics was more reserved. The distinction appears clearly in its reaction to the idea of convening an Arab congress in Egypt. Suggestions for an international Arab gathering in Cairo had come from several sources in 1936: from Palestinian Arabs interested in obtaining Egyptian support; from students at the Egyptian University; and from Pan-Arabist circles in Egypt such as the Arab Bond Society.[71] Nahhas's initial reaction was reported by the British to have been favorable toward efforts to improve Arab cultural ties but apprehensive of any attempt to promote closer political links.[72] When Palestinian Arab spokesmen approached Nahhas concerning a congress which would have had political dimensions, he discouraged its being held in Egypt.[73] In the end no Arab congress materialized.

The best indication of the Wafdist ministry's cautious attitude toward Arab political cooperation appears from its response to Iraqi approaches concerning the conclusion of an Egyptian–Iraqi treaty of mutual cooperation in late 1936–early 1937.[74] Such a pact was first conceived by Iraqi Foreign Minister Nuri al-Sa'id in the summer of 1936. It was Nuri's view that the conclusion of the Anglo-Egyptian Treaty of Alliance had made both Egypt and Iraq formal allies of Great Britain and thereby provided the basis for "joint action by Iraq and Egypt" to counter Italian ambitions in the Middle East.[75] Nuri soon fell from power, and nothing came of his original ideas. Only in January 1937 was a proposal for an Egyptian–Iraqi treaty of alliance put to the Egyptian government by Nuri's successor Naji al-Asil.[76]

The Egyptian response to the proposal for an Iraqi–Egyptian alliance was negative. In March 1937, Nahhas informed the British that he had discouraged the idea of an alliance with Iraq. The reasons he provided for doing so are instructive. As he told Sir Walter Smart, in practical terms "he [Nahhas] was too busy with other things for the moment"; on a more abstract level, "[h]e did not wish to get involved in general complications: he wished first to consolidate Egypt's own position."[77] Internal Egyptian concerns, the pressures of domestic affairs, and the prospect that a positive response would have meant that Egypt was following rather than leading the way, appear to have been sufficient to deter the Wafdist government from entering into formal political cooperation with Iraq in 1937. Despite its encouragement of Egyptian economic and cultural interaction with its Arab neighbors, the party's horizons had not yet expanded enough to lead it to concur in the conclusion of a formal treaty of alliance with another Arab state.

The ministries of Muhammad Mahmud, 1938–1939

Much the same reserve toward regional political involvement marked the foreign policy of the primarily Liberal-Sa'dist ministries headed by Muhammad Mahmud which governed Egypt from the beginning of 1938 until the eve of war in August 1939. Save in the important area of inter-Arab coordination concerning the Palestine issue, there is little in the way of the practical encouragement of Arab political cooperation which can be identified with the ministries of Muhammad Mahmud.

One possible option for Egypt by 1938–9 was adherence to the Middle East Non-Aggression Pact, often called the Saadabad Pact, which had been concluded among Turkey, Iraq, Iran, and Afghanistan in 1937. Reports to the effect that Egypt had been invited to adhere to the Pact appeared early in 1938, when the Turkish Foreign Minister Dr. Rüstü Aras visited Egypt. When queried by the British about the prospect, however, Prime Minister Mahmud denied any Egyptian intention to affiliate with the Saadabad group; as he put it, there was "no advantage" for Egypt in such an action save "a slight moral gain."[78] Nearly a year later Mahmud appears to have changed this view: according to the memoirs of Muhammad Husayn Haykal, in early 1939 the prime minister brought the idea of Egyptian adherence to the Saadabad Pact before his Cabinet. The ministry split evenly on the issue, half feeling that current international conditions necessitated Egypt's participation in regional defense arrangements, the other half holding the view that political association with the non-contiguous states represented in the pact would not serve Egyptian national interests.[79] In view of this division of opinion, the premier chose not to force the issue and withdrew his suggestion for Egyptian entry into the Pact.[80]

The Mahmud ministry was no more enthusiastic about the concept of a specifically Arab alliance when that idea was brought to its attention. In 1939, the government of Iraq again proposed an alliance providing for mutual assistance between the two countries.[81] No more came of the offer than had come from the earlier Iraqi approach to the Egyptians for an alliance in 1937. Muhammad Mahmud's later explanation to the British as to why his ministry had not pursued the Iraqi approach illustrates the indifference of all Egyptian governments to formalized inter-Arab political agreements in the 1930s: "if the spirit of cooperation was there, that was all that really mattered."[82] Prior to World War II, no Egyptian government concluded a formal agreement of a political character with another Arab state.

The Egyptian Palace and the Caliphate, 1937–1939

Yet to search for major regional initiatives on the part of the Muhammad Mahmud ministries of 1938–9 is to look in the wrong place. The dominant position in Egyptian politics in the late 1930s was held by the Egyptian Palace. With his portly figure, poor Arabic, and general contempt for things Egyptian, King Fu'ad had never been a genuinely popular figure in Egypt. His son and successor Faruq at first possessed quite a different image. Young, attractive, and with a reputation for religiosity which was assiduously nurtured by Palace propaganda, Faruq generated much more enthusiasm among the Egyptian public in the early years of his reign. The epithets used to characterize Faruq in the later 1930s capture the aura of piety and progress which he radiated to many Egyptians: the "renovator" or "sword" of Islam; "the pious king [al-malik al-salih]"; "the beloved king [al-malik al-mahbub]."[83]

The political power of the Egyptian Palace in the later 1930s did not stem solely from the personal appeal of the new monarch. King Faruq also possessed the same constitutional prerogatives which had allowed his father, despite his general unpopularity, to dominate Egyptian politics much of the time. He also benefited greatly from the political skills of his advisors. Primary among these was his tutor Shaykh Muhammad Mustafa al-Maraghi, Rector of al-Azhar in the early years of Faruq's reign. In the later 1930s Maraghi was a leading advocate of the desirability of a more religiously grounded, less fractious, political system for Egypt and a promoter of extending the prerogatives of the Egyptian monarchy *vis-à-vis* those of the political parties.[84] Faruq's other key advisor in the early years of his reign was 'Ali Mahir, Chief of the Royal Cabinet through much of the later 1930s. Mahir's agenda appears to have been more purely political than that of Maraghi: to enhance his own political position through a combination of promoting the authority of the monarchy and of appealing to newer groups then emerging on the Egyptian political scene by becoming the champion of efficient but also "reformist" rule.[85]

Together, King Faruq, his tutor Shaykh Maraghi, and his chamberlain 'Ali Mahir possessed an impressive assortment of political assets. Faruq contributed his personal popularity as well as the constitutional powers and the financial resources of the monarchy; Maraghi brought the authority of his position as Rector of al-Azhar plus his ability to manipulate its student body as a political force; while Mahir added tactical skill and a network of contacts with both the politicians of the establishment parties and the growing protest movements of the new generation. The combined power of all this was formidable, ranging from the high ground of religious authority and constitutional prerogatives to the lower terrain occupied by the influence of money and the street in politics.

The policies promoted by the Egyptian Palace in the later 1930s mark a new departure in Egyptian politics during the parliamentary era. Where King Fu'ad had dominated Egyptian public life through a blend of constitutional position, political guile, and British support, King Faruq and those around him attempted to establish royal ascendancy on a more ideological basis. Internally, Palace strategy employed religious symbols and arguments in an effort to promote the authority of the monarch over that of the political parties. The specifics of this endeavor included the presentation of King Faruq as a pious, progressive, and altogether worthy ruler; the leveling of sectarian, anti-Coptic propaganda against the Wafd; royal support for newer and anti-Wafdist political organizations such as Young Egypt and the Muslim Brotherhood; and an attempt, particularly by Shaykh Maraghi, to argue for the need to restructure Egyptian public life along more "Islamic" lines which would have diminished the place of parliament and the parties at the same time as it would have asserted the centrality of the monarchy in the Egyptian political order.[86] Most importantly for our purposes, the Palace coalition also developed an external component in its campaign to enhance the position of the monarchy. The regional policy of the Palace was cast in the ambitious terms of the promotion of Egyptian leadership of the wider Muslim world, and more specifically toward the goal of attaining the Caliphate for King Faruq.

The first Egyptian intimation of a Palace intention to promote Faruq as Caliph came in March 1937, when 'Aziz 'Izzat, one of the three members of the Regency Council directing Palace affairs until the young king should attain his majority, suggested to the British that the establishment of the Caliphate in Egypt would be a useful counter to recent Italian attempts to present Mussolini as a champion of Islam.[87] By mid-1937, it seems that the Palace coterie around Faruq had decided to develop a religiously grounded position for the king of Egypt. Certainly the partially religious trappings with which the Palace surrounded Faruq's coronation ceremonies upon his attaining his majority in July 1937 – the wish to have the Rector of al-Azhar gird the king with the sword of Muhammad 'Ali; the idea of Faruq following his official coronation with a religious ceremony; the references to Faruq as "the pious king" and a "renewer" of Islam expressed by Palace supporters at the time – indicate a conscious effort to surround the young and popular monarch with an Islamic aura.[88]

It was only after its victory over the Wafd in late 1937 that the Egyptian Palace openly promoted the idea of King Faruq as Caliph. The central figure in what by 1938 was a definite campaign to obtain the Caliphate for Faruq was Shaykh Maraghi. Maraghi had long taken an active interest in the Caliphate question.[89] By the later 1930s, his thoughts concerning the nature of the institution were quite different from traditional conceptions of the office. As he presented his ideas to interlocutors in 1938, Maraghi's conception was that of several "territorial Caliphates" in which the rulers of individual Muslim states would assume religious authority within their own countries.[90] Superimposed on top of these local caliphates would be a "Supreme Islamic Council," headquartered at Cairo, which would debate issues of mutual concern and formulate common policies for its member states.[91] Rather than envisaging the reestablishment of a single and universal Caliphate, the concept was thus one in which "each Ruler's Caliphate would be specifically confined to his own territorial limits."[92] The domestic implications of Maraghi's caliphal ideas were noted by Sir Miles Lampson: "His idea seems to be that popular support can best be directed from the Wafd to the King by religious attraction. The King of Egypt, as Caliph, would be religiously entitled to the devotion of his Moslem subjects."[93]

With Maraghi playing the central role, various private and public initiatives aimed at promoting King Faruq's claims to the Caliphate were undertaken in 1938-9. Maraghi presented his own ideas about modified "territorial Caliphates" to at least one foreign Muslim leader visiting Egypt, the Agha Khan.[94] Even more ambitious were his private negotiations with an Iraqi Shi'i leader, 'Abd al-Karim al-Zanjani, toward the convening of a general Muslim congress which would discuss Sunni–Shi'i reconciliation.[95] Egyptian religious missions in other Muslim countries also appear to have been involved in the effort to promote an Egyptian caliphate. In 1937, al-Azhar had dispatched groups of *'ulama'* to other Muslim countries

(Kenya; Nigeria; India) to provide religious instruction and to foster a knowledge of Arabic. These missions may also have had a relationship to the caliphal gambit; a report from India commented on Egyptian 'ulama' propagandizing for the selection of regional caliphs in different Muslim countries.[96]

Within Egypt, considerable propaganda favorable to the idea of the Caliphate being reestablished in Egypt came from Palace sources or groups linked to it in 1938 and 1939. Immediately upon the Wafd's ouster from office, Faruq's attendance at Friday prayers at al-Azhar in January 1938 witnessed the students of that institution hailing the king as "Caliph of the Muslims."[97] Through 1938, Shaykh Maraghi spoke publicly of the need to reorient Egyptian society in a more Islamic direction, with Muslim principles being made the animating force behind Egyptian society and its legal system, and referred to the Muslim world as "a single nation."[98] Propaganda favorable to the idea of Faruq as Caliph also came from organized groups linked to the Palace. 'Abd al-Hamid Sa'id of the YMMA wrote of the necessity of the revival of the Caliphate as an anti-imperialist force among Muslim peoples, asserting that Faruq's virtues as well as his known "concern for Islam" gave the Egyptian monarch "an unquestioned right" to the Caliphate.[99] More explicit pro-Caliphate propaganda came from spokesmen of Young Egypt. In June 1938, Ahmad Husayn identified Egypt as the best site for a reestablished Caliphate and Faruq as "the most suitable" candidate for the position.[100] By early 1939 Young Egypt's journal was calling for "Egypt to be the leader of Islam and for Faruq to be its Caliph."[101]

The major public initiatives aimed at testing the caliphal waters on behalf of King Faruq occurred in late 1938–early 1939. At the opening session of the Parliamentary Congress held in Egypt in October 1938 the largely Egyptian crowd, itself drawn in good part from the youth of the YMMA, acclaimed King Faruq with the appellation "Commander of the Faithful [amir al-mu'minim]," a title traditionally used for the Caliph.[102] The second major public event relating to Faruq and the Caliphate occurred in January 1939, on the occasion of the gathering in Cairo of the delegations from the several independent Arab states prior to their proceeding to London to attend the St. James Conference concerning Palestine. When, on January 20, Faruq joined these Arab representatives in Friday prayer, the king himself led those assembled in prayer (a traditional prerogative of the Caliph), and after the prayer was hailed by the Egyptian crowd outside the mosque with cries of "Long Live the Caliph."[103] Both incidents prompted public speculation concerning the possibility of a congress being convened in the future to select a new Caliph.[104]

Yet in the end, the Egyptian Palace's efforts directed toward obtaining the Caliphate for King Faruq were unsuccessful. When the Palace's maneuvers in the direction of the Caliphate met with significant opposition both inside and outside Egypt, the idea was quickly abandoned. Much of the Egyptian political establishment was hostile to the idea of the Caliphate being brought to Egypt. As in the 1920s, the Wafd naturally opposed the concept of its main rival attaining a religious and presumably more powerful stature.[105] When the issue surfaced in a major way early in 1938, Wafdist spokesmen were quick to criticize the revival of the Caliphate question on the combined grounds of its being "a deliberate maneuver to distract the Egyptian people" from more pressing internal political matters and its representing a development which would be "viewed with misgiving by the other Arabic-speaking nations."[106]

The Palace's Caliphate campaign was also coolly received by the leadership of the Liberal and Sa'dist parties in control of the ministry in 1938–9. Prime Minister Muhammad Mahmud and other ministerial figures several times privately expressed their doubts over a development which would weaken not only the Wafd but also the entire parliamentary regime in Egypt.[107] Newspapers associated with the Liberals and Sa'dists argued against the idea of the Caliphate being brought to Egypt. For 'Abd al-Qadir Hamza of *al-Balagh*, the institution of the Caliphate would only be a "heavy burden" which, rather than bringing any advantage to Egypt, would saddle the country with unnecessary international obligations it could ill afford to assume.[108] The Sa'dist spokesman 'Abbas Mahmud al-'Aqqad echoed Hamza's arguments. As he saw the issue, two conditions had to be met for Egypt to assume the Caliphate: first the assent of other Muslim countries, next that of the Caliphate being of utility to Egypt itself. In his view neither condition had been realized; other Muslim governments opposed recent Egyptian initiatives concerning the Caliphate, and his opinion of the usefulness of the office for Egypt itself was that it would only be "a burden added to our responsibilities."[109] Egyptian publicists of a secular inclination were also well aware of the political implications of an Egyptian Caliphate; as Hamza put it in 1939, the restoration of the Caliphate in Egypt could well undermine the parliamentary system and lead to a "religious regime" dominated by the Egyptian Palace.[110]

Probably the most important factor scuttling the Palace's Caliphate campaign was external opposition. From the first rumblings of Palace designs on the Caliphate, British reports commented on the likelihood of opposition from other Muslim countries, in particular from Sa'udi Arabia and Turkey.[111] The Palace-backed maneuvers toward the Caliphate at the Interparliamentary Congress in October 1938 appear not to have drawn protests from abroad, probably in part because no representatives from the Sa'udi or Turkish governments were present.[112] By early 1939, King ibn

Sa'ud's suspicions that Egypt was mounting a campaign to attain the Caliphate for Faruq had had to be assuaged by the Egyptian Minister to Sa'udi Arabia 'Abd al-Rahman 'Azzam's strenuous denials of the whole idea as "fantastic."[113] Both the Turkish and the Sa'udi governments were quick to voice their opposition to Faruq's claims to the Caliphate when his supporters hailed the king as Caliph in the presence of the Arab delegations to the St. James Conference in Cairo in January 1939. The Sa'udi and Yemeni representatives present at the Friday prayers led by Faruq were reported to have been "considerably annoyed" by the incident, into which they felt "their participation had been maneuvered."[114] Despite its absence from this specifically Arab gathering, the Turkish government promptly responded with a formal statement "strongly denouncing any caliphate movement."[115]

This international opposition appears to have been the crucial factor in halting the Palace's caliphal campaign of the late 1930s. Within a few days of the incident of 20 January, the Egyptian embassy in London issued an official disclaimer of any Egyptian ambition to gain the Caliphate for King Faruq: "there was no question whatever of His Majesty as Caliph of the Muslims."[116] Reports reaching the British after the incident claimed 'Ali Mahir now felt the caliphal issue to be "premature" in view of the opposition it had aroused.[117] The notion of King Faruq as Caliph effectively died early in 1939.

It had had little prospect of success from the beginning. In retrospect, the Caliphate gambit of the Egyptian Palace of the later 1930s was an ephemeral episode in the evolution of Egypt's regional relations. Its long-term significance may lie in its failure. By trying but failing to establish an Egyptian claim to regional leadership on a Muslim basis, Faruq's Caliphate campaign of 1938–9 paved the way for Egyptian regional leadership within an Arab framework in the years to come. The abandonment of the idea of King Faruq as Caliph and Egypt as leader of the Muslim world left Arab solidarity and cooperation as the only practical, meaningful Egyptian regional policy from the later 1930s onwards. With its less problematic domestic implications, Arab interaction and cooperation became the only realistic option available to Egyptians who wished to define a more prominent regional role for their country. An Arab orientation, while lacking in the emotional appeal which the Caliphate still possessed for some Egyptians, had the great advantage of being seen as capable of realization. It was thus a policy of Egyptian leadership of the Arab rather than the wider Muslim world which was pursued by both the Wafd and the Palace in the early 1940s, once wartime conditions were such as to allow Egypt to play an aggressive regional role.

Conclusion

A disjuncture is visible in the position of the Egyptian political establishment toward Egyptian participation in regional politics by the later
1930s. As the preceding discussion indicates, Egyptian involvement in
regional political affairs throughout the decade was quite limited in scope.
Save for the abortive attempt of the Palace to promote the caliphal claims of
King Faruq and the more substantial Egyptian involvement in the issue of
Palestine which will be examined in the following chapter, Egyptian politicians and policy-makers by and large avoided committing Egypt to the
extended external role which the new supra-Egyptian movements were
beginning to demand for it. Yet this practical hesitance to involve Egypt in
regional affairs contrasts with a growing rhetorical acceptance of a more
forward regional position on the part of the same individuals. By the closing
years of the interwar period, Egyptian politicians of differing political
inclinations were coming to speak the language of supra-Egyptianism.

It is hardly surprising to find the Wafd playing the Arab card when it was
in the political wilderness in the later 1930s. The most assertive Wafdist
exponent of Egyptian regional leadership at the time was the party's second-
in-command Makram 'Ubayd. In a famous article entitled "Egyptians are
Arabs!" of 1939,[118] the Wafdist leader expanded on his personal belief in
the necessity of Arab solidarity. It was the existential basis of Arab unity to
which he gave greatest emphasis: how "We are Arabs" because of sharing
the same hopes and fears as well as having the same desires for freedom and
progress as Arabs elsewhere, and how "the Arab East is in need of unity in
the face of the torrential European current." It was particularly the latter
which led Makram to call for the creation of "one patriotic league" uniting
all the independent Arab states in the defense of their common interests.

The Wafd's leader Mustafa al-Nahhas was speaking in much the same
terms by the close of the 1930s. In an interview in July 1938, Nahhas
referred to "Arab unity" as "a worthy and good idea," and spoke approv-
ingly of Arab cultural, economic, but also political cooperation as long as
each Arab people retained its independent political status.[119] In an address
to delegates to the Parliamentary Congress in October 1938, the Wafdist
leader lauded his own country as "the protector of Arabs and Arabism."[120]
By January 1939, again in an address to a largely Arab audience, Nahhas
envisaged the emergence of "an Egyptian-Syrian-Palestinian bloc" working
for mutual interests.[121] Thus the Wafd's rhetorical turn toward an Arab
policy clearly antedates its tenure in office in the later years of World War
II, when it took the lead in the creation of the League of Arab States.

Nor were such statements restricted to movements currently in opposition such as the Wafd. Prime Minister Muhammad Mahmud's public

rhetoric concerning Arab political interaction was little different from that of his rival Nahhas by 1938 and 1939. In an interview with a Syrian journalist on the eve of his coming to power, Mahmud floridly proclaimed how "Egypt is Arab, and exults in its Arabism," explicitly dissociating himself from the Pharaonic outlook with which his party had been associated in the past ("Pharaonicism is neither a racial concept [*jinsiyya*] nor a nationalism [*qawmiyya*] in their proper sense").[122] In his speech to the delegates attending the Parliamentary Congress which met in Cairo in October 1938, Mahmud expressed "the closest feelings of friendship" for the Arab and Muslim worlds, cited the common culture and interests which united the peoples of these regions, and concluded by voicing his support for "all efforts at cooperation."[123] Similarly in his reception for Arab delegations meeting in Cairo before proceeding to the St. James Conference in January 1939, the Egyptian prime minister again emphasized Egypt's historical role as leader of the Arab world and expressed both his and King Faruq's desire to "see this [Arab] collaboration strengthened in all matters of mutual concern."[124]

Several factors seem to account for the considerable gap between this rhetorical acceptance of, but practical reserve about, a more supra-Egyptianist regional stance on the part of Egyptian politicians. In part it can be attributed to the gap between rhetoric and praxis which is observable, perhaps even normal, in many political situations. The institutional context in which Egyptian policy-makers formulated their views also played a part. Prime ministers such as Mustafa al-Nahhas or Muhammad Mahmud were operating from the "inside" of the Egyptian state when they were in power. Institutions produce their own imperatives. Beyond the "external" pressures (from their political rivals; from the broader Egyptian public; from the situational constraints both domestic and foreign within which they governed) which undoubtedly influenced their policies, their position at the helm of the ship of state also had a role in defining their practical policies. The bias of state policy is inherently separatist, oriented toward enhancing the autonomy and power of the state itself. In the context of Egyptian foreign policy in the 1930s, this provided a powerful drag on the adoption of policies which would involve the Egyptian state in commitments which might limit its autonomy and freedom of action.

Both the content and the social basis of supra-Egyptianism also help explain the hesitance of Egypt's political leadership in adopting a more activist regional policy. The supra-Egyptianist outlook developed first and with particular force in a cultural rather than a political framework, its adherents placing greatest emphasis on the cultural bonds linking Egyptians to other Muslims and Arabs rather than on their political ties. On the whole, the advocacy of political cooperation lagged behind the promotion of cultural interaction. This served to dilute the force of supra-Egyptianism on Egyptian politics.

Beyond this, although several establishment politicians such as Muhammad 'Ali 'Alluba, 'Abd al-Rahman 'Azzam, or Makram 'Ubayd participated in the new supra-Egyptian discourse of the 1930s, supra-Egyptianist views developed particularly in oppositional circles. Representatives of the Egyptian younger generation or new effendiyya played the leading role in formulating the new perspective. Supra-Egyptianism was a trickle-up phenomenon, an outlook articulated first at the middle levels of society which came to influence the political elite of the older generation, largely as they responded to the demands of new social groups possessing a different vision of Egypt. In brief, Egypt's political leadership came to speak in more supra-Egyptian terms largely because they were under pressure to do so; thus their rhetorical commitment considerably exceeded their practical enthusiasm. The precise extent and nature of that pressure appears most clearly through an examination of growing Egyptian involvement in the one regional issue where the Egyptian government did commit itself in a major way by the later 1930s. That is the question of Palestine.

8 Palestine, public opinion, and Egyptian policy, 1936–1939

The Palestine Arab Revolt of 1936–9 was the crucial catalyst in reorienting Egyptian foreign policy toward active involvement in Arab politics. Yet the Palestine issue should not be regarded as the "cause" of the adoption of a more forward Egyptian regional policy. The basic reasons for the evolution of Egyptian nationalism in a supra-Egyptian direction lie in domestic Egyptian developments, particularly in the emergence of a larger educated public with a more Arab and Muslim outlook and values. The contribution of the Palestine issue was its role in transforming what had hitherto been a primarily cultural orientation on the part of this cohort into a *political* one. The growing identification of many Egyptians with the struggle of the Palestinian Arabs from the later 1930s onwards and their extension of moral support and material assistance to the Palestinians contributed decisively to the politicization of supra-Egyptianism. The Palestine issue became the mobilizing force impelling both Egyptian public opinion and Egyptian governments into involvement in regional politics.

What allowed the Palestine question to play such a central role in Egyptian politics? Several aspects of the conflict in Palestine made it of particular significance to Egyptians. First, it was primarily an anti-imperialist revolt, and indeed was directed against the same imperial power (Great Britain) which had for so long dominated Egypt. Thus it possessed a powerful emotional resonance for many Egyptians. It also had manifest religious dimensions – Muslim against Jew, a perceived threat to a core Muslim region with important Muslim shrines – which made it a central issue for the increasingly assertive Muslim religious organizations of Egypt. At the same time there were features of the question which made it of grave concern to more secular elements in Egyptian public life, specifically the challenges to Egyptian political and economic interests which a new Jewish state in neighboring Palestine might pose to Egypt. Geography played a role; Palestine was Egypt's eastern neighbor, and existing economic and social links between the two areas as well as its obvious strategic significance for Egypt resulted in its fate attracting greater Egyptian attention than was generated by events in more distant Arab or Muslim lands. On the political level, the involvement of the other Arab states in the problem acted as a magnet to draw the government of "big brother" Egypt into similar commitment. For all these reasons, the Palestine question kindled a much greater Egyptian response than did other aspects of regional relations. Indeed, the question of Palestine became a major national issue in Egypt in the later 1930s.

The impact of the Palestinian general strike and revolt of 1936

The main outlines of the Egyptian response to the Palestine issue through the later 1930s were apparent during the first phase of the Arab Revolt, the urban general strike and rural violence of April to October 1936. The accelerating crisis in Palestine became a major concern of the Egyptian press in the spring and summer of 1936, receiving daily, often front-page, coverage by Egypt's major newspapers. Press interpretations of the Arab Revolt were overwhelmingly sympathetic to the Palestinian Arab position. Accounts and pictures of British "atrocities" and Jewish "terror," some inspired by Palestinian Arab materials and others reportedly encouraged by Italian agents,[1] soon drew protests from the Jewish community in Egypt as well as the British Residency and eventually became the object of government warnings against the publication of inflammatory material.[2] Major newspapers associated with Egypt's political parties called for Egyptian assistance to the Palestinian Arabs. The Wafdist al-Jihad repeatedly urged Egyptian financial contributions to the Palestinian Arabs;[3] the Liberal al-Siyasa wrote of aid for the Palestinians as a "patriotic duty" for Egyptians;[4] and the Liberal-leaning al-Balagh called on Egyptians to render "humanitarian aid" to the Arabs of Palestine in their moment of need.[5]

The most committed organizational support for the Palestinian Arab cause on the part of Egyptians in 1936 came from the Young Men's Muslim Association and the Muslim Brotherhood. The situation in Palestine had drawn the attention of the YMMA throughout the 1930s.[6] That attention intensified when the Arab Revolt erupted in 1936. Editorials and articles in support of the Palestinian Arab position were soon followed by mass meetings aimed at gathering popular support for the Palestinian Arabs as well as by fundraising campaigns on their behalf.[7] The YMMA's president 'Abd al-Hamid Sa'id was perhaps the most visible Egyptian champion of the Palestinian Arabs in 1936, writing, speaking, and convening meetings on the issue. His efforts on behalf of the Arab cause did not go unappreciated by the Palestinian Arabs; later in 1936, the Gaza authorities renamed a street in his honor.[8]

The Muslim Brotherhood called for Egyptian support for the Palestinian

Arabs from the inception of the general strike in April 1936.[9] At a public meeting in mid-May, it was decided to make a major effort in support of the general strike in Palestine through public petitions, fundraising, and the formation of local groups working on the issue.[10] A few days later, a manifesto in the Brotherhood's journal by its General Guide Hasan al-Banna called for a boycott of Jewish merchants as an expression of solidarity with the Palestinian Arabs.[11] From May 1936 onwards the central focus of the Brotherhood for the remainder of the year was activity relating to the Palestine question: the formation of national and local committees to propagandize and raise funds on behalf of the Palestinian Arabs; public appeals to the British as well as to prominent Egyptians protesting the course of events in Palestine and calling for action on the issue; the organization of public rallies to express Egyptian sympathy with the Palestinian Arab cause; and repeated fundraising campaigns to collect financial assistance for the Palestinians.[12]

Numerous other groups and organizations in Egypt became involved in the Palestine issue in 1936. Groups based on the Fertile Crescent Arab population resident in Egypt agitated on the issue, engaging both in the sponsorship of protest meetings and in fundraising on behalf of the Palestinian Arab cause.[13] The students of al-Azhar held meetings concerning Palestine; eventually they went on a one-day strike from class as a demonstration of solidarity with the Palestinians.[14] Friday prayer in Egyptian mosques during the first stages of the revolt in mid-1936 led to the dispatch of pro-Palestinian telegrams sent to the British authorities in Egypt.[15] Activism on the Palestine question in 1936 extended to the Egyptian Women's Union which, after receiving requests for support from a Palestinian Arab women's group, appealed to the British for the cessation of Jewish immigration into Palestine and to the Egyptian government for its diplomatic support for the Palestinian Arab cause.[16]

Considerable financial assistance for the Palestinian Arabs was raised in Egypt in mid-1936. Appeals and/or organized fundraising campaigns on behalf of the Palestinian Arabs were undertaken by various bodies in Egypt: Islamic societies like the YMMA, the Muslim Brotherhood, and the Islamic Guidance Society; newspapers and magazines such as *al-Jihad*, *al-Balagh*, and *al-Rabita al-'Arabiyya*; Azharite and other student groups; and the Egyptian Women's Union.[17] The YMMA and the Muslim Brotherhood were the organizations most active in raising funds, with the former undertaking thirteen and the latter fifteen separate fundraising drives during the spring and summer of 1936.[18]

At the end of May, the YMMA took the lead in convening a meeting of the major pro-Palestinian figures and organizations in Egypt in order to coordinate Palestinian relief efforts. The result of the meeting was the establishment of a standing committee, the High Committee for Assisting Palestinian Victims (al-Lajna al-ʿUlya li-Iʿanat Mankubi Filastin), to co-ordinate fundraising efforts on behalf of the Palestinian Arabs. The High Committee's membership – among others, its president ʿAbd al-Hamid Saʿid of the YMMA; Hasan al-Banna of the Brotherhood; Muhammad Husayn Haykal of the Liberals; the former Wafdist Hamid al-Basil – is an indication of the growing salience of the Palestine issue in Egyptian public life.[19] Its activities were not without material results. It reported sending a total of £E 3650 to the Palestinian Arabs between June and November 1936.[20] Even Prime Minister Nahhas is reported to have donated £E 40 for Palestinian relief.[21]

Until 1936, Egyptian governments had avoided becoming officially involved in the Palestine issue. It was only with the general strike and revolt in 1936 that this began to change, as the Wafdist ministry of Mustafa al-Nahhas found itself drawn into both public and private efforts in support of the Palestinian Arabs.

The Palestinian position of the Wafdist ministry developed within both an internal and an external context. By the later 1930s, the Wafd was a different institution from what it had been in its halcyon days in the 1920s. Other political forces were making inroads into social groups which pre-viously had been predominantly Wafdist (the Saʿdists with urban business elements; the Muslim Brotherhood and Young Egypt with students, the middle class, and the new effendiyya population being created by education and urbanization).[22] As these urban-based elements turned away from the Wafd, large landlords came to be represented in greater numbers among its leadership.[23] In the countryside, a British report of 1937 spoke of "a decline in enthusiasm" for the Wafd under way by the later 1930s.[24] Despite its electoral victory in May 1936, the party could not remain immune to the considerable agitation developing within the Egyptian public over Palestine in 1936.

The external context related to Egypt's regional position. Revolt in Palestine soon set off an involved round of diplomatic contacts among the Arab states as each endeavored to shape prospective Arab intervention in the crisis to its own advantage.[25] Thus the Wafdist government, itself involved in the Anglo-Egyptian negotiations which would result in the Treaty of 1936 and with it a greater measure of independence in foreign policy for Egypt, also had an external incentive to involve itself in the Palestine issue.

Public statements by Wafdist leaders concerning the situation in the Mandate during the general strike were sympathetic to the Arab position. In June, Prime Minister Nahhas spoke at a public meeting on Palestine and declared himself in favor of a temporary cessation of Jewish immigration as a way to end the general strike.[26] In July, the Wafdist president of the Egyptian Senate, Mahmud Basyuni, publicly called on the British to change their policy and to meet Palestinian Arab demands.[27] The most official public statements from the Egyptian government on the Palestine issue in 1936 were parallel resolutions unanimously adopted by the Egyptian Chamber of Deputies and Senate on 20 and 27 July respectively, voicing their "sympathy with the Palestinian nation, which is sacrificing its sons for freedom and honour," and which expressed the hope that "this crisis will be resolved in accordance with principles of justice and fairness."[28]

In actuality, the crisis in Palestine placed the Wafdist ministry in a difficult position. On the one hand, as the authority responsible for the maintenance of law and order in Egypt and as a government then involved in diplomatic negotiations with Great Britain, the ministry took action to keep public manifestations of concern over Palestine within manageable limits. Nahhas responded promptly to the British complaints about mendacious press coverage of the unrest in Palestine, personally warning the editors of some of the offending journals to temper their treatment of the situation in the Mandate.[29] He was also reported to have issued instructions to Egyptian mosque officials not to comment on Palestinian affairs, and to have prohibited public meetings in support of the Palestinian Arab cause.[30] As Sir Miles Lampson summarized Egyptian efforts, "there is no doubt that the Egyptian authorities ... have definitely tried – and with considerable success – to control manifestations of Egyptian feeling against British policy in Palestine."[31]

Actions aimed at restricting the expression of pro-Arab sentiment in Egypt did not go unnoticed by the opponents of the Wafd and the supporters of the Palestinian Arabs. The ministry's efforts to muzzle the press brought complaints of censorship from the Liberal opposition in parliament.[32] The general tenor of public criticism of the Egyptian government's policy in regard to the Palestine conflict in 1936 came down heavily against the perceived inaction of the Wafdist ministry: as Ibrahim 'Abd al-Qadir al-Mazini put it, government officials "talk" about Palestine, yet "the government of Egypt is not participating in any other way [than talk] to stop the bloodshed and to achieve justice."[33] Implicit in this type of commentary was a new and an important notion: that the government of Egypt should become directly involved in the Palestine imbroglio.

This is precisely what the Wafdist ministry was doing. At four separate meetings with British representatives in June 1936, Nahhas approached the British in regard to their policies in Palestine. Speaking at length on the situation in the Mandate and its potential repercussions in Egypt, the substance of his remarks consisted of several interrelated points: admonitions that the unrest in Palestine was due to solid Arab grievances; recommendations that the British temporarily suspend Jewish immigration in order to ease the tension; warnings that his own government was sitting on an "oven" because of the situation in Palestine, with violent agitation and anti-Jewish violence inside Egypt being distinct possibilities; and pointed reminders to the British that "we [Egyptians] also are Arabs" and thus should not be expected to remain aloof from the problem.[34]

With the conclusion of the Anglo-Egyptian Treaty of Alliance in August 1936, Nahhas approached the British with offers to serve as a mediator between them and the Palestinian Arabs.[35] The crux of his position was that, in exchange for a confidential commitment from the British for a suspension of Jewish immigration, the Egyptian government would make "every effort" to convince the Palestinian Arab leadership to terminate the strike and stop the revolt in Palestine.[36] When the prospect of multilateral intervention by the Arab states in the crisis was broached to Nahhas, his response was to emphasize the need for Egyptian primacy in any joint mediation: "his own intervention with the Mufti, combined with [the] declaration of [the] Arab rulers, would certainly restore order immediately for he (Nahas) is regarded as 'the chief Arab leader.'"[37] Ultimately, however, Nahhas rejected Egyptian participation in a multilateral effort at mediation. As he explained his position to a British diplomat,

He feels it will be better in the circumstances for the King of Egypt not to join in declaration to Arab rulers. This will leave Egypt as a card to be played later in case that declaration proves fruitless. Meanwhile Nahas will be ready to intervene personally at any time and in any manner that may seem best to His Majesty's Government. His one wish, as our ally and a friend of the Arabs, is for order to be re-established at the earliest possible moment.[38]

Nahhas's words and actions concerning Palestine in 1936 carry a double-edged message. "The chief Arab leader"; "Egypt as a card to be played later"; "intervene personally . . . as a friend of the Arabs": certainly the tone of his conversations with the British indicates a considerable Egyptian sense of separateness from, and superiority to, the other Arab states in regard to the issue of Palestine. On the other hand, his repeated personal intervention in the issue far exceeded what had been undertaken by previous Egyptian premiers.

The popular Egyptian attitude toward the Palestine issue in particular and the Arab world in general was undergoing significant change by 1936. British reports from Egypt by the fall of that year, as the first phase of the Arab Revolt approached its end, comment on the appreciable shift in outlook occurring in Egypt. In August Sir Miles Lampson, while commenting that the Pan-Arab movement had "very little real strength in Egypt," nonetheless asserted that "a considerable amount of feeling was aroused against what was regarded as a gross injustice being done to the Arabs of Palestine by Great Britain," and estimated that "there can be no doubt that all educated and uneducated opinion in Egypt is convinced that Great Britain is committing a cruel injustice to a neighbouring Moslem country."[39] A month later Sir David Kelly began a report by commenting on the "superficial" nature of Egypt's past involvement with other Arab countries; but he then went on to emphasize that "there are definite signs of a changing outlook in this respect" and to speculate that, had it not been for the preoccupation of the Egyptian public with the treaty negotiations of 1936, disturbances similar to the large-scale demonstrations of late 1935 might have developed over the Palestine question in Egypt.[40]

The Peel Commission and the partition of Palestine, 1937

The general strike in Palestine ended in October 1936, after a public appeal from the governments of Iraq, Transjordan, and Sa'udi Arabia; rural violence subsided through the fall of 1936. In the latter months of 1936 and the first half of 1937, center stage in the Palestine issue was held by the Royal Commission headed by Lord Peel. With a temporary lull in the tension in Palestine while the Royal Commission deliberated, both public and private Egyptian manifestations of concern with the issue also diminished. It was in July 1937, with the release of the final report of the Royal Commission, with its Gordian recommendation for the partition of Palestine between Arab and Jew, that Palestine again became a major subject of concern in Egypt.

The Peel Report received massive attention in Egypt in mid-1937. As Sir Miles Lampson summarized Egyptian public opinion two weeks after the release of the report, "there is universal public condemnation of the idea of partition."[41] The outside Arab community resident in Egypt reacted vehemently, with Arab organizations in Egypt frequently protesting the Peel proposals.[42] Protests against the partition of Palestine came from various Egyptian organizations as well – the Egyptian Women's Union; the Association for the Revival of the Arab Tribes – as well as from *ad hoc* groupings such as the "merchants of Bab al-Lugh."[43] Student and youth groups were vocal on the issue. Statements denouncing the report were issued by such organizations as the youth group of the Watani Party or the association of secondary school students, while the students of both al-Azhar and the Egyptian University held meetings to protest the report.[44] Positive public commentary on the Peel Report in Egypt in July 1937 appears to have been limited to representatives of the Zionist movement and portions of the European-language press.[45]

Egyptian rejection of the partition of Palestine was based on various grounds. The opinions expressed in a poll of prominent Egyptians by the journal *al-Rabita al-'Arabiyya* and in several articles on the subject in the journal *al-Risala* together give a good indication of the range of views being expressed on the Palestine question in mid-1937. Basic to the position of many commentators was the view that the partition of Palestine between Arabs and Jews was unjust; that "Palestine is Arab" and that "another people" had "no right" to it,[46] or that partition was a "gross aggression" against the "national and historical rights" of the Palestinian Arabs.[47] Religious arguments were crucial to some; 'Ali Shawqi held that "partition would mean the loss of Palestine and the loss of the Holy Places," while 'Abd al-Hamid Sa'id proclaimed that it was "the duty of every Muslim to defend Palestine."[48] More secular arguments appeared as well, as commentators noted the strategic implications of the creation of a Jewish state in Palestine; that hostility between the Jewish state and its Arab neighbors would be a source of constant tension in the area,[49] and that this regional unrest would in turn generate repeated foreign intervention in the Middle East.[50] A variant of this position was the idea that a Jewish state in Palestine would be an obstacle to Egypt's improving her relationship with the Arab world, portending "the end of all Egypt's hopes of leading the Arab lands culturally and economically, for the Jewish state would be a barrier between her and those lands."[51] The Jewish state as an economic threat to Egypt was developed by others, including the warning that a Jewish state would seek to make the Arab East its "economic colony."[52]

Some Egyptians saw social or cultural turmoil resulting from the partition of Palestine: that a Jewish state was a "social danger" because of the Western character of its population;[53] that the Jewish immigrants to Palestine were "Bolsheviks";[54] that they carried "a revolutionary, destructive spirit" which would infect the Arab world.[55] Several commentators raised the spectre of expansionism on the part of a Jewish state. Within Palestine itself, the pressure of Jewish immigration would compel it to expand into its poorer and weaker Arab neighbor, until the latter too would become Jewish and its Arab population would be ousted from their lands.[56] The same threat was seen by one commentator as extending beyond Palestine as well; in his view the ultimate goal of Zionism was "the creation of a Jewish state stretching from the Nile to the Euphrates."[57]

Both of the major Wafdist dailies, *al-Misri* and *al-Jihad*, expounded at length on the adverse implications of the Peel Report. *Al-Misri*'s commentary repeatedly emphasized that "the Palestine question does not concern its people alone, but concerns the Arabs collectively,"[58] and noted "the necessity of the participation of all the Arab peoples in working to aid Palestine."[59] *Al-Jihad*'s editor Muhammad Tawfiq al-Diyab also stressed that "the Palestine question is not a local one, but is a general Arab Islamic question,"[60] developing the theme of an expansionist Zionism which threatened to "spread into all the Arab lands" in order to accommodate continued Jewish immigration.[61] Beyond this danger to the region as a whole, Diyab also saw specific Egyptian interests which would be placed in jeopardy by partition. Politically, a Jewish state in Palestine would be a "barrier" between Egypt and the other Arab lands with whom Egypt was now trying to strengthen her relations; a Jewish state also represented a possible future threat to Egypt's national security. Diyab also argued that a Jewish state in Palestine would be a rival to Egypt economically, hindering the expansion of Egyptian commerce into regional markets.[62]

Similar opinions about the partition of Palestine and its potential implications for Egypt were expressed by the Wafd's rivals in the Liberal Party. To the veteran Liberal leader Muhammad Husayn Haykal, Egyptians needed to concern themselves with the situation in Palestine not only because of their historical ties with the Arab East, but also because of "an exclusively Egyptian national consideration":

This new situation [of partition] is far-reaching in its influence for the future of Egypt and its people, this future which is firmly linked to the destinies of the lands which neighbor us and are influenced by us as we are influenced by them – in the security of our country, in the sale of our products, in the shaping of our international relations, in the organization of our self-defense, and in the definition of our policy in the Mediterranean.[63]

Haykal's associate on *al-Siyasa*, Hafiz Mahmud, went further, arguing that a Zionist state in Palestine would be inherently expansionist due to the imperatives of accommodating new immigration, and warning that some day its people could "direct their Zionism toward Egypt" on the basis of Egypt having been a place of Jewish residence in the past.[64] Like Haykal, Mahmud therefore urged his readers that it was necessary for Egyptians to regard Palestine "as an Egyptian Arab cause" and to work to "save Palestine" from the threat of partition.

The political movements based on the new effendiyya population of Egypt were even more vehement in denouncing the Peel Report and calling for Egyptian support of the Palestinian Arabs. The Young Men's Muslim Association officially called for "an Islamic covenant [*mithaq Islami*]" or "an Arab Islamic covenant [*mithaq Islami 'Arabi*]" in which all Arabs and Muslims would pledge themselves to the defense of Palestine.[65] An editorial in the Muslim Brotherhood's journal in July called for Muslim and Arab support of the Arabs of Palestine on both the nationalist basis that "Palestine is an indivisible part of the general Arab *watan*" and the religious necessity to protect "the rights of the Muslims in the Holy Land."[66] Young Egypt's position was that Zionism was a British instrument for the division of the Arabs, "a British thorn stuck in the side of the Arab lands."[67] For Young Egypt, it was the implications of the Palestine question for Egypt which mattered most: "The impact of what is happening today in Palestine is not limited to Palestine alone. Rather, it is directed against Egypt, against the Arab lands, and against their unity in general. We cannot stand with our hands tied in the face of the creation of a Jewish state on the borders of our land which threatens our future."[68]

Egyptian opposition to the Peel Report was not confined to verbal criticism. A new Committee for the Defense of Palestine (Lajnat al-Difa' 'an Filastin) was formed under YMMA initiative as early as 10 July 1937 as an umbrella organization for coordinating efforts for assisting the Palestinian Arabs.[69] As had been the case during the general strike in 1936, assemblies concerning the issue were sponsored by religious and student groups in the latter months of 1937; perhaps the most notable of these occurred on 2 November 1937, when both the YMMA and the Muslim Brotherhood held mass meetings protesting the Balfour Declaration on the twentieth anniversary of its issuance.[70] A significant feature of Egyptian concern with the Palestine question in the latter half of 1937 was marches and demonstrations on the issue at al-Azhar, at the Egyptian University, and in some provincial towns (Mit Ghamr; Tanta; al-Mansura; Jirga); one of the former led to a march on the Palace, clashes with the police, and arrests.[71]

The furore over the Peel Report had almost immediate repercussions for Egyptian political life. Within a few days of the report's release the Liberal leader Muhammad Mahmud dispatched a message of support to Hajj Amin al-Husayni. Speaking in the name of his party, Mahmud rejected the recommendations of the report and asserted the solidarity of Egyptians with the Palestinian Arabs in the struggle of the latter for "their sacred rights."[72] Similar messages of support to the Palestinian leader were sent by spokesmen for the YMMA, the Muslim Brotherhood, Young Egypt, and the Egyptian Women's Union.[73] Soon petitions opposing the Peel Report, in addition to being addressed to the Palestinian Arab leadership or the British, were being directed to the Egyptian government, calling on it to take action on behalf of the Palestinian Arab cause.[74] Opposition parties soon began to use the issue of Palestine as a club with which to beat the ministry, indicting it for its apparent inaction on the matter.[75]

Faced with this public pressure, the Wafdist ministry of Mustafa al-Nahhas did involve itself in the issue. On 20 July Nahhas responded to parliamentary criticism of his ministry's apparent passivity on Palestine, for the first time revealing that the Egyptian government had been discussing the crisis in Palestine with the British since the general strike of 1936 and declaring that his ministry intended to continue devoting its attention to "the defense of the rights and interests of the Arabs of Palestine."[76] The text of his statement was sent to Hajj Amin al-Husayni in Palestine, accompanied by a telegram in which Nahhas assured the Mufti of "the amount of interest I take in maintaining the rights of Arabs and their interests in Palestine."[77]

Nahhas carried through on these statements of intent. The prime minister's substantive view of the Peel Report was expressed to Lampson on 24 July. Speaking "with great seriousness," Nahhas told the ambassador that "he could not too strongly deplore [the] suggestion of partition. To start with, Egypt could not regard with equanimity [the] prospect of an independent Jewish State as her neighbour. Apart from questions of defence, etc., who could say the voracious Jews would not claim Sinai next? Or provoke trouble with [the] Jewish community in Egypt itself?"[78] Suggesting that the only acceptable solution in Palestine was a unitary independent state with mutual tolerance and normal immigration policies for all, Nahhas concluded his presentation by protesting against the Arab population of Palestine being "plucked up by the roots to make way for strangers in their native land." Nahhas's intervention of 24 July is interesting both for its definite sense of Egyptian security, both external and internal, being threatened by the emergence of a Jewish state in Palestine, and for its equally strong sense of the injustice of the Palestinian Arabs being displaced on behalf of "strangers." In this confidential presentation of July 1937, Nahhas expressed many of the same apprehensions concerning the partition of Palestine as were being voiced by Egyptian commentators in the public arena.

But Nahhas's willingness to involve Egypt in the Palestine issue did not yet extend to collaboration with other Arabs. When the organizers of the inter-Arab conference on Palestine which met in Bludan, Syria, in September 1937 solicited official Egyptian participation, Nahhas declined, informing his petitioners that "he preferred to work independently and in his own way towards a solution to the Palestine problem."[79] The six Egyptians in attendance at Bludan went as private individuals. Most prominent among them were Muhammad 'Ali 'Alluba and 'Abd al-Hamid Sa'id. 'Alluba's address to the gathering defined Zionism as "a cancer in the body of our Arab nation," asserted that "the existence of a Jewish nation in Palestine threatens Egyptian existence in particular just as it threatens the existence of the Arabs as a whole," and rhetorically committed "Egypt, government and people, to the defense of Palestine."[80] 'Alluba was selected as one of the two vice-presidents of the conference; Sa'id served as the chairman of its Political Committee.[81] The impact of the Bludan conference on the Palestine question in general and Egypt's involvement in it in particular is problematic; the British evaluation was that it had made "little impression" on the Egyptian public.[82]

The most definitive statement of the Egyptian government's position on the Palestine question in 1937 came at the annual meeting of the Assembly of the League of Nations in September. Foreign Minister Wasif Butrus Ghali's speech of 18 September argued forcefully against the partition of Palestine on the grounds of "right and justice," both of which demanded that "Palestine remain for the Palestinians" and that the dispute be resolved within the framework of a unitary Palestinian state.[83] Within Egypt, Ghali's statements before the League appear to have had a favorable impact; by publicly opposing British policy in Palestine, the Wafdist ministry had demonstrated Egypt's "real independence" and thereby "gained considerable credit" for itself.[84]

From September 1937 onwards, official Egyptian involvement in the Palestine issue slackened. The only official Egyptian initiative on the Palestine question in the last three months of 1937 came from the Egyptian parliament, when in November fifty-eight parliamentarians (fifty-five deputies and three senators) drafted a petition to the British Embassy expressing how "the Egyptian nation is tied to the Palestinian Arab people by many firm bonds of language, blood, religion, traditions, and geographical propinquity," and protesting both partition and British repression in Palestine.[85] This diminution of Palestine-related activity was undoubtedly connected to the internal political crisis which developed within Egypt in the latter months of 1937, and which by the end of the year had resulted in the ouster of the Wafdist ministry from power.

Why did the Egyptian government intervene in the Palestine question in 1937? Part of the answer is to be found in the opportunity for international prestige which successful intervention in the issue would bring to Egypt. Both the Palestinians and other Arabs were looking to Egypt for assistance in reversing the recommendation for partition in 1937; if Egypt on its own could achieve this result, it would confirm its position of predominance in regional affairs.[86]

Of equal or greater importance was the domestic agitation occurring in Egypt over Palestine. Concern over the issue of Palestine was being expressed by much of the Egyptian public, and was particularly intense on the part of the Egyptian younger generation and the new effendiyya population of Egypt. Both through the formation of alternative political organizations and through public protest, these elements were manifesting a considerable degree of alienation from the existing order – the Wafd included – by the later 1930s. Now faced with a powerful rival in the young king as well as with a declining appeal to the newer elements which were entering Egyptian public life, the ministry could not afford to ignore popular concern over Palestine.

Certainly Nahhas was telling the British that he was under growing public pressure and constraint in regard to Palestine. In negative terms, he told

Lampson that "he cannot say one word which might be read as implying he approves recommendation of [the] Royal Commission."[87] As Sir David Kelly evaluated Nahhas's situation by September 1937, "it was difficult for him, in the face of Arab opinion generally and his own position in internal Egyptian politics, to refuse from active intervention on behalf of his fellow Moslems."[88] A contemporary observer in contact with Nahhas in 1937 accurately captured the reactive aspect of the Palestine policy of the Nahhas ministry:

> You may say if you wish (though I think it untrue) that Egyptian politicians do not really care what happens in Palestine, that they raise the question only for demagogic reasons in order to deflect popular attention from the crying need for internal reforms ... But does not the very fact that the cabinet feels obliged to defend the Arab case indicate that there must be many Egyptians who do have a lively interest in Arab nationalism? There is no use dragging a red herring across the path unless the cat likes herrings.[89]

Another dimension of that involvement was the fact that the partition of Palestine into Arab and Jewish states would have created a new regional situation, and new situations demand new policies. To a considerable degree, Nahhas shared the emerging conventional wisdom concerning the gravity of the implications of the partition of Palestine for Egypt itself. There is no reason to question the sincerity of Nahhas's presentation to Lampson of July 24 (made, in Lampson's words, "with great seriousness") about the potentially adverse implications of partition.[90] As he told Kelly later, "far from wishing to make trouble he was most anxious to intervene in dual role as friend and ally of His Majesty's Government *yet deeply interested in Arab cause.*"[91] Kelly did not question the genuineness of this concern; in his opinion, "there is little doubt that he [Nahhas] feels strongly on the subject. If his time were not completely taken up with his anxieties as P.M. he would gladly play a role as leader of Arab opinion."[92]

The Muhammad Mahmud ministries and Palestine, 1938–1939

By the last years of the 1930s, the Palestine question had become a matter of wide and deep concern in Egypt. British reports offer frequent testimony to the extent of Egyptian public concern with the Palestine issue in 1938 and 1939. In May 1938, Sir Miles Lampson's evaluation was that "every Egyptian is pro-Arab" and that all of the Arabic press in Egypt was "criticizing our Palestine policy."[93] His opinion in October was that "there is not a soul, however friendly to us, that is not against our policy," and that "anti-British agitation" over the subject was "assuming serious proportions";[94] in November, he was reporting on "the universal sympathy in Egypt for the Palestinian Arabs";[95] and a report of January 1939 asserted that "practically all Egyptians sympathize with the Arabs in their struggle."[96]

The most prominent place in Egyptian activism relating to Palestine in 1938 and 1939 was again occupied by the Young Men's Muslim Association and the Muslim Brotherhood. The president of the YMMA, 'Abd al-Hamid Sa'id, issued numerous public manifestoes protesting against British repression and "atrocities" in Palestine on the one hand and summoning Arabs and Muslims everywhere to do their "sacred duty" in support of the Palestinian Arabs on the other.[97] The YMMA's headquarters in Cairo served as a clearing-house for pro-Palestinian propaganda in Egypt, being the seat of fundraising committees as well as the scene of mass meetings concerning Palestine.[98] In the complex of pro-Palestinian publicity, protests, and fundraising activities occurring in Egypt in 1938 and 1939, the YMMA was at the center.

The Palestinian Arab cause was a central concern of the Muslim Brotherhood in 1938 and 1939. The Brotherhood undertook many of the same activities as the YMMA; protests to the British concerning their "atrocities" in Palestine, appeals to the Egyptian government to involve itself in defense of the Palestinian Arab cause, mass meetings to demonstrate Egyptian solidarity with the Palestinian Arabs.[99] But the involvement of the Muslim Brotherhood in the issue was more intense, and penetrated deeper into the fabric of Egyptian society, than that of the YMMA. As had been the case in 1936, Brotherhood activism reached out into the provincial cities of Egypt. This was particularly the case in mid-1938, when mass meetings and demonstrations organized by the Brotherhood occurred in such towns as Suez, Isma'iliyya, Zifta, Bani Suwayf, Mit Ghamr, Manfalut, and al-Manzila as well as in Cairo and Alexandria.[100] In May 1938, a meeting at the Cairo headquarters of the society boiled over into a violent march through central Cairo and the arrest of thirty-four participants, and several of the Brotherhood-sponsored demonstrations concerning Palestine in the summer of 1938 resulted in clashes with the police and the arrest of demonstrators.[101] The Muslim Brotherhood's Palestine-related activism had a great deal to do with its phenomenal growth in the later 1930s; in early 1939 the Egyptian Ministry of the Interior was reporting that the organization "provides the most strenuous agitators" against British policy in Palestine and that it was "gaining influence" in Egypt through its efforts on the issue.[102]

Palestine was an issue of major concern to Egyptian students by 1938–9. Special assemblies concerning Palestine were held at al-Azhar in April, May, and August 1938 as well as in March and May 1939.[103] The first of these resulted in a march through the city to the Ministry of the Interior and a confrontation with the prime minister.[104] A similar Azharite demonstration in the following month led to another march and the arrest of nineteen demonstrators.[105] A one-day student assembly and suspension of classes occurred at the Egyptian University in November 1938; it resulted in the passage of anti-Zionist resolutions and the creation of a student fundraising committee.[106] By November 1938, Lampson was referring to the Egyptian University as "a centre of this anti-British movement [focused on Palestine], in which students of all parties are taking part."[107] At the peak of Egyptian concern with the Palestine question in late 1938, meetings and demonstrations concerning the subject were held at Dar al-'Ulum, vocational, and secondary schools as well.[108]

Quite diverse segments of the Egyptian public involved themselves in the Palestine issue in 1938–9. In January 1939, the Arab doctors' conference made the situation in Palestine a major subject of discussion at its annual meeting.[109] An organization which undertook a major initiative relating to Palestine by 1938–9 was the Egyptian Women's Union headed by Huda Sha'rawi. The Women's Union initiated and hosted a "Conference of Eastern Women for the Defense of Palestine" in October 1938. Delegations of women from Palestine, Syria, Lebanon, Iraq, and Iran as well as Egypt participated in the meeting. The final resolutions of the Conference called for the annulment of the Balfour Declaration, the cessation of Jewish immigration to Palestine, a rejection of partition in any form, support for the establishment of a sovereign Palestinian state, and a summons to both the publics and the governments throughout the Arab and Muslim worlds to assist the Palestinian Arabs in their realization of their national rights.[110] The Women's Union continued its Palestine-related activities into 1939, with Huda Sha'rawi sending protests to the British and with meetings and fundraising efforts being undertaken by the organization itself.[111]

Young Egypt had not played a major role in Egyptian agitation on the Palestine issue in 1936–7. Only in 1938 and 1939 did the organization choose to make Palestine a major item on its agenda. It participated in organizing the protests at the Egyptian University in late 1938, and by mid-1939 was devoting much of its activity to a combination of vitriolic attacks on Zionism and Jews as well as the sponsoring of a boycott of Jewish merchants within Egypt.[112] The timing of this pro-Palestinian activism is important. Young Egypt became vitally involved in the Palestine issue only after broad concern with the problem had developed among the Egyptian public. It took up the cause of Palestine at the same time as its main rival the Muslim Brotherhood was rapidly growing, in part because of its prominence in championing the Palestinian Arab cause; Young Egypt's emphasis on Palestine also coincided with a shift in its public orientation in a more Islamic direction.[113] Thus it appears that Young Egypt's Palestine-related activism of 1938–9 was prompted in large measure because the question of Palestine had become an important issue to those segments of the Egyptian public – students; youth; the new effendiyya population in general – to whom it wished to appeal.

The growing importance of the Palestine issue in Egyptian public life is also attested by the activities of the Wafd when in opposition in 1938–9. The Wafdist press repeatedly emphasized the past efforts of the previous Wafdist ministry concerning Palestine, contrasting these with what it presented as the insufficient and ineffective methods of the present government.[114] In his address to a Wafdist party conference in July 1938 Nahhas similarly defended the record of his own ministries on the issue, belittled that of the incumbent ministry, and declared his and his party's commitment to the defense of Arab Palestine.[115] The same conference inaugurated a Wafdist fundraising drive on behalf of the Palestinians.[116] In a private conversation with a British official in the same month Nahhas declared the Wafd's intention to "take the lead against British policy in Palestine" in the future; he went on to protest against Great Britain allowing "Jews to thrust Arabs off their native soil" and to warn that British policy in Palestine would only "unite the Arab world against her."[117]

By the fall of 1938, information reaching the British indicated that the Wafd was financially supporting Muslim Brotherhood activism on Palestine, and that it was behind agitation on the issue at the Egyptian University.[118] In his public address on 13 November 1938 commemorating the Revolution of 1919, Nahhas called for the cessation of Jewish immigration to Palestine and the creation of an independent Palestinian state.[119] When exiled Palestinian Arab leaders passed through Cairo on their way to the St. James Conference in January 1939, the Wafd held a reception in their honor. Both Nahhas and Makram 'Ubayd spoke, the former comparing the Palestinian exiles to Sa'd Zaghlul during the Revolution of 1919 and pledging that Egypt, "its people and its Wafd, will work for the good, glory, and benefit of sisterly Palestine," the latter extolling the brotherhood existing between Palestine and Egypt.[120]

The Wafd was not the only Egyptian organization to undertake fundraising activities on behalf of the Palestinian Arabs in 1938–9. A variety of organizations and institutions in Egypt – Muslim religious societies; Arabist journals; the Egyptian Women's Union; student groups – also mounted fundraising campaigns.[121] The High Committee for Assisting Palestinian Victims reportedly raised a total of £E 7675 on behalf of the Palestinian Arabs between its inception in May 1936 and early 1939.[122] Information reaching the British indicated that approximately £E 3000 had been sent to the Palestinian Arabs as of October 1938.[123]

Egyptian material assistance to the Palestinian Arabs may not have been limited to financial aid. From late 1938, the Muslim Brotherhood issued public appeals for volunteers to join the Palestinians in their *jihad* against the British.[124] The same may have been done by Young Egypt in 1939.[125] In addition to fundraising, the High Committee for Assisting Palestinian Victims by 1939 had created a "committee for volunteers" and was calling on Egyptian youth to volunteer to go to Palestine.[126]

Another form of assistance was the pressure exerted by Egyptian organizations upon the Egyptian government to involve itself directly in the Palestine question. Many of the frequent public declarations by Egyptian organizations on Palestine in 1938–9 were addressed to the Egyptian government, expressing the concern of these groups with the situation in Palestine and calling directly upon the authorities to intervene on behalf of the Palestinian Arab cause.[127] Opposition deputies in the Chamber of Deputies and the Senate raised the Palestine issue in parliament several times in the spring of 1938.[128]

As had been the case with its Wafdist predecessor, the Muhammad Mahmud ministries responded to the pressures being placed upon them in several ways. Ministers in the coalition ministry spoke out publicly in support of the Palestinian Arabs.[129] Despite British objections over the nature of Egyptian press coverage of the situation in Palestine, through early 1938 the government generally gave the Egyptian press a free hand to speak out against British policy in the Mandate. At the same time, the ministry also attempted to restrain the more inflammatory aspects of popular agitation over Palestine. In the spring of 1938, Prime Minister Mahmud is reported to have told a delegation of Azharite students which visited him to present their views on the Palestine issue that "he wished to have no demonstrations and that they should refrain from mixing themselves up in Palestinian business."[130] By the later months of 1938 government efforts to damp down pro-Palestinian activism within Egypt included warnings to the editors of major journals to restrain their criticism of British policy in Palestine, the occasional confiscation of materials which it regarded as inflammatory, and (at least according to its critics) the muting of Egyptian state radio coverage of the revolt in Palestine.[131]

In conjunction with warning of the popular pressure building up within Egypt over the Palestine question in 1938, Prime Minister Mahmud also appealed to the British to do something to alleviate this potentially dangerous situation. In May he asked Lampson to call on his government to "do something to remove this cause of Moslem discontent" before it led to serious problems in Egypt itself.[132] When in London in July, he again advised the British of the need for them to "do something which might effect improvement in the present anxious situation."[133] In a subsequent meeting with Colonial Secretary Malcolm MacDonald, Mahmud warned the British that "if we adopted the policy of partition we should never have peace" and called upon them to arrange a general Arab–Jewish conference in order to reach a mutually-acceptable "agreed settlement" to the Palestine crisis.[134] This effort at direct mediation by Mahmud marks the beginning of a new phase in the involvement of the Egyptian government in the Palestine issue, one in which its own actions increasingly demonstrated a greater willingness for Egypt to play an official role in the resolution of the situation in Palestine.

A more active Palestine policy by the Mahmud ministry developed in conjunction with a major non-ministerial Egyptian initiative concerning the Palestine question: the "World Parliamentary Congress of Arab and Muslim Countries for the Defense of Palestine" of October 1938. In May 1938 a meeting of several Egyptian parliamentarians resulted in a decision to organize an international assembly of Arab and Muslim parliamentarians to take action in support of the Palestinian Arab cause.[135] An Executive Committee headed by Muhammad 'Ali 'Alluba worked through the summer in organizing the gathering. Invitations to both foreign and Egyptian parliamentarians to attend a conference in Cairo in October were sent out in August.[136]

The World Parliamentary Congress met in Cairo between 7 and 11 October 1938. Some 130 delegates from eleven Arab or Muslim countries attended.[137] Despite the attendance of numerous Egyptian parliamentarians and the presidents of the Iraqi and Syrian Chambers of Deputies, the assembly was an unofficial one at which governments were unrepresented. The Egyptian delegation was led by the ex-Wafdist Muhammad Bahiy al-Din Barakat, Speaker of the Chamber of Deputies, and came overwhelmingly from the Liberal and Sa'dist parties then cooperating in the coalition ministry. The non-Wafdist parliamentarians organizing the meeting had not invited the few Wafdist deputies in parliament to attend.[138] Much of the manpower which served as ushers and a large part of the crowd which attended its first session came from the supporters of the YMMA and the Muslim Brotherhood.[139] The Congress resolutions adopted on 11 October proclaimed the Balfour Declaration null and void, called for the cessation of Jewish immigration into Palestine, rejected the partition of the Mandate, and demanded the establishment of a "patriotic constitutional government" for the country.[140]

The organization of the Congress demonstrates the central place which Egyptians were coming to occupy in collaborative Arab efforts concerning the Palestine question. Congress sessions were chaired by Bahiy al-Din Barakat of Egypt. The five-person Executive Committee of the Congress had three Egyptian members (Muhammad 'Ali 'Alluba, Hamid al-Basil, and 'Abd al-Hamid Sa'id) and an Egyptian president ('Alluba). The Permanent Committee selected at the close of the Congress had four Egyptians (the above three and Tawfiq Dus) among its eleven members.[141]

The Parliamentary Congress was received with widespread approval in Egypt.[142] The Wafd's *al-Misri* took pains to assure the delegates to the assembly that Wafdist non-participation in the event was not due to a lack of dedication to the Palestine cause, on the contrary asserting that "the Wafd was the first in Egypt to sympathize with it [Palestine] and to work for the desires of its people."[143] Nahhas himself arranged a reception for the foreign delegates to the Congress; donning the Palestinian *kaffiyya*, he declared his and his party's devotion to "the most worthy cause in recent Arab and Muslim history."[144]

The reception accorded the Congress in Egyptian official circles was more ambivalent. King Faruq, Prime Minister Mahmud, and the Rector of al-Azhar, Shaykh Maraghi, all hosted receptions for the delegates to the Congress. Reviewing Egypt's historic position as a leader of "the East" and his own government's past activities on behalf of Palestine, Prime Minister Mahmud's welcoming address pledged his government's continued efforts to the further consolidation of friendly relations between Egypt and other Arab and Muslim states.[145] Maraghi's speech similarly asserted Egypt's Arab and Muslim character and expressed the need for continued Arab-Muslim cooperation concerning Palestine.[146]

But the official Egyptian position to the Congress was less than wholly supportive. Prime Minister Mahmud viewed the Congress as a diversion cutting across his own efforts at promoting a governmental conference on Palestine; he also saw it as a manifestation of the "increasingly religious aspect" being taken by agitation over Palestine.[147] Despite these reservations, however, he felt himself unable to obstruct the Congress in view of the state of Egyptian public opinion concerning Palestine.[148] The prime minister worked behind the scenes to temper the proceedings of the Parliamentary Congress. He informed the British that he had spoken privately to the event's organizers and warned them to keep the proceedings in a moderate vein.[149] Similar efforts to control the deliberations of the Congress came from Palace circles. Both the Royal Chamberlain 'Ali Mahir and the former Regent Prince Muhammad 'Ali are reported to have spoken to 'Alluba, counseling him to keep the Congress under control.[150]

The practical results of the Parliamentary Congress were marginal. The party which had first encouraged the Egyptians to sponsor the event, the Palestinian Arabs themselves, was "somewhat disappointed at the results of the Congress" since it (the Congress) generated no significant increase in material support for their cause.[151] It led to nothing on the diplomatic level;

the British dismissed the efforts of the representatives of the Permanent Committee of the Congress to negotiate with them.[152] Although the Committee continued to issue declarations concerning Palestine until well into 1939,[153] these appear to have had little impact on the evolution of the Palestine issue.

The Congress's significance was largely symbolic. That Egyptian parliamentarians played the central role in organizing an international conference devoted to the Palestine question was precisely what Arab-oriented Egyptian activists wished: that Egypt end her regional isolation and become a leader in Arab and Muslim political life. The Congress demonstrated that this process was well under way. As a British appreciation of the event put it, the convening of the Congress in Egypt indicated how Egypt was "increasingly becoming the nerve-centre of the Moslem world."[154]

An opportunity for the Egyptian government to do more concerning the question of Palestine developed in early 1939, in relation to the British planning and implementation of the St. James Conference of Palestinian Arab, Zionist, and Arab governmental representatives in London. The Mahmud ministry at the end of December 1938 invited the other Arab parties attending the conference to have their delegates gather in Cairo for the development of a common Arab approach to the talks. In January 1939, Cairo became the diplomatic center of the Arab world. Early in the month the Palestinian Arab leaders who had been interned in the Seychelles passed through Cairo on their way to attend the conference. They were the object of well-publicized receptions by both the Wafd and the prime minister.[155] In the middle of the month the representatives of all the Arab states save Transjordan who were to attend the St. James Conference arrived in Cairo for prior consultations. Prime Minister Mahmud's speech of welcome at what may be termed the first Arab summit was Arabist in tone: after invoking the glories of their common Arab past, referring to the language, history, and customs which they all shared, and declaring that "Egypt has never forgotten this past and the unbroken friendship between herself and the Arab countries through history," Mahmud concluded by asserting the desire of all Egyptians to strengthen inter-Arab cooperation in all spheres.[156] To Lampson, this speech in particular was a clear indication of Muhammad Mahmud's new desire to play a leading role in inter-Arab politics:

The Prime Minister's speech goes much further than was strictly necessary on an occasion of this kind ... The presence together in Cairo of all these representatives from the Arab world has afforded a heaven-sent opportunity for the propagation of an idea long dear to the heart of the Egyptian monarchy, namely the idea of a great future of the Arab peoples under the leadership of the King of Egypt.[157]

The St. James Conference convened on 7 February and lasted until 15 March 1939. The titular head of the Egyptian delegation was Prince Muhammad 'Abd al-Mun'im; its actual leader was the Royal Chamberlain 'Ali Mahir, assisted by the Egyptian ambassador in London Hasan Nash'at and Egypt's Minister to Iran, Iraq, and Sa'udi Arabia 'Abd al-Rahman 'Azzam.

The Egyptian delegation initially took a back seat at St. James. The first Egyptian statement of substance came only in the sixth plenary meeting between Arab and British representatives, and was limited to 'Ali Mahir stating that Egypt "fully shared" the views being expressed by the other Arab delegations.[158] Mahir presented a more detailed statement of the Egyptian position on the Palestine issue in the ninth plenary session. Its measured tone differed considerably from the vehement criticisms of British policy which characterized other Arab presentations. While it put forth the agreed-upon Arab demand for "the establishment of an independent Palestinian state," it coupled this with an acknowledgment of the need for "reasonable guarantees and safeguards" for both the existing Jewish community in Palestine and the "vital interests of Great Britain in the country."[159]

The fullest exposition of the official Egyptian position at St. James came in the three confidential meetings arranged by the British between leading Arab and Zionist delegates. Mahir was present at each of these, offering formal presentations at the first and last. His statement at the first was largely an appeal to the Zionist leaders present to realize the need to fit themselves into an Arab Palestine. Beginning with a reference to Arab–Jewish harmony as he knew it to exist in Egypt ("He himself as a boy at school had a Jew sitting beside him"), it went on to caution his audience that, although there could be no Jewish "sovereignty or control," no "Jewish state," in Palestine, nonetheless "[t]he present Jewish inhabitants of the country were welcome" and the Arabs were willing both to give them "guarantees" and to "co-operate" with them in a future Palestinian state. "The only way to peace was for the Jews to acquire Arab friendship by pacific penetration," by which Mahir meant that Jewish immigration to Palestine should be determined only "on its merits," as in other countries.[160]

Mahir's presentation at the third meeting demonstrated the same combination of conciliatory tone and pro-Arab substance. Saying that he "appreciated and respected the Zionist ideal" and that he acknowledged "the perseverance and the ability of the Jews" present in Palestine, Mahir nonetheless urged the Zionist leaders present to "recognize realities, and in particular the fact of the existing inhabitants of Palestine." "[T]here could never be peace" if the feelings of the Arabs were ignored, he warned; thus he called on his listeners to "call a halt in the realization of their ideal" by accepting the limitation or cessation of Jewish immigration, and expressed his own conviction that this would result in winning "the goodwill of the Arabs."[161]

The position of the Egyptian delegation at St. James provides the best indication of how the official stance of Egypt toward the Palestine issue was evolving by the close of the interwar period. The Egyptian spokesman 'Ali Mahir left the initial definition of the joint Arab position to others; when later he did speak, he expressed the Egyptian position in relatively moderate terms. His statements were less negative toward Great Britain and Zionism than were those of the other Arab delegations, being both more conciliatory in tenor and in substance more optimistic about the prospects for the conference arriving at a mutually satisfactory resolution of the problem. Wedded to no firm position of its own, the main Egyptian concern at the St. James Conference seems to have been to assist the other more involved parties to find a mutually acceptable compromise solution to a festering crisis which threatened continuing instability on Egypt's eastern border. Thus, while its official involvement in inter-Arab politics in general and the Palestine question in particular had increased greatly by 1939, Egypt's augmented role in diplomatic negotiations concerning Palestine resembled that of a disinterested "big brother" assisting both Arabs and Jews to resolve this issue which concerned them more than it concerned Egypt itself.

The effort to reach an agreed-upon resolution to the Palestine issue at St. James failed; when the conference concluded in mid-March, both the Arab and the Jewish delegations had rejected British proposals for the future of Palestine. But the failure at St. James did not end Egyptian efforts to serve as an intermediary on the issue. Immediately after the end of the London negotiations, Mahmud approached the British to express his dismay over the failure of the conference and to offer the services of the Egyptian government to mediate between the British and the Arab positions.[162] Prime Minister Mahmud demonstrated a definite exasperation with the Palestinian Arabs in the wake of St. James, on 13 April telling the British that, if they accepted a set of compromise recommendations offered by the Arab states, he would summon the Mufti to Cairo and "make him toe the line."[163] When Palestinian Arab representatives came to Cairo at the end of April to discuss new proposals for an independent Palestinian state with the delegations of the Arab governments, the meeting was a charged one. Muhammad Mahmud and 'Ali Mahir both spoke in terms of the necessity of compromise: where Mahmud used the example of how Egypt itself had had at one point to accept British supervision on its road to independence in an effort to persuade the Palestinians to accept the British proposals, Mahir concentrated on warning the Palestinians of the dire consequences of rejection and that compromise was imperative to "relieve Palestine from extermination and ruin."[164]

The post-St. James efforts of the Arab states at mediation failed to bridge the gap between the Palestinian Arab demand for the immediate establishment of a responsible Palestinian ministry and the British reluctance to do more than appoint Palestinian Arab department heads within the Mandatory regime. The British White Paper of 17 May promising Palestinian independence within ten years posed the dilemma of whether or not to accede to this statement of British intent. The White Paper was received with denunciations by activist groups such as the High Committee for Assisting Palestinian Victims, the Muslim Brotherhood, and the Permanent Committee of the Parliamentary Congress; in the Egyptian press "[t]here was little distinction between the opposition, independent, and government press in their general attitude of condemnation of the 'White Paper'."[165] The initial reaction of the Egyptian government was disappointment and frustration over the apparent near miss of their effort to serve as intermediary; Prime Minister Mahmud is reported by Lampson to have "looked upset" upon his advance perusal of the document, and to have told the British Ambassador that the Egyptian government had no choice but to join Iraq and Sa'udi Arabia in the formal rejection of its terms.[166] On the day after the White Paper's public release, the premier made a public statement on behalf of his own as well as the other Arab governments in which he announced that the Arab regimes would not recommend the acceptance of the terms of the White Paper to the Palestinian Arabs.[167]

In actuality, the position of the Egyptian government toward the White Paper of May 1939 was not as clear-cut as this. Both the Egyptian and Iraqi governments are reported to have counselled the Palestinian Arab leadership against total rejection of the White Paper after its issuance.[168] Mahmud was still in contact with the Palestinians as late as July 1939, by his own testimony endeavoring to persuade them to "take full advantage of what the White Paper gave them";[169] at one point he informed the British that he was "not without hope of success" in winning them over to acceptance of the White Paper.[170] Only his replacement as prime minister by 'Ali Mahir in August 1939 effectively ended Muhammad Mahmud's repeated efforts to act as an intermediary between Egypt's British ally and its Arab neighbors.

What accounts for the intensive involvement in the Palestine issue on the part of the coalition ministries of 1938–9 led by Egyptian politicians who previously had had little to do with regional Arab affairs? As had been the case with the Wafdist ministries in 1936–7, domestic political factors were an important component in the deepening involvement of the Egyptian government in the Palestine question in 1938–9. Prime Minister Mahmud himself frequently pointed to domestic political considerations as a major reason behind the growing involvement of his ministries in the Palestine question. In June, he stated that the Palestine question was "causing him increasing disquiet" and that he was "finding himself in an extremely difficult position" over the issue.[171] During a visit to London in July, Mahmud warned the British Foreign Secretary that Palestine was "becoming in an increasing degree a source of anxiety to him in Egypt," and informed the British Colonial Secretary that "feeling in Egypt against our [British] policy in Palestine was growing stronger and stronger" and that "he felt it would get worse."[172] British reports largely accepted the Egyptian premier's assertions; as an Embassy evaluation of May 1938 put it, "the Palestine question has to all intents and purposes become a domestic political issue."[173] Well into 1939 Ambassador Lampson's own evaluations took the same line, stating that the concern of the Egyptian public with Palestine was a matter which was now "seriously preoccupying the Government."[174]

The question of the validity of these statements can of course be raised. Indeed it was raised at the time, particularly by Zionist leaders who challenged the accuracy of Lampson's judgments and who attributed such warnings of the gravity of public concern with the Palestine issue in Egypt countries to the pro-Arab inclinations of the British officials involved. The tendency to disparage reports from the Cairo Embassy was sometimes shared by British officials in London as well; in December 1938, Colonial Secretary Malcolm MacDonald referred to Lampson's "out-Arabing the Arabs" and to his "simply giving rein to his own preconceived ideas" in his reports.[175]

In retrospect, the testimony of Mahmud and Lampson seems to have been a closer reflection of Egyptian realities than the scepticism of their critics. Both the timing and the nature of Mahmud's policies support the view that popular sentiment played a major role in producing those policies. The Palestine initiatives of the Mahmud ministries, like those of its Wafdist predecessors, developed only gradually, were far from unreserved in their commitment to the Palestinian Arab position, and even at the height of Egyptian involvement during the diplomatic negotiations of early 1939 were marked by a relative moderation about substantive issues. This hesitant and ambivalent character of the Egyptian government's involvement in the Palestine question reinforces the conclusion that it occurred in large measure in response to external stimuli rather than as a result of the inclinations or convictions of its leaders.

Official Egyptian involvement in the Palestine question was not motivated solely by such "external" considerations, to be sure. Prime Minister Mahmud's explanations for his government's involvement in the question also emphasized the strategic implications of the situation in the Mandate; that the partition of Palestine between Jews and Arabs would mean that "we should never have peace" in the region, or that his desire for a negotiated settlement was prompted primarily by the threat of world war and the corresponding need to free British troops currently tied down in Palestine to meet that threat.[176] The same theme was stressed by 'Ali Mahir at the St. James Conference, when he remarked that "there would never be peace" in Palestine as well as the Middle East as a whole if the grievances of the Arabs were ignored.[177] The general impression given by such statements is that, in addition to the domestic political context for their actions, both Muhammad Mahmud and 'Ali Mahir genuinely feared the destabilizing quality of the Palestine problem, its capacity for sparking uncontrollable trends within Egypt as well as its potential for menacing Egyptian interests in the international arena.

But it was the domestic implications and the domestic agitation building up over the Palestine issue which received primary emphasis in the explanations offered by Egyptian leaders for their concern with the Palestine problem. Given the growth of Egyptian public concern with the Palestine issue by 1938–9, we see no reason to doubt that popular pressure was a key factor leading the ministries of Muhammad Mahmud to assume a central role in the diplomacy of the Palestine problem. Here political development paralleled the course of Egyptian intellectual evolution in the 1930s. Just as Egyptian intellectuals had had to adapt to a more populist and supra-Egyptian style of discourse which was capable of appealing to the desires of their changing literate audience, so Egyptian politicians also found themselves compelled to take a more supra-Egyptian position in response to the demands of the same public. By the later 1930s, this meant the endorsement of Egyptian involvement in the main Arab-Muslim issue of the day, the Palestine question.

Due primarily to the circumstances of war, little in the way of extending Egypt's links with its Arab and Muslim neighbors was achieved during the early years of the war. Significant movement in the direction of greater Egyptian regional involvement only occurred from 1942 onwards, as war receded from the Middle East. Early in 1943, the Wafdist ministry of Mustafa al-Nahhas initiated prolonged diplomatic consultations with other Arab governments concerning the establishment of a new association of independent Arab states. As a result of further negotiations conducted by the non-Wafdist ministries of Ahmad Mahir and Mahmud Fahmi al-Nuqrashi in 1944–5, the League of Arab States was established in March 1945. Egypt was the unquestioned leader in the involved inter-Arab diplomatic negotiations resulting in the formation of the Arab League. Negotiations commenced with an Egyptian initiative in the spring of 1943; Egypt to a large degree controlled the course of negotiations over the next two years; the character of the new international organization was in good measure determined by Egypt, corresponding with Egyptian conceptions of what Arab "unity" should mean in the postwar world; and Egyptian primacy within the body was symbolized by the selection both of Cairo as its headquarters and an Egyptian, 'Abd al-Rahman 'Azzam, as its first Secretary-General.

Egyptian regional policy from 1939 to 1941

The outbreak of war in September 1939 had immediate repercussions for Egyptian political life. Although Egypt did not formally enter the war in September 1939, the Egyptian government severed relations with Germany, declared a state of siege, and imposed strict censorship on the press; full martial law came into effect a year later.[1] Particularly affected by censorship and martial law were the popular movements which had taken the lead in promoting a supra-Egyptianist outlook in the 1930s. Both Young Egypt and the Muslim Brotherhood had their freedom of expression severely restricted from late 1939 onwards. By 1941–2, both organizations had their political activities totally suppressed because of their anti-British inclinations.[2] The political involvement of the third major body which had championed an Arab-Muslim orientation in the 1930s, the Young Men's Muslim Association, also slackened with the death of the society's activist president, 'Abd al-Hamid Sa'id, in 1940.

The ministry of 'Ali Mahir, in office from August 1939 to May 1940, has frequently been evaluated as having attempted to promote Egyptian regional leadership. This interpretation seems to have originated with Sir Miles Lampson, who as early as 1940 evaluated Mahir and his associates as "rabid pro-Arabists" who "undoubtedly hoped to see Egypt taking a prominent if not dominant role in any discussions" about inter-Arab unity.[3] Later historians have echoed Lampson's view.[4]

When the words and actions of 'Ali Mahir and his colleagues are examined in detail, however, a supra-Egyptianist orientation on the part of his ministry becomes problematic. A sampling of Mahir's public statements when he was prime minister in 1939–40 does not demonstrate any great personal commitment to an active regional policy. A radio address by the new prime minister upon the outbreak of the war in September 1939 focused on the need for Egyptian national unity and solidarity in the face of the ominous circumstances of world war. The speech made no mention of Egypt's relationship with the Arab and Muslim worlds, rather employing the integralist slogan "Egypt Over All [misr fawqa al-jami']" as the basis of future government policy.[5] The Speech from the Throne of November 1939 treated regional relations only in passing: while it praised the fact that Egypt's ties with its "eastern neighbors" were improving and promised continued governmental efforts to strengthen regional contacts, nonetheless it established the national interest of Egypt itself as the criterion of the ministry's foreign policy.[6]

'Ali Mahir's Cabinet included two definitely Arab-inclined members; 'Abd al-Rahman 'Azzam (Minister of Awqaf and later of Social Affairs) and Muhammad 'Ali 'Alluba (Minister for Parliamentary Affairs). 'Alluba continued to advocate increased Arab cooperation, especially in the cultural realm, while serving as a minister in the Mahir government.[7] 'Azzam may have done more. According to his later memoirs, 'Azzam opposed unconditional Egyptian entry into the war in September 1939. Rather than Egypt automatically declaring war on Germany as the ally of Great Britain, his position was that Egypt should attempt to extract political concessions from Great Britain as the price of entering the war. 'Azzam's suggested list of Egyptian desiderata as the price of Egyptian entry into the war included the definitely Arabist demand that Great Britain should give "support for the aspirations of the Egyptian people concerning Arab unity."[8]

The one area in which Mahir did pursue an active regional policy was that of Palestine. Through the fall of 1939, the Egyptian prime minister made several interventions with the British concerning clemency for Palestinian Arab rebels and an amnesty for exiled Palestinian Arab leaders.[9] These unilateral Egyptian actions were paralleled by Egyptian–Iraqi consultations in the fall of 1939 regarding possible negotiations with the British concerning an amnesty in Palestine and modifications of the terms of the White Paper of 1939.[10] Similar inter-Arab diplomatic efforts concerning both Palestine and Syria occurred in the spring of 1940 when the governments of Egypt, Iraq, and Saudi Arabia collaborated to pressure the British and French mandatory regimes for amnesties for imprisoned nationalists in the Palestine and Syrian Mandates.[11] But these Palestine-related activities of the Mahir ministry were hardly new departures by 1939–40; all had precedents in the policies pursued by previous Egyptian governments.

Nor did the Mahir ministry demonstrate greater initiative than its predecessors in other areas of regional interaction. There is no indication that the Mahir ministry developed new initiatives in the cultural area in 1939–40. Indeed, its lack of an active "Egyptian Arab policy" in the cultural realm drew the repeated criticism of the Arabist spokesman Karim Thabit of al-Muqattam.[12] In regard to politics, the Mahir ministry declined involving Egypt in projects for regional cooperation in 1939–40. When the possibility of Egyptian entry into the Saadabad Pact was raised in the Egyptian Parliament in late 1939, the idea was rejected.[13] Similarly, when Nuri al-Saʿid suggested the possibility of a Turkish–Iraqi–Egyptian alliance on a visit to Egypt in November 1939, the prime minister was not responsive to the proposal. In his discussion of the approach with Sir Miles Lampson, "[h]e seemed, if anything, disinclined towards this idea, but would encourage it if we thought it helpful to us."[14] The British immediately discouraged the proposal, and nothing came of it.[15]

From the dismissal of the Mahir ministry in June 1940 until the Wafd's assumption of office in February 1942, Egypt was governed by ministries headed by the independents Hasan Sabri (June–November 1940) and Husayn Sirri (November 1940–February 1942). Both the Sabri and Sirri ministries bore the stamp of British approval. The former was installed after the British demanded the resignation of the Mahir ministry because of the perceived pro-Axis sympathies of the former; the latter remained a cooperative ally in the Allied war effort until pressured out of office by King Faruq because of its decision to suspend diplomatic relations with Vichy France early in 1942.

In these circumstances, it is hardly surprising that little was attempted in the way of new Egyptian regional initiatives in 1940–1. In the summer of 1940 yet another approach by the indefatigable Nuri al-Saʿid for inter-Arab political collaboration, this time in the form of an international Arab conference to be held in Baghdad, was not favorably received by Prime Minister Sabri. According to Lampson, Sabri "was definitely inclined to pooh-pooh the idea of a direct Egyptian interest in an 'Arab state,'" and reportedly responded to Nuri's approach with an instruction limiting Egyptian cooperation with Iraq to non-political areas such as technical assistance.[16]

A similar indifference to regional relations characterized the ministry of Husayn Sirri. In January 1941 Sirri rejected an approach by the new Iraqi ministry of Rashid 'Ali al-Kaylani for a joint protest against British policy in Palestine, instead counselling the Iraqis that their interests would be best served by fidelity to their alliance with Great Britain.[17] The attitude of the Sirri ministry in regard to the Anglo-Iraqi conflict which developed in the spring of 1941 was solidly pro-British. When Rashid 'Ali returned to the premiership in mid-April at the head of an overtly anti-British ministry, the Egyptian government accorded his ministry only *de facto* recognition, and Sirri himself is reported to have summarized the Egyptian attitude toward Iraqis in general as being that they were "a very poor lot."[18]

The only areas in which specific regional initiatives can be credited to the Sirri ministry are those of economics and culture. In late 1940 the Ministry of Commerce and Industry was reported to have been considering the convening of an Arab economic conference in Cairo.[19] The subsequent crises of early 1941 in both Iraq and Syria-Lebanon prevented this initiative from being realized. In late 1941, the Sirri ministry began another non-political initiative which was to have concrete results. This was the idea of convening an inter-Arab cultural conference promoted particularly by Sirri's Minister of Education Muhammad Husayn Haykal. Haykal's efforts in this direction included the Ministry of Education's bringing together representatives from the government and academe to commence planning for a cultural conference; externally, the Egyptian government began contacting other Arab governments concerning their participation in such a gathering.[20] Just prior to the ministry's dismissal in early 1942, Haykal informed the British of the Egyptian government's intention to invite representatives of other Arab countries to a cultural conference in Cairo in December 1942.[21] Although not realized in the form envisaged by Haykal, under the following Wafdist ministry this initiative did mature in the form of an inter-Arab bureau established to promote Arab cultural coordination.

The new Arab policy of the Wafd, 1942–1943

The famous incident of 4 February 1942, in which the British authorities in Egypt forced a reluctant King Faruq to install a Wafdist ministry headed by Mustafa al-Nahhas, was a crucial event in Egyptian history in many ways.

Its internal consequences are well known: the tarnishing of the image of both the king and the Wafd; the further disillusionment of many Egyptians with the existing political order; the embitterment of parliamentary politics and their descent into an increasingly rancid "game of revenge" until terminated by a military coup precisely a decade later.[22] Less appreciated are the international repercussions of the installation of the Wafdist ministry of 1942–4. In brief, it was during its wartime tenure in office that Egypt's leading political party committed the country to an institutionalized role in the political life of the surrounding Arab world.

The Wafd's new Arab policy during 1942–4 was clearly related to its domestic position. Suffering an erosion of popular enthusiasm and support since the late 1930s, the Wafd's assumption of office through the action of the British irreparably stained its image as a movement whose *raison d'être* was Egyptian national liberation. Lacking a clear social and economic program which addressed the manifold socio-economic disparities existing in Egypt by the 1940s, the party had lost much of its appeal to the urban new effendiyya population, who found the more authentic and reformist message of the Muslim Brotherhood better attuned to their perceptions and needs. Compromised by its coming to power with the assistance of the British and devoid of an internal reformist message capable of appealing to a changing Egyptian public, the Wafd needed a new popular initiative through which it could rehabilitate its image, restore its prestige, and regain its position as the central force in Egyptian public life. It eventually found that initiative in its new policy toward the Arab world.

The ministry's movement in the direction of a more active regional policy began in the area of cultural cooperation. As noted earlier, the ministry of Husayn Sirri had begun to plan for an Arab cultural conference in 1941. The Wafd expanded upon the idea. In the summer of 1942, the Egyptian Ministry of Education conducted discussions with the Iraqi Legation in Egypt for the creation of a joint agency to coordinate cultural and educational affairs in the two countries.[23] A Bureau of Cultural Cooperation (Maktab al-Ta'awun al-Thaqafi) was established in late 1942; consisting of representatives from Egypt and Iraq but open to membership by any other Arab state which should wish to affiliate in the future, it was charged with such matters as curricular coordination, the exchange of students, teachers, and educational materials, and the convening of periodic Arab cultural conferences.[24] Parallel with this bilateral Egyptian–Iraqi undertaking, the ministry also pursued its predecessor's plan for an Arab cultural conference which would promote educational cooperation.[25]

There is clear evidence that the Wafd was moving closer to an Arabist political orientation by the end of 1942. A benchmark in the definition of the Arab policy of the Wafd was a speech by Nahhas on 13 November 1942. In it, the Egyptian premier announced his ministry's intention of working to realize the national aspirations of the Arabs in general, and specified a new goal for the states of the region: the need for "Arab and Eastern" countries to band together to form "a strong and cohesive block" in the postwar world.[26] A few days later, Nahhas privately told Lampson of his government's desire for "Egyptian 'leadership' of the neighbouring Arab states who would certainly be looking to Egypt to lead a solid Arab block in [postwar] peace discussions."[27] Nahhas's references of November 1942 as to the desirability of the creation of some sort of Egyptian-led regional organization are an important indicator of the direction in which the Wafdist leader's thinking about Middle Eastern affairs was evolving. Egypt's leadership of her Arab neighbors was coming to be seen as an indispensable element in the country's assumption of a larger international role in the postwar era.

But vague aspirations for the creation of a postwar Arab block did not yet comprise a positive policy of Egyptian regional leadership. That developed only in 1943. Three developments occurring early in 1943 provided the immediate stimuli to the adoption of an Arab policy by Egypt. The first came from Iraq. In January 1943, Prime Minister Nuri al-Sa'id of Iraq presented the details of his plans for Fertile Crescent unity to the British for their consideration. Recommending first the total union of Syria, Lebanon, Palestine, and Transjordan, then the creation of an Arab League between this new state and Iraq as well as other Arab states which might wish to affiliate, the details of the plan did not necessarily exclude Egypt from participation in this Arab alliance.[28] Yet the creation of a new Arab League according to an Iraqi plan and under Iraqi sponsorship presumably was unsettling to an Egyptian government now thinking in terms of Egypt as the leader of a regional block. More definite is the fact that a parallel Iraqi initiative of January 1943, its declaration of war against the Axis, was interpreted by Nahhas as part of an Iraqi effort to assume regional leadership in the postwar world, and accordingly angered the Egyptian leader.[29] An Egyptian riposte to counter Iraqi ambitions was in order.

The second stimulus came from the British. In response to a question in parliament on 24 February 1943, Foreign Secretary Sir Anthony Eden declared British sympathy for the idea of Arab federation.[30] Although intended merely as a placebo to assuage Arab public opinion, Eden's statement was immediately interpreted by Arabs as British encouragement to undertake discussion of closer political cooperation.

The third and probably the most important trigger to the Wafdist ministry's adoption of a new Arab policy in early 1943 was internal. Nahhas's statement about the creation of an Arab bloc of November 1942 kindled considerable public speculation within Egypt about the subject of regional relations, prompting veteran Egyptian Arabists within the opposition such as 'Abd al-Rahman 'Azzam and Muhammad 'Ali 'Alluba to call for greater efforts toward the promotion of Arab political cooperation to be undertaken by the Egyptian government.[31] By early 1943, the same figures were reported to be attempting to organize in order to pressure the ministry to "adopt a more active Arab policy."[32]

This was also the goal of a new organization created specifically to promote the concept of Arab unity in Egypt, the Arab Union Club (Nadi al-Ittihad al-'Arabi), which had been established by the director of the royal estates Fu'ad Abaza in May 1942.[33] Dedicated to "the fostering of relations, the strengthening of bonds, the protection of interests, and the defense of the rights of the Arab regions,"[34] the society resembled earlier Arab-oriented organizations in Egypt. With its leadership composed of a blend of native Egyptians and non-Egyptian Arab publicists resident in Egypt, it sponsored public meetings and receptions devoted to Arab subjects, issued manifestoes and protests concerning current Arab problems such as French repression in Syria and Lebanon or the situation in Palestine, and joined other non-Wafdist voices calling on the Egyptian government to extend its involvement in Arab affairs and the movement for Arab federation.[35]

Eden's statement provided these elements with the opportunity to bring public pressure to bear on the government. On 28 February 1943, less than a week after Eden's statement in parliament, 'Azzam published an article in al-Ahram calling on the Arabs to follow up on Eden's encouragement of the "historic aspirations" of the Arab nation for unity by organizing "a free [i.e., non-governmental] Arab conference" to meet and discuss the subject of Arab political cooperation.[36] The issue of inter-Arab cooperation immediately became a major concern of the Egyptian press.[37] Most ominously for the Wafdist ministry, this pressure for an unofficial inter-Arab conference seems to have had the support of the Egyptian Palace.[38]

These efforts to generate a non-governmental inter-Arab conference at which there was a good prospect of the Wafdist ministry being over-shadowed by its historically more Arabist rivals were an obvious embarrassment to Nahhas and his colleagues. The ministry's initial response was to discourage the idea; journalists associated with the Wafd wrote articles opposing the idea of an inter-Arab conference which in their view was premature and might prove a setback to more realistic hopes of Arab economic and cultural cooperation.[39] Eventually, the ministry used the censorship to limit public debate on the subject.[40]

Public pressure for the ministry to adopt a more Arab policy was reinforced by Iraqi action. On 17 March 1943, Nuri al-Sa'id wrote to Nahhas suggesting the convening of an inter-Arab conference, either official or unofficial, to discuss the subject of Arab unity.[41] Nuri soon dispatched his colleagues Jamil al-Midfa'i and Tahsin al-'Askari to Egypt to discuss the subject of political coordination with the Egyptian government. The Iraqi envoys met with Prime Minister Nahhas on 27 March 1943. No agreement on inter-Arab cooperation was reached.[42]

At this point, Nahhas boldly imposed a *fait accompli* upon both his internal and external rivals. Speaking on behalf of the ministry before the Egyptian Senate on 30 March 1943, the Minister of Justice Sabri Abu 'Alam announced the Egyptian government's intention to begin individual consultations with the other Arab governments concerning Arab political cooperation. Upon the completion of these bilateral negotiations, the Egyptian government would then take the initiative in sponsoring an official Arab conference which would institutionalize the measures necessary to realize the common goal of "Arab unity."[43]

The Wafdist gambit of 30 March succeeded. With this declaration, the ministry both effectively forestalled the possibility of an unofficial conference on Arab unity at which its domestic rivals might have been represented, and also neatly moved to ensure that Egypt rather than Iraq would take the lead in the diplomatic negotiations which eventually resulted in the formation of the Arab League. The statement also marked the definitive adoption of an Arabist program by the Egyptian Wafd. There was no going back for the Wafd after March 1943; its prestige was clearly committed to an Arabist program.

That an Arab orientation had become a basic tenet of the Wafd by 1943 is made clear in subsequent party declarations. In November 1943, the Wafd held its first party conference since 1935. Nahhas's speech before the assembly orated at length on the various efforts on behalf of Arab causes undertaken by his several ministries in the past, and reviewed the efforts toward institutionalizing Arab political cooperation under way in his current consultations with other Arab governments.[44] The final resolutions of the conference not surprisingly endorsed the ministry's ongoing efforts to realize "friendship and cooperation among the Arab countries."[45] On the following day, the Speech from the Throne delivered by Nahhas voiced the newfound Arabism of the Wafd in even stronger terms, expressing the ministry's "special concern for the project of Arab unity" and pledging to continue its efforts on behalf of the same goal in the future.[46]

Contemporary comments viewed the Wafdist initiative of March 1943 as being produced primarily by short-term political considerations. A British report saw it as a maneuver by Nahhas designed to "maintain for himself the leading role as against Nuri Pasha and at the same time to obviate any danger that the Opposition and the Palace would steal his thunder at a conference run on a non-official basis."[47] Nuri al-Sa'id of Iraq and King 'Abd Allah of Transjordan also attributed the move to personal political advantage.[48]

Subsequent judgments by historians have generally accepted this interpretation, seeing the Wafdist initiative primarily as a response to Palace and opposition pressure – a measure taken by Nahhas, as Elie Kedourie put it, in order to "dish his opponents by adopting their policy."[49]

Unquestionably, political factors provide much of the explanation for the Wafdist ministry's Arab initiative of March 1943. But to see the Wafd's initiative as no more than a response to immediate political stimuli is to take too narrow and too venal a view. Previous chapters have noted the gradual adoption by many Egyptians, Wafdist leaders included, of less isolationist views as to what constituted the most effective foreign policy for Egypt itself. Wartime developments contributed to this evolution. The establishment in Cairo of the Middle East Supply Centre in April 1941 had made Egypt the hub of wartime Middle Eastern economic life, underlining its centrality in the region and thereby encouraged Wafdist leaders to think in terms of a greater regional role for Egypt.[50] Egyptian leadership of the Arab world was also viewed as a way of obtaining Egyptian participation in any postwar peace conference, an important consideration in Wafdist foreign policy from late 1942 onwards.[51] Nahhas's references of November 1942 to Egyptian leadership of a block of Arab nations did not occur in a vacuum; they reflected this growing Egyptian perception of a more interdependent postwar world both within and beyond the Middle East. Thus, while the timing of the Wafd's Arab initiative of March 1943 was largely determined by short-term political considerations, the new policy also reflected a gradual shift in the general outlook of the party from its earlier position that Egypt had little or nothing to gain from regional political cooperation to a new stance of perceiving that a great deal of advantage was to be gained from such a policy.

Inter-Arab negotiations and the Alexandria Conference, 1943–1944

The Wafdist ministry's statement of 30 March 1943 marked the beginning of its leadership of the movement toward Arab federation. Over the next year, the Egyptian government undertook bilateral negotiations with each of the technically independent Arab states aimed at soliciting their views on the subject of Arab political cooperation. In June 1944 Nahhas issued a formal invitation to the other Arab regimes to attend a conference in Alexandria. In September–October 1944, representatives of the independent Arab states as well as a Palestinian delegate met in Alexandria. By 7 October, they had drafted the Alexandria Protocol, the preliminary charter for a new League of Arab States. One day later, King Faruq dismissed the Wafdist ministry from office.

Based primarily on the minutes of the bilateral meetings between Nahhas and Arab representatives as well as those of the Alexandria Conference, several recent studies have analyzed the course of the inter-Arab negotiations of 1943–4 which resulted in the Alexandria Protocol.[52] Our focus in what follows will be upon the Egyptian role in those negotiations and what the Egyptian position indicates about Egyptian attitudes toward Arab collaboration by the early 1940s.

The central figure in these negotiations was Prime Minister and Foreign Minister Mustafa al-Nahhas. Nahhas conducted the bilateral negotiations with the Arab representatives visiting Egypt in 1943–4; eventually he led the Egyptian delegation to the Alexandria Conference. As a British observer summarized his central role, "Nahhas was the unchallenged master of the Wafd and of his Government. He could therefore decide upon a policy and execute it."[53]

Equally in the eyes of Arab, British, and American diplomats in contact with him at this time, personal ambition in the form of the desire to be recognized as paramount leader in the Arab world was assumed to have been the driving force behind Nahhas's adoption of an active Arab policy. Arab and British diplomats who discussed the subject with him in 1943 found him "very ignorant of Arab countries and problems" and commented on the "simplicity or crudeness" of his views on Arab affairs.[54] His vanity was proverbial. The Wafdist press was fulsome in their praise of "the leader of Arabism" or "the only leader of the East."[55] Arab diplomats who negotiated with him went out of their way to cater to his conceits, the Syrians expounding on how "the name of Nahas would be inscribed in the annals of all Arab countries,"[56] the Iraqis publicly acclaiming him as the "leader of the leaders of the Arabs."[57]

Nahhas's effectiveness as a diplomat is debatable. At one time or another in the course of the negotiations of 1943–4, Nahhas's personalized diplomacy succeeded in upsetting most of the other Arab governments. In 1943 the incomplete Egyptian summary of recent Egyptian–Sa'udi communications, a summary which presented Nahhas in a more and King ibn Sa'ud in a less favorable light, outraged the latter and delayed agreement on the convening of an Arab conference.[58] Nahhas and Nuri al-Sa'id of Iraq are reported to have had a "marked personal dislike for each other,"[59] and certainly Nahhas had a penchant for annoying the Iraqis in particular. His limited knowledge of Arab affairs did not prevent him from expounding at length on the subject; the Iraqis came away from their first discussions with Nahhas in March 1943 complaining that, despite his lack of knowledge, he had "perorated at them without allowing them to get a word in edgeways."[60] His ministry's declaration of 30 March 1943, made without prior notice to the Iraqis with whom he had just met, not unnaturally upset the

Iraqis.[61] Prior to the Alexandria Conference Nahhas again infuriated the Iraqis by suggesting that Nuri al-Sa'id should not represent Iraq.[62]

Nahhas's repeated use of the diplomatic *fait accompli* was also a problematic tactic. The declaration of 30 March 1943 came as a surprise to all the Arab states; in addition to upsetting the Iraqis, it drew an icy response from ibn Sa'ud who felt he should have been consulted in advance.[63] In June 1944, Nahhas's formal invitation to the other Arab governments to attend a conference at Alexandria was again issued without prior warning to other governments, in this case angering both the British and the Sa'udis.[64] Nahhas's most extreme use of preemptive tactics came at the end of the Alexandria Conference, when he publicly released the preliminary text of the Alexandria Protocol to the press in order to forestall possible changes in the text agreed upon by the Egyptian, Iraqi, Syrian, Lebanese, and Transjordanian representatives but not yet approved by the Sa'udi and Yemeni governments.[65]

Against these vagaries must be set the indisputable facts that none of his *gaucheries* derailed the inter-Arab consultations of 1943–4; that he was ultimately successful in arranging an international conference attended by seven disparate and often opposed states; and that the conference did result in a formal agreement providing for the establishment of the League of Arab States.[66] Whether this result came about because of, or in spite of, the diplomatic abilities of Mustafa al-Nahhas is an open question.

In the initial stages of the bilateral negotiations of 1943–4 the substantive Egyptian position was, as both Arab and British observers noted, "very vague" and "hazy";[67] it took time for a firm Egyptian concept of Arab federation to emerge. But certain Egyptian preferences were apparent during the discussions. These may be summarized under four headings: (1) initial uncertainty as to Egypt's own role in institutionalized Arab political cooperation; (2) reserve as to the feasibility or even desirability of Arab political union; (3) firm opposition to schemes of Fertile Crescent unity; (4) a desire for Egyptian primacy in the inter-Arab negotiating process.

The Egyptian government did not automatically assume that Egypt would be a member of whatever organization might emerge from Arab negotiations concerning federation. The questionnaire which Nahhas presented to other Arab governments initially left the matter of Egyptian participation for their decision. In the negotiations with Iraq in July– August 1943, the Egyptian position was that Egyptian participation in an Arab organization was not assured and that there was still "the possibility that Egypt may not adhere to the Arab Union."[68] Nahhas expressed even stronger reservations to the Lebanese in January 1944, taking the position that Egypt did not wish to be "drawn into the orbit of a Pan-Arab consortium of Asiatic States" but rather envisaged herself as playing a role in the

Arab world analogous to that of the United States in relation to Latin America.[69]

The Egyptian position on the precise form which institutionalized Arab cooperation should take was a minimalist one. Already in the Egyptian–Iraqi negotiations in the summer of 1943, it was the view of both governments that "[u]nion under a central Government was ruled out as unrealizable owing to external difficulties and internal differences and disagreements."[70] The envoy sent by Nahhas to King ibn Sa'ud in the fall of 1943 informed the British that the Egyptian government was not anticipating political unity as a result of the negotiations:

Arab Federation as such could never assume a strong political character and that Nahas was not in favour of it so doing. He added that he could not see Egypt or any other Arab country surrendering any of its prerogatives in favour of a political Arab Federation. He thought that the question could never pass beyond the bounds of cultural, social, and perhaps economic collaboration and that certainly Nahas Pasha had no ideas beyond these three forms.[71]

The Egyptian viewpoint as expressed in meetings with the Transjordanian and Lebanese delegations was equally skeptical about the possibility of political integration; only in the discussions with the Syrians – who themselves were the only Arab government willing to consider actual schemes of union in 1943–4 – was the possibility of a more tightly meshed form of Arab political cooperation left open.[72]

The Egyptian government expressed a concrete conception of Arab political cooperation only at the Alexandria Conference in October 1944. The precise formula for the Arab League embodied in the Alexandria Protocol was Nahhas's, and was a compromise between looser Sa'udi and more unitary Syrian views about the nature of Arab federation. Nahhas's proposal postulated an organization of independent and equal states. It rejected the idea of a League council with the power to make decisions binding on its members; only when two members of the League should choose to refer a dispute between them to the council would that body's decisions be "effective and binding" upon the parties involved.[73]

The Wafdist ministry was more definite about what it did not want. At the head of that list stood the rival projects for Fertile Crescent unity which had been proposed by the governments of Iraq and Transjordan in the early 1940s. As a "reliable source" informed the British in September 1943, Nahhas was "strongly opposed to the idea of any union between Iraq and Syria, lesser or greater, because he thinks that such a state might take the place of Egypt as the predominant local power in the Levant."[74] Nahhas himself told the Syrians in October 1943 that he was extremely skeptical about the possibility of Fertile Crescent unity in view of the differences in local conditions among the regions involved.[75]

The final feature of the Wafdist ministry's position in the inter-Arab diplomatic negotiations of 1943–4 was its insistence on the maintenance of Egyptian leadership of the negotiating process. Several points noted above – Nahhas's disavowal of any form of Arab unity which would have limited existing state sovereignty; his opposition to schemes of Fertile Crescent unity which would have threatened the Egyptian position of ascendancy in the Arab world; the image of the Egyptian position in the Arab world as similar to that of the United States in relation to the Americas – reflect an assumption of Egyptian autonomy from and hegemony over its neighbors. There were other indications of such an outlook as well. The form imposed by the Egyptian government on the negotiations is a case in point: its initial seizure of the initiative from the Iraqis in March 1943 as well as its later insistence on Egyptian management of the bilateral negotiations of 1943–4 both demonstrate a firm desire for Egyptian leadership.[76] The same commitment to Egyptian leadership in inter-Arab politics was apparent in the Egyptian rejection of a Sa'udi suggestion that Mecca be the site of the inter-Arab conference; although justified on the grounds that Christian Arabs would be disbarred from attending a conference at Mecca, the only alternative venue mentioned by the Egyptians was Egypt itself.[77] The Wafdist government, even as it assumed leadership of the movement toward Arab federation, retained a strong sense of Egyptian distinctiveness within the Arab world.

The Egyptian Palace was only tangentially involved in discussions concerning Arab cooperation being conducted by the Wafdist ministry. Kept uninformed save in a general way of the course of the bilateral negotiations of late 1943–early 1944,[78] King Faruq's views on the inter-Arab negotiations were understandably reserved. Speaking with Lampson in August 1943, Faruq deprecated the recent Egyptian–Iraqi talks as "a competition between Nahhas and Nuri"; as for himself, "he was purposely keeping aloof from these Pan-Arab discussions which had no substantiality."[79] In January 1944, a Lebanese leader who met with the king found the latter's views on Arab federation "even more moderate" [i.e., skeptical] than those of the Egyptian government.[80]

Nonetheless, the Palace did not publicly challenge the Wafdist ministry over its Arab policy. Instead, it periodically attempted to use Arab issues to enhance its own popularity. As the issue of the possible representation of non-independent Arab countries in the future Arab conference became a matter of contention between the Arabs and the British early in 1944, the Palace pressured the ministry to insist upon such participation.[81] It similarly attempted to use the issue of Palestinian representation in the Alexandria Conference to embarrass the Wafdist ministry, treating Musa al-'Alami of Palestine as a recognized participant in the Conference even prior to the question of his participation having been decided upon.[82] More constructive was the Palace role in arranging a royal reception during the Conference as a device for soothing Syrian sensibilities after Nahhas had disturbed the Syrians with his suggestion that the minutes of the earlier inter-Arab bilateral negotiations be made public.[83]

The Egyptian opposition took a similar position in 1943–4. Opposition leaders echoed some of the same criticisms of the new Arab policy of the Wafdist ministry which were offered by contemporary diplomats, crediting the motives behind the ministry's Arab initiative to purely domestic political considerations.[84] Yet, rather than opposing the new Arab policy of the Wafd, the Egyptian opposition more often followed a policy of competing with the ministry in support of the movement toward Arab federation. In July 1943, major opposition figures such as Ahmad Mahir of the Sa'dist Party and the Watanist leader Hafiz Ramadan joined with Arabist politicians such as 'Azzam, 'Alluba, and Hamid al-Basil to issue a public denunciation of existing Arab boundaries as "artificial" and to call for an inter-Arab conference with both official and popular representation.[85] In the early months of 1944, when the issue of the participation of Palestinian and North African representatives in any future conference on Arab unity became a matter of discussion in the press, opposition leaders joined the Palace in calling on the government to hold firm in support of such participation.[86]

Considered together, the policies of the Egyptian Palace and opposition confirm the growing popularity of an Arab political orientation in Egypt. Arab federation was not an issue between Egypt's major political forces in 1943–4. Despite private reservations, the public stance of Palace and opposition alike was to compete with the Wafd as public enthusiasts of the idea.

The formation of the Arab League, 1944–1945

The Alexandria Conference did not by itself create the Arab League. Stating that a "League will be formed of the independent Arab states," the Protocol drafted at Alexandria was merely an agreement to agree.[87] While it laid down preliminary principles for the new organization, it left the drafting of the league's statutes for future negotiations. It was only in the early months of 1945 that these negotiations were completed and the "League of Arab States" finally established.

The Egyptian position in the diplomatic negotiations which defined the precise character of the Arab League in late 1944–early 1945 was shaped by the coalition ministries of non-Wafdist parties headed first by the Sa'dist Ahmad Mahir until his assassination in February 1945, then by his Sa'dist Foreign Minister and successor as premier, Mahmud Fahmi al-Nuqrashi.

Neither Mahir nor Nuqrashi came to office with a record of advocacy of Egyptian involvement in Arab politics; according to a British evaluation, Foreign Minister Nuqrashi began his tenure as Foreign Minister "with the disadvantage of knowing almost nothing of Arab affairs."[88] Divided among several competing parties and usually preoccupied with domestic affairs, notably the electoral campaign of late 1944–early 1945, the ministries of 1944–5 were both internally weaker than their Wafdist predecessor and less concerned with the Arab issue in which Nahhas had invested so much personal prestige in 1943–4.[89]

Nonetheless, the new regime did maintain an official commitment to the realization of institutionalized Arab political cooperation. Ahmad Mahir's first official statement upon forming his new ministry in October 1944 stated support for "the Arab cause and Arabism" to be one of the basic principles of his ministry.[90] Public statements by members of the coalition ministry reiterated an intention to work for Arab unity, as did the electoral platforms of coalition parties during the campaign of late 1944.[91] The Speech from the Throne after the election of January 1945 codified the ministry's formal commitment to Arab unity, declaring that "Arab unity is considered an important aspect of national policy."[92]

The practical realization of this goal was a slow process. The Alexandria Protocol had called for a subcommittee of representatives of the Arab states to meet in order to draft the statutes of the League of Arab States. Convening such a meeting took several months. Only in February 1945 did a political subcommittee composed of representatives of all the independent Arab states save the Yemen meet in Cairo in order to determine the concrete structure of the Arab League. It took sixteen sessions to reach agreement. The resulting Pact of the Arab League departed in significant ways from the Protocol agreed upon in Alexandria in the previous year; in particular, it virtually eliminated the ability of the League and its Council to determine policies binding upon League members or to intervene in disputes between members save with their consent. As a caustic British evaluation put it, "the [Arab League] Council now becomes little more than a debating society . . .; the Royal Automobile Club has more power."[93]

It is the Egyptian position in the discussions which is our concern here. Nuqrashi's own inexperience in Arab affairs and absence from the later sessions after becoming prime minister limited his role. On the question of how to resolve disputes between League members, his own position was a relatively strong one favoring compulsory arbitration of inter-Arab disputes in all cases save those involving domestic matters or affecting non-League members.[94] On the issue of how to agree upon joint action to resist aggression he took a milder stance, favoring unanimity by League members in order to adopt binding measures to counter aggression against a member state.[95] His views on the controversial question of the League relationship with non-independent Arab states were also cautious; when queried by the British on the subject, he responded that for the League to involve itself in the affairs of non-independent Arab countries would be an "error."[96]

The most important Egyptian in the negotiations of February–March 1945 was Minister for Arab Affairs 'Abd al-Rahman 'Azzam, who chaired the discussions after Nuqrashi's assumption of the premiership in late February. 'Azzam was responsible for formulating several of the key provisions of the Pact of the Arab League. He shaped the compromise wording of the proviso relating to non-interference by League members in the internal affairs of other members,[97] and was the author of the crucial provision which made League arbitration in inter-Arab disputes contingent upon the approval of the parties involved, a major dilution of the terms of the Alexandria Protocol.[98] Equally significant was his contribution regarding the League's relationship with non-independent Arab regions. It was his arguments on behalf of Palestinian membership which convinced the delegates to recommend the appointment of a Palestinian representative to the League Council.[99] He took a similar position in relation to the non-independent Arab countries of North Africa, arguing for their being allowed to participate in League affairs and for the League itself to concern itself with assisting them to achieve independence.[100] On the whole, the Egyptian role in the negotiations of February 1944–March 1945 as shaped primarily by 'Azzam was, as a British evaluation noted, one of "arbiter" between the conflicting viewpoints of the other parties present.[101]

'Azzam's leading role in the negotiations of February–March 1945 was resented by the Iraqis, and his vigorous advocacy of League involvement in the affairs of non-independent Arab regions upset the Lebanese.[102] The British were equally critical of 'Azzam. In the view of Sir Miles Lampson, 'Azzam was "an Arab enthusiast and not at all practical"; the prospect of his becoming the Secretary-General of the League was thus "not at all reassuring" to the British ambassador.[103] His selection for the post was due to strong support from three Arab states. One was the government of Sa'udi Arabia. Ibn Sa'ud had reportedly been favorably impressed with 'Azzam during the latter's negotiations with the king; 'Azzam himself later claimed that ibn Sa'ud had made his selection as Secretary-General a condition of Sa'udi participation in the League.[104] 'Azzam's personal support for the Greater Syrian idea seems to have won him Syrian support for his appointment as Secretary-General.[105] For the Egyptian government, the choice of an Egyptian as Secretary-General of the League was only fitting in view both of Egypt's preeminent place in the Arab world and its role in the creation of the League. Nuqrashi pushed hard for the designation of his countryman 'Azzam as Secretary-General; a British report termed the choice "practically imposed by Nokrashi Pasha."[106] With the Egyptian government having led the recent discussions which had created the League and with Cairo selected as its headquarters, it was almost inevitable that an Egyptian would be chosen as the chief executive officer of the new organization.

The Cairo discussions of February–March 1945 determined the shape of the League of Arab States. All that remained were formalities. On 17 March, the full Preparatory Committee composed of representatives of all Arab states save the Yemen approved the final text of the Pact of the League of Arab States.[107] On 22 March the same representatives transformed themselves into a "General Arab Congress" and signed the Pact, at the same time sending a copy of the document to the Yemen for its consideration.[108] Both chambers of the Egyptian parliament held one-day debates on the Pact early in April and gave their unanimous approval to the document; the king signed it on 5 April.[109] Article 20 of the Pact stipulated that it would come into effect when four member states had ratified the document. This occurred on 10 May, 1945.[110]

Contemporary Egyptian opinion about the League of Arab States often demonstrated an awareness of the limitations of the organization. The statements of the Egyptian government leaders involved in the League's formation were frequently apologetic in tenor, presenting it as an imperfect and incomplete vehicle for the realization of Arab unity but nonetheless the best that was possible given current circumstances. Terming the Arab League "a necessity called for by contemporary international conditions," Prime Minister Nuqrashi's speech on the occasion of the signing of the League's Pact on 22 March acknowledged that the new body was but a partial step toward Arab unity; but he defended it on the grounds that it was necessary to make progress cautiously lest more ambitious attempts at cooperation collapse in failure.[111] His Foreign Minister 'Abd al-Hamid Badawi defended what critics of the Pact were terming its imprecision as a pragmatic "flexibility" which would allow for future development. While some had wanted a stronger, more unitary League, Badawi argued that the historical record demonstrated that union could only come through a long process of evolution. In this process, the present League was a realistic beginning.[112] The new organization's Secretary-General 'Abd al-Rahman 'Azzam admitted that the League was only a beginning step toward true Arab unity; whether it would remain a federation or evolve into the sort of Arab "empire" which he had long been advocating was a matter which could only be determined by "future generations."[113]

Each chamber of the Egyptian parliament debated the terms of the Pact. The report of the Foreign Affairs Committee of the Chamber of Deputies termed the new body "an acceptable start towards the high goal to which we all aspire, namely the achievement of a strong Arab unity," and unanimously recommended parliamentary approval.[114] The few questions raised in the lower chamber focused on the Pact's annexes on Palestine and the other non-independent Arab regions, which were criticized as too weak; other comments noted the feeble procedures for mediating disputes between members and emphasized that the requirement of unanimity in security matters had led to the failure of the League of Nations. Prime Minister Nuqrashi's response admitted weaknesses in the Pact and that the League itself would need strengthening in the future. Approval by the Chamber was unanimous.

In the Senate's debate on the following day, Senate President Muhammad Husayn Haykal observed that, while the text of the Pact of the League may not have pleased some and the new organization's goal may not be acceptable to others, he found the Arab League a beneficial "first step uniting these Arab states in an official league."[115] The leader of the Wafdist opposition, Sabri Abu 'Alam, delivered a lengthy speech criticizing the differences between the references to Palestine in the Alexandria Protocol of the preceding year and those of the Pact of the League; in his view, the Pact's Annex on Palestine was an insufficient commitment on the vital Arab and Egyptian issue of Palestine. The defense of the Palestine Annex was left to 'Azzam, who attempted to counter Abu 'Alam's criticism by maintaining that the commitment in the Pact was a "real" one where that in the Protocol had been only verbal. Only one Senator – the Nationalist 'Abd al-Rahman al-Rafi'i – expressed any reservations about the text of the Pact itself. As had been the case in the lower chamber, Senate approval of the terms of the Pact was unanimous.

The Egyptian press is reported to have greeted the creation of the Arab League with "enthusiasm."[116] Endorsement of the concept of Arab federation was widespread across the political spectrum. But many commentators also noted the limitations of the new body. A veteran pro-Arab publicist like Ibrahim 'Abd al-Qadir al-Mazini on the one hand rejoiced "both as an Egyptian and as an Arab" at the creation of the Arab League;[117] on the other, he also characterized its present structure as representing only "a cautious step" in the direction of the Arab unity which he desired, and counseled that not much should be expected from it in the immediate future.[118] For Fikri Abaza of al-Musawwar, the "gaping wound" in the Pact was its relative neglect of the Palestine issue: "no Arab will believe in the Pact of the League save when its 'core and essence' is a clear text concerning the necessity of expanding united cooperative efforts to effectuate and complete the independence of the Arab East."[119] Muhammad 'Ali 'Alluba was more favorably disposed toward the Pact of the League, but also termed it but a "first step" which had to be followed by "further steps" before Arab unity would be realized in actuality.[120]

Wafdist commentary was particularly critical of the compromises of 1945 which had created a weaker federation than that envisaged when it had been in power. The Wafdist press naturally stressed that it was the Wafd which had begun the movement toward Arab federation.[121] Two lengthy analyses of the Pact of the League in the Wafdist daily *al-Wafd al-Misri* were supportive of the League in principle but critical of its specifics. One reviewed the security provisions of the Pact which demanded unanimity before becoming effective, terming this a "point of weakness" which would have to be corrected in the future.[122] The other discussed the Annex on Palestine, criticizing it for its failure to state the Arab case with sufficient vigor and calling on the League to move to meaningful intervention in the Palestine question.[123]

In general, two common themes can be found in contemporary Egyptian opinion about the new League of Arab States. One was the admission that the organization actually established in March 1945 was but a partial and imperfect realization of the concept of Arab unity as it had been articulated up to that time. The other was the expectation that the League was but a first step in the direction of such unity, and that its creation needed to be followed by further measures extending and consolidating Arab integration. Both the admission and the expectation testify to the now widely shared acceptance of the goal of Arab unity as a desirable one in Egyptian political discourse.

Sir Miles Lampson's appraisal of the Arab League was a nuanced one.[124] The ambassador cast his evaluation in terms of inter-Arab rivalries. The movement for Arab federation began in 1943 as a contest for Arab primacy between Iraq and Egypt. Egypt itself had become involved in the movement "largely by reasons of internal politics": the desire of both Nahhas and King Faruq to strengthen their positions internally by becoming leaders of the Arab world. As the negotiations progressed, most of the other Arab regimes chose to align themselves with what Lampson termed "the Egyptian *bloc*." Each had its reasons for doing so: ibn Sa'ud because of his previous rivalries with the Hashemites, Lebanon because its Christians viewed Egypt as "more modernized and less fanatical," Syria because of its fears of being absorbed by Iraq. Only Transjordan, also Hashemite, inclined toward Iraq. The new Arab League was thus an Egyptian triumph, and marked a new era of Egyptian ascendancy within inter-Arab politics.

In terms of what the formation of the Arab League meant for Egyptian nationalism, two points deserve emphasis. The first is that the creation of the League in the mid-1940s did mark an important change in modern Egypt's historical relationship with the Arab world. Independent Egypt had been developing closer relations with the neighboring Arab lands since the 1930s. Politically, Egypt's substantive role in inter-Arab affairs dates from the late 1930s. But the emergence in 1945 of an Arab inter-governmental organization largely inspired by Egypt, located in Egypt, and directed by an Egyptian placed that relationship on an institutionalized basis.

The terms upon which Egypt was formally brought into Arab political life during the process of the formation of the Arab League in 1943–5 also need to be stressed. In brief, Egypt came into the League as its leader. As Lord Killearn noted at the time, the manner in which the Arab League had been formed demonstrated beyond a doubt that "the influence of Egypt is a determining factor in the present evolution of [the] Arab states."[125] This position of Egyptian leadership of the Arab world both reflected and was fully congruent with the hegemonic concepts of supra-Egyptian nationalism which had developed in Egypt in the 1930s and 1940s.

10 Conclusion: from Egyptian territorial to supra-Egyptian nationalism

Benedict Anderson has characterized nationalism as the creation of "an imagined political community." "Communities," he observed, "are to be distinguished not by their falsity/genuineness, but by the style in which they are imagined."[1] Anderson's approach is useful for understanding the complex evolution of Egyptian national identity over the first half of the twentieth century. On one level nationalism in Egypt in this period was a network of several imaginings, in part overlapping but also partially incommensurate, which vied for primacy as the dominant conception of what Egypt was and should be.

The collapse of Ottoman religio-political order after World War I, along with the more extended social processes of the weakening and/or dissolution of the traditional family, village, and tribal communities, religious brotherhoods, and urban solidarities of quarter and guild, eroded the basis of the older concepts of community held by previous generations of Egyptians. These processes created an urgent need to redefine the collective image of Egypt in terms congruent with current conditions. It was this need which gave birth to the different new imaginings of Egypt which developed in the early twentieth century.

Structurally, these alternative images of Egypt can be divided into two major systems. The first was a territorially bounded imagining with a Western coloration; the second was a set of cultural and ethnic imaginings based on Islamic, Arab, and Eastern materials. In the immediate post-1919 era, it was the territorial and Western-influenced image of Egypt which achieved dominance in Egyptian cultural and political life. This outlook was based on the revivification of the Egyptian *ethnie* as it had emerged and had been shaped into a unique national community by the particular environment and the distinctive history of the people living in the Nile Valley.[2] In as far as this territorial nationalist imagining accepted external affiliations for Egypt, they were with the culture and values of Mediterranean civilization and the modern West. Socially, it was the creation of Egypt's Westernized elite striving to reconstruct Egyptian society on a Western model. Politically it assumed a necessary identity between the state and the nation, and drew sharp lines between that nation-state and the world around it.

In the 1930s and 1940s, alternative ways of imagining Egypt developed. The supra-Egyptian nationalism of the post-1930 era was composed of several variants with common premises. This set of imaginings was based on cultural, religious, and linguistic sources rather than on materials deriving from Egypt's geographical setting and its ancient history. Supra-Egyptian nationalism drew its nourishment from the Islamic-Arab heritage which Egypt shared with peoples outside the Nile Valley, and viewed Egypt's proper external affiliations as being not with the West, which it defined as alien and aggressive, but with the peoples of the Arab, Muslim, and Eastern worlds. In the supra-Egyptianist view, Egyptian national identity transcended Egypt alone. Created through a process of social and intellectual interaction between the Egyptian elite and emerging new urban literate groups, these variants of nationalism were, like cultural and ethnic nationalisms elsewhere, more "demotic and plebeian" in character[3] and were shared by a broader segment of Egyptian society than had been the case with the earlier elitist territorial nationalism. Politically, while no supra-Egyptian national imagining totally rejected the existence of a distinct Egyptian state, all presupposed the existence of a larger community to which Egyptians also belonged.

Why this radical shift in the nature of the imagining of Egypt in the 1930s and 1940s? We have argued that changing Egyptian concepts of national identity had their roots in several interlocking factors. The most obvious was the change in the Egyptian environment over the interwar period. The economic and political crises experienced by Egypt, the Middle East, and the world as a whole in the 1930s had direct effects for Egyptian nationalism. Internally, the economic depression of the early 1930s and its wrenching social ramifications; the prolongation of British dominance over Egypt and the resultant perception that the Revolution of 1919 had not achieved Egyptian independence; the repressive Sidqi regime, later Palace manipulation of political life, more generally the corrupt character of the political establishment and the consequent loss of faith in the parliamentary and Western-derived order erected in the 1920s: all this served to undermine Egyptian territorial nationalism and to lead Egyptians to search for other, presumably more effective, nationalist alternatives. Externally, the crisis of democracy in Europe in the 1930s and the new movement toward Arab cooperation which developed in the same decade on the one hand sapped the perceived attractiveness of the European model from which territorially based nationalism had in large part derived, and on the other hand posed new regional prospects which led Egyptians to reevaluate their relationship to their neighbors.

These internal and external crises were paralleled by a more subtle crisis of Egyptian nationalism at the cultural level. Like other nationalisms, Egyptian nationalism from its birth was endowed with partially contradictory functions. Its original function – present throughout the period under discussion – was that of political liberation from foreign domination, most urgently the struggle against the British occupation of Egypt and more generally the effort to resist Western control over many spheres of Egyptian life. A second function – one which became more prominent over time – was the social and economic imperative of nation-building, of creating a modern polity, economy, and society in Egypt. Given the circumstances of the time, this of necessity involved emulating or borrowing from the West many of the institutions and practices which had first been developed in the West and had made it "modern." Yet a third function of Egyptian nationalism was the psychological one of developing and disseminating an independent and Egyptian sense of identity shared by the whole Egyptian community and thus capable of providing the feelings of national solidarity, pride, and self-confidence necessary for both successful political struggle and socio-economic nation-building. In short, Egyptian nationalism had simultaneously to fight the West, to borrow appropriate models for modern community from the West, and to establish its cultural and psychological distinctiveness from the West. Not an easy task.

Prior to World War I as well as during the territorialist heyday of the 1920s, Egyptian nationalists largely ignored the contradictions inherent in the nationalist situation. Originating among the small Westernized elite of Egypt, the prevalent assumption of early Egyptian nationalists was that one could struggle politically against the West while at the same time drawing from its culture in order to promote nation-building. This approach presumed a natural bond between Egypt and the West, between the cultural heritage of historic Egypt and the Greco-Roman legacy in which the culture of the modern West had its roots. It posited that Western ideas and institutions were not entirely alien to Egypt; indeed, many had had their origins in the civilization of the Nile Valley, and thus could be reintegrated into the fabric of Egyptian life. Based on this premise, it was the Western ideas of liberalism, secularism, and science as well as the European model of the territorially derived nation-state which were viewed as the only possible basis for building a progressive Egyptian nation and a modern national culture. Massive Westernization was the only road to Egyptian independence and progress.

During the 1930s and 1940s a significant evolution in the Egyptian perception of the West, Western culture, and the Egyptian relationship with the West took place. The ambivalence of political resistance to Western domination but cultural acceptance of its norms was increasingly replaced by a decidedly non-ambivalent image of Europe as an aggressive imperialist civilization which had little to offer to Egypt. On a deeper level, faith in the magic of reason and science and the earlier infatuation with the theories of Darwin, Spencer, and Comte were superseded by the influential concept of the imminent decline of the West popularized by Spengler and by the eclectic philosophy of Bergson asserting the virtues of the intuitive and the necessity of the inclusion of "spiritual" dimensions in modern life and thought. Now it was maintained that Egypt's natural affinities were with the wisdom and values found in the spiritual civilization of the East, not with those of the materialist West.

In part the change was a result of time and the progressive modernization of Egypt which made the emulation of Western models appear less necessary than it had in the past. But in part it stemmed from a growing awareness of the contradiction between an acceptance of Western culture on the one hand and the political as well as psychological need for Egyptian disengagement from the West on the other. More and more a new premise gained currency – that it was impossible to struggle against Western domination while at the same time trying to absorb its culture. This kind of imitative nation-building was now perceived as having produced social and cultural chaos in contemporary Egypt.

In the new nationalist paradigm, Egyptian nationalism was seen as capable of performing its multiple functions only by developing a clearly non-Western and authentically Egyptian character. This meant the denial of the Egyptian = Western equation and the adoption of Islamic, Arab, and Eastern symbols, myths, and values as the basis of Egyptian identity. These manifestly non-Western components were perceived as possessing vital attributes missing in the Pharaonic and Nile Valley imagery associated with territorialism. One was the ability to generate sentiments of collective self-esteem and self-confidence which the Western-oriented and assimilative approach, due to its effacement of the Self and imitation of the Other, could not foster. This was paralleled by the belief that the cultural resources available in Egypt's remote Pharaonic heritage were inadequate for the tasks demanded of nationalism. Furthermore, it was now perceived that the Egyptianist approach deprived Egypt of the power which was to be had through alliance with its Arab, Muslim, and Eastern neighbors in what was a common effort at liberation and development.

Thus it was the resources to be found in Arabic culture and in the legacy of Islamic civilization, as well as the strength which could be mobilized by the cooperation and unity of all Arab and Muslim peoples, which were presented as the basis for an effective struggle against the West and the forging of an independent national existence. Completing political emancipation, moving on to the next phase of socio-economic nation-building, and restoring psychological self-assertion formed a unified field; each was capable of realization only in conjunction with the achievement of the others.

Overlapping with this intellectual reevaluation of the functions of nationalism was the course of Egyptian social change. The "modernist" interpretation of nationalism posits an essential linkage between the development of industrial society and the emergence of nationalism.[4] This approach roots nationalism in the impact of modernization on the numerous localized and compartmentalized mini-communities which were characteristic of agrarian society. It sees the combined effects of technological change, industrialization, urbanization, and especially the expansion of formal education and the spread of literacy as producing an entirely new form of community. In the larger, more homogeneous but also more anonymous collectivities which mark the modern world, the personal, kinship, and local bonds which once shaped a sense of community are weakened or dissolved. In their place the more diffuse and largely mental bonds provided by the shared language, culture, and history disseminated by uniform literate education and the new mass media become the main referents for identity. As Ernest Gellner summarized the change, "culture is now the necessary shared medium, the life-blood or perhaps rather the minimal shared atmosphere, within which alone the members of the society can breathe and survive and produce."[5] Thus the common culture disseminated by universal literacy replaces traditional structures as the primary determinant of collective identity.

The interwar period witnessed significant changes of this nature in Egypt. Accelerating urbanization, the expansion of the educational system, the development of the mass media, and the growth of the commercial and service sectors of the economy together produced a much larger urban, literate, and therefore nationally involved population bound primarily by their shared language and common culture. Over time, what we have termed the "new effendiyya" – a broad social stratum of urban, literate, modern occupational groups – became the most important producers and consumers of nationalist imaginings.

The new effendiyya was the key group in the development of supra-Egyptian nationalism. In part because of their middle or lower class and less Westernized social background, the imagined community found in their nationalist writings was a more Arab and Islamic one. Subjective factors may also have reinforced the importance of language and religion for the new effendiyya. Expanding literacy and the increasing pervasiveness of the impersonal, standardized means of communication represented by the mass media probably accentuated the psychological importance of language as a referent for identity. The expansion of literacy also allowed Egyptian Muslims to acquaint themselves directly with the scriptural texts of Islam, thereby eroding the popular variants of Islam based on oral interpretations and helping to make the shared scripturalist version of the faith a focus of collective self-definition. The prominent economic position of foreigners who were neither Arab nor Muslim and the extensive use of foreign languages by this population as well as by much of the Westernized elite may also have worked to strengthen the linguistic as well as the religious self-awareness of the growing urban and literate native Egyptian population who were both economically and culturally disadvantaged in comparison to the Europeanized *haute bourgeoisie*.

Building on the bonds of religion, language, and culture, the new effendiyya emphasized the Islamic and Arab nature of Egypt. Simultaneously, they rejected as both dysfunctional and inauthentic the local and Western elements upon which Egyptian territorial nationalism had been based. The more this new group of producers and consumers became prominent in the generation of Egyptian nationalism, the more they determined that it would be more Islamic and Arab, as well as less Pharaonic and Western, in character.

The new effendiyya also underwent a process of radicalization over time. The combined effects of educational overproduction resulting in an imbalance between educated professionals and professional jobs, competition with an existing professional class composed partially of foreigners, and political disillusionment with the failures and corruption of the elite-dominated Egyptianist order led them to attempt to solve their own social predicament through an "ethnic solution";[6] i.e., a redefinition of community in a way which would elevate their own position in society. This meant the adoption of concepts of community capable of providing an alternative to the existing social order. The radicalization of the new effendiyya both intensified their opposition to the foreign presence in Egypt and led them to reject what they viewed as corrupt and ineffective Egyptian rulers. Nor was it conceived solely in political terms; it also produced a cultural radicalism which identified Western civilization as the primary enemy, which rebelled against the existing cultural order which was identified with the West, and which sought self-assertion and dignity within an Arab-Islamic context.

In time, the new concepts of the nation developed primarily at the middle levels of society spread both upwards and downwards. Earlier Egyptian nationalist thinkers had defined the nation in primarily Western terms meaningful only to the Westernized elite of Egypt. As Egyptian society changed over the interwar era, a realization of the necessity of the mobilization and integration of broader segments of society into the fabric of the nation gradually developed among Egypt's intellectual establishment. As they addressed this issue, many of Egypt's leading intellectuals were led to alter their elitist outlook. Now acknowledging the imperative of creating a nationalism and national culture which would be genuinely popular in appeal, they began to redefine the components of national identity in more cultural, religious, and linguistic terms. By so doing, they too contributed to the process of imagining an Islamic-Arab Egypt which was more Eastern than Western and in which Pharaonic and Mediterranean elements were secondary. Thus previously Egyptianist intellectuals also contributed to the formulation of supra-Egyptian nationalism.

Another direction of dissemination of the supra-Egyptian outlook which had its central locus in the new effendiyya was downward. This was inevitable for both theoretical and practical reasons. Considered in abstract terms, the *raison d'être* of nationalism is its claim to encompass and represent the entire nation. In the case of Egypt, the desire of supra-Egyptian ideologues to achieve the maximum involvement of all strata of society led them to frame their nationalist concepts in terms which would have mass appeal. In this process of popularization, the content of nationalist thought was reworked to facilitate its acceptance by the broader Egyptian public.

There were also practical considerations which made supra-Egyptian nationalism populist in tone. As the new effendiyya's alienation from the established order increased and took on a radical coloring, they reached out to the lower strata of society in order to mobilize support in what was now presented as the common struggle of the Egyptian people against their oppressors both domestic and foreign. This too led in the direction of a more linguistic and cultural form of nationalism. In attempting to mobilize broader sectors of society, the new effendiyya relied on those components of national memory and consciousness which would be most effective in mass mobilization: the Islamic heritage, the Arabic language and culture, and sentiments of the solidarity of all Eastern peoples exploited by the imperialist West. The effort at mass mobilization reinforced the movement of Egyptian nationalism toward reliance on Islamic-Arab components and its rejection of the archaic and Western elements upon which it had previously been based. The more Egyptian nationalism moved from being the exclusive property of elitist intellectuals and spread among wider strata of society, the more it became less Pharaonic-Western and more Islamic-Arab. Egyptian nationalism was disseminated and popularized only through its Islamification and Arabization.

What is the historical legacy of the supra-Egyptian nationalist outlook which developed in Egypt in the 1930s and 1940s? The processes of political, economic, and social change which had generated the supra-Egyptian perspective did not come to an end with the Egyptian Revolution of 1952. Urbanization; occupational change; the expansion of formal education and the mass media; improved regional communication and interaction; the perception of common political and economic interests linking Egypt and its neighbors: all these factors which had formed the infrastructure behind the emergence of supra-Egyptianism prior to 1952 were still operating in Egypt after 1952, and thus continued to direct both Egyptian ideas and behavior in a supra-Egyptianist direction.

In particular, we hope we have shown that the Pan-Arabist urge which manifested itself most clearly in the rhetoric and policies of the Nasirist regime in the 1950s and 1960s had clear antecedents in the pre-revolutionary era. Certainly in its intellectual aspects, Nasirism was not a new phenomenon. The central theoretical premises – that Egypt was destined by geography and history to play a leading role in the affairs of the Arab nation of which it was a part, the Islamic community with which it was linked by faith and culture, and the wider Eastern or Asian/African world to which it was joined in a common struggle for liberation from imperialism – which underlay Egypt's activist regional stance in the post-1952 era had been articulated in Egypt before 1952. Nasir further popularized and institutionalized Egyptian Arabism, of course, translating ideology into the language of political action, radicalizing the content of supra-Egyptianism through the inclusion of a socialist component, and harnessing the resources of the Egyptian state behind Egyptian leadership of the Arab world. He also went further than supra-Egyptian ideologues of the earlier period had conceived of going; the creation of the United Arab Republic in 1958 (largely under Syrian prodding) was a development not foreshadowed in the nationalist thought and behavior of the pre-1952 era. But, while Nasir unquestionably moved supra-Egyptian nationalism to a new level of prominence, he was not its progenitor. He was its heir.

Notes

PREFACE

1 James Tully (ed.), *Meaning and Context: Quentin Skinner and His Critics* (Oxford, 1988), 75–6.
2 See ibid., 7–25; J. G. A. Pocock, *Virtue, Commerce, and History: Essays on Political Thought and History Chiefly in the Eighteenth Century* (Cambridge, 1985), 1–34.
3 David A. Hollinger, "Historians and the Discourse of Intellectuals," in John Higham and Paul K. Conkin (eds.), *New Directions in American Intellectual History* (Baltimore, 1979), 42–63; Hollinger, "The Return of the Prodigal: The Persistence of Historical Knowing," *American Historical Review*, 94 (June 1989), 610–21.
4 On the reproduction of culture by its consumers, see Roger Chartier, "Intellectual History or Socio-Cultural History?: The French Trajectories," in Dominick LaCapra and Steven L. Kaplan (eds.), *Modern European Intellectual History: Reappraisals and New Perspectives* (Ithaca, 1982), 13–46; Dominick LaCapra, *History and Criticism* (Ithaca, 1985), 45–94; La Capra, *Soundings in Critical Theory* (Ithaca, 1989), 1–29; John E. Toews, "Intellectual History after the Linguistic Turn: The Autonomy of Meaning and the Irreducibility of Experience," *American Historical Review*, 92 (Oct. 1987), 879–907; David F. Lidenfeld, "On Systems and Embodiments as Categories for Intellectual History," *History and Theory*, 27 (1988), 30–50.
5 Israel Gershoni and James Jankowski, *Egypt, Islam, and the Arabs: The Search for Egyptian Nationhood, 1900–1930* (New York, 1986), 89–94.

1 THE ROOTS OF SUPRA-EGYPTIAN NATIONALISM IN MODERN EGYPT

1 A. E. Crouchley, *The Economic Development of Modern Egypt* (London, 1938), 215.
2 Samir Radwan, *Capital Formation in Egyptian Industry and Agriculture, 1882–1967* (London, 1974), 188.
3 Bent Hansen, "Income and Consumption in Egypt, 1886–1887 to 1937," *International Journal of Middle East Studies*, 10 (1979), 29, 43–4.
4 Alan Richards, *Egypt's Agricultural Development, 1800–1980: Technical and Social Change* (Boulder, 1982), 159, 163.
5 On the politics of the early 1930s, see Marius Deeb, *Party Politics in Egypt: The*

Wafd and Its Rivals, 1919–39 (London, 1979), 240–50; P. J. Vatikiotis, *The Modern History of Egypt* (New York, 1969), 280–5; Afaf Lutfi al-Sayyid Marsot, *Egypt's Liberal Experiment 1922–1936* (Berkeley, 1977), 138–64.

6 For accounts of Egyptian politics in the later 1930s, see Muhammad 'Abd al-'Azim Ramadan, *al-Sira' bayna al-Wafd wa al-'Arsh, 1936–1939* (Cairo, 1979), *passim*; Jacques Berque, *Egypt: Imperialism and Revolution* (trans. by Jean Stewart; London, 1972), 519–36, 559–63; Vatikiotis, *Egypt*, 285–91; Deeb, *Party Politics*, 332–44.

7 See Gershoni and Jankowski, *Egypt, Islam, and the Arabs*, 83–9.

8 The text of the letter is available in Sabri Ghunaym, *'Abd al-Nasir Dhalika al-Insan* (Cairo, 1970), 53–7. See also Georges Vaucher, *Gamal Abdel Nasser et son équipe* (Paris, 1959), 71–5.

9 Ghunaym, *'Abd al-Nasir*, 54.

10 Tawfiq al-Hakim, *Tahta Shams al-Fikr* (2nd edn; Cairo, 1941).

11 Ibid., 186–200.

12 Tawfiq al-Hakim, *Yawmiyyat Na'ib fi al-Aryaf* (Cairo, 1937), 143. English trans. by Abba Eban, *Maze of Justice: Diary of a Country Prosecutor* (2nd edn; Austin, 1989), 112.

13 Muhammad 'Awad Muhammad, "al-Dimuqratiyya bayna al-Shu'ub," *HI*, Dec. 1941, 22.

14 Ramsis Shahata, "Da'wa ila al-Thawra," *MJ*, 1 March 1938, 49–51.

15 *MF*, 31 March 1938, 5.

16 *MF*, 18 July 1938, 5.

17 Tawfiq al-Hakim, *Shajarat al-Hukm* (Cairo, 1945), 11, 13.

18 For systematic critiques of the party system, see Hafiz 'Afifi, *'Ala Hamish al-Siyasa* (Cairo, 1938), 6–8; Mirrit Butrus Ghali, *Siyasat al-Ghad* (Cairo, 1938), 14–20; Mirrit Butrus Ghali and Ibrahim Madkur, *al-Ada al-Hukumiyya* (Cairo, 1943), 81–94.

19 Developed in detail in Hakim, *Tahta Shams al-Fikr*, 184–222.

20 Ibid., 219–20.

21 Ibid., 218; for similar themes, see Ahmad Hasan al-Zayyat writing in *RI*, 4 April 1938, 561–2.

22 Ibrahim al-Misri, "Li-man Yaktubu al-Katib fi Misr," *HI*, July 1938, 987–91 (quotation from 989).

23 Ahmad Husayn, *Imani* (2nd edn; Cairo, 1946), 74–5.

24 Ibid., 75.

25 'Abd al-'Aziz al-Bishri, "Athar al-Siyasa al-Hizbiyya fi al-Akhlaq," *RI*, 17 Dec. 1934, 2041–2; 24 Dec. 1934, 2081–3.

26 Salama Musa, "Ihtiram al-Mu'arada," *MJ*, 1 July 1934, 25; see also his articles in *MJ*, 1 May 1936, 9–10 and 1 Jan. 1937, 17–23.

27 Hakim, *Tahta Shams al-Fikr*, 184.

28 Hakim, *Shajarat al-Hukm*, 11.

29 Hakim, *Tahta Shams al-Fikr*, 160–70.

30 Ibid., 169.

31 Hakim, *Shajarat al-Hukm*, 13.

32 Hakim, *Tahta Shams al-Fikr*, 177; Ahmad Hasan al-Zayyat, "La Taqulu Ayna al-Kuttab wa Qulu Ayna al-Qada'," *RI*, 24 Nov. 1941, 1417–18; Shahata, "Da'wa ila al-Thawra," 49.

33 Ahmad Hasan al-Zayyat, "al-Thaqafa al-Mudhabdhaba," *RI*, 28 Jan. 1935, 121–2.
34 Sayyid Qutb, "Mustaqbal al-Thaqafa fi Misr," *Sahifat Dar al-'Ulum*, 5 (April 1939), 28–79 (quote from 45).
35 Amin al-Khuli, "al-Asalib," *RI*, 4 Dec. 1933, 5–6, 42.
36 Fikri Abaza, "al-Mar'a: Malak wa Shaytan," *HI*, Nov. 1934, 65–8.
37 Khuli, "al-Asalib," 42.
38 'Abd al-'Aziz al-Bishri, "Hajatuna ila Tawhid al-Ziyy," *MJ*, 1 March 1934, 43–4.
39 Muhammad 'Abd al-Wahid Khalaf, "Bayna Jilayn," *TQ*, 28 March 1939, 14–16 (quotation from 14).
40 Zaki Mubarak, *al-Lugha wa al-Din wa al-Taqalid fi Hayat al-Istiqlal* (Cairo, 1936), 89.
41 Ibid.
42 Najib Mahfuz, *al-Maraya* (Cairo, 1972), 11; English translation *Mirrors* (trans. by Roger Allen; Chicago, 1977), 6.
43 See Ellis Goldberg, *Tinker, Tailor, and Textile Worker: Class and Politics in Egypt, 1930–1952* (Berkeley, 1986), 27.
44 Deeb, *Party Politics*, 11; for the nineteenth-century use of the term, see Ehud R. Toledano, *State and Society in Mid-Nineteenth-Century Egypt* (Cambridge, 1990), 69, 155–80.
45 al-Mamlaka al-Misriyya, Wizarat al-Maliyya, Maslahat 'Umum al-Ihsa' wa al-Ta'dad, *Ta'dad Sukkan al-Qutr al-Misri Sanat 1937* (2 vols.: Cairo, 1942), II, 34–5.
46 Charles Issawi, *Egypt at Mid-Century: An Economic Analysis* (London, 1954), 60; al-Mamlaka al-Misriyya, *Ta'dad, 1937*, II, 34–5.
47 Egypt, Ministry of Finance, Statistical and Census Department, *Population Census of Egypt, 1947* (Cairo, 1954), 46–9.
48 Ghali, *Siyasat al-Ghad*, 145 (English translation *The Policy of Tomorrow* (trans. by Isma'il R. el Faruqi; Washington, 1953), 102).
49 Jean-Jacques Waardenburg, *Les Universités dans le monde arabe actuel* (2 vols.: The Hague, 1966), II, 80; Issawi, *Egypt at Mid-Century*, 67.
50 al-Mamlaka al-Misriyya, Wizarat al-Maliyya, Maslahat 'Umum al-Ihsa' wa al-Ta'dad, *Ta'dad Sukkan al-Qutr al-Misri Sanat 1927* (2 vols.; Cairo, 1931), II, 186–9; Egypt, *Census, 1947*, 400–3.
51 Waardenburg, *Les Universités*, II, 80.
52 Ibid., II, 121.
53 For an overview see Daniel Crecelius, "Non-Ideological Responses of the Egyptian Ulama to Modernization," in Nikki R. Keddie (ed.), *Scholars, Saints, and Sufis: Muslim Religious Institutions since 1500* (Berkeley, 1972), 167–209, especially 195–204.
54 Issawi, *Egypt at Mid-Century*, 61–2; Deeb, *Party Politics*, 319.
55 Morroe Berger, *Bureaucracy and Society in Modern Egypt: A Study of the Higher Civil Service* (Princeton, 1957), 82.
56 Waardenburg, *Les Universités*, II, 81.
57 Ibid.
58 See Eric Hobsbawm and Terence Ranger (eds.), *The Invention of Tradition* (Cambridge, 1983).

59 See Deeb, *Party Politics*, 151; Ahmed Abdalla, *The Student Movement and Nationalist Politics in Egypt, 1923–1973* (London, 1985), 34; Haggai Erlich, *Students and University in Twentieth Century Egyptian Politics* (London, 1989), 99; Raoul Makarius, *La Jeunesse intellectuelle d'Egypte au lendemain de la deuxième guerre mondiale* (The Hague, 1960), 11.

60 'Ali Shalabi, *Misr al-Fatah wa Dawruha fi al-Siyasa al-Misriyya* (Cairo, 1982), 277–303.

61 *TH*, 14 Oct. 1937, 2.

62 *TH*, 19 July 1937, 4.

63 *TH*, 21 Oct. 1937, 6; *MF*, 27 Dec. 1938, 8.

64 See Hasan al-Banna, *Mudhakkirat al-Da'wa wa al-Da'iya* (Cairo, n.d.), 10–59.

65 Richard P. Mitchell, *The Society of the Muslim Brothers* (London, 1969), 329.

66 Ibid.

67 Ellis Goldberg, "Muslim Union Politics in Egypt: Two Cases," in Edmund Burke III and Ira Lapidus (eds.), *Islam, Politics, and Social Movements* (Berkeley, 1988), 228–43, especially 235, 240.

68 Uri M. Kupferschmidt, "The Muslim Brothers and the Egyptian Village," *Asian and African Studies*, 16 (1982), 157–70.

69 Mitchell, *Society of Muslim Brothers*, 329; see also Donald M. Reid, *Cairo University and the Making of Modern Egypt* (Cambridge, 1990), 148.

70 Russell Galt, *The Effects of Centralization on Education in Modern Egypt* (Cairo, 1936), 127–9.

71 See Waardenburg, *Les Universités*, II, 225–6; Erlich, *Students and University*, 65–71.

72 Ahmad Amin, *Yawm al-Islam* (Cairo, 1952), 153; cited in Nadav Safran, *Egypt in Search of Political Community* (Cambridge, 1961), 207.

73 Quoted in Fahmy Mahmoud Hussein, "Aims and Objectives of Teaching World History in American and Egyptian Secondary Schools" (Ph.D. dissertation, School of Education, Syracuse University, 1974), 164.

74 Ahmad Husayn, *Imani* (Cairo, 1936), 43.

75 'Abd al-Tawwab 'Abd al-Hayy, *'Asir Hayati* (Cairo, 1966), 55.

76 In his recollections of his youth as given in ibid., 31–3.

77 Husayn, *Imani* (1936 edn), 43–4; (1946 edn), 99.

78 Mahmud Kamil, "Azmat al-Muta'allimin fi Misr," *HI*, Jan. 1931, 177–88; the theme was repeated in an article entitled "Nahdatuna al-Sina'iyya wa Kayfa Nushajji'uha," *HI*, March 1931, 828–31.

79 Issawi, *Egypt at Mid-Century*, 261.

80 The Egyptian *Annuaire Statistique* for 1952 as quoted in Daniel Lerner, *The Passing of Traditional Society: Modernizing the Middle East* (New York, 1958), 238.

81 See Berque, *Egypt: Imperialism and Revolution*, 456–7; Abdalla, *Student Movement*, 34–5.

82 Abdalla, *Student Movement*, 35–6.

83 Deeb, *Party Politics*, 320–2; Erlich, *Students and University*, 100–2.

84 Deeb, *Party Politics*, 261–3.

85 James Jankowski, *Egypt's Young Rebels: "Young Egypt," 1933–1952* (Stanford, 1975), 12.

86 *SA*, 9 Dec. 1933, 7.

87 Quoted in G. Kampffmeyer, "Egypt and Western Asia," in H. A. R. Gibb (ed.), *Whither Islam?* (London, 1932), 101–70 (quote from 136).
88 Quoted in James Heyworth-Dunne, *Religious and Political Trends in Modern Egypt* (Washington, 1950), 108–9.
89 *SA*, 21 Oct. 1933, 5–6; 9 Dec. 1933, 7.
90 Mitchell, *Society of Muslim Brothers*, 8.
91 See ibid., 207–8; Jankowski, *Egypt's Young Rebels*, 13–15, 72–8.
92 Discussed in Safran, *Egypt in Search of Political Community*, 148–50.
93 See Makarius, *La Jeunesse intellectuelle*, 9–14.
94 *HI*, April 1936, 603.
95 See Berque, *Egypt: Imperialism and Revolution*, 520, 534–5.
96 *MF*, 7 April 1938, 2.
97 Speech of June 1938 as quoted in *MF*, 6 June 1938, 6.
98 For examples, see Husayn, *Imani* (1936 edn), 44; Fathi Radwan, '*Asr wa Rijal* (Cairo, 1967), 250–1, 466–8.
99 See 'Abd al-Hayy, '*Asir Hayati*, 54–5; *SI*, 1 Sept. 1929, 5; Husayn, *Imani* (1936 edn), 66–7; Deeb, *Party Politics*, 261–2.
100 Jankowski, *Egypt's Young Rebels*, 11–12.
101 See Abu al-Hajjaj Hafiz, *al-Shahid Kamal al-Din Salah* (Cairo, n.d.), 24–5; Radwan, '*Asr wa Rijal*, 99, 164–5, 401, 468, 601.
102 See Jankowski, *Egypt's Young Rebels*, 12–14.
103 Ibid., 14–16.
104 See Erlich, *Students and University*, 125–32; James Jankowski, "The Egyptian Blue Shirts and the Egyptian Wafd, 1935–1938," *Middle Eastern Studies*, 6 (1970), 77–95.
105 On the founding and early activities of the YMMA see *FH*, 17 Nov. 1927, 11; 1 Dec. 1927, 5–15; Kampffmeyer, "Egypt and Western Asia," 103–12. For the inception of the Brotherhood, see Mitchell, *Society of Muslim Brothers*, 7–11.
106 *RS*, 15 Oct. 1929, 27.
107 Mitchell, *Society of Muslim Brothers*, 328.
108 Heyworth-Dunne, *Religious and Political Trends*, 30.
109 Albert Hourani, *A History of the Arab Peoples* (Cambridge, 1991), 339.
110 al-Mamlaka al-Misriyya, *Ta'dad 1927*, I, 40–3. On Syrians in Egypt, see Albert Hourani, "The Middleman in a Changing Society: Syrians in Egypt in the Eighteenth and Nineteenth Centuries," in his *The Emergence of the Modern Middle East* (Berkeley, 1981), 112.
111 Occupational data on some 300 prominent Syrian residents of Egypt show roughly 20 per cent to have regarded themselves as "journalists" or "writers"; Thomas Philipp, "Demographic Patterns of Syrian Immigration to Egypt during the Nineteenth Century – An Interpretation," *Asian and African Studies*, 16 (1982), 187.
112 Anis Sayigh, *al-Fikra al-'Arabiyya fi Misr* (Beirut, 1959), 178.
113 Hafiz Mahmud, *al-Ma'arik fi al-Sihafa wa al-Siyasa wa al-Fikr bayna 1919–1952* (Cairo, 1969), 55–7.
114 Ahmad Husayn, *Nisf Qarn ma'a al-'Uruba wa Qadiyyat Filastin* (Sidon, 1971), 58.
115 *Bayan* of the Preparatory Committee of the Jam'iyyat al-Wahda al-'Arabiyya in 1931 as quoted in *FH*, 2 Safar 1350, 8.

116 As'ad Daghir, *Mudhakkirati 'ala Hamish al-Qadiyya al-'Arabiyya* (Cairo, 1959), 9–10.
117 Russell to Keown-Boyd, 10 Sept. 1930, FO 141/625, 808/4/30.
118 See *MU*, 10 May 1931, 3; 15 June 1931, 1.
119 *FI*, 15 Dec. 1931, 3.
120 Discussed in Daghir, *Mudhakkirati*, 242–5.
121 Program in *FH*, 27 Rajab 1357, 29.
122 See *RI*, 20 Feb. 1939, 378–9.
123 For its formation, organization, and goals see *RA*, 27 May 1936, 1; 22 July 1936, 20–1.
124 For examples of its activities, see *RA*, 9 Sept. 1936, 22–3; 14 April 1937, 960–2; 23 June 1937, 4–9; 26 Jan. 1938, 16–17; 17 May 1939, 1200–13.
125 Sayigh, *al-Fikra al-'Arabiyya*, 180.
126 For examples, see *SM*, 4 (1932–3), 516–19; 5 (1933–4), 47–52, 128.
127 Discussed in Husayn, *Nisf Qarn*, 71.
128 See the annual British Pilgrimage Reports as contained in FO 371/5094, E15761/38/44; FO 371/9999, E25/11/91; FO 371/11436, E5283/155/91; FO 371/12999, E4867/58/91; FO 371/20055, E5367/27/25; FO 371/23267, E7015/98/25.
129 Anwar al-Jundi, *Ahmad Zaki* (Cairo, 1964), 81–2.
130 For 'Azmi's journalistic travels, see *SU*, 11 Dec. 1926, 14–15, and subsequent issues; for Mazini's, *RI*, 26 Aug. 1935, 1363–4.
131 See *IM*, 6 Aug. 1935, 6.
132 Testimony in *SU*, 2 Aug. 1930, 13, 26; 9 Aug. 1930, 22.
133 For Harb's travels in Arab countries in the 1920s, see *RS*, 15 July 1929, 26–8; for Shafiq's trip to the Hijaz, see Ahmad Shafiq, *A'mali ba'da Mudhakkirati* (Cairo, 1941), 275–85.
134 For examples, see Ibrahim 'Abd al-Qadir al-Mazini, *Rihlat al-Hijaz* (Cairo, 1930); Muhammad Sulayman, *Rasa'il Sa'ir* (Cairo, 1935); Muhiy al-Din Rida, *Rihlati ila al-Hijaz* (Cairo, 1935); Muhammad Thabit, *Jawwala fi Rubu' al-Sharq al-Adna* (Cairo, 1936); Ahmad Kamil, "Rihlat al-'Iraq," *MT*, 15 June 1936, 111–20; Zaki Mubarak, *Wahy Baghdad* (Cairo, 1938); 'Abd al-Wahhab 'Azzam, *Rihalat* (Cairo, 1939).
135 *RS*, 15 Feb. 1930, 9.
136 For examples, see *SM*, 5 (1933–4), 47–52; 6 (1934–5), 194–9, 584; *RA*, 10 March 1937, 33; 20 Aug. 1938, 30.
137 See below, Chapter 8.
138 *RA*, 17 Feb. 1937, 611.
139 See *Apulu*, Nov. 1932, 286–8; Dec. 1932, 503–4; Oct. 1933, 151–3; Nov. 1933, 170–1; June 1934, 896–7; Sept. 1934, 4–8.
140 Ibid., Oct. 1933, 152; March 1934, 615.
141 *MU*, 4 Nov. 1933, 5–6.
142 *RI*, 11 Jan. 1937, 73.
143 Account in *RA*, 6 Jan. 1937, 278–9.
144 *RA*, 8 April 1938, 9–10, 49; Shafiq, *A'mali*, 161–2.
145 Sayigh, *al-Fikra al-'Arabiyya*, 184.
146 See *MT*, 17 Jan. 1936, 334–5; *BL*, 11 March 1936, 1, 11; Mubarak, *Wahy Baghdad*, 409–17; Khalil al-Hindawi and 'Umar al-Daqqaq, *al-Muqtabis min*

Wahy al-Risala: Ahmad Hasan al-Zayyat, Dirasa wa Mukhtarat (Aleppo, 1965), 5–6; 'Abd al-Razzaq al-Hilali, *Zaki Mubarak fi al-'Iraq* (Beirut, 1969), 45–8.

147 Ahmad Hasan al-Zayyat, "Shabab al-'Iraq fi Misr," *RI*, 2 March 1936, 321–2; 'Abd al-Wahhab 'Azzam, *Rihalat*, 40–8, 181–9, 360–4; 'Abd al-Mun'im Muhammad Khalaf, "Min al-Nil ila al-Rafidayn," *RI*, 9 Nov. 1936, 1836–7; Mubarak, *Wahy Baghdad*, 54–65, 121–3, 151–2, 250–8, 272–303, 396–417; Nabih Bayyumi 'Abd Allah, *Tatawwur Fikrat al-Qawmiyya al-'Arabiyya fi Misr* (Cairo, 1975), 86–7.

148 Mahmud 'Azmi, "al-'Alam al-Asmar: Ta'rifuhu wa Tanzimuhu," *HI*, May 1929, 1039–44 (quotation from 1042).

149 Husayn, *Nisf Qarn*, 37–40.

150 Ahmad Hasan al-Zayyat, "Misr wa Akhawatuha," *RI*, 4 March 1935, 321–2.

151 *RS*, 15 Oct. 1930, 40.

152 See *BL*, 8 to 26 July 1934, and *RI*, 26 Aug. 1935, 1363–4.

153 Quoted in *FH*, 9 Safar 1355, 9.

154 As quoted in *RA*, 26 Jan. 1938, 32.

155 Reports in *MR*, 6 Jan. 1931, 465–74, and *FH*, 27 Rajab 1349, 2.

156 "Hadaratuna al-Qadima: Fir'awniyya am 'Arabiyya am Gharbiyya," *HI*, April 1931, 817–27.

157 In his regular column in *KS*, 28 Aug. 1933, 6.

158 Many of the contributions to the debate which appeared in late 1933 are republished, in abbreviated form, in Anwar al-Jundi, *al-Ma'arik al-Adabiyya fi al-Shi'r wa al-Nashr wa al-Thaqafa wa al-Lugha al-Qawmiyya al-'Arabiyya* (Cairo, 1961), 17–43.

159 For examples, see *BL*, 6 Sept. 1933, 7; 8 Sept. 1933, 1, 8; 12 Sept. 1933, 1, 3.

160 'Abd al-Qadir al-Mazini, "al-Balagh wa al-Duktur Taha: Hawla Maqal 'Misr wa al-'Arab,'" *BL*, 9 Sept. 1933, 7.

161 Hasan al-Banna, "Misr 'Arabiyya," *IM*, 1 Jumada al-Akhira 1352, 2.

162 'Abd al-Qadir Hamza, "Misr wa al-'Arab," *BL*, 7 Sept. 1933, 7.

163 'Abd al-Rahman 'Azzam, "Alaysat Misr 'Arabiyya," *BL*, 29 Aug. 1933, 7.

164 Muhammad Amin Hassuna, "Misriyyun Yunaduna bi al-Fir'awniyya, wa Isbaniyyun Da'una li-al-'Arabiyya!," part 1, *MSU*, 29 Sept. 1933, 21–3; part 2, *MSU*, 1 Nov. 1933, 16–17.

165 Ahmad Hasan al-Zayyat, "Fir'awniyyun wa 'Arab!," *RI*, 1 Oct. 1933, 3–4.

166 Banna, "Misr 'Arabiyya," 3.

167 'Ali al-'Inani, "Bayan 'Amm li-al-'Arab," *NF*, 1 Nov. 1933, 3–4.

168 'Abd al-Rahman 'Azzam, "Alaysat Misr 'Arabiyya," part 1, *BL*, 29 Aug. 1933, 7.

169 'Abd al-Rahman 'Azzam, "Alaysat Misr 'Arabiyya," part 2, *BL*, 11 Sept. 1933, 7.

170 Ibid.

171 In his column in *KS*, 8 Sept. 1933, 7.

172 Hasan Subhi, "Hadith al-Masa'," *BL*, 16 Sept. 1933, 1, 3; Muhammad Zaki Ibrahim, "Thaqafat Misr," *BL*, 24 Sept. 1933, 1, 9.

173 Muhammad Kamil Husayn, "La Fir'awniyya wa La 'Arabiyya," *KS*, 2 Oct. 1933, as reprinted in Jundi, *al-Ma'arik*, 42–3; Hasan 'Arif, "'Arabiyya am Fir'awniyya," *BL*, 11 Oct. 1933, 7.

174 Muhammad Husayn Haykal, "Fir'awniyya wa 'Arabiyya," *MSU*, 29 Sept. 1933, 24–8.

175 'Abd al-Qadir Hamza, "Makan Misr min al-'Arab wa al-Qawmiyya al-'Arabiyya,"
      BL, 13 Sept. 1933, 1.
176 Mahmud 'Azmi, "Ayyuha Nuqaddimu: al-Rabita al-Sharqiyya am al-Rabita
      al-Islamiyya am al-Rabita al-'Arabiyya," *HI*, Nov. 1933, 53–8.
177 Letter from 'Azzam to Mr. Hamilton, Oct. 1933; contained in FO 141/744,
      834/2/33.

2 NOW IS THE TURN OF THE EAST

 1 The phrase was used by Fathi Radwan in his article "Mu'tamar al-Talaba
     al-Sharqiyyin wa Fajr al-Sharq," *MSU*, 8 July 1932, 8.
 2 The concept of orientations is ours. Our discussion of ideology is based primarily
     on the "culturalist-hermeneutic" approach expounded by such authors as Paul
     Ricoeur, Clifford Geertz, and Dominick LaCapra. See Paul Ricoeur, *Herme-
     neutics and the Human Sciences* (ed. and trans. by John B. Thompson; Cambridge,
     1981); Ricoeur, *Lectures on Ideology and Utopia* (ed. by George H. Taylor;
     Chicago, 1986); John B. Thompson, *Studies in the Theory of Ideology* (Cam-
     bridge, 1984), especially 1–6, 173–204; Thompson, *Critical Hermeneutics; A
     Study of the Thought of Paul Ricoeur and Jurgen Habermas* (Cambridge, 1983),
     36–70, 115–49; Clifford Geertz, *The Interpretation of Cultures* (New York, 1973),
     193–254.
 3 Thompson rephrasing Ricoeur, in his *Studies*, 174.
 4 See Gershoni and Jankowski, *Egypt, Islam, and the Arabs*, Part II.
 5 Yahya Ahmad al-Dardiri, "Asas Nahdat al-Muslimin wa al-Sharqiyyin," *SM*,
     Nov. 1929, 81–6.
 6 Hasan al-Banna, "Inna fi Dhalika li-'Ibra," *FH*, 7 Feb. 1929, 1–2 (quotation from
     2).
 7 Hasan al-Banna, "al-Sabil ila al-Islah fi al-Sharq," *FH*, 25 April 1929, 1–3.
 8 Ibrahim 'Abd al-Qadir al-Mazini, "al-Hayat al-Misriyya wa Hajatuha ila 'Anasir
     al-Quwwa wa al-Khayal," *HI*, March 1930, 549–52.
 9 Ahmad Amin, "Bayna al-Ya's wa al-Raja'," *RI*, 1 Sept. 1933, 7–8.
10 Mansur Fahmi, "Mawqif al-Sharq min Hadarat al-Gharb," *HI*, Nov. 1931,
     49–50, 56.
11 Mansur Fahmi, "Nahwa Thaqafa Sharqiyya Khalisa," *RA*, 21 July 1937, 16–17.
12 Zayyat, "al-Thaqafa al-Mudhabdhaba," 121–2.
13 'Abd al-Wahhab 'Azzam, "al-Nahda al-Turkiyya al-Akhira," part 2, *RI*, 24 June
     1935, 1009.
14 Ibid.
15 Dardiri, "Asas Nahdat," 82.
16 Ibid.
17 Banna, "Inna fi Dhalika," 2.
18 Banna, "al-Sabil," 2.
19 Banna, "Inna fi Dhalika," 2.
20 Mansur Fahmi, "al-Sharq wa al-Hadara al-Gharbiyya," *MQ*, Oct. 1930, 257–63
     (quotation from 261).
21 Fahmi, "Nahwa," 17. See also his "al-Sharq fi al-Mathal al-A'la," *MSU*, 14 Oct.
     1932, 1.
22 'Abd al-Wahhab 'Azzam, "Wajib al-Sharqiyyin al-Yawm," *MSU*, 14 Oct. 1932, 5.

23 Ibid.
24 Zayyat, "al-Thaqafa al-Mudhabdhaba," 122.
25 Mazini, "al-Hayat al-Misriyya," 552.
26 Mustafa Sadiq al-Rafi'i, *Wahy al-Qalam* (3 vols., 5th edn; Cairo, 1954), III, 203–4.
27 Qutb, "Mustaqbal al-Thaqafa fi Misr," 45–6.
28 Muhammad Husayn Haykal, *Fi Manzil al-Wahy* (Cairo, 1937), 22. For Haykal's changing attitude in the late 1920s and early 1930s, see his articles "al-Nur al-Jadid," *HI*, Feb. 1928, 399–403, and "al-'Aql wa al-Ruh," *SU*, 18 May 1929, 3–4; Charles Smith, *Islam and the Search for Social Order in Modern Egypt: A Biography of Muhammad Husayn Haykal* (Albany, 1983), 96–113; David Semah, *Four Egyptian Literary Critics* (Leiden, 1974), 97–100.
29 Haykal, *Fi Manzil al-Wahy*, 629–37.
30 Ibid., 22.
31 Ibid.
32 For examples, see Muhammad Amin Hassuna, *Wara'a al-Bihar* (Cairo, 1936), 52–64; Ahmad Hasan al-Zayyat, "al-Ghazi Kamal Ataturk," *RI*, 14 Nov. 1938, 1841–2; Mubarak, *al-Lugha*, 98–103; Fathiyya 'Azmi, "Istithmar Nahdat al-Mar'a al-Misriyya," *RI*, 13 April 1936, 581–3.
33 Ahmad Hasan al-Zayyat, "Ila Ayna Yusaq al-Atrak?", *RI*, 11 March 1935, 361–2.
34 Ahmad Amin, "Nahdatuna al-Fikriyya," *HI*, April 1937, 653–6.
35 'Abd al-Wahhab 'Azzam, "al-Nahda al-Turkiyya al-Akhira," part 7, *RI*, 5 Aug. 1935, 1254.
36 Muhammad 'Abd Allah 'Inan, "Harb Munazzama Yashharuha al-Kamaliyyun 'ala al-Islam," *RI*, 14 Jan. 1935, 45–7.
37 Ibid., 46.
38 Muhammad Husayn Haykal, *Thawrat al-Adab* (Cairo, 1933), 12.
39 Haykal, *Fi Manzil al-Wahy*, 23.
40 Ibid., 23–5; also Charles Smith, "The 'Crisis of Orientation': The Shift of Egyptian Intellectuals to Islamic Subjects in the 1930s," *International Journal of Middle East Studies*, 4 (1973), 382–410.
41 Haykal, *Fi Manzil al-Wahy*, 24.
42 Banna, "al-Sabil," 3.
43 Muhammad Lutfi Jum'a, *Hayat al-Sharq* (Cairo, 1932), 14–16.
44 Qutb, "Mustaqbal al-Thaqafa fi Misr," 46.
45 See Muhammad Lutfi Jum'a, "Nahdat al-Sharq al-'Arabi," *HI*, Dec. 1922, 237–42; Jum'a, "al-Nahda al-Sharqiyya al-Haditha," *MQ*, Aug. 1927, 141–3; Jum'a, "al-Hayat al-Jadida fi Misr," *BU*, 27 March 1929, 8–9.
46 Jum'a, *Hayat al-Sharq*, 6–20.
47 Ibid., 12.
48 See ibid., 11–17.
49 See particularly Mansur Fahmi, *Khatarat Nafs* (Cairo, 1930).
50 Fahmi, "al-Sharq," 257–63; Fahmi, "Mawqif al-Sharq," 49–59.
51 Fahmi, "al-Sharq," 262–3.
52 Ibid.; Fahmi, "al-Sharq fi al-Mathal al-A'la," 3; Fahmi, "Masir al-Madaniyya wa Mawqif al-Sharq minha fi Ma'al," *HI*, Feb. 1932, 513–20.
53 See Hafiz Mahmud, "Misr bi-Majdiha Ula," *MJ*, Feb. 1931, 474–6; Mahmud, "Misr lil-Misriyyin," ibid., April 1931, 733–6.

54 Hafiz Mahmud, "al-Maddiyya fi Urubba," *SU*, 21 Jan. 1939, 4–5.
55 Ibid., 5.
56 Ibid.
57 Muhammad Husayn Haykal, "al-Sharq wa al-Gharb," part 1, *MSU*, 29 Sept.
    1933, 33–4; part 2, *MSU*, 1 Nov. 1933, 12–13; part 3, *MSU*, 30 Nov. 1933, 8–10;
    republished in Haykal, *al-Sharq al-Jadid* (2nd edn; Cairo, 1962), 13–69 (refer-
    ences to the latter).
58 Haykal, *al-Sharq al-Jadid*, 13.
59 Ibid., 16–17.
60 Ibid., 69.
61 Ibid., 50–3.
62 Ibid., 65.
63 Ibid., 69.
64 Ibid., 67.
65 Ibid., 67–8.
66 Ibid., 68.
67 See *IM*, 2 Rabi' al-Awwal 1353, 1–3; 3 Safar 1353, 1–3; 19 May 1936, 19; 14 Oct.
    1938, 3; *KL*, 16 Dec. 1938, 1–6.
68 See *IM*, 2 Rabi' al-Awwal 1353, 2–3; 3 Safar 1953, 2–3; 5 Nov. 1935, 12–14; 26
    May 1936, 1–3; 11 Aug. 1936, 1–3; 24 June 1938, 1–2.
69 Salih Mustafa 'Ashmawi, "al-Kufr Milla Wahida wa al-Isti'mar Dhull Wahid,"
    ND, 29 Muharram 1358, 4.
70 Ibid., 4.
71 Ibid., 3.
72 Banna, *Bayna al-Ams wa al-Yawm*, 24; trans. in Charles Wendell, *Five Tracts of
    Hasan al-Banna' (1906–1949)* (Berkeley, 1978), 13–39.
73 Ibid., 24 (Eng. trans. 31).
74 Ibid., 20–1 (Eng. trans. 28).
75 Ibid., 22 (Eng. trans. 29).
76 Haykal, "al-Nur al-Jadid," 399–400.
77 Muhammad Husayn Haykal, "Hadarat al-Sharq," *SU*, 29 Dec. 1928, 3–4.
78 Haykal, "al-'Aql wa al-Ruh," 4.
79 "Nihayat al-Hadara al-Gharbiyya," *HI*, Nov. 1929, 57–60.
80 Ibid. For similar editorials in *al-Hilal*, see *HI*, April 1932, 817–21; Aug. 1933,
    1385–8.
81 Jum'a, *Hayat al-Sharq*, 5–17.
82 Ibid., 16.
83 Ibid.
84 Radwan, "Mu'tamar al-Talaba al-Sharqiyyin," 8.
85 Ibid.
86 Husayn, *Imani* (1946 edn), 46–7.
87 Ibid., 47.
88 Ibid.
89 'Abd al-Wahhab 'Azzam, "'Ibrat al-Hadathat," *RI*, 30 Sept. 1935, 1561.
90 Ibid., 1562.
91 Ibid.; see also his "Madaniyya Za'ifa!," *RI*, 8 Jan. 1934, 21.
92 Ahmad Hasan al-Zayyat, "Khaybat al-Madaniyya," *RI*, 28 Oct. 1935, 1721–2.
93 Ahmad Hasan al-Zayyat, "al-Risala fi 'Ammiha al-Khamis," *RI*, 4 Jan. 1937, 1.
94 'Abbas Mahmud al-'Aqqad, "Masir al-Hadara," *RI*, 6 Sept. 1937, 1444–5.

95 Ibid., 1445.
96 'Azzam, "'Ibrat al-Hadathat," 1562.
97 Ahmad Hasan al-Zayyat, "Min al-Dhikrayat al-Jamila," *RI*, 18 July 1938, 1162.
98 'Aqqad, "Masir al-Hadara," 1445.
99 Tawfiq al-Hakim, '*Usfur min al-Sharq* (2nd. edn; Cairo, 1941), 222. For discuss-
     ions of the novel, see M. M. Badawi, *Modern Arabic Literature and the West*
     (London, 1985), 83–97; Paul Starkey, *From the Ivory Tower: A Critical Study of
     Tawfiq al-Hakim* (London, 1987), 108–29.
100 Hakim, '*Usfur*, 227.
101 Ibid.
102 Hasan al-Banna, *Nahwa al-Nur* (Cairo, 1937), 7; trans. in Wendell, *Five Tracts*,
     103–32 (Eng. trans. 106).
103 Banna, *Bayna al-Ams wa al-Yawm*, 17 (Eng. trans. 25).
104 Banna, *Nahwa al-Nur*, 8 (Eng. trans. 107).
105 Banna, *Bayna al-Ams wa al-Yawm*, 24 (Eng. trans. 31).
106 For examples, see Salama Musa, "al-Sharq Sharq wa al-Gharb Gharb," *MJ*,
     May 1930, 882–8; Musa, "Tatawwur al-Wataniyya," *MJ*, May 1937, 61–9;
     Musa, "al-Sharq wa al-Gharb," *MJ*, April 1938, 9–14.
107 See Muhammad Ahmad al-Sawi's editorials in *MT*, 1 Dec. 1934, 2; 1 June 1935,
     front page; 15 Feb. 1937, 498–505.
108 Husayn Fawzi, *Sindibad 'Asri* (Cairo, 1938); Fawzi, "Kayfa Na'mal 'ala Ihya'
     al-Thaqafa al-'Arabiyya," *MJ*, Feb. 1938, 87–93; Isma'il Ahmad Adham, "al-
     Tatawwur al-Hadith fi Misr wa Turkiya," *MJ*, April 1937, 17–28; Adham,
     "Misr wa al-Thaqafa al-Urubbiyya," *MJ*, May 1937, 17–31; Amir Buqtur,
     "Imtizaj al-Thaqafa - Hal Hunaka Thaqafa Sharqiyya wa Ukhra Gharbiyya?,"
     HI, April 1933, 777–83; Amin al-Khuli, "al-Sharq wa al-Gharb Yaltaqiyan,"
     HI, Feb. 1934, 444–8.
109 Taha Husayn, *Mustaqbal al-Thaqafa fi Misr* (2 vols; Cairo, 1938), I, 10–11. For
     a condensed translation, see Taha Hussein, *The Future of Culture in Egypt*
     (trans. by Sidney Glaser; New York, 1954).
110 Ibid., I, 14–15 (Eng. trans. 5).
111 Ibid., I, 25–6 (Eng. trans. 9).
112 Ibid., I, 69–70 (Eng. trans. 22).
113 Ahmad Amin, "Bayna al-Gharb wa al-Sharq aw al-Maddiyya wa al-
     Ruhaniyya," *TQ*, 10 Jan. 1939, 2–5.
114 Mahmud, "al-Maddiyya fi Urubba," 4.
115 Qutb, "Mustaqbal al-Thaqafa fi Misr," 28–79.
116 Ibid., 47–9.

3 THE RETURN OF ISLAM

1 The phrase was coined by Bernard Lewis in his essay "The Return of Islam,"
    Commentary, 61 (Jan. 1976), 39–49.
2 Account in *SU*, 30 Jan. 1937, 1.
3 Muhammad Rida, *Abu Bakr al-Siddiq* (Cairo, 1935), 4.
4 Muhammad Husayn Haykal, *Hayat Muhammad* (Cairo, 1935); English trans. by
    Isma'il Maji A. el Faruqi, *The Life of Muhammad* (n.p., 1976). The following
    discussion is based on the second edition (Cairo, 1936).

5 For the work's publication history, see *Hayat Muhammad*, 582–3; Antonie Wessels, *A Modern Arabic Biography of Muhammad: A Critical Study of Muhammad Husayn Haykal's "Hayat Muhammad"* (Leiden, 1972), 37–41.

6 Husayn, *Mustaqbal*, II, back page.

7 Interview with Muhammad Husayn Haykal in *MT*, 1 March 1935, 610–11; Muhammad Husayn Haykal, *al-Siddiq Abu Bakr* (Cairo, 1942), 9–11; interviews with Hafiz Mahmud, 2–3 Feb. 1981.

8 Particularly Wessels, *Biography of Muhammad*, *passim*; Smith, *Haykal*, 109–30.

9 Haykal, *Hayat Muhammad*, 245–6; see also ibid., 61–2, 506–9; Wessels, *Biography of Muhammad*, 68–9, 92–3.

10 Haykal, *Hayat Muhammad*, 72; see also Wessels, *Biography of Muhammad*, 79–80.

11 Haykal, *Hayat Muhammad*, 71–3, 202–9; see also Wessels, *Biography of Muhammad*, 78–86.

12 Haykal, *Hayat Muhammad*, 416–31, 446–55; see also Wessels, *Biography of Muhammad*, 123.

13 Haykal, *Hayat Muhammad*, 139–40, 245–7, 515, 544–5; see also Wessels, *Biography of Muhammad*, 95.

14 Haykal, *Hayat Muhammad*, 166; see also Wessels, *Biography of Muhammad*, 56.

15 Haykal, *Hayat Muhammad*, 165; see also Wessels, *Biography of Muhammad*, 91.

16 Haykal, *Fi Manzil al-Wahy*, 14–17, 634–7.

17 Haykal, *Fi Manzil al-Wahy*, 166–89; see also M. M. Badawi, "Islam in Modern Egyptian Literature," *Journal of Arabic Literature*, 2 (1971), 164–5; Smith, *Haykal*, 133–4.

18 Haykal, *Fi Manzil al-Wahy*, 634.

19 Ibid., 635; see also Smith, *Haykal*, 135.

20 Haykal, *al- Siddiq Abu Bakr*; Haykal, *al-Faruq 'Umar* (2 vols.; Cairo, 1944); Haykal, *'Uthman ibn 'Affan* (4th edn; Cairo, 1977).

21 See Haykal, *Abu Bakr*, 10–22, 28, 372–7; Haykal, *'Umar*, I, 1–22; II, 237–8, 300–2, 334–48.

22 *MT*, Nov. 1936, 935.

23 Tawfiq al-Hakim, *Muhammad* (Cairo, 1936), 31–46, 143–9, 301–16, 329–35; also Wessels, *Biography of Muhammad*, 12–13; Badawi, "Islam," 168–9.

24 'Abd al-Rahman 'Azzam, *Batal al-Abtal aw Abraz Sifat al-Nabiy Muhammad* (Cairo, 1938).

25 Ibid., vii–viii, 1–4, 106–17.

26 'Abd al-Rahman 'Azzam, *al-Risala al-Khalida* (2nd edn; Cairo, 1954), 3, 223–5, 240–6, 302–3.

27 'Abbas Mahmud al-'Aqqad, *'Abqariyyat Muhammad* (2nd edn; Cairo, 1942), 3.

28 'Aqqad, *Muhammad*, 5–7; see also Wessels, *Biography of Muhammad*, 14–15.

29 'Aqqad, *Muhammad*, 10–16, 116–28, 284–96.

30 Ibid., 34–48; 'Abbas Mahmud al-'Aqqad, *'Abqariyyat 'Umar* (Cairo, 1942), 3–8; al-'Aqqad, *'Abqariyyat al-Siddiq* (Cairo, 1943), 3–9; al-'Aqqad, *'Abqariyyat al-Imam* (Cairo, 1943), 3–8; al-'Aqqad, *'Abqariyyat Khalid*, (Cairo, 1944), 3–16.

31 'Aqqad, *Muhammad*, 28–48 (quotation from 34).

32 Ibid., 6–16, 284.

33 Mahmud Taymur, *al-Nabiy al-Insan wa Maqalat Ukhar* (Cairo, 1945), 13, as quoted in Badawi, "Islam," 162.

34 Taymur, *al-Nabiy al-Insan*, 14, as quoted in Badawi, "Islam," 162.

35 Husayn al-Harawi, *al-Mustashriqun wa al-Islam* (Cairo, 1936), 47–57 (quotation from 53).
36 Muhammad Sa'id Lutfi, *al-Siyar* (Cairo, 1938).
37 From the list of "Book of the Month" publications listed on the back page of Muhammad Subayh, *Faysal al-Awwal* (Cairo, 1945).
38 Husayn's account appeared in *WN*, 19 May to 11 July 1935; for references to the others see above, Chapter 1, n. 134.
39 See Gershoni and Jankowski, *Egypt, Islam, and the Arabs*, 170–5.
40 See Mazini, *Rihlat al-Hijaz*, 5–17, 159–66; Rida, *Rihlati*, 5–8, 124–7; Haykal, *Fi Manzil al-Wahy*, 33–47, 543, 615–27; 'Azzam, *Batal*, 1–3; 'Azzam, *Rihalat*, 334–7.
41 Vatikiotis, *Egypt*, 170.
42 For a discussion of *Nur al-Islam* see Wilfred Cantwell Smith, *Islam in Modern History* (Princeton, 1957), 122–56.
43 See *HI*, Aug. 1935 (al-Mutanabbi); Aug. 1936 (Abu Nuwas).
44 *al-Muqtataf* Library, *Fi Misr al-Islamiyya*, 1.
45 Interviews with Hafiz Mahmud, 18 July 1980 and 6 Feb. 1981.
46 Muhammad Sayyid Muhammad, *al-Zayyat wa al-Risala* (Riyadh, 1982), 48.
47 The first such special issue celebrating the new *hijri* year appeared in *RI*, 26 March 1934; those celebrating the birthday of the Prophet commenced on 25 June 1934.
48 Ahmad Hasan al-Zayyat, "al-Risala," *RI*, 15 Jan. 1933, 1.
49 Ni'mat Ahmad Fu'ad, *Qimam Adabiyya* (Cairo, 1967), 177.
50 See *RI*, 20 May 1935, 840, and Muhammad, *al-Zayyat*, 190.
51 *RI*, 20 May 1935, 177, 182; also Muhammad, *al-Zayyat*, 190.
52 "Note: Sur la presse égyptienne et la presse palestinienne à la fin de 1944," *Cahiers de l'Orient contemporain*, 1 (1945), 124–7.
53 *TQ*, 21 Feb. 1939; 2 May 1939.
54 For examples from the first few months of the journal, see *TQ*, 17 Jan. 1939, 2–3; 14 Feb. 1939, 20–1, 31–4; 28 March 1939, 7–16; 4 April 1939, 26–30; 18 April 1939, 9–11; 25 April 1939, 6–8; 2 May 1939, 1–4, 19–22.
55 Haykal, *Hayat Muhammad*, 37 (Eng. trans. li).
56 Ibid., 36.
57 *MT*, 1 March 1935, 610.
58 Ibid., 610–11; see also Haykal, *Hayat Muhammad*, 36–7.
59 Muhammad Husayn Haykal, "Kayfa wa Limadha Aktubu *Hayat Muhammad*?," *MSU*, 23 May 1932, 2.
60 Muhammad Husayn Haykal, "Thawrat al-Adab: min Haykal ila Taha [Husayn]," *RI*, 15 June 1933, 41–2 (quotation from 41).
61 Tawfiq al-Hakim, "al-Difa' 'an al-Islam," *RI*, 15 April 1935, 576–80.
62 Ibid., 576.
63 Ibid., 577.
64 'Aqqad, *Muhammad*, 8.
65 Ibid., 191.
66 Ibid., 49–103, 182–219.
67 'Abd al-Wahhab Najjar, *Qisas al-Anbiya'* (Cairo, 1932), 8–12.
68 Harawi, *al-Mustashriqun*, 12.
69 Ibid., 16.
70 Muhammad Rida, *al-Imam 'Ali ibn Abi Talib* (Cairo, 1939), 355–60.

71 Muhammad Husayn Haykal, "al-Fir'awniyya wa al-'Arabiyya: Hadir La Madi lahu La Mustaqbal lahu," *MSU*, 29 Sept. 1933, 24–8.
72 Muhammad Husayn Haykal, "al-Ta'awun fi al-Ihya' al-'Arabi," *HI*, May 1935, 768.
73 Haykal, *Abu Bakr*, 10.
74 Haykal, *Fi Manzil al-Wahy*, 24–9.
75 Haykal, *Hayat Muhammad*, 514–15; interview with Haykal, *MT*, 1 March 1935, 610–11; Haykal, *Abu Bakr*, 9–28; Haykal, *'Umar*, I, 1–22.
76 Taha Husayn, *'Ala Hamish al-Sira* (I, 23rd edn, Cairo, 1974; II, 14th edn, Cairo, 1973; III, 9th edn, Cairo, 1968), I, 2–6; see also Pierre Cachia, *Taha Husayn: His Place in the Egyptian Literary Renaissance* (London, 1956), 198.
77 Ahmad Hasan al-Zayyat, "al-Risala fi 'Ammiha al-Rabi'," *RI*, 6 Jan. 1936, 1–2.
78 Ahmad Hasan al-Zayyat, "al-Risala fi 'Ammiha al-Sadis," *RI*, 3 Jan. 1938, 2.
79 'Azzam, *Batal*, 1–2; 'Azzam, *al-Risala al-Khalida*, 3–8.
80 'Abd al-Wahhab 'Azzam, *Mudhakkirat fi Ta'rikh al-Umma al-'Arabiyya* (Cairo, 1932), 2–3, 192–4.
81 Rida, *al-Imam 'Ali ibn Abi Talib*, 355–60.
82 Ahmad Hasan al-Zayyat, *Wahy al-Risala* (multi-vol.; 2nd edn; Cairo, 1954), IV, 72–5. See also Muhammad, *al-Zayyat*, 46–50.
83 Ahmad Hasan al-Zayyat, "al-Risala," 15 Jan. 1933, 1.
84 For examples, see *RI*, 1 Feb. 1933, 1; 1 Jan. 1934, 1–2; 6 Jan. 1936, 1–2; 4 Jan. 1937, 1–2; 3 Jan. 1938, 1–2; 2 Jan. 1939, 1–2.
85 Rida, *Abu Bakr*, 3; Mubarak, *al-Lugha*, 5; 'Abd al-Wahhab 'Azzam, *Mahd al-'Arab* (Cairo, 1946), 5.
86 Husayn, *Hamish*, I, 1; see also Badawi, "Islam," 169.
87 Husayn, *Hamish*, I, 6–7.
88 Haykal, *Fi Manzil al-Wahy*, 22–3.
89 Ibid., 23.
90 Ibid., 25.
91 Ibid., 22.
92 Ibid., 21–9, 629–37; see also Semah, *Four Egyptian Literary Critics*, 99.
93 See Chartier, "Intellectual History?", 32–46.
94 Muhammad 'Awad Muhammad's review in *RI*, 18 Dec. 1933, 40–2.
95 Ibid., 40.
96 Anon., "Kutub Jadida," *HI*, Jan. 1934, 375–6.
97 Ahmad Hasan al-Zayyat, "Muhammad," *RI*, 3 Feb. 1936, 161.
98 Review of "'Ala Hamish al-Sira," in *HI*, Feb. 1934, 526.
99 Hakim, "Difa' 'an al-Islam," 579.
100 Anon., "Kutub Jadida," *HI*, May 1935, 869–71.
101 Anon., "Kitab *Hayat Muhammad*," *RI*, 15 April 1935, 637–9.
102 The event was covered by Radio Cairo and received front-page press coverage; see *AH*, 16 May 1935, 1, and Wessels, *Biography of Muhammad*, 40–1.
103 Anon., "Takrim al-Duktur Muhammad Husayn Haykal," *RI*, 20 May 1935, 837.
104 Ibid.
105 Anon., "Kutub Jadida," *HI*, Feb. 1938, 469–70.
106 Ibid., 469.

107 Muhammad Fahmi 'Abd al-Latif, "Fi Manzil al-Wahy," part 1, *RI*, 31 Jan. 1938, 196–8 (quotation from 197).
108 Muhammad Fahmi 'Abd al-Latif, "Fi Manzil al-Wahy," part 2, 7 Feb. 1938, 237–8.
109 Mustafa Sadiq al-Rafi'i, "Muhammad: Kitab Tawfiq al-Hakim," *RI*, 10 Feb. 1936, 239.
110 Zayyat, "Muhammad," 161.
111 Ibid., 162.
112 Muhammad Sa'id al-'Aryan, "Muhammad: Kitab al-Ustadh Tawfiq al-Hakim," *RI*, 24 Feb. 1936, 318.
113 Muhibb al-Din al-Khatib, "Hayat Muhammad," *MQ*, June 1935, 118–21 (quotation from 119).
114 Ibid., 118–19.
115 Ibid., 119.
116 Hasan al-Banna, "al-Duktur Haykal wa Kitab *Hayat Muhammad*," *IM*, 21 May 1935, 30.
117 Ibid.
118 Ibid.
119 Anon., "Kitab *Hayat Muhammad* li al-Duktur Haykal," *SA*, 4 April 1935, 7, 14.
120 *Tilmidh* (Student) Muhammad 'Abduh, "al-Duktur Muhammad Husayn Haykal bayna al-Ams wa al-Yawm," *ND*, 29 Jumada al-Ula 1358, 3–4.
121 Haykal, *Hayat Muhammad*, 11–17 (quotation from 16). For Maraghi's political associations, see Smith, *Haykal*, 109–13, 145–51.
122 *MT*, 1 Nov. 1935, 1143.
123 Interviews in *HI*, June 1935, 893–8, and *MT*, 1 Nov. 1935, 1138–43; 'Azzam, *Batal*, 4–5.
124 See Wessels, *Biography of Muhammad*, 40.
125 *NI*, 5 (1935), 136–7.
126 Letter by Shaykh Muhammad Zahran in *MR*, 3 May 1935, 789–90.
127 Ibid., 789.
128 Ibid., 790.
129 As noted by Rida in *MR*, 5 May 1935, 788–9.
130 Muhammad Rashid Rida, "Kitab *Hayat Muhammad*," part 1, *MR*, 3 May 1935, 787–93; part 2, *MR*, 1 July 1935, 64–72.
131 Ibid., part 1, 791.
132 Ibid., part 2, 64.
133 Ibid., part 1, 792.
134 Salama Musa, "al-Lugha wa al-Adab al-'Arabiyyan," *MJ*, Sept. 1935, 9–13.
135 Salama Musa, "Masa'il al-Shabab al-Misriyyin," *MJ*, April 1938, 80–7.
136 Ibid., 82–5.
137 Ibid., 82.
138 See *HT*, Jan. 1938, 16–26, 110–15.
139 Ibid., 111.
140 Ibid.

4 EGYPTIAN ISLAMIC NATIONALISM

1 Most of Banna's systematic *rasa'il* originally appeared in the 1930s. The first to be published was *Ila Ayyi Shay' Nad'u al-Nas* (To What Do We Summon People?), which first appeared in *IM* in mid-1934 and was reissued in pamphlet form in 1936. His *Da'watuna* (Our Mission) appeared in *IM* in 1935 and as a pamphlet in 1937. *Nahwa al-Nur* (Towards the Light) was an appeal to the king, the prime minister, and various Muslim leaders which appeared in 1937. Banna's *Bayna al-Ams wa al-Yawm* (Between Yesterday and Today) appeared in 1939. (All four are available in English translation in Wendell, *Five Tracts*). In the same category of *rasa'il* are Banna's address to the fifth congress of the Muslim Brothers in 1938, published as "al-Ikhwan al-Muslimun fi 'Ashr Sanawat" ("The Muslim Brothers in Ten Years"), *ND*, 17 Dhu al-Hijja 1357, 1–34, and his "Ila al-Shabab" ("To the Youth") of 1938 or 1939 (reprinted in *ND* on 15 Jan. 1940, 7–15). Two other *rasa'il* of Banna used in this chapter, *Mushkilatuna fi Daw' al-Nizam al-Islami* (Our Problems in the Light of the Islamic Order) (Cairo, n.d.), and *Da'watuna fi Tawr Jadid* (Our Mission in a New Stage) (Cairo, n.d.), appeared in the 1940s.
2 Quoted by Banna in *Da'watuna*, 20 (Eng. edn 54).
3 Ahmad ibn 'Abd al-Wahhab Warith, "al-Jami'a al-Islamiyya Aqwa Rabita bayna al-Umam," part 1, *ND*, 28 Jumada al-Thaniyya 1358, 6–9.
4 Muhibb al-Din al-Khatib, "Hadir al-Islam wa Mustaqbaluhu," *FH*, 20 Jan. 1927, 1–4. For further examples see Banna, *Nahwa al-Nur*, 10–11; Banna, "Ila al-Shabab," 13; Banna, *Mushkilatuna*, 24–6, 40–1.
5 Anon., "'Alaqat al-Rabita al-Islamiyya wa al-Rabita al-Wataniyya," *FH*, 4 Dhu al-Qa'da 1356, 17; Hasan al-Banna, "La al-Qawmiyya wa La al-'Alamiyya Bal al-Ukhuwwa al-Islamiyya," *IM*, 11 Rabi' al-Thani 1351, 1–2.
6 Mustafa Ahmad al-Rifa'i al-Lubban, "Wajib al-Muslim Nahwa Watanihi al-Khass wa Watanihi al-'Amm," *HD*, Shawwal 1349, 253.
7 Banna, *Da'watuna*, 21 (Eng. trans. 55).
8 Banna, "al-Ikhwan al-Muslimun fi 'Ashr Sanawat," 7–8.
9 Muhibb al-Din al-Khatib, "al-Wataniyya," *FH*, 14 June 1928, 1–3.
10 Ibid., 2.
11 Lubban, "Wajib al-Muslim," 253–5.
12 Banna, *Ila Ayyi Shay'*, 32–4. See also anon., "al-Qawmiyya al-Islamiyya," *IM*, 12 Jan. 1937, 1–3; anon., "Hadhihi Qawmiyyatuna," *IM*, 25 March 1938, 1–3; Banna, *Da'watuna*, 19–22.
13 Lubban, "Wajib al-Muslim," 255; Banna, *Nahwa al-Nur*, 10–11; Muhibb al-Din al-Khatib, "Umma Wahida," *FH*, 16 Dhu al-Hijja 1356, 3–4.
14 Banna, *Da'watuna*, 15 (Eng. trans. 50–1).
15 Ibid., 14 (Eng. trans. 50).
16 See Muhibb al-Din al-Khatib, "Misr al-'Arabiyya," *FH*, 22 Shawwal 1349, 1–2; Hasan al-Banna, "Misr 'Arabiyya," *IM*, 1 Jumada al-Akhira 1352, 1–3; 'Abd al-Hamid Sa'id, "Misr wa al-Wahda al-'Arabiyya," *RA*, 5 April 1939, 8.
17 Muhibb al-Din al-Khatib, "Risalat al-Umma al-'Arabiyya ila al-Bashar," *FH*, 7 Jumada al-Ula 1351, 2.
18 Ibid.
19 Muhibb al-Din al-Khatib, "al-'Uruba wa al-Fir'awniyya," *FH*, 20 Rajab 1349,

1–2; 'Umar Ibrahim Dasuqi, "Salama Musa," *FH*, 6 Feb. 1930, 4; Mustafa Ahmad al-Rifa'i al-Lubban, "Umniyyat Salama Musa," *FH*, 13 Feb. 1930, 6–7.

20 Banna, *Da'watuna*, 18–19 (Eng. trans. 53–4).

21 "The Islamic world is one homeland" was the motto of *al-Fath*; "the people of the *qibla* are one person and one body" was the heading to *Jaridat al-Ikhwan al-Muslimin*'s column on regional news; the other phrase appears in Muhammad Ghazzali, "al-Ikhwan al-Muslimun," *ND*, 3 Rabi' al-Thani 1358, 6–8.

22 Banna, *Ila Ayyi Shay'*, 34 (Eng. trans. 94).

23 Banna, *Da'watuna*, 12–13 (Eng. trans. 48–9).

24 Ibid., 13 (Eng. trans. 49).

25 For this phrase see Isma'il Shalabi Sha'fan, "La Watan Illa bi-Din," *FH*, 5 May 1927, 13–15; Muhibb al-Din al-Khatib, "al-Islam wa al-Watan al-'Arabi," *FH*, 24 Shawwal 1355, 3–4; 'Abd al-'Azim Muhammad Khalil, "Hubb al-Watan min al-Iman," *IM*, 1 Oct. 1935, 18.

26 Sha'fan, "La Watan," 13–14; Khalil, "Hubb al-Watan," 18.

27 As quoted in *FH*, 4 Jumada al-Ula 1355, 10.

28 Sha'fan, "La Watan," 13–15; Lubban, "Wajib al-Muslim," 253–9.

29 Banna, *Da'watuna*, 11–17; Ghazzali, "al-Ikhwan al-Muslimun," 6–8.

30 Sha'fan, "La Watan," 14.

31 Ibid.

32 See Lubban, "Wajib al-Muslim," 253–9; Banna, *Nahwa al-Nur*, 12.

33 Banna, "Ila al-Shabab," 12; also 'Abd al-Hamid Sa'id, "Limadha Ta'assasat Jam'iyyat al-Shubban al-Muslimin," *FH*, 22 Dec. 1927, 8–9.

34 Lubban, "Wajib al-Muslim," 253–9; Banna, "al-Ikhwan al-Muslimun fi 'Ashr Sanawat," 24–7.

35 Banna, *Da'watuna fi Tawr Jadid*, 12.

36 "All believers are brothers" was the motto appearing on the front page of *Jaridat al-Ikhwan al-Muslimin* in the 1930s.

37 Warith, "al-Jami'a al-Islamiyya," 6.

38 'Abd al-Rahman al-Sa'ati al-Banna, "al-'Alam Tha'ir fa-Limadha La Nathur?," *IM*, 17 Sept. 1935, 2–5.

39 Banna, *Da'watuna*, 21 (Eng. trans. 52).

40 Ibid., 24 (Eng. trans. 56).

41 Banna, *Bayna al-Ams wa al-Yawm*, 3–16 (Eng. trans. 14–29).

42 Ibid., 3–4 (Eng. trans. 14).

43 Ibid., 7 (Eng. trans. 17).

44 Ibid.

45 Ibid., 7–8 (Eng. trans. 17–18). For further examples of this focus on early Islam, see Mustafa Rahhal, "Dhikra al-Hijra," *FH*, 2 Rabi' al-Awwal 1353, 7–9; Muhammad al-Hadi 'Atiyya, "Nahdat al-Umma al-'Arabiyya," *IM*, 23 June 1936, 6–8; Muhammad al-Khadir Husayn, "Hayat al-Da'wa al-Islamiyya bi-Jazirat al-'Arab," *HD*, July 1937, 641–52.

46 Banna, *Bayna al-Ams wa al-Yawm*, 8–11 (Eng. trans. 18–20).

47 Ibid., 11–16 (Eng. trans. 20–4). For similar accounts, see Muhibb al-Din al-Khatib, "Quwwat al-'Arab al-Mu'attala," *FH*, 19 Sha'ban 1352, 2–3; Muhammad Sulayman, "al-'Arabiyya wa al-Islam," *FH*, 19 Rabi' al-Awwal 1354, 6–7; Mustafa Ahmad al-Rifa'i al-Lubban, "Hayat al-Umma wa al-Ihtifaz bi-Adabiha wa Taqalidiha," *HD*, Rajab 1355, 47–56.

48 Banna, *Bayna al-Ams wa al-Yawm*, 27 (Eng. trans. 33).

49 Ibid., 17 (Eng. trans. 24).

50 See Gershoni and Jankowski, *Egypt, Islam, and the Arabs*, 150–62.

51 *Mudhakkira fi al-Ta'lim al-Dini bi al-Madaris al-Misriyya* (Cairo, 1932), 8–9; the appeal was repeated in *al-Mudhakkira al-Thaniyya fi al-Ta'lim al-Dini bi al-Madaris al-Misriyya* (Cairo, 1935).

52 Anon., "al-Ta'rikh al-Qawmi wa Ta'rikh al-'Arab," *ND*, 15 Jumada al-Ula 1358, 7.

53 For examples, see Khatib, "al-Wataniyya," 1–3; 'Atiyya, "Nahdat al-Umma al-'Arabiyya," 7–8, 18; Lubban, "Umniyyat Salama Musa," 6–7.

54 Banna, "Misr 'Arabiyya," 2.

55 See Khatib, "Misr 'Arabiyya," 1–2; 'Ali Afandi al-Jundi, "Misr 'Arabiyya wa lan Takuna Ghayr Dhalika," *FH*, 15 Jumada al-Akhira 1352, 4–5, 13; Muhammad Zaki Hasan and 'Abd al-Rahman Zaki, *Fi Misr al-Islamiyya* (Cairo, 1937), preface and 10–11.

56 Hasan and Zaki, *Fi Misr*, 2–5; Banna, *Bayna al-Ams wa al-Yawm*, 12, and *Mudhakkira fi al-Ta'lim* (1932), 3, 8–11; Salih Mustafa 'Ashmawi, "Za'amat Misr Islamiyya: La Sharqiyya wa La 'Arabiyya," *ND*, 24 Rajab 1357, 3–5.

57 Hasan and Zaki, *Fi Misr*, 5–6; Banna, *Bayna al-Ams wa al-Yawm*, 9–11.

58 Hasan and Zaki, *Fi Misr*, 5.

59 Ibid., 5–6.

60 Ibid., 6. For a similar emphasis, see Isma'il Muhammad Abu al-'Aynayn, "Misr al-Islamiyya fi al-'Usur al-Wusta," *FH*, 28 Jumada al-Ula 1351, 5, 28; Banna, "al-Ikhwan al-Muslimun fi 'Ashr Sanawat," 17.

61 Hasan and Zaki, *Fi Misr*, 7.

62 Banna, *Bayna al-Ams wa al-Yawm*, 12–13.

63 Ibid., 24–5 (Eng. trans. 30–1).

64 Shaykh 'Abd Allah 'Afifi, "Watan wa 'Ashira," *FH*, 19 Sha'ban 1352, 3.

65 Sulayman, "al-'Arabiyya wa al-Islam,", 6–7.

66 Cited in Warith, "al-Jami'a al-Islamiyya," 14.

67 Hamza Faraj, "La Ikhtilaf Bayna al-Wahda al-'Arabiyya wa al-Jami'a al-Islamiyya," *ND*, 21 Rajab 1358, 18.

68 Ibid.; Khatib, "Quwwat al-'Arab al-Mu'attala," 1–3; Ibrahim al-Jabbali, "Limadha Ikhtara Allah al-'Arab li-Haml Amanat al-Islam ila Umam al-Ard?," *FH*, 30 Jumada al-Ula 1354, 6–8.

69 See Hasan al-Banna, "al-'Uruba wa al-Islam," *SJ*, 1 June 1945, 31; Ghazzali, "al-Ikhwan al-Muslimun," 6–8; Dardiri, "Asas Nahdat al-Muslimin," 84; 'Atiyya, "Nahdat al-Umma al-'Arabiyya," 6–8.

70 See Muhibb al-Din al-Khatib, "al-Akhlaq Hiya Allati Intasarat," *FH*, 26 Muharram 1353, 1–3; Husayn, "Hayat al-Da'wa al-Islamiyya," 641–52; Jabbali, "Limadha Ikhtara Allah al-'Arab," 6–8.

71 Banna, *Da'watuna*, 20–1 (Eng. trans. 55).

72 'Azzam, *Mudhakkirat*, 193.

73 See Muhammad Sa'id 'Urfi, "al-Lugha al-'Arabiyya Rabitat al-Shu'ub al-Islamiyya," part 1, *HD*, Sha'ban 1349, 113–22; part 2, *HD*, Ramadan 1349, 203–6; part 3, *HD*, Shawwal 1349, 260–4; Sulayman, "al-'Arabiyya wa al-Islam," 6–7; Hasan al-Banna, *al-Salam fi al-Islam wa Buhuth Ukhra* (Cairo, n.d.), 21.

74 'Afifi, "Watan wa 'Ashira," 3; Banna, *Da'watuna fi Tawr Jadid*, 15; Muhammad

Ahmad al-Ghamrawi, "al-'Arabiyya Lughat Al Quraysh," *ZA*, Rabi' al-Awwal 1347, 34–40; Sulayman, "al-'Arabiyya wa al-Islam," 6–7.

75 'Urfi, "al-Lugha al-'Arabiyya," part 1, 116–17.
76 Ibid., 206; Ahmad Hasan al-Zayyat, "Risalat al-Azhar," *RI*, 27 March 1939, 607–8.
77 Sulayman, "al-'Arabiyya wa al-Islam," 6–7; Banna, "al-'Uruba wa al-Islam," 31; Sa'id Haydar, "'Arabiyyat Misr," *FH*, 22 Jumada al-Akhira 1352, 6–7; Tantawi Jawhari, "Lughat al-'Arab wa Lughat Qudama' al-Misriyyin," *FH*, 13 Rajab 1352, 17–18.
78 Banna, *al-Salam fi al-Islam wa Buhuth Ukhra*, 21.
79 Banna, "Ila al-Shabab," 11; Banna, *Da'watuna fi Tawr Jadid*, 14–15.
80 Muhibb al-Din al-Khatib, "'Arba'ata 'Ashara Qarnan Tunaji Ummat al-'Arab," *FH*, 18 Dhu al-Hijja 1354, 3–4.
81 See Warith, "al-Jami'a al-Islamiyya," 6–9, 14; 'Atiyya, "Nahdat al-Umma al-'Arabiyya," 6–8; Ahmad Hasan al-Zayyat, "al-Rajul al-Muntazar," *RI*, 27 April 1942, 473–4.
82 *MI*, 4 July 1938, 2.
83 Warith, "al-Jami'a al-Islamiyya," 9; Banna, "al-'Uruba wa al-Islam," 31–2.
84 'Atiyya, "Nahdat al-Umma al-'Arabiyya," 6–8; Banna, "al-Ikhwan al-Muslimun fi 'Ashr Sanawat," 25–6.
85 Banna, "al-Ikhwan al-Muslimun," 25–6.
86 Ibid., 27.
87 Banna, *Da'watuna fi Tawr Jadid*, 12.
88 For other examples, see Muhibb al-Din al-Khatib, "al-Jami'a al-Qawmiyya wa al-Jami'a al-Islamiyya," *FH*, 12 Sha'ban 1349, 2–3; Khatib, "al-Wataniyya al-Misriyya," *FH*, 7 Shawwal 1354, 3–4; anon., "al-Qawmiyya al-Islamiyya Ajla wa Asma min al-Qawmiyya al-Mahalliyya," *IM*, 4 March 1938, 1–2.
89 See Muhammad al-Khadir Husayn's speech at the founding of the YMMA, *FH*, 1 Dec. 1927, 5; Sayyid Qutb, "Bayt al-Maghrib fi Misr," *RI*, 28 Nov. 1938, 1937; Zayyat, "Risalat al-Azhar," 607–8.
90 Hasan al-Banna, "Mudhakkirat al-Ikhwan al-Muslimin ila Rif'at Ra'is al-Wuzara' [Muhammad Mahmud]," *ND*, 14 Rabi' al-Thani 1357, 5–6.
91 For examples, see Muhammad Sulayman, *Rasa'il Sa'ir* (Cairo, 1935), 8–13, 81–3; Zayyat, "Shabab al-'Iraq fi Misr," 321–2; 'Atiyya, "Nahdat al-Umma al-'Arabiyya," 9–12, 17–18.
92 For examples, see Khatib, "Umma Wahida," 3–4; Banna, *Nahwa al-Nur*, 12; Banna, "al-Ikhwan Muslimun fi 'Ashr Sanawat," 25–6.
93 'Ashmawi, "Za'amat Misr Islamiyya," 3–5.
94 Ibid., 5.
95 Banna, "al-Ikhwan al-Muslimun fi 'Ashr Sanawat," 27. See also Banna, *Ila Ayyi Shay'*, 8–9, 28–9; Banna, *Da'watuna fi Tawr Jadid*, 12–13.
96 'Ashmawi, "Za'amat Misr Islamiyya," 5.

5   INTEGRAL EGYPTIAN NATIONALISM

1 Carlton J. H. Hayes, *The Historical Evolution of Modern Nationalism* (New York, 1931), 165 (quotation from Maurras).
2 Peter Alter, *Nationalism* (London, 1985), 38–41.

3 Hayes, *Modern Nationalism*, 202.

4 *TH*, 31 May 1937, 3.

5 Fathi Radwan, "13 'Amman fi Madaris Misr," *HI*, 41 (Aug. 1933), 1358–63 (quotations from 1363).

6 Mahmud al-Manjuri, *Ittijahat al-'Asr al-Jadid fi Misr* (Cairo, 1937), 166–7.

7 Mahmud Kamil, *al-'Amal li-Misr: Ba'th Dawla wa Ihya' Majd* (Cairo, 1945), 18.

8 The first formula is cited in Husayn, *Imani* (1936 edn), 177; the second in *SA*, 30 March 1934, 4.

9 Speech of 1935 as cited in *Imani* (1946 edn), 181.

10 Radwan, "13 'Amman," 1360.

11 See Husayn, *Imani* (1936 edn), 27–32, 103–4, 140–2, 146–54; Mahmud Kamil, *Misr al-Ghad Tahta Hukm al-Shabab* (Cairo, 1939), 110–19; Fathi Radwan, "Hal Nahnu Du'at al-Diktaturiyya?," *MF*, 18 July 1938, 5; 'Abd al-Hamid al-Dib, "al-Quwwa Hayat al-Shu'ub," *MF*, 17 April 1941, 4.

12 *SA*, 21 Oct. 1933, 5–6; 31 March 1934, 4, 13; 12 Nov. 1935, 8.

13 *SA*, 14 Jan. 1935, 1–2; also in Husayn, *Imani* (1936 edn), 142–58.

14 Husayn, *Imani*, 148.

15 Ibid., 150–1.

16 Ibid., 27.

17 Ibid., 18–37 (1946 edn 11–26); Kamil, *al-'Amal li-Misr*, 40–8; Ibrahim Jum'a, *al-Qawmiyya al-Misriyya al-Islamiyya* (Cairo, 1944), 5–15.

18 Husayn, *Imani* (1936 edn), 30.

19 Ibid., 51.

20 Husayn, *Imani* (1936 edn), 52; Kamil, *al-'Amal li-Misr*, 49–50.

21 Jum'a, *Qawmiyya*, 29–37; Husayn, *Imani* (1936 edn), 52–3.

22 Ibid., 112.

23 Jum'a, *Qawmiyya*, 44–69, 123–9 (quotation from 69).

24 Husayn, *Imani* (1936 edn), 53–4.

25 Ibid., 54–5; Jum'a, *Qawmiyya*, 87–92; Kamil, *al-'Amal li-Misr*, 37.

26 Husayn's overview of Egyptian history ignored the Ottoman era; Jum'a's gave it only eight lines (Jum'a, *Qawmiyya*, 92).

27 See ibid., 93–4, 165; Husayn, *Imani* (1936 edn), 56–7; Kamil, *al-'Amal li-Misr*, 89–93; Kamil, *Misr al-Ghad*, 114–19.

28 Husayn, *Imani* (1936 edn), 57. See also Fathi Radwan, "Fi Tariq al-'Ubudiyya al-Jadida," *SA*, 4 April 1935, 3; Radwan, speech as reported in *WN*, 13 June 1935, 1; Kamil, *al-'Amal li-Misr*, 13–16.

29 Husayn, *Imani* (1936 edn), 58–9.

30 *SA*, 21 Oct. 1933, 5.

31 For examples, see Husayn, *Imani* (1936 edn), 58–9, 94, 118, 201, 218, 240–1; Kamil, *al-'Amal li-Misr*, 27–8, 34, 40–3.

32 Husayn, *Imani* (1936 edn), 65–6; Kamil, *al-'Amal li-Misr*, 27, 40–3; Muhammad 'Ali 'Alluba, *Mabadi' fi al-Siyasa al-Misriyya* (Cairo, 1942), 314–18; Sulayman Huzayyin, "Misr Halqat al-Ittisal al-Thaqafi Bayna al-Sharq wa al-Gharb," *KM*, Dec. 1945, 369–84.

33 Jum'a, *Qawmiyya*, 6–8; Husayn, *Imani* (1936 edn), 109–11, 124.

34 'Alluba, *Mabadi'*, 317.

35 Husayn, *Imani* (1936 edn), 54.

36 Ibid., 57.

37 Ibid., 110, 124; Jum'a, *Qawmiyya*, 6.
38 Quoted in Ahmad Husayn, *Ra'y Jam'iyyat Misr al-Fatah fi Mu'ahadat Sanat 1936* (Cairo, 1936), 39.
39 Kamil, *Misr al-Ghad*, 113.
40 Husayn, *Imani* (1936 edn), 152–4; Manjuri, *Ittijahat*, 9–14.
41 Huzayyin, "Misr Halqat al-Ittisal al-Thaqafi," 381.
42 Husayn, *Imani* (1936 edn), 55.
43 Kamil, *al-'Amal li-Misr*, 27–8; Husayn, *Imani* (1936 edn), 102–3, 240–1.
44 'Alluba, *Mabadi'*, 317; Husayn, *Imani* (1936 edn), 240–1.
45 See Gershoni and Jankowski, *Egypt, Islam, and the Arabs*, 205–8.
46 Husayn, *Imani* (1936 edn), 60–1.
47 *SA*, 21 Oct. 1933, 5.
48 *MF*, 3 Aug. 1938, 13.
49 Ahmad Husayn, *Murafa'at al-Ra'is: Misr al-Fatah wa al-Hukuma Amama al-Qada'* (Cairo, 1937), 36–8; Kamil, *Misr al-Ghad*, 113; Fathi Radwan, "Nahnu Hum Nahnu," *MF*, 2 May 1940, 1.
50 Kamil, *Misr al-Ghad*, 113; Kamil, *al-'Amal li-Misr*, 34–5.
51 *MF*, 13 June 1940, 1.
52 See Husayn, *Imani* (1946 edn), 46–7; *SA*, 29 Sept. 1934, 9; *MF*, 14 March 1938, 2.
53 *SA*, 21 Oct. 1933, 5.
54 Huzayyin, "Misr Halqat al-Ittisal al-Thaqafi," 382.
55 Ibid., 383.
56 Ibid.
57 *SA*, 21 Oct. 1933, 5.
58 Fathi Radwan, "La Fir'awniyya wa La 'Arabiyya Ba'da al-Yawm," *BL*, 19 Sept. 1933, 4.
59 Fathi Radwan, "Misr Insaniyya," *MU*, 11 Oct. 1930, 1.
60 Ahmad Husayn, "al-Wahda al-Islamiyya Walidat al-Ittihad al-'Arabi," *FH*, 2 Dhu al-Hijja 1358, 6–8; see also Mustafa Fahmi, "Mawqif Misr min al-Sharq wa al-Sharqiyyin," *MSU*, 29 Sept. 1933, 15. Husayn Mu'nis, "Bayna al-'Uruba wa al-Fir'awniyya," *HT*, Jan. 1939, 39–44.
61 Husayn, *Imani* (1936 edn), 76; Fathi Radwan, "Hawla Ihraq Kutub Taha Husayn," *JI*, 3 Sept. 1933, 1; 15 Sept. 1933, 1.
62 Hafiz Mahmud, "Ayyuha al-'Arab: Misr Misrukum, wa Majduha fi al-Ta'rikh Majdukum," *SU*, 28 Jan. 1939, 5–6.
63 See Salih Mustafa 'Ashmawi, "Za'amat Misr Islamiyya, La Sharqiyya wa la 'Arabiyya," *ND*, 24 Rajab 1357, 3–5; Hasan al-Banna, "Qit'a min Watanina," *ND*, 8 Ramadan 1357, 3–4; Banna, "al-Ikhwan al-Muslimun fi 'Ashr Sanawat," *ND*, 17 Dhu al-Hijja 1357, 24–7.
64 See *SA*, 21 Oct. 1933, 5–7; 9 Dec. 1933, 7; *MF*, 18 Aug. 1938, 16; 10 Nov. 1938, 1; 3 April 1941, 3.
65 *MF*, 9 May 1938, 7.
66 *MF*, 18 March 1940, 4–8.
67 See the references cited in n. 63 above.
68 *MF*, 15 Dec. 1938, 1, 3; 19 Dec. 1938, 1, 4.
69 *MF*, 15 Nov. 1939, 3.
70 *MF*, 15 Sept. 1938, 12.
71 Manjuri, *Ittijahat*, 9–10.

72 Ibid., 24–5.
73 Husayn, *Imani* (1946 edn), 110; see also 269, 274.
74 *SA*, 21 Oct. 1933, 6.
75 *MF*, 18 March 1940, 4, 8.
76 Jum'a, *Qawmiyya*, 3–4, see also 50–86.
77 Husayn, *Imani* (1936 edn), 187; see also "al-'Amal bi-Kull Quwwa," *MF*, 29 Feb. 1940, 1, 4.
78 Ahmad Hussein [Husayn], *Message to Hitler!* (New York, 1947), 1.
79 See Husayn, *Imani* (1936 edn), 61–2, 107–8, 133–4, 147–8.
80 Hussein, *Message to Hitler!*, 5.
81 Ibid., 6.
82 Ibid.
83 *MF*, 14 Nov. 1938, 12.
84 *SA*, 23 Dec. 1933, 2; text in Husayn, *Imani* (1946 edn), 99–110.
85 Husayn, *Imani* (1946 edn), 104.
86 Ibid., 108.
87 Husayn, "al-Wahda al-Islamiyya Walidat al-Ittihad al-'Arabi," 6.
88 Kamil, *Misr al-Ghad*, 110, 117.
89 Jum'a, *Qawmiyya*, 6–9, 50–73, 154–65; Kamil, *al-'Amal li-Misr*, 50–4, 76–84, 90–1; 'Alluba, *Mabadi'*, 317–18.
90 'Alluba, *Mabadi'*, 313–18; Kamil, *Misr al-Ghad*, 110–18.
91 Interview in *Giornale de Genoa* as reprinted in *MF*, 11 Aug. 1938, 3.
92 'Abd al-Hamid Muhammad al-Mashhadi, "Sarayan al-Ruh: al-'Iraq Ba'da Filastin," *WN*, 2 July 1935, 2–3.
93 Ibid., 2.
94 Ibid., 3.
95 *SA*, 21 Oct. 1933, 5.
96 *MF*, 18 March 1940, 4.
97 Ibid., 8; see also Ahmad Husayn, "al-Wahda al-'Arabiyya: Darura La lil-'Arab Faqat, Bal lil-Umam Ajma'," *MF*, 7 March 1940, 1–2; Mustafa al-Wakil, "Misr wa al-'Iraq," *MF*, 17 Oct. 1940, 3–4; Muhammad Subayh, "Wujub al-Ittisal Bayna Hukumat al-'Arabiyya lil-Ittifaq 'Ala Siyasa Muwahhada," *MF*, 2 Jan. 1941, 1–2.

6   EGYPTIAN ARAB NATIONALISM

1 See Albert Hourani, *Arabic Thought in the Liberal Age, 1798–1939* (London, 1962), 260–323; Sylvia G. Haim, *Arab Nationalism: An Anthology* (Berkeley, 1962), 3–49; C. Ernest Dawn, "The Formation of Pan-Arab Ideology in the Interwar Years," *International Journal of Middle East Studies*, 20 (1988), 67–91; William L. Cleveland, *The Making of an Arab Nationalist: Ottomanism and Arabism in the Life and Thought of Sati' al-Husri* (Princeton, 1971), *passim*.
2 See the answer of 'Ali 'Abd al-Raziq in the symposium on "Hadaratuna al-Qadima," *HI*, April 1931, 823–4; Mustafa Fahmi, "al-Rawabit al-Fikriyya bayna al-Umam al-'Arabiyya," *MSU*, 30 Dec. 1933, 10; Mustafa Sadiq al-Rafi'i, "al-Lugha wa al-Din wa al-'Adat bi- I'tibariha min Muqawwimat al-Istiqlal," *RI*, 13 April 1936, 562–3.
3 Muhammad Lutfi Jum'a, "al-Hadara al-'Arabiyya wa Ahamm Muqawwimatiha,"

RA, 10 Nov. 1937, 11. See also Muhammad 'Ali 'Alluba, "'Urubat Misr Aydan," *FH*, 25 Dhu al-Hijja 1354, 13; Muhibb al-Din al-Khatib, "al-'Arab," *FH*, 17 Dhu al-Qa'da 1353, 2–3; Ahmad Hasan al-Zayyat, "Fir'awniyyun wa 'Arab," *RI*, 1 Oct. 1933, 3–4; 'Abd al-Rahman 'Azzam, "Man Hum al-'Arab?," *FH*, 28 Rabi' al-Thani 1358, 18; Fu'ad Mafraj, "Hal Nahnu 'Arab?," *FH*, 6 Rabi' al-Akhir 1358, 19.

4 Ibrahim 'Abd al-Qadir al-Mazini, "al-Qawmiyya al-'Arabiyya," *RI*, 26 Aug. 1935, 1363–4.

5 Muhibb al-Din al-Khatib, "al-Qawmiyya al-'Arabiyya wa Makanat Misr Minha," *FH*, 24 Jumada al-Ula 1352, 6–7, 18–19; 'Alluba, "Fi Sabil al-Wahda al-'Arabiyya," *SU*, 18 Oct. 1930, 7, 25; 'Abd al-Rahman 'Azzam, "Wahdat al-Thaqafa al-Islamiyya," *FH*, 19 Sha'ban 1352, 4–5.

6 'Alluba, "'Urubat Misr Aydan," 13.

7 Ahmad Zaki, "'Araqil fi Sabil al-Nahda al-'Arabiyya," *TQ*, 6 Nov. 1945, 28.

8 Muhibb al-Din al-Khatib, "Misr al-'Arabiyya," *FH*, 22 Shawwal 1349, 1–2. See also Muhammad 'Ali 'Alluba, "Misr wa al-Wahda al-'Arabiyya," *RA*, 15 Feb. 1939, 7–8, 10; Rafiq al-Lababidi, "al-Rabita al-Thaqafiyya bayna Misr wa al-Sharq al-'Arabi," *RI*, 1 Feb. 1936, 222–3; Mahmud 'Azmi, "Jabha min al-Shu'ub al-'Arabiyya," *HI*, Nov. 1938, 1–7; Zaki Mubarak, "Mustaqbal al-Adab al-'Arabi," *HI*, April 1939, 129–31.

9 Ahmad Ramzi, "Misr al-'Arabiyya," *RI*, 10 March 1947, 275.

10 Muhammad 'Ali 'Alluba, "al-Fikra al-Fir'awniyya Fikra 'Aqima," *FH*, 19 Rabi' al-Awwal 1349, 8–9; 'Alluba, "Fi Sabil al-Wahda al-'Arabiyya," *SU*, 18 Oct. 1930, 7, 25; Mazini, "al-Qawmiyya al-'Arabiyya," 1363–4; Jum'a, "al-Hadara al-'Arabiyya," 11–15.

11 Jum'a, "al-Hadara al-'Arabiyya," 11.

12 Hasan 'Arif, "Hal Misr Fir'awniyya?," *MU*, 12 Sept. 1930, 7; 'Azzam, "Man Hum al-'Arab?," 18.

13 Muhibb al-Din al-Khatib, "al-'Uruba wa al-Fir'awniyya," *FH*, 20 Rajab 1349, 1–2; Mafraj, "Hal Nahnu 'Arab?," 19; 'Abd al-Rahman 'Azzam, "al-Wahda al-'Arabiyya wa al-Aqalliyyat," *HT*, May–June 1945, 231–2.

14 'Azzam, "Man Hum al-'Arab?," 18.

15 'Alluba, "Fi Sabil al-Wahda al-'Arabiyya," 7.

16 'Abd al-Rahman 'Azzam, "al-Wahda al-'Arabiyya," *HI*, Oct. 1943, 462–6; see also 'Azzam, "Alaysat Misr 'Arabiyya?," *BL*, 11 Sept. 1933, 7, 11; 'Ali al-'Inani, "al-Wahda al-'Arabiyya," *NF*, 15 May 1933, 2–3.

17 'Ali al-'Inani, "Bayan 'Amm li-al-'Arab," *NF*, 1 Nov. 1933, 3–4, 11; Ahmad Sabri, *Qina' al-Fir'awniyya* (Cairo, 1943), 109–12.

18 Muhibb al-Din al-Khatib, "Ifrat wa Tafrit," *FH*, 28 Jumada al-Ula 1356, 3–4; Ahmad Zaki, "al-Nahda al-'Arabiyya," *TQ*, 13 Nov. 1945, 26.

19 'Abd al-Mun'im Muhammad Khalaf, "'Imlaq Aradu Mishanat Qazaman!" *AA*, 10 May 1947, as reprinted in his *Ma'a al-Qawmiyya al-'Arabiyya fi Rub' Qarn* (Cairo, 1958), 30–6.

20 Makram 'Ubayd, "al-Misriyyun 'Arab," *HI*, April 1939, 32–3.

21 Ibid.

22 'Azzam, "al-Wahda al-'Arabiyya," 463.

23 Khalaf, "'Imlaq Aradu," 34–5; 'Inani, "Bayan 'Amm," 3–4, 11; 'Azzam, "al-Wahda al-'Arabiyya," 462–6.

24 See Hamza, "Makan Misr," 1; Zaki Mubarak, "Misr wa al-Bilad al-'Arabiyya,"

RI, 8 Aug. 1938, 1037–38; Ahmad Ahmad Badawi, "Ma'na al-Qawmiyya fi Misr," *SB*, 20 May 1936, 33–4.

25 Ahmad Ramzi, "'Urubat Mamlakat Wadi al-Nil," *AA*, 10 March 1948, 35–7.
26 Ibid.
27 Ibrahim 'Abd al-Qadir al-Mazini, "al-Fikra al-'Arabiyya," *BL*, 10 July 1934, 1; editorial, "Misr fi Khidmat al-'Arab wa al-Islam," *RA*, 8 May 1940, 4–5.
28 Mazini, "al-Fikra al-'Arabiyya," 1; Zaki Mubarak, "al-'Uruba fi Misr," *RA*, 26 Jan. 1938, 30–1.
29 Zaki Mubarak, *Layla al-Marida fi al-'Iraq* (3 vols.; Cairo, 1938–9), III, 244–5.
30 Mazini, "al-Qawmiyya al-'Arabiyya," 1363.
31 Makram 'Ubayd in *FI*, 24 Sept. 1931, 4; 'Atiyya Muhammad al-Sayyid, "Misr wa al-Buldan al-'Arabiyya," *SU*, 11 Sept. 1938, 17.
32 See Gershoni and Jankowski, *Egypt, Islam, and the Arabs*, 130–42.
33 Ramzi, "'Urubat Mamlakat Wadi al-Nil," 35–7.
34 Sulayman Huzayyin, "Rawabit al-Tabi'a wa al-Ta'rikh fi Wadi al-Nil," *KM*, May 1947, 653–63 (quotations from 660).
35 Sulayman Huzayyin, "Rabitat al-Jins wa al-Thaqafa fi Wadi al-Nil," *KM*, July 1947, 228–42 (quotations from 238).
36 Sulayman Huzayyin, "al-Jami'a al-'Arabiyya wa-Muqawwimatuha al-Jughrafiyya wa al-Ta'rikhiyya," *KM*, Jan. 1946, 529–42.
37 Ramzi, "'Urubat Mamlakat Wadi al-Nil," 35–7.
38 Sulayman Huzayyin, "Misr Halqat al-Ittisal al-Thaqafi bayna al-Sharq wa al-Gharb," *KM*, Dec. 1945, 369–84 (quotation from 372).
39 Huzayyin, "al-Jami'a al-'Arabiyya," 529–42.
40 Fahmi, "al-Rawabit al-Fikriyya," 10.
41 Jum'a, "al-Hadara al-'Arabiyya," 11–12.
42 Mazini, "al-Qawmiyya al-'Arabiyya," 1363–4.
43 Zaki Mubarak, "Fi al-Tariq ila al-Wahda al-'Arabiyya," *RI*, 20 Oct. 1941, 1284–8.
44 'Ali al-'Inani, "al-Wahda al-'Arabiyya," *NF*, 15 May 1933, 2.
45 Jum'a, "al-Hadara al-'Arabiyya," 13–15.
46 Mubarak, "Fi al-Tariq ila al-Wahda al-'Arabiyya," 1285–6.
47 Ibrahim 'Abd al-Qadir al-Mazini, "Misr wa al-Hilf al-'Arabi," *SB*, 28 Oct. 1936, 9–10.
48 As quoted in Muhammad Shakir al-Khardaji, *al-'Arab Fi Tariq al-Ittihad* (Damascus, 1947), 85. This is a collection of interviews about the subject of Arab unity conducted with numerous Egyptian politicians, professionals, and intellectuals in the late 1930s.
49 Fu'ad Abaza, "al-Wahda al-'Arabiyya," *MU*, 16 Sept. 1941, 5.
50 'Azmi, "Jabha," 3.
51 'Alluba, "Fi Sabil al-Wahda al-'Arabiyya," 7.
52 Muhammad Lutfi Jum'a, "Misr bayna al-'Uruba wa al-Fir'awniyya," *RA*, 13 Oct. 1937, 13.
53 Mahmud Muhammad Shakir, "al-Fann," *RI*, 12 Feb. 1940, 260.
54 'Azzam, "Wajib al-'Arab," 29.
55 'Abd al-Rahman 'Azzam, "Nuridu min al-'Arab An Yattahidu li-Yarfa'u min Sha'n al-Islam," *FH*, 14 Sha'ban 1350, 5.
56 Jum'a, "Misr bayna al-'Uruba wa al-Fir'awniyya," 14.

57 Ibid., 12–14.
58 Anon., "Hukumat al-Fir'awniyya al-Istibdadiyya," *AN*, 21 Oct. 1941, 4; see also anon., "Shawahid al-Istibdad wa al-Dhull," *AN*, 21 Nov. 1941, 5–6.
59 Anon., "al-Muttafarra'un wa al-Islam," *AN*, 22 Sept. 1941, 3.
60 See Mubarak, *Wahy Baghdad*, 56–8; 'Abd al-Hamid Sa'id, "Misr wa al-Wahda al-'Arabiyya," *RA*, 5 April 1939, 8; Muhammad Lutfi Jum'a, "al-'Uruba fi Misr," *RA*, 26 Jan. 1939, 30–3.
61 'Azzam, "Alaysat Misr 'Arabiyya?," 11.
62 See Muhammad Lutfi Jum'a, "Misr wa al-Wahda al-'Arabiyya," *RA*, 25 Jan. 1939, 11–13; Zaki Mubarak, "Ila al-Duktur Taha Husayn," *RI*, 23 Jan. 1939, 147–52; 'Abd al-Salam al-Kurdani, "Mustaqbal al-Thaqafa fi Misr," *RI*, 14 Feb. 1939, 9–14; al-Ikhwan al-Muslimun, "Mustaqbal al-Thaqafa fi Misr," *ND*, 6 Safar 1358, 3–7 (an official protest against Husayn's book sent by the Brotherhood to the Minister of Education and the Rector of al-Azhar); 'Abd al-Mun'im Muhammad Khalaf, "Jadal fi al-'Iraq Hawla 'Urubat Misr," *al-Akhbar* (Baghdad), 18 Dec. 1938, as republished in his *Ma'a al-Qawmiyya al-'Arabiyya*, 71.
63 See Gershoni and Jankowski, *Egypt, Islam, and the Arabs*, 191–227.
64 The views of Taha Husayn, Mansur Fahmi, 'Ali 'Abd al-Raziq, and Ahmad Ibrahim in a symposium in *HI*, Jan. 1934, 273–8; the response of Tawfiq al-Hakim in a symposium in *RA*, 8 Sept. 1937, 6–7; 'Ali al-'Inani, "Shababuna al-Jadid: Amaluhu wa Ahlamuhu," *HI*, Nov. 1933, 51; Muhammad 'Abd Allah 'Inan, "Thaqafat Misr al-Mustaqilla," *RI*, 1 March 1937, 321–3; 'Abbas Mahmud al-'Aqqad, "Ihya' al-Adab al-'Arabi," *RI*, 31 Oct. 1938, 1761–3; Taha Husayn, "al-Ittijah al-Hadith fi al-Adab al-Misri," *HT*, Jan. 1939, 17–20, 121–5.
65 Ahmad Hasan al-Zayyat, "Shuruh wa Hawashi," *RI*, 1 May 1933, 4.
66 Mustafa Fahmi, "Wahdat al-Thaqafa fi al-Sharq al-'Arabi," *MSU*, 5 Nov. 1932, 16–17; Ahmad Ahmad Badawi, "al-Wahda al-'Arabiyya wa al-Adab al-Qawmi," *MA*, Feb. 1932, 1213–16; Jum'a, "al-Hadara al-'Arabiyya," 12.
67 Taha Husayn, "al-Adab al-'Arabi wa Makanatuhu bayna al-Adab al-Kubra al-'Alamiyya," in his *Min Hadith al-Shi'r wa al-Nathr* (Cairo, 1936), 1–23 (quotation from 21).
68 Taha Husayn, "Ila al-Ustadh Tawfiq al-Hakim," *RI*, 15 June 1933, 9.
69 Amin al-Khuli, *Fi al-Adab al-Misri* (Cairo, 1943), 9–37.
70 Ibid., 35–6.
71 'Abd al-Wahhab 'Azzam, "Athar al-Thaqafa al-'Arabiyya fi al-Thaqafa al-Misriyya al-Haditha," *TQ*, 29 June 1943, 623–8 (quotation from 624–5).
72 See Salama Musa, "Islah al-Lugha," *BL*, 23 Feb. 1935, 1; Musa, "al-Khatt al-Latini li al-Lugha al-'Arabiyya," *MJ*, Nov. 1935, 69–70; Isma'il Adham, "Misr wa al-Thaqafa al-Urubbiyya," *MJ*, May 1937, 17–31.
73 'Alluba, "al-Fikra al-Fir'awniyya," 8.
74 Husayn, *Mustaqbal*, II, 304 (Eng. trans. 83).
75 Badawi, "al-Wahda al-'Arabiyya," 1215.
76 Mahmud Taymur, "al-Niza' bayna al-Fusha wa al-'Ammiyya fi al-Adab al-Misri al-Hadith," *HI*, July 1933, 1186.
77 See Muhammad 'Ali 'Alluba, "Ahammiyyat al-Mu'tamarat al-'Arabiyya," *HI*, April 1939, 50–2; Fahmi, "Wahdat al-Thaqafa," 16–17; Mubarak, "Mustaqbal al-Adab al-'Arabi," 130–1.

78 Muhammad al-'Ashmawi as cited in "Tawhid al-Thaqafa bayna al-Aqtar al-'Arabiyya," *HI*, Jan. 1939, 250–2; Mansur Fahmi, "Zu'ama' al-Thaqafa bi-Misr Yatahaddathun 'An al-Wahda al-'Arabiyya," *RA*, 18 May 1939, 14–15; Muhammad 'Ali 'Alluba, "Ud'u bi-Quwwa ila Wahdat al-Thaqafa bayna al-Aqtar al-'Arabiyya," *RA*, 6 March 1940, 4–5.
79 See Giora Eliraz, "Tradition and Change: Egyptian Intellectuals and Linguistic Reform, 1919–1939," *Asian and African Studies*, 20 (1986), 233–62.
80 'Alluba, "Hawla al-Qamus wa al-Mawsu'a al-'Arabiyya," *JA*, 12 Dec. 1931, 1, 4; Ahmad Amin, "Ta'awun al-'Arab fi Wad' Da'irat Ma'arif 'Arabiyya," in his *Fayd al-Khatir* (2nd edn; 10 vols.; Cairo, 1946), X, 78–82; 'Abd al-Rahman 'Azzam as interviewed in *AD*, Sept. 1946, 75–6.
81 See Shlomit Shraybom-Shivtiel, "The Arabic Language Academy in Egypt: Trends and Actions, 1932–1982" (Hebrew), Ph.D. dissertation, Tel Aviv University, 1993.
82 Sasun Sumikh [Sasson Somekh], "Masrah Mahmud Taymur: Lughat al-Hiwar fi Siyaghatayn," in Sasun Sumikh (ed.), *Abhath fi al-Lugha wa al-Uslub* (Tel Aviv, 1980), 23–43; Sasson Somekh, "Two Versions of Dialogue in Mahmud Taymur's Drama," Princeton Near East Paper no. 21 (Princeton, 1975), 1; M. M. Badawi, *Modern Arabic Drama in Egypt* (Cambridge, 1987), 93–5; J. Brugman, *An Introduction to the History of Modern Arabic Literature in Egypt* (Leiden, 1984), 257–8.
83 Sasun Sumikh [Sasson Somekh], "Hawla Lughat al-Hiwar fi Masrahiyyat al-Hakim," in Dafid Simah (ed.), *Adwa' 'Ala Adab Tawfiq al-Hakim* (Haifa, 1979), 73–85; Sasson Somekh, "The Diglottic Dilemma in the Drama of Tawfiq al-Hakim," *Israel Oriental Studies*, 9 (1979), 392–403; Badawi, *Arabic Drama*, 14–26; Starkey, *From the Ivory Tower*, 195–9.
84 See Gershoni and Jankowski, *Egypt, Islam and the Arabs*, 221–4.
85 See Brugman, *Modern Arabic Literature*, 291, 295–8, 316; Hamdi Sakkut, *The Egyptian Novel and Its Main Trends, 1919–1952* (Cairo, 1971), 72–84; Mattityuhu Peled, *Religion, My Own: The Literary Works of Najib Mahfuz* (New Brunswick, 1983), 28–67.
86 Sakkut, *The Egyptian Novel*, 52–3.
87 Ibid.; Brugman, *Modern Arabic Literature*, 312; Muhammad 'Abd al-Mun'im Khatir, *Muhammad Farid Abu Hadid* (Cairo, 1979), 128–84.
88 Sakkut, *The Egyptian Novel*, 60–2; Brugman, *Modern Arabic Literature*, 315.
89 See Sakkut, *The Egyptian Novel*, 63–4; Brugman, *Modern Arabic Literature*, 314.
90 Brugman, *Modern Arabic Literature*, 316.
91 See *Apulu*, Nov. 1932, 286–8; Dec. 1932, 336–7; Oct. 1933, 101–2, 152–3; Nov. 1933, 170–1; March 1934, 615; June 1934, 896–900, 1050–5; Sept. 1934, 4–8. On romanticism in modern Arabic poetry, see Brugman, *Modern Arabic Literature*, 151–204; M. M. Badawi, *A Critical Introduction to Modern Arabic Poetry* (Cambridge, 1975), 115–78; Salma Khadra Jayyusi, *Trends and Movements in Modern Arabic Poetry* (2 vols.; Leiden, 1977), II, 361–474.
92 *Apulu*, May 1933, 1046–7; Sept. 1933, 63–4; *FH*, 15 Muharram 1355, 7.
93 *MU*, 18 Oct. 1933, 3.
94 *RI*, 15 June 1936, 989; 27 July 1936, 1232; 16 Jan. 1939, 134.
95 *TQ*, 18 March 1941, 28–9; *RI*, 5 Oct. 1942, 948–9; 19 April 1943, 310; 1 Jan. 1945, 17.

96 *RI*, 5 Nov. 1945, 1213; 26 Nov. 1945, 1297; 21 Jan. 1946, 86–7; *TQ*, 21 May 1946, 587; *RI*, 29 July 1946, 842–3.

97 See Badawi, *Critical Introduction*, 137–45; Brugman, *Modern Arabic Literature*, 173–81; Jayyusi, *Trends and Movements*, II, 397–410; Nazik al-Mala'ika, *Shi'r 'Ali Mahmud Taha: Dirasa wa Naqd* (Cairo, 1965); Anwar al-Ma'addawi, *'Ali Mahmud Taha: al-Sha'ir al-Insan* (Baghdad, 1965); al-Sayyid Taqiy al-Din al-Sayyid, *'Ali Mahmud Taha: Hayatuhu wa Shi'ruhu* (Cairo, 1965).

98 The following is based on the anthology of his works entitled *Diwan 'Ali Mahmud Taha* (Beirut, 1972).

99 Ma'addawi, *'Ali Mahmud Taha*, 79.

100 See 'Ali Mahmud Taha, *Sharq wa Gharb* (Cairo, 1947), 69–78, 79–85, 86–91, 121–53, 157–64, 165–7, 175–8.

101 Ibid., 111–20 (quotation from 113).

102 For these points, see 'Inani, "Bayan 'Amm," 3–4; Jum'a, "Misr wa al-Wahda al-'Arabiyya," 11–13; Mubarak, "Mustaqbal al-Adab al-'Arabi," 129–31; 'Abd al-Rahman 'Azzam, "al-Imbiraturiyya al-'Arabiyya wa Hal Ana an Tatahaqqaqa," *HI*, Feb. 1934, 385–9; Ahmad Husayn, "Ayyuha al-'Arab fi Anha' al-Dunya Ittahidu," *RA*, 5 Oct. 1938, 8, 47–8; 'Abd al-Ghani al-Rafi'i, "Mata Tantazimu Halat al-'Arab?," *RA*, 27 March 1940, 1–2; 'Abd al-Mun'im Muhammad Khalaf, "Mazamir lil-Nafs al-'Arabiyya," *RI*, 1 April 1940, 565–8; 'Abd al-Wahhab 'Azzam, "Nahdat al-'Arab," *AD*, May 1945, 18.

103 As quoted in Khardaji, *al-'Arab*, 121.

104 See ibid., 81, 98, 101, 131–2; 'Azzam, "Man Hum al-'Arab?," 18; Ahmad Hasan al-Zayyat, "Misr wa al-Wahda al-'Arabiyya," *RI*, 12 April 1943, 282.

105 'Abd al-Rahman 'Azzam, "al-'Arab Ummat al-Mustaqbal," *AR*, 27 Aug. 1932, 6, 16; 'Azzam, "al-Imbiraturiyya al-'Arabiyya," 385–9; Mubarak, *Wahy Baghdad*, 56–8, 409–17; Ibrahim 'Abd al-Qadir al-Mazini, "Misr wa Shaqiqatuha," *BL*, 11 March 1936, 1; Mahmud Muntasir, "al-Qawmiyya al-'Arabiyya," *RA*, 28 July 1937, 20–2; Khardaji, *al-'Arab*, 100, 109, 173, 191–2.

106 'Azzam, "al-Imbiraturiyya al-'Arabiyya," 389.

107 'Azzam, "Wajib al-'Arab," 28.

108 Husayn, "al-Wahda al-Islamiyya Walidat al-Ittihad al-'Arabi," 6.

109 'Abd al-Rahman 'Azzam, "Darurat al-Wahda al-'Arabiyya lil-Salam al-'Alami," *RA*, 24 March 1937, 784–6; Lababidi, "al-Rabita al-Thaqafiyya," 222–3; 'Alluba, "Ahammiyyat al-Mu'tamarat al-'Arabiyya," 50–2; Khardaji, *al-'Arab*, 87–8, 91, 157–8.

110 'Azzam, "al-'Arab Ummat al-Mustaqbal," 16.

111 'Azzam, "Wajib al-'Arab," 29.

112 Tawfiq Muhammad al-Shawi, "Ahdafuna al-Qawmiyya wa al-Qadaya al-'Arabiyya," *RI*, 24 Sept. 1945, 1023–4; Khalaf, *Ma'a al-Qawmiyya al-'Arabiyya*, 37; 'Abd al-Rahman 'Azzam, *al-Jami'a al-'Arabiyya wa al-Wahda al-'Alamiyya* (Cairo, 1946), 4–12.

113 'Azzam, *al-Jami'a al-'Arabiyya*, 5; Khalaf, *Ma'a al-Qawmiyya al-'Arabiyya*, 35–6.

114 'Azzam, "al-'Arab Ummat al-Mustaqbal," 16.

115 See Fahmi, "Wahdat al-Thaqafa," 16–17; 'Azmi, "Jabha," 1–7; 'Alluba, "Ahammiyyat al-Mu'tamarat al-'Arabiyya," 50–2.

116 Muhammad Husayn Haykal, "al-Ittihad al-Thaqafi bayna al-Umam al-'Arabiyya," *HI*, April 1939, 12.

117 Muhammad 'Abd Allah al-'Arabi, "Kayfa Nunazzimu Silatana al-Thaqafiyya Ma'a Bilad al-'Arabiyya?," *RA*, 20 Jan. 1937, 373; see also Muhammad 'Abd Allah 'Inan, "Fikrat al-Jami'a al-'Arabiyya," *MSU*, 14 June 1933, 1; Ahmad Amin as cited in the symposium on "Tawhid al-Thaqafa bayna al-Aqtar al-'Arabiyya," *HI*, Jan. 1939, 253–4.

118 Khatib, "al-Wataniyya al-Misriyya," 3–4; Ahmad Hasan al-Zayyat, "Istiqlal al-Lugha," *RI*, 7 Dec. 1936, 1981–2; Zayyat "Tawhid al-Thaqafa al-'Amma," *RI*, 30 May 1938, 881–2; Zaki Mubarak, "al-Lugha al-'Arabiyya wa al-Jami'a al-Misriyya," *RA*, 27 May 1936, 23–5.

119 The first phrase is Tal'at Harb's as cited in *FH*, 17 Shawwal 1355, 22, the second 'Abd al-Qadir Hamza's in *BL*, 30 March 1936, 1.

120 'Azzam, "al-Imbiraturiyya al-'Arabiyya," 388.

121 Mazini, "al-Qawmiyya al-'Arabiyya," 1364.

122 Ibrahim 'Abd al-Qadir al-Mazini, "Filastin al-Tha'ira," *SB*, 16 Sept. 1936, 7–8.

123 Mazini, "al-Qawmiyya al-'Arabiyya," 1364.

124 Editorial by 'Abd al-Qadir Hamza, *BL*, 3 April 1936, 1.

125 Tal'at Harb, "al-Ta'awun al-Iqtisadi bayna al-Umam al-'Arabiyya," *HI*, April 1939, 34–5.

126 'Alluba, *Mabadi'*, 27–9.

127 'Abd al-Rahman 'Azzam, "al-Wahda al-'Arabiyya: Darura li al-'Arab wa Sa'ada li al-Bashar," *AR*, 15 Oct. 1932, 2–3.

128 Mazini, "al-Qawmiyya al-'Arabiyya," 1363.

129 Ibrahim 'Abd al-Qadir al-Mazini, "al-Injiliz wa al-'Arab," *SB*, 30 Sept. 1936, 6–7.

130 Ibrahim 'Abd al-Qadir al-Mazini, "Misr wa al-Qadiyya al-'Arabiyya," part 1, *SB*, 7 Oct. 1936, 6; part 2, 14 Oct. 1936, 5–6.

131 Mazini, "al-Qawmiyya al-'Arabiyya," 1364.

132 Mazini, "Filastin al-Tha'ira," 7–8.

133 Mazini, "Misr wa al-Qadiyya al-'Arabiyya," part 1, 6.

134 Mazini, "Misr wa al-Qadiyya al-'Arabiyya," part 2, 7.

135 'Abd al-Ghani al-Rafi'i, "al-Ittihad al-'Arabi," *ARB*, 23 April 1930, 1.

136 See Muhibb al-Din al-Khatib, "Watan Wahid, Umma Wahida, Lugha Wahida," *FH*, 22 Muharram 1357, 3–4; 'Umar Naji, "Nida' ila al-Wahda al-Arabiyya al-'Amma," *FH*, 24 Jumada al-Akhira 1358, 10–11.

137 Khalaf, *Ma'a al-Qawmiyya al-'Arabiyya*, 35.

138 For examples see Khardaji, *al-'Arab*, 113, 152–3; 'Alluba, "Misr wa al-Wahda al-'Arabiyya," 7–8; 'Alluba, *Mabadi'*, 314–15; 'Abbas Mahmud al-'Aqqad, "Bayna al-Haqa'iq wa al-Asatir," *RI*, 16 Oct. 1944, 921–3.

139 *RA*, 18 Nov. 1936, 19, 26.

140 See 'Inan, "Fikrat al-Jami'a al-'Arabiyya," 1; Mazini, "Misr wa al-Hilf al-'Arabi," 9–10; 'Alluba, "al-Hilf al-'Arabi," 2–6; editorial, "al-Jami'a al-'Arabiyya," *TQ*, 31 Jan. 1939, 1–4; Ahmad Amin, "al-Hilf al-'Arabi," *TQ*, 5 Aug. 1941, 1001–3; Muhammad Farid Abu Hadid, "Hawla al-Hilf al-'Arabi," *TQ*, 12 Aug. 1941, 1037–40; 'Abd al-Wahhab 'Azzam, "al-Hilf al-'Arabi," *TQ*, 2 Sept. 1941, 1135–7.

141 See anon., "al-Jami'a al-'Arabiyya," *TQ*, 31 Jan. 1939, 1–4; 'Alluba, *Mabadi'*, 312–18; 'Abd al-Ghani al-Rafi'i, "al-Hilf al-'Arabi Kama Yanbaghi an Yakuna," *RA*, issues of 1 Jan.–26 March 1941; Abu Hadid, "Hawla al-Hilf al-'Arabi,"

248 Notes to pages 138–40

9–11; Ahmad Hasan al-Zayyat, "Misr wa al-Wahda al-'Arabiyya," *RI*, 12 April 1943, 281–2.

142 'Abd al-Rahman 'Azzam, "Qadiyyat Filastin wa al-Wahda al-'Arabiyya," *FH*, 21 Rabi' al-Awwal 1358, 83; 'Abd al-Ghani al-Rafi'i, "al-Qawmiyya al-'Arabiyya al-Kubra," *RA*, 21 Aug. 1940, 1–2.

143 Zaki Mubarak, "al-'Uruba fi Misr," *RA*, 26 Jan. 1938, 30–2.

144 'Ubayd, "al-Misriyyun 'Arab," 33.

145 Ibid.

146 See Khatib, "al-Qawmiyya al-'Arabiyya wa Makanat Misr Minha," 6–7; 'Abd Allah 'Afifi as quoted in "Misr wa al-Qadiyya al-'Arabiyya," *MU*, 18 Oct. 1933, 7; Zaki Mubarak, "Misr wa al-Bilad al-'Arabiyya," *RI*, 8 Aug. 1938, 1036–8.

147 Ibrahim 'Abd al-Qadir al-Mazini, "Kayfa Yataharraru al-'Arab min al-Nufudh al-Ajnabi," *HI*, May–June 1946, 291.

148 Ibid.

149 See 'Abd al-Rahman 'Azzam, "al-Wahda al-'Arabiyya," *AR*, 15 Oct. 1932, 2–3; speech by Makram 'Ubayd as published in *MU*, 10 March 1936, 1, 4; Khalaf, *Ma'a al-Qawmiyya al-'Arabiyya*, 4–5.

150 For examples, see Mazini, "Filastin al-Tha'ira," 8; Jum'a, "Misr bayna al-'Uruba wa al-Fir'awniyya," 12–14; 'Azzam, "al-Wahda al-'Arabiyya: Darura li al-'Arab," 2; Ahmad Hasan al-Zayyat, "Misr wa Akhawatuha," *RI*, 5 March 1935, 321–2; Mubarak, "Misr wa al-Bilad al-'Arabiyya," 1036–8; 'Azzam, "Misr wa al-Bilad al-'Arabiyya," 1521–2; 'Abd al-Ghani al-Rafi'i, "Risalat Misr al-Ta'rikhiyya al-Khalida," *RA*, 1 May 1940, 1–2.

151 'Alluba, "Misr wa al-Wahda al-'Arabiyya," 8.

152 For the term, see Mazini, "Misr wa Filastin," 13; 'Azzam, "Misr wa al-Bilad al-'Arabiyya," 1521–2; editorials in *RA*, 31 Jan. 1940, 14–16, and 18 June 1941, 1–2; Khardaji, *al-'Arab*, 125–6, 167–8.

153 *Mudhakkira fi al-Ta'lim al-Dini bi al-Madaris al-Misriyya*, 3; Amin, *Fayd al-Khatir*, X, 69; editorial in *Apulu*, Sept. 1934, 6–8; Rafi'i, "Risalat Misr al-Ta'rikhiyya al-Khalida," 1–2; Siyasi 'Arabi, "Misr wa Bala'uhu fi Khidmat al-'Arab wa al-Islam," *RA*, 8 May 1940, 4–5.

154 Husayn, *Mustaqbal*, II, 519 (Eng. trans. 149).

155 Mubarak, *Wahy Baghdad*, 412.

156 Ahmad Hasan al-Zayyat, "Shuruh wa Hawashi," *RI*, 1 May 1933, 4; Zayyat, "Misr wa al-Umam al-Sharqiyya," *RI*, 2 Sept. 1935, 1401–2; Ahmad Ramzi, "Mazahir al-Ta'awun al-Thaqafi bayna Misr wa al-Aqtar al-'Arabiyya," *HT*, March 1941, 95–7; Rafi'i, "al-Hilf al-'Arabi," part 9, 10–12.

157 Muhammad Ghallab, "Misr wa al-Wahda al-'Arabiyya," *NF*, 15 Sept. 1933, 1–2, 6; Ahmad Hasan al-Zayyat, "Misr wa al-Sharq al-Islami," *RI*, 12 Aug. 1935, 1281–2; 'Atiyya Muhammad al-Sayyid, "Misr wa al-Buldan al-'Arabiyya," *SU*, 18 Sept. 1938, 17; Sayyid Qutb, "al-Ta'awun al-Thaqafi bayna al-Aqtar al-'Arabiyya," *RI*, 30 April 1945, 442.

158 Interview with 'Abd al-Razzaq al-Sanhuri in *RA*, 12 Aug. 1936, 5; Harb, "al-Ta'awun al-Iqtisadi," 34–5; Khardaji, *al-'Arab*, 110–11; editorial by 'Abd al-Qadir Hamza in *BL*, 19 March 1936, 1.

159 Editorial by 'Abd al-Qadir Hamza, *BL*, 3 April 1936, 1; see also Mazini, "Misr wa al-Hilf al-'Arabi," 9–10.

160 Siyasi 'Arabi, "Misr wa Bala'uhu fi Khidmat al-'Arab wa al-Islam," 4–5.

161 The first phrase is from an editorial in *RA*, 13 March 1940, 13–14, the second from 'Abd al-Rahman 'Azzam, "Wajib al-Fard Nahwa al-Watan," *RA*, 19 June 1940, 1–2.

162 *AH*, 13 Oct. 1938, 1. See also 'Azzam, "Misr wa al-Bilad al-'Arabiyya," 1521–2; Ghallab, "Misr wa al-Wahda al-'Arabiyya," 1–2, 6; Jum'a, "Misr wa al-Wahda al-'Arabiyya," 11–12; Karim Thabit, "Misr wa al-Aqtar al-'Arabiyya," *RA*, 28 Feb. 1940, 3–4.

163 Ahmad Hasan al-Zayyat, "Misr wa al-Umam al-Sharqiyya," *RI*, 2 Sept. 1935, 1402.

7 EGYPT, ARAB ALLIANCE, AND ISLAMIC CALIPHATE, 1930–1939

1 See Khaldun S. Husry, "King Faisal I and Arab Unity, 1930–1933," *Journal of Contemporary History*, 10 (1975), 323–40; Arnold Toynbee assisted by V. M. Boulter, *Survey of International Affairs, 1934* (London, 1935), 174–94; Ahmed M. Gomaa, *The Foundation of the League of Arab States* (London, 1977), 5–7; Yehoshua Porath, *In Search of Arab Unity, 1930–1945* (London, 1986), 4–6, 10–12; Philip S. Khoury, *Syria and the French Mandate: The Politics of Arab Nationalism, 1920–1945* (Princeton, 1987), 351–9.

2 *SI*, 9 July 1930, 1; *BL*, 7 July 1930, 7; *KS*, 5 July 1930, 3.

3 First quotation from an interview in *SU*, 9 Aug. 1930, 11; second from a speech in Damascus as published in *SU*, 18 Oct. 1930, 7, 25.

4 In a speech of early 1931 as quoted in *RS*, March 1931, 15.

5 *MU*, 8 May 1931, 1.

6 Minute on "Pan-Arabism and Pan-Islamism," 24 Feb. 1931; FO 141/763, 495/1/31; Campbell (Cairo) to Humphreys (Baghdad), 4 May 1933, FO 141/705, 635/3/33.

7 As quoted in *FH*, 3 Ramadan 1349, 2.

8 For the contents of the treaty see FO 141/769, file 458.

9 Horne (Cairo) to Henderson, 27 Feb. 1931; FO 371/15282, E1205/1205/65.

10 See Gershoni and Jankowski, *Egypt, Islam, and the Arabs*, 250–4.

11 See *FI*, 26 April 1931; 3 May 1931; *MS*, 29 April 1931.

12 For examples, see *FI*, 8 Sept. 1931, 1; 12 Sept. 1931, 4.

13 *FI*, 3 Sept. 1931, 2 (following material from this report).

14 For a similar speech in Jaffa, see *FI*, 12 Sept. 1931, 4.

15 *FI*, 18 Sept. 1931, 1, 4 (following material from this report).

16 *FI*, 17 Sept. 1931; see also Thomas Mayer, *Egypt and the Palestine Question, 1936–1945* (Berlin, 1983), 31–2.

17 See FO 141/728, 1132/11/31; Thomas Mayer, "Egypt and the General Islamic Conference of Jerusalem in 1931," *Middle Eastern Studies*, 18 (1982), 313; Muhammad 'Ali al-Tahir, *Nazarat al-Shura* (Cairo, 1932), 97; Fakhr al-Din al-Ahmadi al-Zawahiri, *al-Siyasa wa al-Azhar: min Mudhakkirat Shaykh al-Islam al-Zawahiri* (Cairo, 1945), 317–18; Ralph Moses Coury, "Abd al-Rahman Azzam and the Development of Egyptian Arab Nationalism" (Ph. D. dissertation, Princeton University, 1983), 410–11; Coury, "Egyptians in Jerusalem: The Role of the General Islamic Conference of 1931," *Muslim World*, 82 (1992), 37–54.

18 FO 141/728, 1132/6/31 (Sidqi–Sir Walter Smart conversation).

19 Memorandum by George Rendel on a conversation with Ambassador Hafiz 'Afifi, 4 Nov. 1931; FO 371/15282, E5495/1205/65.
20 FO 371/15282, E5696/1205/65; *SI*, 2 Dec. 1931, 4.
21 FO 371/15282, E5665/1205/65; Mayer, "Conference," 314.
22 See FO 141/728, 1132/27/31; FO 371/15282, E5696/1205/65; Tahir, *Nazarat al-Shura*, 98.
23 Shakib Arslan, *Sayyid Rashid Rida aw Ikha' Arba'in Sana* (Damascus, 1937), 564–5; Mayer, "Conference," 314.
24 Mayer, "Conference," 316.
25 The Congress is discussed in FO 141/489, 82/5/32; H. A. R. Gibb, "The Islamic Congress at Jerusalem in December 1931," in Toynbee, *Survey, 1934,* 99–109; Uri M. Kupferschmidt, "The Supreme Muslim Council 1921–1937: Islam under the British Mandate for Palestine" (Ph. D. dissertation, Hebrew University of Jerusalem, 1978), 349–63.
26 FO 141/489, 82/5/32; Mayer, "Conference," 316.
27 See *SM*, 3 (1931–1932), 33; Kupferschmidt, *Council*, 350.
28 *SI*, 9 Dec. 1931, 4; *BL*, 16 Dec. 1931, 4; FO 141/489, 82/5/32.
29 FO 141/489, 82/5/32.
30 *BL*, 8 Dec. 1931, 1; FO 141/728, 1132/48/31; Coury, *Azzam*, 414–16.
31 See the speech reported in *FH*, 14 Sha'ban 1350, 5.
32 *FH*, 14 Sha'ban 1350, 10; Coury, *Azzam*, 429–30.
33 See *BL*, 16 Dec. 1931, 4; FO 371/15283, E6216/1205/65; 'Azzam's interview in *JA*, 13 Sha'ban 1350; Coury, *Azzam*, 421–5.
34 FO 371/15283, E6276/1205/65; FO 141/728, 1132/56/31; *BL*, 18 Dec. 1931, 4; see also Martin Kramer, *Islam Assembled: The Advent of the Muslim Congresses* (New York, 1986), 135; Coury, *Azzam*, 426–7.
35 *SH*, 1 Dec. 1931, 5; 10 Dec. 1931, 5; 11 Dec. 1931, 5; 13 Dec. 1931, 5.
36 *SI*, 7 Dec. 1931, 4.
37 *SI*, 15 Dec. 1931, 4.
38 *BL*, 10 Dec. 1931, 1; 15 Dec. 1931, 1.
39 *SH*, 7 Dec. 1931, 5; see also 10 Dec. 1931, 5.
40 *SI*, 2 Dec. 1931, 4; see also 7 Dec. 1931, 4.
41 *BL*, 10 Dec. 1931, 1.
42 See Gershoni and Jankowski, *Egypt, Islam, and the Arabs*, 246–7.
43 Mayer, *Egypt*, 35.
44 From a speech by Sidqi as reported in *MS*, 13 April 1932, 1.
45 Loraine (Cairo) to Oliphant, 20 Jan. 1933; FO 141/756, 137/2/33.
46 "Memorandum on the Proposed ARAB CONGRESS," 30 Dec. 1932; FO 141/768, 1190/2/32.
47 See ibid.; FO 141/756, 137/2/33; Porath, *Arab Unity*, 16–17.
48 See Humphrys to Simon, 9 March 1933, in Kenneth Bourne and D. Cameron Watt (eds.), *British Documents on Foreign Affairs: Reports and Papers from the Foreign Office Confidential Print, Part II: From the First to the Second World War. Series B: Turkey, Iran, and the Middle East, 1918–1939* (Washington, 1986) (hereafter *BDFA*), 8, no. 295; Simon to Ogilvie-Forbes, 1 July 1933, *BDFA*, 9, no. 76.
49 "Attitude of His Majesty's Government towards the Question of Arab Unity," 13 June 1933; FO 371/16855, E3119/347/65.

50 Apparently developed first in Heyworth-Dunne, *Religious and Political Trends*, 23–7.
51 Ralph M. Coury, "Who 'Invented' Egyptian Arab Nationalism?," *International Journal of Middle East Studies*, 14 (1982), 257, 261, 273; Mayer, *Egypt*, 41–3, 118–22, 138–47.
52 Wahid al-Dali, *Asrar al-Jami'a al-'Arabiyya wa 'Abd al-Rahman 'Azzam* (Cairo, 1982), 18; Coury, "Who Invented," 273; Coury, *Azzam*, 519.
53 See Clive Leatherdale, *Britain and Saudi Arabia, 1925–1939: The Imperial Oasis* (London, 1983), 264–7.
54 Porath, *Arab Unity*, 181–2.
55 Ibid., 183.
56 Telegram from Lampson, 8 April 1936, FO 371/20061, E1898/202/25.
57 "Negotiations between the Hijaz and Egypt," by Sir Walter Smart, 21 April 1936, FO 141/536, 398/5/36; see also *BL*, 21 April 1936, 1.
58 Text in FO 406/74, no. 24, and in Mahmud 'Azmi, *al-Ayyam al-Mi'a* (Cairo, 1936), 102–6.
59 *AH*, 25 April 1936, 1.
60 *MU*, 9 May 1936, 4; *IM*, 12 May 1936, 21.
61 *SI*, 9 May 1936, 4.
62 Excerpt in *BL*, 6 May 1936, 9 (italics added).
63 "Negotiations between the Hijaz and Egypt," by Sir Walter Smart, 1 April 1936, FO 141/536, 398/5/36.
64 Deeb, *Party Politics*, 345–50.
65 *HI*, Nov. 1936, 2–5.
66 Husayn, *Mustaqbal*, I, 2 (Eng. trans. vii).
67 Quoted in Muhammad Shafiq Ghurbal, *Ta'rikh al-Mufawadat al-Misriyya al-Biritaniyya, 1882–1936* (Cairo, 1952), 312.
68 Dali, *Asrar*, 18.
69 FO 407/219, no. 53; *RA*, 2 Dec. 1936, 95–7.
70 For these measures, see Kelly to Eden, 4 Sept. 1936, FO 371/19980, E5831/381/65; *RA*, 27 May 1936, 7; 9 Dec. 1936, 104–6; 16 Dec. 1936, 154; *MGQ*, Dec. 1936, 64; Lampson to Eden, 28 May 1937, FO 371/20801, E3080/698/93.
71 Report on the "Pan Arab Congress," 30 Dec. 1936, FO 371/20786, E577/351/65; see also Lampson to Eden, 17 Dec. 1936, *BDFA*, 12, no. 83.
72 Letter from Hamilton of the European Department, Ministry of the Interior, FO 141/537, 403/251/36.
73 "Pan Arab Congress," 30 Dec. 1936, FO 371/20786, E577/351/65.
74 Discussed in Mayer, *Egypt*, 60–3; Porath, *Arab Unity*, 184–5.
75 Bateman (Baghdad) to Eden, 21 Aug. 1936, FO 141/455, 861/1/36.
76 Letter from Kerr (Baghdad), 18 Jan. 1937, FO 141/481, 181/2/37.
77 Kelly to Eden, 26 March 1937, FO 371/20801, E1870/698/93.
78 Lampson to Halifax, 24 Feb. 1938, FO 407/222, no. 67.
79 Muhammad Husayn Haykal, *Mudhakkirat fi al-Siyasa al-Misriyya* (3 vols.; Cairo, 1951, 1953, 1978), II, 147–8.
80 Ibid., 148.
81 Foreign Secretary to Peterson (Baghdad), 24 Feb. 1939, FO 371/23213, E1503/712/93.

82 Telegram from Bateman, 30 Aug. 1939, FO 371/23211, E6167/474/93 (quoted in Porath, *Arab Unity*, 185).

83 See Berque, *Egypt: Imperialism and Revolution*, 534–5, 561–2; Marcel Colombe, *L'Evolution de l'Egypte* (Paris, 1951), 68–9.

84 For sketches, see Elie Kedourie, "Egypt and the Caliphate, 1915–52," in his *The Chatham House Version and Other Middle-Eastern Studies* (New York, 1970), 199–202; Smith, *Haykal*, 146–7.

85 See Berque, *Egypt: Imperialism and Revolution*, 460–5; Ramadan, *Sira'*, 194–5.

86 For detailed accounts of this campaign, see Tariq al-Bishri, *al-Muslimun wa al-Aqbat fi Itar al-Jama'a al-Wataniyya* (Cairo, 1980), 557–68; Kedourie, "Egypt and the Caliphate," 199–205; Berque, *Egypt: Imperialism and Revolution*, 559–64; Barbara Lynn Carter, *The Copts in Egyptian Politics* (London, 1986), 260–9.

87 Memorandum by Smart, 31 March 1937, FO 141/445, 494/2/37.

88 Berque, *Egypt: Imperialism and Revolution*, 534–5; Kedourie, "Egypt and the Caliphate," 199.

89 See Kedourie, "Egypt and the Caliphate," 178–81; Gershoni and Jankowski, *Egypt, Islam, and the Arabs*, 64–6.

90 Maraghi in a conversation with the Agha Khan, as reported in a dispatch from Lampson, 17 Feb. 1938, FO 371/21838, E1114/1034/16.

91 Maraghi in a conversation with Lord Lloyd, as reported in Lampson to Halifax, 25 March 1938, FO 371/21838, E1870/1034/16.

92 Maraghi in a conversation with the Agha Khan, as reported in a dispatch from Lampson, 17 Feb. 1938, FO 371/21838, E1114/1034/16.

93 Ibid.

94 Ibid.

95 Discussed in Kramer, *Islam Assembled*, 102–4.

96 Lampson to Halifax, 25 March 1938, FO 371/21838, E1870/1034/16.

97 Ramadan, *Sira'*, 196.

98 Lampson to Eden, 17 Feb. 1938, FO 371/21945, J893/6/16.

99 *HI*, April 1939, 14–15.

100 *MF*, 6 June 1938, 9.

101 *MF*, 28 Jan. 1939, 3; see also 2 Feb. 1939, 5.

102 *BL*, 8 Oct. 1938, 9–10; see also Kedourie, "Egypt and the Caliphate," 204.

103 Telegram from Lampson, 25 Jan. 1938, FO 371/23304, J358/1/16.

104 See *BL*, 16 Oct. 1938, 8; *AH*, 9 Feb. 1939, 9.

105 On the Wafdist opposition, see *RA*, 2 Feb. 1938, 18–19; Lampson to Brooke-Popham (Nairobi), 18 Jan. 1938, FO 371/21838, E1034/1034/16.

106 Tawfiq Diyab writing in *al-Jihad*, as cited in a memorandum on the Egyptian Press, 6 Jan. – 14 Feb. 1938, FO 371/22000, J748/264/16.

107 See FO 371/22004, J2691/2014/16; FO 371/22004, J2792/2014/16; FO 371/23304, J377/1/16.

108 *BL*, 16 Oct. 1938, 8; see also *DS*, 26 Jan. 1939, 1.

109 *HI*, March 1939, 481–4.

110 Writing in *HI*, April 1939, 14–15.

111 Dispatch from Lampson, 17 Feb. 1938, FO 371/21838, E1114/1034/16; Baggallay to Lampson, 4 April 1938, FO 371/21838, E1527/1034/16; note by Cavendish-Bentnick, 9 May 1938, in FO 371/22004, J2014/2014/16.

112 Dispatch from Lampson, 24 Oct. 1938, FO 371/21883, E6508/10/31.
113 Bullard (Jedda) to Halifax, 19 Jan. 1939, *BDFA*, 13, no. 326.
114 Lampson to Halifax, 3 Feb. 1939, FO 371/23361, J564/364/16.
115 Ibid.
116 Extract from *The Times*, 25 Jan. 1939, in FO 371/23361, J364/364/16.
117 Lampson to Halifax, 3 Feb. 1939, FO 371/23361, J564/364/16.
118 *HI*, April 1939, 32–3 (following material from this article).
119 Quoted in Khardaji, *al-'Arab*, 76.
120 *MI*, 12 Oct. 1938, 1.
121 *MU*, 6 Jan. 1939, 7.
122 Quoted in Khardaji, *al-'Arab*, 76–7.
123 *BL*, 11 Oct. 1938, 8.
124 *MU*, 19 Jan. 1939, 1.

8 PALESTINE, PUBLIC OPINION, AND EGYPTIAN POLICY

1 Residency minute sheet, 6 June 1936, FO 141/536, 403/28/36; memo contained in
   FO 141/536, 403/38/36.
2 See FO 141/536, 403/13/36 and 403/38/36.
3 *JH*, 19 May 1936, 1; 21 May 1936, 8; 28 May 1936, 1.
4 *SI*, 27 May 1936, 4.
5 *BL*, 29 May 1936, 1.
6 *SM*, V (1933–4), 185–8 and 309–14; VI (1934–5), 166–78 and 517–18.
7 *SM*, VII (1935–6), 556–63, 629–34; VIII (1936–7), 41–60, 83–91, 160, 250–53.
8 See *SM*, VIII (1936–7), 83.
9 *IM*, 28 April 1936, 17.
10 Secret memo, Public Security Department, Special Section, contained in FO141/
   536, 403/12/36.
11 *IM*, 19 May 1936, 19–20.
12 Israel Gershoni, "The Muslim Brothers and the Arab Revolt in Palestine,
   1936–39," *Middle Eastern Studies*, 22 (1986), 367–97.
13 See *JH*, 23 May 1936, 1, 7, for one example.
14 Telegram from Lampson, 25 May 1936, FO 371/20108, J4727/2/16; telegram
   from Lampson, 26 May 1936, FO 371/20108, J4766/2/16; Kelly to Eden, 4 June
   1936, FO371/20035, E3507/3217/31.
15 Ten such protests were received by the British after Friday prayer on 12 June
   1936; FO 141/536, 403/34/36.
16 Telegram from Huda Sha'rawi; in FO 371/20035, E3610/3217/31.
17 See *RA*, 27 May 1936, 18; *JH*, 21 May 1936, 8; *BL*, 29 May 1936, 1.
18 *SM*, VIII (1936–7), 60; *IM*, 6 Oct. 1936, 22.
19 Founding discussed in *SM*, VII (1935–6), 558–63. See also *IM*, 2 June 1936, 17;
   11 Aug. 1936, 9–11; *FH*, 21 Rabi' al-Awwal 1355, 23; 25 Jumada al-Ula 1355,
   16–17; 15 Rajab 1355, 6–7.
20 *SM*, VIII (1936–7), 160.
21 'Awatif 'Abd al-Rahman, *Misr wa Filastin* (Cairo, 1980), 265.
22 Deeb, *Party Politics*, 345–50.
23 See Gabriel Baer, *A History of Landownership in Modern Egypt, 1800–1950*
   (London, 1962), 145–6.

24 Quoted in Deeb, *Party Politics*, 349.
25 See Yehoshua Porath, *The Palestinian Arab National Movement, 1929–1939: From Riots to Rebellion* (London, 1977), 199–219; Norman Rose, "The Arab Rulers and Palestine, 1936: The British Reaction," *Journal of Modern History*, 44 (1972), 213–31; Michael J. Cohen, *Palestine: Retreat from the Mandate; The Making of British Policy, 1936–1939* (New York, 1978), 18–31.
26 Reported in David Ben-Gurion, *My Talks with Arab Leaders* (trans. by Aryeh Rubenstein and Misha Louvish; New York, 1973), 105–6.
27 *RA*, 22 July 1936, 20–1.
28 Texts in *AH*, 28 July 1936, 1; *RA*, 29 July 1936, 7.
29 Telegram from Kelly, 6 June 1936, FO 371/20110, J5227/2/16; telegram from Kelly, 9 June 1936, FO 371/20110, J5232/2/16.
30 *SB*, 7 Oct. 1936, 6–7; Mayer, *Egypt*, 51.
31 Lampson to Eden, 12 Aug. 1936, FO 371/20023, E5207/94/31.
32 Discussed in Ghurbal, *Ta'rikh*, 312.
33 *SB*, 21 Oct. 1936, 5–6.
34 Discussed in Kelly's telegrams of 4 June, 16 June, 22 June, and 29 June 1936; FO 371/20035, E3483/3217/31, E3598/3217/31, E3753/3217/31, E3990/3217/31.
35 Telegram from Lampson, 12 Aug. 1936, FO 371/20035, E5160/3217/31; FO minute by Campbell, 28 Aug. 1936, FO 371/20024, E5492/94/31.
36 Quotation from a memorandum by Rendel summarizing Nahhas's views, 8 Sept. 1936, FO 371/20024, E5691/94/31.
37 Telegram from Phipps (Berlin), 29 Sept. 1936, FO 371/20026, E6131/94/31. (Nahhas was visiting Berlin at the time.)
38 Telegram from Phipps, 2 Oct. 1936, FO 371/20026, E6240/94/31.
39 Lampson to Eden, 12 Aug. 1936, FO 371/20023, E5207/94/31.
40 Kelly to Eden, 4 Sept. 1936, FO 371/19980, E5831/381/65.
41 Telegram from Lampson, 21 July 1937, FO 371/20809, E4194/22/31.
42 *RA*, 14 July 1937, 4–6; *AH*, 15 July 1937, 9; 16 July 1937, 9; 18 July 1937, 2; *FH*, 14 Jumada al-Ula 1356, 3–4; 5 Jumada al-Akhira 1356, 3–4; *MU*, 15 July 1937, 11; *SI*, 16 July 1937, 8.
43 See *AH*, 15 July 1937, 9; 23 July 1937, 10; 14 July 1937, 9; 17 July 1937, 11.
44 See *MU*, 15 July 1937, 11; *AH*, 17 July 1937, 11; FO 371/20809, E4206/22/31.
45 Memorandum on the Egyptian press, 7–26 July 1937, FO 371/20811, E4746/22/31.
46 Ibrahim 'Abd al-Qadir al-Mazini in *RA*, 11 Aug. 1937, 7.
47 *RI*, 5 July 1937, 1086–8.
48 Both quotations from *RA*, 4 Aug. 1937, 16–17.
49 Hasan Nabih al-Misri as quoted in *RA*, 11 Aug. 1937, 6; Sayyid Khashaba as quoted in *RA*, 18 Aug. 1937, 5–6.
50 Ibrahim 'Abd al-Qadir al-Mazini in *RA*, 11 Aug. 1937, 7.
51 *RI*, 2 Aug. 1937, 1266–7.
52 Ibid.
53 'Abd al-Hamid Sa'id in *RA*, 4 Aug. 1937, 16–17.
54 Fu'ad Abaza in *RA*, 25 Aug. 1937, 7.
55 *RI*, 2 Aug. 1937, 1247–9.
56 See *RA*, 18 Aug. 1937, 6; *RI*, 2 Aug. 1937, 1247–9.
57 *RI*, 2 Aug. 1937, 1267.
58 *MI*, 9 July 1937, 1; see also 16 July 1937, 1.

59 *MI*, 19 July 1937, 1; see also 12 July 1937, 1.

60 *JH*, 10 July 1937, 1.

61 *JH*, 13 July 1937, 1.

62 *JH*, 14 July 1937, 1.

63 *SU*, 17 July 1937, 3.

64 *JH*, 24 July 1937, 10.

65 *SM*, IX (1937–8), 56–7.

66 *IM*, 16 July 1937, 6; 5 Nov. 1937, 12–13.

67 *TH*, 12 July 1937, 2.

68 Ibid.; see also *TH*, 19 July 1937, 7, 10.

69 *AH*, 11 July 1937, 1; 12 July 1937, 8; *SM*, IX (1937–8), 57–8.

70 *FH*, 8 Ramadan 1356, 17, 21–2; *IM*, 10 Dec. 1937, 24; *SM*, IX (1937–8), 157–65; FO 141/676, 52/221/37.

71 *FH*, 9 Sha'ban 1356, 20; 16 Sha'ban 1356, 19; 8 Ramadan 1356, 17, 21–2; *IM*, 15 Oct. 1937, 5; 10 Dec. 1937, 24.

72 *AH*, 14 July 1937, 9.

73 See *TH*, 19 July 1937, 7, 10; FO 371/20811, E4746/22/31.

74 *AH*, 14 July 1937, 9; 15 July 1937, 9; 17 July 1937, 11.

75 See *BL*, 15 July 1937, 1; *TH*, 26 July 1937, 4, 12.

76 *MI*, 21 July 1937, 8; FO 141/678, 52/95/37.

77 Translated from *al-Jihad*, 3 Aug. 1937, in Kelly to Eden, 21 Aug. 1937, FO 371/20812, E5054/22/31.

78 Telegram from Lampson, 25 July 1937, FO 371/20810, E4320/22/31.

79 Minute by Kelly on a conversation with Amin 'Uthman of 9 Sept. 1937; FO 141/678, 52/153/37. On Bludan generally, see Fu'ad Khalil Mufarraj, *al-Mu'tamar al-'Arabi al-Qawmi fi Buludan, 1937* (Damascus, n.d.), *passim*; Elie Kedourie, "The Bludan Congress on Palestine, September 1937," *Middle Eastern Studies*, 17 (1980), 107–25.

80 Quotations from Mufarraj, *al-Mu'tamar*, 46–8.

81 Kedourie, "Bludan," 114.

82 "Memorandum on the Egyptian press, 2 Sept. – 1 Oct. 1937," FO 371/20903, J4334/148/16.

83 Text in *RA*, 22 Sept. 1937, 6–7.

84 Kelly to Eden, 28 Sept. 1937, FO 371/20816, E5903/22/31.

85 Text in *RA*, 2 Feb. 1938, 47–8; copy received by the British enclosed in Lampson to Eden, 9 Jan. 1938, FO 371/21872, E443/10/31.

86 See Mayer, *Egypt*, 73–4.

87 Telegram from Lampson, 21 July 1937, FO 371/20809, E4194/22/31.

88 Kelly to Eden, 28 Sept. 1937, FO 371/20816, E5903/22/31.

89 Robert Gale Woolbert, "Pan-Arabism and the Palestine Problem," *Foreign Affairs*, 16 (Jan. 1938), 319.

90 Telegram from Lampson, 25 July 1937, FO 371/20810, E4320/22/31.

91 Telegram from Kelly, 25 Aug. 1937, FO 371/20812, E4985/22/31.

92 Kelly to Eden, 27 Oct. 1937, FO 141/678, 52/221/37.

93 Telegram from Lampson, 3 May 1938, FO 371/21876, E2575/10/31; telegram from Lampson, 4 May 1938, FO 371/21876, E2576/10/31.

94 Telegram from Lampson, 9 Oct. 1938, FO 371/21881, E5895/10/31; telegram from Lampson, 31 Oct. 1938, FO 371/21883, E6429/10/31.

95 Lampson to Halifax, 7 Nov. 1938, FO 407/222, no. 48.
96 Lampson to Halifax, 16 Jan. 1939, FO 371/23304, J377/1/16.
97 For his numerous statements of 1938–9, see *SM*, IX (1937–8) and X (1938–9), *passim*.
98 *FH*, 12 Rabi' al-Awwal 1357, 30–1; 23 Jumada al-Ula 1357, 9; 15 Jumada al-Akhira 1357, 17; 5 Sha'ban 1357, 6–8.
99 See Gershoni, "Muslim Brothers," 382–9.
100 See *ND*, issues of Rajab 1357.
101 *FH*, 24 Rabi' al-Thani 1357, 15.
102 Telegram from Lampson, 1 April 1939, FO 371/23232, E2444/6/31.
103 *RA*, 4 May 1938, 10; 24 Aug. 1938, 41; *FH*, 25 Muharram 1358, 6; 13 Rabi' al-Akhir 1358, 5; Lampson to Halifax, 17 May 1938, FO 371/21877, E3172/10/31.
104 Telegram from Lampson, 28 April 1938, FO 371/21875, E2462/10/31.
105 Lampson to Halifax, 17 May 1938, FO 371/21877, E3172/10/31.
106 *RA*, 2 Nov. 1938, 6–8; 9 Nov. 1938, 47–8; Bateman to Halifax, 10 Nov. 1938, FO 371/21866, E6905/1/31.
107 Lampson to Halifax, 7 Nov. 1938, FO 407/222, no. 48.
108 *FH*, 10 Rabi' al-Awwal 1357, 17; 25 Ramadan 1357, 20; FO 371/21883, E6494/10/31.
109 Tariq al- Bishri, *al-Haraka al-Siyasiyya fi Misr, 1945–1952* (Cairo, 1972), 247.
110 *al-Mu'tamar al-Nisa'i al-Sharqi lil-Difa''an Filastin* (Cairo, 1938), 46–54. See also *BL*, 15 Oct. 1938, 8; 19 Oct. 1938, 10.
111 Letter from Huda Sha'rawi enclosed in FO 371/21867, E7110/1/31; see also *RA*, 1 March 1939, 8; 26 April 1939, 14.
112 Jankowski, *Egypt's Young Rebels*, 40–3.
113 Ibid., 37–9, 72–8.
114 Memorandum on the Egyptian Press, 28 June – 27 July 1938, FO 371/22000, J3207/264/16; see also Mayer, *Egypt*, 88–9.
115 *RA*, 13 July 1938, 44; Lampson to Halifax, 8 July 1938, FO 407/222, no. 4.
116 *RA*, 27 July 1938, 44.
117 Report of a conversation between Nahhas and Mr. Chapman Andrews, July 1938, contained in CO 733/368, 75156/16.
118 Telegram from Lampson, 7 Oct. 1938, FO 371/21881, E5868/10/31; telegram from Lampson, 27 Oct. 1938, FO 371/21883, E6327/10/31.
119 Cited in Bateman to Halifax, 16 Nov. 1938, FO 407/222, no. 46.
120 *MU*, 6 Jan. 1939, 7–9.
121 For examples, see *FH*, 23 Dhu al-Hijja 1356, 19; *RA*, 9 Nov. 1938, 47–8; 26 April 1939, 14.
122 *SM*, X (1938–9), 271–2.
123 MacKereth to Tegart, 27 Oct. 1938, as reprinted in Michael G. Fry and Itamar Rabinovich, *Despatches from Damascus: Gilbert MacKereth and British Policy in the Levant, 1933–1938* (Jerusalem, 1985), 188–92.
124 Bateman to Halifax, 26 Sept. 1938, FO 371/21881, E5898/10/31; *FH*, 27 Rajab 1357, 30; Gershoni, "Muslim Brothers," 384.
125 Reported but discounted in *FH*, 17 Jumada al-Ula 1358, 14.
126 *RI*, 27 Feb. 1939, 425–6.
127 For examples see Lampson to Halifax, 9 May 1938, FO 371/21876, E2983/10/

31; *RA*, 4 May 1938, 10; 11 May 1938, 46; *FH*, 12 Rabi' al-Awwal 1357, 13, 30–1; 15 Jumada al-Akhira 1357, 20.

128 *FH*, 26 Rabi' al-Awwal 1357, 22; 3 Rabi' al-Thani 1357, 12; Lampson to Halifax, 2 June 1938, FO 371/21877, E3509/10/31.

129 See Mayer, *Egypt*, 87.

130 Telegram from Lampson, 28 April 1938, FO 371/21875, E2462/10/31.

131 See *RA*, 27 July 1938, 44–7; 24 Aug. 1938, 41; Lampson to Halifax, 3 Oct. 1938, FO 371/22004, J3930/2014/16; telegram from Lampson, 31 Oct. 1938, FO 371/21883, E6429/10/31.

132 Telegram from Lampson, 3 May 1938, FO 371/21876, E2575/10/31.

133 Halifax to Lampson, 23 July 1938, FO 371/21878, E4415/10/31.

134 "Note of Interview with the Egyptian Prime Minister on Friday, the 29th July 1938," FO 371/21879, E4618/10/31.

135 Lampson to Halifax, 2 June 1938, FO 371/21877, E3510/10/31.

136 Telegram from Lampson, 26 July 1938, FO 371/21879, E4441/10/31.

137 According to the official document of the Congress, *Khutub Haflat al-Iftitah al-Kubra lil-Mu'tamar al-Barlamani al-'Alami lil-Difa' 'an Filastin* (Cairo, 1938), 142–8. See also Ettore Rossi, "Il congresso interparlamentare arabo e musulmano pro Palestina al Cairo (7–11 Ottobre)," *Oriente Moderno*, 18 (1938), 589.

138 *MI*, 6 Oct. 1938, 6; see also telegram from Lampson, 7 Oct. 1938, FO 371/21881, E5868/10/31.

139 See *MU*, 3 Oct. 1938, 9; 5 Oct. 1938, 6.

140 *MU*, 8 Oct. 1938, 6; *BL*, 10 Oct. 1938, 9; *FH*, 4 Ramadan 1357, 14–17; *Khutub*, 126–41; Rossi, "Il congresso interparlamentare," 593–9.

141 *Khutub*, 141; Rossi, "Il congresso interparlamentare," 591, 599.

142 See FO 371/22000, J3628/264/16, J3978/264/16, and J4641/264/16; *MU*, 8 Oct. 1938, 1; *AH*, 13 Oct. 1938, 1; *BL*, 12 Oct. 1938, 1.

143 *MI*, 8 Oct. 1938, 6.

144 *MI*, 12 Oct. 1938, 1, 2, 7, and *FI*, 12 Oct. 1938.

145 *MI*, 11 Oct. 1938, 8.

146 *BL*, 15 Oct. 1938, 10.

147 Telegram from Bateman, 7 Sept. 1938, FO 371/21880, E5238/10/31.

148 Telegram from Lampson, 3 Oct. 1938, FO 371/21881, E5787/10/31.

149 Telegram from Lampson, 6 Oct. 1938, FO 371/21881, E5844/10/31; telegram from Lampson, 6 Oct. 1938, FO 371/21881, E5849/10/31; telegram from Lampson, 9 Oct. 1938, FO 371/21881, E5895/10/31; telegram from Lampson, 9 Oct. 1938, FO 371/21881, E5907/10/31.

150 Telegram from Lampson, 4 Oct. 1938, FO 371/21881, E5816/10/31; telegram from Lampson, 7 Oct. 1938, FO 371/21881, E5868/10/31.

151 Report by the Palestine Police, 1 Nov. 1938, CO 733/359, 75021. See also Khayriyya Qasimiyya (ed.), *'Awni 'Abd al-Hadi: Awraq Khassa* (Beirut, 1974), 97.

152 Telegram from Lampson, 27 Oct. 1938, FO 371/21882, E6306/10/31; note on the conversation between 'Alluba and MacDonald, 22 Nov. 1938, contained in FO 371/21866, E6986/1/31.

153 See *FH*, 13 Dhu al-Hijja 1357, 17, and 27 Rabi' al-Akhir 1358, 15.

154 Dispatch from Lampson, 24 Oct. 1938, FO 371/21883, E6908/10/31.

155 Details in Lampson to Halifax, 16 Dec. 1939, FO 371/23304, J377/1/16; *MU*,

4 Jan. 1939, 4; 6 Jan. 1939, 7–9; 8 Jan. 1939, 9; *MI*, 6 Jan. 1939, 1, 2, 7; Muhammad 'Ali al-Tahir, *Zalam al-Sajn: Mudhakkirat wa Mufakkirat Sujayn Harib* (Cairo, 1951), 467.

156 *BL*, 19 Jan. 1939, 1, 11.

157 Lampson to Halifax, 20 Jan. 1939, FO 371/23221, E754/6/31.

158 Report on the sixth meeting between the British and the Arab delegations, 15 Feb. 1939, FO 371/23224, E1220/6/31.

159 Report on the ninth meeting between the British and the Arab delegations, 20 Feb. 1939, FO 371/23224, E1342/6/31.

160 "Conferences on Palestine, 1939. Informal Discussions with Arab and Jewish Delegates," 23 Feb. 1939, FO 371/23225, E1448/6/31.

161 "Conferences on Palestine, Note of Informal Conversation with Arab and Jewish Delegates," 7 March 1939, FO 371/23228, E1875/6/31.

162 Telegram from Lampson, 18 March 1939, FO 371/23230, E2051/6/31; telegram from Lampson, 23 March 1939, FO 371/23231, E2218/6/31.

163 Telegram from Lampson, 13 April 1939, FO 371/23233, E2724/6/31.

164 From the *procès-verbaux* of the meeting of 29 April as contained in FO 371/23236, E3945/6/31.

165 Telegram from Lampson, 22 May 1939, FO 371/23236, E3743/6/31; "Memorandum. The Egyptian Press. 3rd May, 1939, to 5th August, 1939," FO 371/23364, J3399/774/16; *FH*, 6 Rabi' al-Akhir 1358, 14–17; 13 Rabi' al-Akhir 1358, 5; 20 Rabi' al-Akhir 1358, 3–4; *SM*, X, no. 9 (June 1939), 578; *MF*, 25 May 1939, 1.

166 Telegram from Lampson, 17 May 1939, FO 371/23235, E3618/6/31.

167 Telegram from Lampson, 18 May 1939, FO 371/23235, E3673/6/31.

168 Porath, *Palestinian Arab National Movement*, 291.

169 Lampson to Halifax, 4 July 1939, FO 371/23238, E5102/6/31.

170 Telegram from Lampson, 6 July 1939, FO 371/23238, E4904/6/31.

171 Telegram from Lampson, 8 June 1938, FO 371/21877, E3389/10/31.

172 Halifax to Lampson, 23 July 1938, FO 371/21878, E4415/10/31; "Note of an Interview with the Egyptian Prime Minister," 29 July 1938, contained in FO 371/21879, E4618/10/31.

173 "Memorandum. The Egyptian Press. 16th April, 1938 - 22nd May, 1938," FO 371/22000, J2254/264/16.

174 Dispatch from Lampson, 16 Jan. 1939, FO 371/23304, J377/1/16; dispatch from Lampson, 19 May 1939, FO 371/23305, J2132/1/16.

175 Quoted in Cohen, *Palestine*, 68; see also Norman Rose, *The Gentile Zionists: Anglo-Zionist Diplomacy, 1929–1939* (London, 1973), 157–8.

176 The quoted phrase was used by Mahmud in a conversation with Malcolm MacDonald in July 1938; note by MacDonald, 29 July 1938, FO 371/21879, E4618/10/31. The latter perception was expressed by Mahmud in a conversation with Lampson in April 1939; telegram from Lampson, 30 April 1939, FO 371/23234, E3160/6/31.

177 In the Arab–Jewish meeting of 7 March 1939; see above, n. 161.

9 THE ROAD TO THE ARAB LEAGUE, 1939–1945

1 George Kirk, *The Middle East in the War*, vol. II of *Survey of International Affairs, 1939–1946* (London, 1952), 34, 195.
2 Mitchell, *Society of Muslim Brothers*, 21–6; Jankowski, *Egypt's Young Rebels*, 79–85.
3 Lampson to Eden, 25 Aug. 1940, FO 371/24548, E2511/953/65.
4 Heyworth-Dunne, *Religious and Political Trends*, 23; Gomaa, *League of Arab States*, 43–5.
5 *RA*, 27 Sept. 1939, 2–4.
6 *RA*, 22 Nov. 1939, 1–2.
7 See his articles in *RA*, 3 March 1940, 4–5, and 3 April 1940, 13.
8 As published in Jamil 'Arif (ed.), *Safahat min al-Mudhakkirat al-Sirriyya li-Awwal Amin 'Amm lil-Jami'a al-'Arabiyya, 'Abd al-Rahman 'Azzam* (2 vols.; Cairo, 1978–), I, 251–7 (quotation from 255).
9 See Mayer, *Egypt*, 138–40.
10 See FO 371/23242, E7854/6/31, E7886/6/31, and E7932/6/31.
11 *AH*, 25 April 1940, 4; *RA*, 5 May 1940, 4–5; Mayer, *Egypt*, 146–7.
12 See his article in *RA*, 28 Feb. 1940, 3–4.
13 'Asim Ahmad al-Dasuqi, *Misr fi al-Harb al-'Alamiyya al-Thaniya, 1939–1945* (Cairo, 1976), 286.
14 Lampson to Halifax, 16 Nov. 1939, FO 407/223, no. 40.
15 Halifax to Lampson, 18 Nov. 1939, FO 407/223, no. 41.
16 Lampson to Eden, 25 Aug. 1940, FO 371/24548, E2511/953/65.
17 See Mayer, *Egypt*, 152–3.
18 Lampson to Foreign Office, 21 April 1941, FO 371/27066, E1643/1/93; same to same, 15 May 1941, FO 371/27070, E2333/1/93.
19 From a report in *RA*, 23 Oct. 1940, 2.
20 See Lampson to Eden, 1 Dec. 1941, FO 371/27045, E8275/53/65; *RA*, 6 Dec. 1941, 4; 13 Dec. 1941, 6–8.
21 *RA*, 13 Dec. 1941, 8; 7 Feb. 1942, 1–2; Lampson to MacMichael, 23 Jan. 1942, FO 371/31337, E1786/49/65.
22 Vatikiotis, *Egypt*, 349.
23 See *RI*, 13 July 1942, 712; 3 Aug. 1942, 770; *RA*, 27 June 1942, 15; 25 July 1942, 15; 15 Aug. 1942, 18; dispatch from Lampson, 16 Dec. 1942, FO 371/35528, J125/2/16; dispatch from Lampson, 5 March 1943, FO 371/35530, J1464/2/16.
24 Statutes published in *RA*, 2 Jan. 1942, 3; see also dispatch from Lampson, 2 Jan. 1943, FO 371/35528, J490/2/16.
25 Lampson to Eden, 1 Dec. 1942; FO 371/27045, E8275/53–65.
26 Text in *RA*, 21 Nov. 1942, 10–11, and summarized in a telegram from Lampson, 13 Nov. 1942, FO 371/31575, J4665/38/16.
27 Telegram from Lampson, 16 Nov. 1942, FO 371/31575, J4692/38/16.
28 See Gomaa, *League of Arab States*, 99–100.
29 Mayer, *Egypt*, 172.
30 Discussed in Porath, *Arab Unity*, 255–6.
31 *MSR*, 11 Dec. 1942, 1 ('Azzam); 18 Dec. 1942, 1 ('Alluba).
32 Telegram from Jidda, 14 Feb. 1943, FO 141/866, 149/10/43.
33 For its founding meeting, see *RA*, 27 May 1942, 14–15; its statutes are contained

in Nadi al-Ittihad al-'Arabi, *al-Ittihad al-'Arabi wa Qanunuhu al-'Amm* (Cairo, 1942).

34 Quotation from its charter as cited in *RA*, 27 May 1942, 14–15.

35 For examples of its activities in 1942–4, see *RA*, 21 Nov. 1942, 12; 28 Nov. 1942, 32–3; 6 Feb. 1943, 14; 6 March 1943, 3–11; 17 April 1943, 1–4; 12 June 1943, 6–7; 18 Sept. 1943, 8; 24 Oct. 1943, 3; 22 Jan. 1944, 17–18; *AH*, 7 March 1944, 2; 13 March 1944, 3.

36 *AH*, 28 Feb. 1943, 3; also available in FO 921/113, 90(2)43/32.

37 See *BL*, 1 March 1943, 1; *AH*, 2 March 1943, 3; 3 March 1943, 3; and the material in FO921/113, 90(2)43/32, 90(2)43/33, 90(2)43/38, FO 921/114, 90(2)43/42, and FO 371/35530, J1322/2/16.

38 Weekly report, Cairo, 4–10 March 1943, FO 371/35530, J1366/2/16; telegram from Lampson, 13 March 1943, FO 371/35530, J1203/2/16; telegram from Lampson, 31 March 1943, FO 141/866, 149/39/43.

39 FO 921/113, 90(2)43/38 and 90(2)43/33; FO 371/35530, J1322/2/16.

40 Weekly report, Cairo, 6 March 1943, FO 371/35530, J1070/2/16.

41 Copy enclosed in FO 371/34956, E2027/506/65.

42 Lampson to Eden, 16 June 1943, FO 371/35536, J2855/2/16.

43 Text in *AH*, 31 March 1943, 3; copy in a dispatch from Lampson, 1 April 1943, FO 371/34957, E2096/506/65.

44 *AH*, 15 Nov. 1943, 5.

45 *AH*, 17 Nov. 1943, 3.

46 *AH*, 18 Nov. 1943, 3.

47 Weekly report, 25–31 March 1943, FO 371/35531, J1615/2/16.

48 For Nuri's view, see memo by Clayton, 7 Aug. 1943, FO 141/866, 149/90/43; for 'Abd Allah, see Patrick Seale, *The Struggle for Syria: A Study in Post-War Arab Politics, 1945–1958* (London, 1965), 13.

49 Elie Kedourie, "Pan-Arabism and British Policy," in *The Chatham House Version and Other Middle-Eastern Studies* (New York, 1970), 218; see also Gomaa, *League of Arab States*, 161; Porath, *Arab Unity*, 258.

50 See Gomaa, *League of Arab States*, 99.

51 For ideas of postwar regional cooperation in Egypt, see Eran Lerman, "The Egyptian Question, 1942–1947: The Deterioration of Britain's Postwar Position in Egypt, Al-Alamein to the U.N. Debate of 1947" (Ph.D. dissertation, University of London, 1982), 152–7.

52 See Gomaa, *League of Arab States*, 153–234; Mayer, *Egypt*, 195–215; Porath, *Arab Unity*, 257–84.

53 "Note on the Present Stage of the Arab Unity Conversations," 11 March 1945, FO 141/1010, 32/77/45.

54 Iraqi views as summarized in "Memorandum: Egypt and the Arab World," by Sir Walter Smart, 3 May 1943, FO 141/866, 149/2/43; the view of Col. S. F. Newcombe, FO 141/866, 149/138/43.

55 For examples see *RA*, 23 Oct. 1943, 5–8; 25 Dec. 1943, 6–7; 19 Aug. 1944, 4–6; FO 371/35535, J1951/2/16 and J2693/2/16; FO 371/35536, J2954/2/16; FO 371/41319, J3749/14/16.

56 Minutes of the Syrian–Egyptian discussions, Oct.–Nov. 1943, FO 371/34963, E7981/506/65.

57 Cited in Seale, *Struggle for Syria*, 22–3.

58 Shone to Eden, 14 Sept. 1943, FO 371/34962, E5770/506/65; Jordan to Eden, 11 Sept. 1943, FO 371/34962, E5822/506/65.
59 "Conflicts and Agreements of Interest to the United States in the Near East," 10 Jan. 1944, United States, State Department, Offices of Strategic Services, Research and Analysis Branch (hereafter OSS/R&A), report no. 1206.
60 Lampson to Eden, 16 June 1943, FO 371/35536, J2855/2/16.
61 Telegram from Lampson, 4 April 1943, FO 371/35531, J1519/2/16.
62 Telegram from Baghdad, 13 Sept. 1944, FO 921/221, 48(2)44/120.
63 See the statement of the king's views as transmitted to the British in May 1943, FO 371/34959, E3595/506/65.
64 Discussed in Gomaa, *League of Arab States*, 202–11.
65 *AH*, 8 Oct. 1944, 3; see also the memo by Smart, 10 Oct. 1944, FO 141/949, 151/234/44; Gomaa, *League of Arab States*, 225.
66 For a defense of Nahhas's diplomacy see Gomaa, *League of Arab States*, 190, 216.
67 For Arab impressions of Nahhas's vagueness, see FO 371/45237, E1709/3/65; "hazy" is a British evaluation in FO 371/45241, E9471/3/65.
68 Minutes of the discussions, in FO 371/34961, E5376/506/65.
69 From an account of the negotiations relayed to the British by the Lebanese Foreign Minister in FO 371/39987, E871/41/65.
70 Minutes of the discussions, in FO 371/34961, E5376/506/65.
71 Dispatch from Jordan, 2 Oct. 1943, FO 371/34962, E6264/506/65.
72 FO 371/34962, E6291/506/65; FO 371/34963, E7981/506/65; FO 371/39987, E1349/41/65.
73 Minutes of the sixth session of the conference, in FO 371/45235, E455/3/65.
74 Telegram from Shone, 5 Sept. 1943, FO 371/34961, E5352/506/65.
75 Minutes of the discussions, in FO 371/34963, E7981/506/65.
76 For an example see the minutes of the Nahhas–Nuri meetings contained in FO 371/34961, E5376/506/65.
77 Dispatch from Shone, 28 Oct. 1943, FO 371/94963, E6706/506/65.
78 Ibrahim Faraj, *Dhikrayyat Siyasiyya* (Giza, 1983), 138 (Faraj was Nahhas's personal assistant during the early 1940s).
79 Telegram from Lampson, 31 Aug. 1943, FO 371/34961, J3849/2/16.
80 Furlonge to Spears, 21 Jan. 1944, FO 371/39987, E871/41/65.
81 See Gomaa, *League of Arab States*, 197, 200.
82 Ibid., 212; Mayer, *Egypt*, 254.
83 Dispatch from Lampson, 10 Oct. 1944, FO 141/949, 151/232/44.
84 See *AH*, 14 Nov. 1943, 3; Mayer, *Egypt*, 200.
85 Report from the CID, Palestine Police, 6 July 1943, FO 816/43, pp. 50–50A; report on "The Opposition," 17 July 1943, FO 816/43, p. 86B.
86 Gomaa, *League of Arab States*, 189–90, 197, 200.
87 Text in *AH*, 8 Oct. 1944, 3.
88 "Note on the Present Stage of the Arab Unity Conversations," 11 March 1945, FO 141/1010, 32/77/45.
89 Ibid.; memo by Smart, 10 Oct. 1944, FO 141/949, 151/234/44.
90 *AH*, 9 Oct. 1944, 3.
91 See *RA*, 11 Nov. 1944, 7; *al-Dustur*, 8 Feb. 1945, as quoted in FO 141/1045, 781/1/45; Mayer, *Egypt*, 258.
92 *Egyptian Gazette*, 18 Jan. 1945, 3.

93 "Note on the Present Stage of the Arab Unity Conversations," 11 March 1945, FO 141/1010, 32/77/45.
94 See Gomaa, *League of Arab States*, 252–4.
95 Ibid., 256.
96 "Weekly Appreciation," 3 March 1945, FO 371/45930, J871/10/16; telegram from Lampson, 17 March 1945, FO 371/45237, E1859/3/65.
97 Dali, *Asrar*, 456–7; Gomaa, *League of Arab States*, 242.
98 Dispatch from Lampson, 24 Feb. 1945, FO 371/45236, E1337/3/65.
99 Dispatch from Lampson, 3 March 1945, FO 371/45236, E1479/3/65.
100 Gomaa, *League of Arab States*, 260–1; Dali, *Asrar*, 460–2.
101 The word is used in a draft telegram by Lampson, 21 Feb. 1945, (FO 141/1010, 3253a45), and in the weekly political and economic report for 22–28 Feb. 1945 (FO 371/45930, J1003/10/16).
102 Minute by Clayton, received 3 March 1945, FO 141/1010, 32/65/45; dispatch from Lampson, 3 March 1945, FO 371/45236, E1484/3/65.
103 Dispatch from Lampson, 9 March 1945, FO 371/45237, E1930/3/65.
104 See Porath, *Arab Unity*, 288–9; Dali, *Asrar*, 63–4.
105 Porath, *Arab Unity*, 289.
106 Weekly political and economic report, 15–21 March 1945, FO 37/45930, J1234/10/16.
107 Weekly political and economic report, 15–21 March 1945, FO 371/45930, J1234/10/16; *MI*, 17 March 1945, 2; 18 March 1945, 2.
108 Accounts in *AH*, 23 March 1945, 2–4; *SI*, 23 March 1945, 1–3; telegram from Lampson, 24 March 1945, FO 371/45237, E2010/3/65.
109 The debate in the Chamber of Deputies (2 April) is reported in *AH*, 3 April 1945, 3–4, and FO 141/1011, 32/139/45; the Senate debate (3 April) in *AH*, 4 April 1945, 3–4, and FO 921/324, 48(1)45/85.
110 *AH*, 11 May 1945, 2.
111 *SI*, 23 March 1945, 2, and *AH*, 23 March 1945, 4.
112 Quoted in Michel Laissy, *Du Panarabisme à la Ligue Arabe* (Paris, 1948), 138–41; see also Gomaa, *League of Arab States*, 263.
113 *KW*, 16 March 1945, 3–4.
114 *AH*, 3 April 1945, 3–4.
115 *AH*, 4 April 1945, 3–4.
116 Weekly Political and Economic Report, 22–28 March 1945, FO 371/45930, J1303/10/16.
117 *BL*, 21 March 1945, 3.
118 *BL*, 24 March 1945, 3.
119 *MSR*, 30 March 1945, 1.
120 Ibid., 3.
121 *WM*, 26 Feb. 1945, 3.
122 *WM*, 29 March 1945, 1.
123 *WM*, 30 March 1945, 1.
124 Lord Killearn to Eden, 23 March 1945, FO 371/45237, E2091/3/65.
125 Ibid.

CONCLUSION

1 Benedict Anderson, *Imagined Communities: Reflections on the Origin and Spread of Nationalism* (2nd edn, London, 1991), 6.
2 Here we use *ethnie* as defined by Anthony Smith – as a collectivity which "unites an emphasis upon cultural differences with a sense of historical community"; Anthony D. Smith, *The Ethnic Origins of Nations* (Oxford, 1986), 21–2.
3 Ibid., 137.
4 See Anderson, *Imagined Communities*, 16–49, and Ernest Gellner, *Nations and Nationalism* (London, 1983), 8–52.
5 Gellner, *Nations*, 37–8.
6 Anthony D. Smith, *The Ethnic Revival* (Cambridge, 1981), 116–21.

Select bibliography

UNPUBLISHED ARCHIVAL MATERIALS

GREAT BRITAIN, PUBLIC RECORD OFFICE, SERIES

FO 141 – Embassy and Consular Archives, Egypt, Correspondence
FO 371 – General Correspondence, Political
FO 406 – Confidential Print, Eastern Affairs
FO 407 – Confidential Print, Egypt and the Sudan
FO 816 – Embassy and Consular Archives, Jordan, Correspondence
FO 921 – Minister of State, Cairo.

UNITED STATES, NATIONAL ARCHIVES, OFFICE OF STRATEGIC SERVICES

Research and Analysis Branch Reports.

ARABIC-LANGUAGE PERIODICALS (PUBLISHED IN EGYPT UNLESS OTHERWISE NOTED)

al-Adib (Lebanon), *al-Ahram, al-'Alam al-'Arabi, al-Ansar, al-'Arab, al-'Arab* (Palestine), *al-Balagh, al-Balagh al-Usbu'i, al-Dustur, al-Fath, Filastin* (Palestine), *al-Hadith* (Syria), *al-Hidaya al-Islamiyya, al-Hilal, al-Ikhwan al-Muslimun, al-Jami'a al-'Arabiyya* (Palestine), *al-Jami'a al-Islamiyya* (Palestine), *al-Jihad, al-Jil al-Jadid, al-Katib al-Misri, Kawkab al-Sharq, al-Kitab, al-Khulud, al-Kutla al-Wafdiyya, Liwa' al-Islam, al-Majalla al-Jadida, Majallat Ghurfat al-Qahira, Majallati, al-Makshuf* (Lebanon), *al-Manar, al-Ma'rifa, Mir'at al-Sharq, Misr al-Fatah, al-Misri, Mulhaq al-Siyasa, al-Muqattam, al-Muqtataf, al-Musawwar, al-Nadhir, al-Nahda al-Fikriyya, Nur al-Islam, al-Rabita al-'Arabiyya, al-Rabita al-Sharqiyya, al-Risala, Ruz al-Yusuf, al-Sarkha, al-Sha'b, al-Shabab, al-Sharq al-Jadid, al-Shubban al-Muslimun, al-Sirat al-Mustaqim* (Palestine), *al-Siyasa, al-Siyasa al-Usbu'iyya, al-Thaqafa, al-Thughr, Wadi al-Nil, al-Wafd al-Misri, al-Zahra'.*

DOCTORAL DISSERTATIONS

Coury, Ralph Moses. "Abd al-Rahman Azzam and the Development of Egyptian Arab Nationalism." Princeton University, 1983.
Hussein, Fahmy Mahmoud. "Aims and Objectives of Teaching World History in American and Egyptian Secondary Schools." Syracuse University, 1974.

Kupferschmidt, Uri M. "The Supreme Muslim Council, 1921–1937." Hebrew University of Jerusalem, 1978.

Lerman, Eran. "The Egyptian Question, 1942–1947: The Deterioration of Britain's Position in Egypt, Al Alamein to the U.N. Debate of 1947." London University, 1982.

Shroybom-Shivteil, Shlomit, "The Arabic Language Academy in Egypt: Trends and Actions, 1932–1982" (in Hebrew). Tel Aviv University, 1993.

WORKS IN ARABIC CITED IN THE TEXT

'Abd Allah, Nabih Bayyumi. *Tatawwur Fikrat al-Qawmiyya al-'Arabiyya fi Misr.* Cairo, 1975.

'Abd al-Hayy, 'Abd al-Tawwab. *'Asir Hayati.* Cairo, 1966.

'Abd al-Rahman, 'Awatif. *Misr wa Filastin.* Cairo, 1980.

'Afifi, Hafiz. *'Ala Hamish al-Siyasa.* Cairo, 1938.

'Alluba, Muhammad 'Ali. *Mabadi' fi al-Siyasa al-Misriyya.* Cairo, 1942.

Amin, Ahmad. *Fayd al-Khatir: Majmu' Maqalat Adabiyya wa Ijtima'iyya.* 2nd edn, 10 vols.; Cairo, 1946.

    Yawm al-Islam. Cairo, 1952.

al-'Aqqad, 'Abbas Mahmud. *'Abqariyyat Muhammad.* 2nd edn; Cairo, 1942.

    'Abqariyyat 'Umar. Cairo, 1942.

    'Abqariyyat al-Imam. Cairo, 1943.

    'Abqariyyat al-Siddiq. Cairo, 1943.

    'Abqariyyat 'Amr ibn al-'As. Cairo, 1944.

    'Abqariyyat Khalid. Cairo, 1944.

    'Abqariyyat 'Uthman. Cairo, 1954.

'Arif, Jamil. *Safahat min al-Mudhakkirat al-Sirriyya li-Awwal Amin 'Amm li al-Jami'a al-'Arabiyya 'Abd al-Rahman 'Azzam.* Part 1; Cairo, 1978.

Arslan, Shakib. *Sayyid Rashid Rida aw Ikha' Arba'in Sana.* Damascus, 1937.

al-'Aryan, Muhammad Sa'id. *Qatr al-Nada'.* Cairo, 1945.

    'Ala Bab al-Zuwayla. Cairo, 1947.

    Shajarat al-Durr. Cairo, 1947.

'Azmi, Mahmud. *al-Ayyam al-Mi'a.* Cairo, 1936.

'Azzam, 'Abd al-Rahman. *Batal al-Abtal aw Abraz Sifat al-Nabiy Muhammad.* Cairo, 1939.

    al-Jami'a al-'Arabiyya wa al-Wahda al-'Alamiyya. Cairo, 1946.

    al-Risala al-Khalida. 2nd edn; Cairo, 1954.

'Azzam, 'Abd al-Wahhab. *Mudhakkirat fi Ta'rikh al-Umma al-'Arabiyya.* Cairo, 1932.

    Rihalat. Cairo, 1939.

    Mahd al-'Arab. Cairo, 1946.

Bakathir, 'Ali Ahmad. *Salamat al-Qass.* Cairo, 1943.

    Wa' Islamah. Cairo, 1945.

al-Banna, Hasan. *Ila Ayyi Shay' Nad'u al-Nas?.* Cairo, 1936.

    Da'watuna. Cairo, 1937.

    Nahwa al-Nur. Cairo, 1937.

    Bayna al-Ams wa al-Yawm. Cairo, 1939.

    Da'watuna fi Tawr Jadid. Cairo, n.d.

    Mudhakkirat al-Da'wa wa al-Da'iya. Cairo, n.d.

Mushkilatuna fi Daw' al-Nizam al-Islami. Cairo, n.d.
al-Salam fi al-Islam wa Buhuth Ukhra. Cairo, n.d.
al-Bishri, Tariq. *al-Haraka al-Siyasiyya fi Misr, 1945–1952.* Cairo, 1972.
al-Muslimun wa al-Aqbat fi Itar al-Jama'a al-Wataniyya. Cairo, 1980.
Daghir, As'ad. *Mudhakkirati 'Ala Hamish al-Qadiyya al-'Arabiyya.* Cairo, 1959.
al-Dali, Wahid. *Asrar al-Jami'a al-'Arabiyya wa 'Abd al-Rahman 'Azzam.* Cairo, 1982.
al-Dasuqi, 'Asim Ahmad. *Misr fi al-Harb al-'Alamiyya al-Thaniya, 1939–1945.* Cairo, 1976.
Fahmi, Mansur. *Khatarat Nafs.* Cairo, 1930.
Faraj, Ibrahim. *Dhikrayyat Siyasiyya.* Giza, 1983.
Fawzi, Husayn. *Sindibad 'Asri.* Cairo, 1938.
Fu'ad, Ni'mat Ahmad. *Qimam Adabiyya.* Cairo, 1967.
Ghali, Mirrit Butrus. *Siyasat al-Ghad.* Cairo, 1938.
Ghali, Mirrit Butrus and Ibrahim Madkur. *al-Ada al-Hukumiyya.* Cairo, 1943.
Ghunaym, Sabri. *'Abd al-Nasir: Dhalika al-Insan.* Cairo, 1970.
Ghurbal, Muhammad Shafiq. *Ta'rikh al-Mufawadat al-Misriyya al-Biritaniyya, 1882–1936.* Part 1; Cairo, 1952.
Hafiz, Abu al-Hajjaz. *al-Shahid Kamal al-Din Salah.* Cairo, n.d.
al-Hakim, Tawfiq. *Muhammad.* Cairo, 1936.
   Yawmiyyat Na'ib fi al-Aryaf. Cairo, 1937.
   Tahta Shams al-Fikr. 2nd edn; Cairo, 1941.
   'Usfur min al-Sharq. 2nd edn; Cairo, 1941.
   Shajarat al-Hukm. Cairo, 1945.
al-Harawi, Husayn. *al-Mustashriqun wa al-Islam.* Cairo, 1936.
Hasan, Muhammad Zaki and 'Abd al-Rahman Zaki. *Fi Misr al-Islamiyya.* Cairo, 1937.
Hassuna, Muhammad Amin. *Wara'a al-Bihar.* Cairo, 1936.
Haykal, Muhammad Husayn. *Thawrat al-Adab.* Cairo, 1933.
   Hayat Muhammad. Cairo, 1935; 2nd edn Cairo, 1936.
   Fi Manzil al-Wahy. Cairo, 1937.
   al-Siddiq Abu Bakr. Cairo, 1942.
   al-Faruq 'Umar. 2 vols.; Cairo, 1944.
   Mudhakkirat fi al-Siyasa al-Misriyya. 3 vols.; Cairo, 1951, 1953, 1978.
   al-Sharq al-Jadid. 2nd edn; Cairo, 1962.
   'Uthman ibn 'Affan. 4th edn; Cairo, 1977.
al-Hilali, 'Abd al-Razzaq. *Zaki Mubarak fi al-'Iraq.* Beirut, 1969.
al-Hindawi, Khalil and 'Umar al-Daqqaq. *al-Muqtabis min Wahy al-Risala: Dirasa wa Mukhtarat.* Aleppo, 1965.
Husayn, Ahmad. *Imani.* 1st edn; Cairo, 1936; 2nd edn Cairo, 1946.
   Ra'y Jam'iyyat Misr al-Fatah fi Mu'ahadat Sanat 1936. Cairo, 1936.
   Murafa'at al-Ra'is: Misr al-Fatah wa al-Hukuma Amama al-Qada. Cairo, 1937.
   Nisf Qarn ma'a al-'Uruba wa Qadiyyat Filastin. Sidon, 1971.
Husayn, Taha. *Min Hadith al-Shi'r wa al-Nathr.* Cairo, 1936.
   Mustaqbal al-Thaqafa fi Misr. 2 vols.; Cairo, 1938.
   'Ala Hamish al-Sira. 3 vols.; Cairo, 1968–1974.
Jum'a, Ibrahim. *al-Qawmiyya al-Misriyya al-Islamiyya.* Cairo, 1944.
Jum'a, Muhammad Lutfi. *Hayat al-Sharq.* Cairo, 1932.
al-Jundi, Anwar. *al-Ma'arik al-Adabiyya fi al-Shi'r wa al-Nashr wa al-Thaqafa wa al-Lugha al-Qawmiyya al-'Arabiyya.* Cairo, 1961.

Ahmad Zaki al-Mulaqqab bi-Shaykh al-'Uruba. Cairo, 1964.
Kamil, Mahmud. *Misr al-Ghad Tahta Hukm al-Shabab.* Cairo, 1939.
al-'Amal li-Misr: Ba'th Dawla wa Ihya' Majd. Cairo, 1945.
Khalaf, 'Abd al-Mun'im Muhammad. *Ma'a al-Qawmiyya al-'Arabiyya fi Rub' Qarn.* Cairo, 1958.
al-Khardaji, Muhammad Shakir. *al-'Arab fi Tariq al-Ittihad.* Damascus, 1947.
Khatir, Muhammad 'Abd al-Mun'im. *Muhammad Farid Abu Hadid.* Cairo, 1979.
al-Khuli, Amin. *Fi al-Adab al-Misri: Fikra wa Manhaj.* Cairo, 1943.
Khutub Haflat al-Iftitah al-Kubra li al-Mu'tamar al-Barlamani al-'Alami li al-Difa' 'an Filastin. Cairo, 1938.
Lutfi, Muhammad Sa'id. *al-Siyar.* Cairo, 1938.
al-Ma'addawi, Anwar. *'Ali Mahmud Taha: al-Sha'ir al-Insan.* Baghdad, 1965.
Mahfuz, Najib. *al-Maraya.* Cairo, 1972.
Mahmud, Hafiz. *al-Ma'arik fi al-Sihafa wa al-Siyasa wa al-Fikr bayna 1919–1952.* Cairo, 1969.
Maktabat *al-Muqtataf. Fi Misr al-Islamiyya.* Cairo, 1937.
Nawahi Majida min al-Thaqafa al-Islamiyya. Cairo, 1938.
al-Mala'ika, Nazik. *Shi'r 'Ali Mahmud Taha: Dirasa wa Naqd.* Cairo, 1965.
al-Mamlaka al-Misriyya, Wizarat al-Maliyya, Maslahat 'Umum al-Ihsa' wa al-Ta'dad.
   Ta'dad Sukkan al-Qutr al-Misri Sanat 1927. 2 vols.; Cairo, 1931.
   Ta'dad Sukkan al-Qutr al-Misri Sanat 1937. 2 vols.; Cairo, 1942.
al-Manjuri, Mahmud. *Ittijahat al-'Asr al-Jadid fi Misr.* Cairo, 1937.
al-Mazini, Ibrahim 'Abd al-Qadir. *Rihlat al-Hijaz.* Cairo, 1930.
Mubarak, Zaki. *al-Lugha wa al-Din wa al-Taqalid fi Hayat al-Istiqlal.* Cairo, 1936.
   Layla al-Marida fi al-'Iraq. 3 vols.; Cairo, 1938–9.
   Wahy Baghdad. Cairo, 1938.
al-Mudhakkira fi al-Ta'lim al-Dini bi al-Madaris al-Misriyya. Cairo, 1932.
al-Mudhakkira al-Thaniya fi al-Ta'lim al-Dini fi al-Madaris al-Misriyya. Cairo, 1935.
Mufarraj, Fu'ad Khalil. *al-Mu'tamar al-'Arabi al-Qawmi fi Buludan, 1937.* Damascus, n.d.
Muhammad, Sayyid Muhammad. *al-Zayyat wa al-Risala.* Riyadh, 1982.
al-Mu'tamar al-Nisa'i al-Sharqi li al-Difa' 'an Filastin. Cairo, 1938.
Nadi al-Ittihad al-'Arabi. *al-Ittihad al-'Arabi wa Qanunuhu al-'Amm.* Cairo, 1942.
al-Najjar, 'Abd al-Wahhab. *Ta'rikh al-Islam: al-Khulafa' al-Rashidun.* Cairo, 1930.
   Qisas al-Anbiya'. 2nd edn; Cairo, 1936.
Qasimiyya, Khayriyya (ed.). *'Awni 'Abd al-Hadi: Awraq Khassa.* Beirut, 1974.
Radwan, Fathi. *'Asr wa Rijal.* Cairo, 1967.
   Tal'at Harb: Bahth fi al-'Azama. Cairo, 1970.
al-Rafi'i, Mustafa Sadiq. *Wahy al-Qalam.* 5th edn, 3 vols.; Cairo, 1954.
Ramadan, 'Abd al-'Azim. *al-Sira' bayna al-Wafd wa al-'Arsh, 1936–1939.* Cairo, 1979.
Rida, Muhammad. *Abu Bakr al-Siddiq.* Cairo, 1935.
   al-Imam 'Ali ibn Abi Talib. Cairo, 1939.
   Muhammad Rasul Allah. 2nd edn; Cairo, 1939.
Rida, Muhiy al-Din. *Rihlati ila al-Hijaz.* Cairo, 1935.
Sabri, Ahmad. *Qina' al-Fir'awniyya.* Cairo, 1943.
Sayigh, Anis. *al-Fikra al-'Arabiyya fi Misr.* Beirut, 1959.
al-Sayyid, Taqiy al-Din. *'Ali Mahmud Taha: Hayatuhu wa Shi'ruhu.* Cairo, 1965.

Shafiq, Ahmad. *A'mali ba'da Mudhakkirati*. Cairo, 1941.
Shalabi, 'Ali. *Misr al-Fatah wa Dawruha fi al-Siyasa al-Misriyya*. Cairo, 1982.
Subayh, Muhammad. *Faysal al-Awwal*. Cairo, 1945.
Sulayman, Muhammad. *Rasa'il Sa'ir*. Cairo, 1935.
Sumikh, Sasun. "Hawla Lughat al-Hiwar fi Masrahiyyat al-Hakim." In Dafid Simah (ed.), *Adwa' 'Ala Adab Tawfiq al-Hakim* (Haifa, 1979), 73–85.
  "Masrah Mahmud Taymur: Lughat al-Hiwar fi Siyaghatayn." In his *Abhath fi al-Lugha wa al-Uslub* (Tel Aviv, 1980), 23–43.
Taha, 'Ali Mahmud. *Sharq wa Gharb*. Cairo, 1947.
  Diwan 'Ali Mahmud Taha. Beirut, 1972.
al-Tahir, Muhammad 'Ali. *Nazarat al-Shura*. Cairo, 1932.
  Zalam al-Sajn. Cairo, 1951.
Taymur, Mahmud. *al-Nabiy al-Insan wa Maqalat Ukhar*. Cairo, 1945.
Thabit, Muhammad. *Jawwala fi Rubu' al-Sharq al-Adna*. Cairo, 1936.
al-Zawahiri, Fakhr al-Din al-Ahmadi. *al-Siyasa wa al-Azhar: min Mudhakkirat Shaykh al-Islam al-Zawahiri*. Cairo, 1945.
al-Zayyat, Ahmad Hasan. *Wahy al-Risala*. Multi-vol.; 2nd edn; Cairo, 1954.

WORKS IN WESTERN LANGUAGES CITED IN THE TEXT

Abdalla, Ahmed. *The Student Movement and Nationalist Politics in Egypt, 1923–1973*. London, 1985.
Alter, Peter. *Nationalism*. London, 1985.
Anderson, Benedict. *Imagined Communities: Reflections on the Origin and Spread of Nationalism*. London, 1983. 2nd edn, revised, 1991.
Badawi, M. M. "Islam in Modern Egyptian Literature." *Journal of Arabic Literature*, 2 (1971), 154–77.
  A Critical Introduction to Modern Arabic Poetry. Cambridge, 1975.
  Modern Arabic Literature and the West. Ithaca, 1985.
  Modern Arabic Drama in Egypt. Cambridge, 1987.
Baer, Gabriel. *A History of Landownership in Modern Egypt, 1800–1950*. London, 1962.
Ben-Gurion, David. *My Talks with Arab Leaders*. New York, 1973.
Berger, Morroe. *Bureaucracy and Society in Modern Egypt*. Princeton, 1957.
Berque, Jacques. *Egypt: Imperialism and Revolution*. London, 1972.
Bianchi, Robert. *Unruly Corporatism: Associational Life in Twentieth-Century Egypt*. New York, 1989.
Bourne, Kenneth and D. Cameron Watt (eds.). *British Documents on Foreign Affairs: Reports and Papers from the Foreign Office Confidential Print. Part II: From the First to the Second World War. Series B: Turkey, Iran, and the Middle East, 1918–1939*. 13 vols.; Washington, 1986.
Brugman, J. *An Introduction to the History of Modern Arabic Literature in Egypt*. Leiden, 1984.
Cachia, Pierre. *Taha Husayn: His Place in the Egyptian Literary Renaissance*. London, 1956.
Carter, Barbara Lynn. *The Copts in Egyptian Politics*. London, 1986.
Chartier, Roger. "Intellectual History or Socio-Cultural History? The French Trajectories." In Dominick LaCapra and Steven L. Kaplan (eds.), *Modern*

European Intellectual History: Reappraisals and New Perspectives (Ithaca, 1982), 13–46.

Cleveland, William L. *The Making of an Arab Nationalist: Ottomanism and Arabism in the Life and Thought of Sati' al-Husri.* Princeton, 1971.

Cohen, Michael J. *Palestine: Retreat from the Mandate; The Making of British Policy, 1936–1945.* New York, 1978.

Colombe, Marcel. *L'Evolution de l'Egypte.* Paris, 1951.

Coury, Ralph M. "Who 'Invented' Egyptian Arab Nationalism?." *International Journal of Middle East Studies,* 14 (1982), 249–81, 459–79.

"Egyptians in Jerusalem: The Role of the General Islamic Conference of 1931." *Muslim World,* 82 (1992), 37–54.

Crecelius, Daniel. "Non-Ideological Responses of the Egyptian Ulama to Modernization." In Nikki R. Keddie (ed.), *Scholars, Saints, and Sufis: Muslim Religious Institutions Since 1500* (Berkeley, 1972), 167–209.

Crouchley, A. E. *The Economic Development of Modern Egypt.* London, 1938.

Dawn, C. Ernest. "The Formation of Pan-Arab Ideology in the Interwar Years." *International Journal of Middle East Studies,* 20 (1988), 67–91.

Deeb, Marius. *Party Politics in Egypt: The Wafd and Its Rivals, 1919–1939.* London, 1979.

Egypt, Ministry of Finance and Economy, Statistical and Census Department. *Population Census of Egypt, 1947.* Cairo, 1954.

Eliraz, Giora. "Tradition and Change: Egyptian Intellectuals and Linguistic Reform, 1919–1939." *Asian and African Studies,* 20 (1986), 233–62.

Erlich, Haggai. *Students and University in Twentieth Century Egyptian Politics.* London, 1989.

Fry, Michael G. and Itamar Rabinovich, *Despatches from Damascus: Gilbert Mac-Kereth and British Policy in the Levant, 1933–1939.* Jerusalem, 1985.

Galt, Russell. *The Effects of Centralization on Education in Modern Egypt.* Cairo, 1936.

Geertz, Clifford. *The Interpretation of Cultures.* New York, 1973.

Gellner, Ernest. *Nations and Nationalism.* London, 1983.

Gershoni, Israel. "The Muslim Brothers and the Arab Revolt in Palestine, 1936–39." *Middle Eastern Studies,* 22 (1986), 367–97.

Gershoni, Israel and James Jankowski. *Egypt, Islam, and the Arabs: The Search for Egyptian Nationhood, 1900–1930.* New York, 1986.

Ghali, Mirrit Boutros. *The Policy of Tomorrow.* Washington, 1953.

Gibb, H. A. R. "The Islamic Congress at Jerusalem in December 1931." In Arnold J. Toynbee, *Survey of International Affairs, 1934* (London, 1935), 99–109.

Goldberg, Ellis. *Tinker, Tailor, and Textile Worker: Class and Politics in Egypt, 1930–1952.* Berkeley, 1986.

"Muslim Union Politics in Egypt: Two Cases." In Edmund Burke III and Ira Lapidus (eds.), *Islam, Politics, and Social Movements* (Berkeley, 1988), 228–43.

Gomaa, Ahmed M. *The Foundation of the League of Arab States.* London, 1977.

Haim, Sylvia G. *Arab Nationalism: An Anthology.* Berkeley, 1962.

al-Hakim, Tawfiq. *Maze of Justice: Diary of a Country Prosecutor.* 2nd edn; Austin, 1989.

Hansen, Bent. "Income and Consumption in Egypt, 1886/1887 to 1937." *International Journal of Middle East Studies,* 10 (1979), 27–47.

Hayes, Carlton J. H. *The Historical Evolution of Modern Nationalism.* New York, 1931.

Haykal, Muhammad Husayn. *The Life of Muhammad.* N.p., 1976.

Heyworth-Dunne, James. *Religious and Political Trends in Modern Egypt.* Washington, 1950.

Hobsbawm, Eric and Terence Ranger (eds.). *The Invention of Tradition.* Cambridge, 1983.

Hollinger, David A. "Historians and the Discourse of Intellectuals." In John Higham and Paul K. Conkin (eds.), *New Directions in American Intellectual History* (Baltimore, 1979), 42–63.

"The Return of the Prodigal: The Persistence of Historical Knowing." *American Historical Review,* 94 (1989), 610–21.

Hourani, Albert. *Arabic Thought in the Liberal Age, 1798–1939.* London, 1962.

"The Middleman in a Changing Society: Syrians in Egypt in the Eighteenth and Nineteenth Centuries." In his *The Emergence of The Modern Middle East* (Berkeley, 1981), 103–23.

A History of the Arab Peoples. Cambridge, MA, 1991.

Husry, Khaldun S. "King Faisal I and Arab Unity, 1930–33." *Journal of Contemporary History,* 10 (1975), 323–40.

Hussein, Ahmad. *Message to Hitler!* New York, 1947.

Hussein, Taha. *The Future of Culture in Egypt.* 2nd edn; New York, 1975.

Issawi, Charles. *Egypt at Mid-Century: An Economic Analysis.* London, 1954.

Jankowski, James. "The Egyptian Blue Shirts and the Egyptian Wafd, 1935–1938." *Middle Eastern Studies,* 6 (1970), 77–95.

Egypt's Young Rebels: "Young Egypt," 1933–1952. Stanford, 1975.

Jayyusi, Salma Khadra. *Trends and Movements in Modern Arabic Poetry.* 2 vols.; Leiden, 1977.

Kampffmeyer, G. "Egypt and Western Asia." In H. A. R. Gibb (ed.), *Whither Islam?* (London, 1932), 101–70.

Kedourie, Elie. "Egypt and the Caliphate, 1915–52." In his *The Chatham House Version and Other Middle-Eastern Studies* (New York, 1970), 177–207.

"Pan-Arabism and British Policy." In his *The Chatham House Version and Other Middle-Eastern Studies* (New York, 1970), 213–35.

"The Bludan Congress on Palestine, September 1937." *Middle Eastern Studies,* 17 (1980), 107–25.

Khoury, Philip S. *Syria and the French Mandate, 1920–1945.* Princeton, 1987.

Kirk, George. *The Middle East in the War.* Volume II of *Survey of International Affairs, 1939–1945.* London, 1952.

Kramer, Martin. *Islam Assembled: The Advent of the Muslim Congresses.* New York, 1986.

Kupferschmidt, Uri M. "The Muslim Brothers and the Egyptian Village." *Asian and African Studies,* 16 (1982), 157–70.

LaCapra, Dominick. *History and Criticism.* Ithaca, 1985.

Soundings in Critical Theory. Ithaca, 1989.

Laissy, Michel. *Du Panarabisme à la Ligue Arabe.* Paris, 1948.

Leatherdale, Clive. *Britain and Saudi Arabia, 1925–1939: The Imperial Oasis.* London, 1983.

Lerner, Daniel. *The Passing of Traditional Society: Modernizing the Middle East.* New York, 1958.

Lewis, Bernard. "The Return of Islam." *Commentary*, 61 (Jan. 1976), 39–49.
Lidenfeld, David F. "On Systems and Embodiments as Categories for Intellectual History." *History and Theory*, 27 (1988), 30–50.
Mahfuz, Nagib. *Mirrors*. Trans. by Roger Allen; Chicago, 1977.
Makarius, Raoul. *La Jeunesse intellectuelle d'Egypte au lendemain de la deuxième guerre mondiale*. The Hague, 1960.
Marsot, Afaf Lutfi al-Sayyid. *Egypt's Liberal Experiment, 1922–1936*. Berkeley, 1977.
Mayer, Thomas. "Egypt and the General Islamic Conference of Jerusalem in 1931." *Middle Eastern Studies*, 18 (1982), 311–22.
Egypt and the Palestine Question, 1936–1945. Berlin, 1983.
Mitchell, Richard P. *The Society of the Muslim Brothers*. London, 1969.
"Note: Sur la presse égyptienne et la presse palestinienne à la fin de 1944." *Cahiers de l'Orient contemporain*, 1 (1945), 124–7.
Peled, Mattityahu. *Religion, My Own: The Literary Works of Najib Mahfuz* (New Brunswick, 1983).
Phillip, Thomas. "Demographic Patterns of Syrian Immigration to Egypt during the Nineteenth Century – An Interpretation." *Asian and African Studies*, 16 (1982), 171–95.
Pocock, J. G. A. *Virtue, Commerce, and History: Essays on Political Thought and History Chiefly in the Eighteenth Century*. Cambridge, 1985.
Porath, Yehoshua. *The Palestinian Arab National Movement, 1929–1939: From Riots to Rebellion*. London, 1977.
In Search of Arab Unity, 1930–1945. London, 1986.
Radwan, Samir. *Capital Formation in Egyptian Industry and Agriculture, 1882–1967*. London, 1974.
Reid, Donald M. *Cairo University and the Making of Modern Egypt*. Cambridge, 1990.
Richards, Alan. *Egypt's Agricultural Development, 1800–1980*. Boulder, 1982.
Ricoeur, Paul. *Hermeneutics and the Human Sciences*. Ed. and trans. by John B. Thompson; Cambridge, 1981.
Lectures on Ideology and Utopia. Ed. by George H. Taylor; Chicago, 1986.
Rose, Norman. "The Arab Rulers and Palestine, 1936: The British Reaction." *Journal of Modern History*, 44 (1972), 213–31.
The Gentile Zionists: Anglo-Zionist Diplomacy, 1929–1939. London, 1973.
Rossi, Ettore. "Il congresso interparlamentare arabo e musulmano pro Palestina al Cairo (7–11 Ottobre)." *Oriente Moderno*, 18 (1938), 587–601.
Safran, Nadav. *Egypt in Search of Political Community*. Cambridge, 1961.
Sakkut, Hamdi. *The Egyptian Novel and Its Main Trends, 1913 to 1952*. Cairo, 1971.
Seale, Patrick. *The Struggle for Syria: A Study of Post-War Arab Politics, 1945–1958*. Oxford, 1965.
Semah, David. *Four Egyptian Literary Critics*. Leiden, 1974.
Smith, Anthony D. *The Ethnic Revival*. Cambridge, 1981.
The Ethnic Origins of Nations. Oxford, 1986.
Smith, Charles D. "The 'Crisis of Orientation': The Shift of Egyptian Intellectuals to Islamic Subjects in the 1930s," *International Journal of Middle East Studies*, 4 (1973), 382–410.
Islam and the Search for Social Order: A Biography of Muhammad Husayn Haykal. Albany, 1983.

Smith, Wilfred Cantwell. *Islam in Modern History*. Princeton, 1957.

Somekh, Sasson. "Two Versions of Dialogue in Mahmud Taymur's Drama." Princeton Near East Paper no. 21; Princeton, 1975.

"The Diglottic Dilemma in the Drama of Tawfiq al-Hakim." *Israel Oriental Studies*, 9 (1979), 392–403.

Starkey, Paul. *From the Ivory Tower: A Critical Study of Tawfiq al-Hakim*. London, 1987.

Thompson, John B. *Critical Hermeneutics: A Study of the Thought of Paul Ricoeur and Jurgen Habermas*. Cambridge, 1983.

Studies in the Theory of Ideology. Oxford, 1984.

Toews, John E. "Intellectual History after the Linguistic Turn: The Autonomy of Meaning and the Irreducibility of Experience." *American Historical Review*, 92 (1987), 879–907.

Toledano, Ehud R. *State and Society in Mid-Nineteenth-Century Egypt*. Cambridge, 1990.

Toynbee, Arnold J., assisted by V. M. Boulter. *Survey of International Affairs, 1934*. London, 1935.

Tully, James (ed.). *Meaning and Context: Quentin Skinner and His Critics*. Oxford, 1988.

Vatikiotis, P. J. *The Modern History of Egypt*. New York, 1969.

Vaucher, Georges. *Gamal Abdel Nasser et son équipe*. Paris, 1959.

Waardenburg, Jean-Jacques. *Les Universités dans le monde arabe actuel*. 2 vols.; The Hague, 1966.

Wendell, Charles (ed. and trans.). *Five Tracts of Hasan al-Banna' (1906–1949)*. Berkeley, 1978.

Wessels, Antonie. *A Modern Arabic Biography of Muhammad: A Critical Study of Muhammad Husayn Haykal's Hayat Muhammad*. Leiden, 1972.

Woolbert, Robert Gale. "Pan-Arabism and the Palestine Problem." *Foreign Affairs*, 16:2 (Jan. 1938), 309–22.

Index